Japan's Holy War

ASIA-PACIFIC: CULTURE, POLITICS,
AND SOCIETY

*Editors: Rey Chow, H. D. Harootunian,
and Masao Miyoshi*

WALTER A. SKYA

Japan's Holy War

THE IDEOLOGY OF RADICAL SHINTŌ

ULTRANATIONALISM

Duke University Press Durham and London 2009

© 2009 Duke University Press
All rights reserved
Printed in the United States of America
on acid-free paper ∞
Designed by C. H. Westmoreland
Typeset in Arno with Magma Compact display
by Keystone Typesetting, Inc.
Library of Congress Cataloging-in-
Publication Data appear on the last printed
page of this book.

DEDICATED TO

MY WIFE, MARIKO,

DAUGHTER, AMY, AND

SON, MARK

Contents

Acknowledgments

I am deeply grateful to a number of scholars in the United States, Japan, and Europe who have taught me and enthusiastically supported me and my research projects over the past two decades. First, and foremost, however, I owe a special debt of gratitude to Professor Harry Harootunian, my main advisor at the University of Chicago. I wish to thank this remarkable scholar once again for welcoming me to Chicago. I could not have asked for a better mentor. It has been said that higher education is America's greatest industry because the American system is better than any other at developing the critical faculties of the mind. I am convinced that scholars like Harootunian deserve credit for this nation's great innovation because they teach their students to think. The volume of ideas coming from the mind of this prolific writer over the years has never ceased to amaze me. Equally important, he has had the intellectual vigor and personal courage to challenge entrenched orthodoxies. Without his encouragement and support, this book on Shintō nationalism, a topic that has been conspicuously shunned by American academics, would have not been possible. Also, I feel I was extremely fortunate to have had the privilege to attend the University of Chicago during a time when Chicago was an intellectual powerhouse of world-class scholars in the field of Japanese studies. In addition to Harry Harootunian, I had the opportunity to learn from professors Tetsuo Najita, Akira Iriye, Norma Field, and Bernard Silberman, all of whom contributed a nexus of courses, lectures, visiting scholars, symposiums, and study groups that made for a truly stimulating and exciting intellectual climate for graduate studies.

Many other scholars offered me advice and assistance throughout the various stages in the preparation of this book. However, I would first like to thank Reynolds Smith, Executive Editor of Duke University Press, for providing three conscientious anonymous readers for my manuscript whose careful and diligent reading greatly improved my work. My special thanks and appreciation go to the following individuals: Professor Bruce

Reynolds of San Jose State University, a loyal friend and colleague, for closely reading several versions of the manuscript and offering me innumerable suggestions for improvement; Professor Tamara Hunt, University of Southern Indiana, for her intellectual companionship and for painstakingly reading early versions of this work and for saving me from making embarrassing errors; independent scholar Dr. Scott Myerly, also for his intellectual companionship and unfailing support for my research; Professor George Wilson for reading an earlier version of my chapter on the thought of Kita Ikki; the late David A. Titus at Wesleyan University for his support and enthusiasm for my research on Kakehi Katsuhiko; Reverend James Fredericks, Department of Religion, Loyola Marymount University, for sharing with me his insights on comparative religion; Professor Stefan Tanaka, University of California, San Diego, for offering many suggestions on how to organize my material and for his kind remarks on my chapter on Minobe Tatsukichi; and Dr. Christopher Szpilman for his useful comments on several chapters. I was first attracted to Japanese intellectual history during my undergraduate years by Professor Kenneth Pyle at the University of Washington. For my ideas on religious nationalism, I am grateful to Professor Mark Juergensmeyer, Director of the Orfalea Center for Global and International Studies at the University of California, Santa Barbara, who graciously read an early draft of my work and gave me precious support and encouragement.

In Japan, I owe a special intellectual debt of gratitude to the writings of Professor Nagao Ryūichi, a scholar of the history of Japanese constitutional legal thought, who taught for many years at the University of Tokyo. I first stumbled across the writings of Nagao one day while I was browsing through the large collection of Japanese language materials in the University of Chicago's Regenstein Library. It was there that I discovered his early work *Nihon Kokka Shisō Shi Kenkyū* (*A Study of the History of Japanese State Thought*) (1982). I took it off the bookshelf and sat down on the floor in the aisle between the stacks and started flipping through the pages. Intrigued, I checked it out and spent the next few weeks poring over it. It was through this work that I first became aware of the significance of the political thought of Uesugi Shinkichi and Kakehi Katsuhiko, and I discovered that these two Japanese constitutional legal scholars were writing something very different from that of their Meiji predecessors. Extremely excited about this work, I initiated a correspondence with Nagao. I later flew to Tokyo to meet with him. That would be the beginning of my long-term relationship with this noted scholar across the Pacific. I wish to publicly thank him again for all the exciting conversations we have had together over the years; for kindly taking the time to send me manuscripts, books, and other materials; and also for offering me invaluable comments on my chapters, saving me from factual errors and mistaken readings of Japanese characters. Professor Ida Terutoshi, formally of the Department of Law, Kitakyūshū University, kindly invited me to his home in Kyūshū for a stimulating discussion on Uesugi Shinkichi.

The late Professor Sagara Tōru initially got me interested in Shintō nationalism while I attended his lectures on early modern and modern Japanese history and his seminar course on Tokugawa thought when I was a foreign student in the Ethics Department at the University of Tokyo (I believe I was the first foreigner to have formally studied for any length of time in that department). It was in Sagara's seminar course that I met and made friends with a number of students who are currently well-accomplished professors at the University of Tokyo, including Kurozumi Makoto, Takeuchi Seiichi, and Kanno Kakumyō. I also benefited immensely from a summer research grant awarded to me from Kokugakunin University's International Guest Research Program. It was at Kokugakuin University that I was able to gather invaluable documents, especially on Kakehi Katsuhiko. I want to thank Professor Yokoyama Minoru, Dean of the School of Law at Kokugakuin University, and his spouse, Professor Yahagi Yumiko, for supplying me with important Japanese language documents and books. Librarian Isogai Yukihiko was kind enough to find for me materials on the authors of *Kokutai no Hongi*. But I owe even more to my good friend Professor Sugai Masuro, Department of Economics, who helped me arrange for my accommodations and who was a great companion while I was doing research at Kokugakuin University. My six years at the University of Tokyo would not have been so enjoyable without the friendship of Professor Richard Zgusta of the Department of Comparative Culture at the Osaka University of Foreign Studies. Thanks, Richard, for all the fun we had together in Tokyo.

I owe a debt of gratitude to several European scholars as well. At the top of the list is Professor Dr. Klaus Antoni of Eberhard Karls Universität Tübingen, Germany, for inviting me to present my research at an international symposium, "Religion and National Identity in the Japanese Context," which was held at Hohentübingen Castle in Tübingen in February 2001, and for helping me with German grammar and German language materials used in this book. Michael Wachutka was an especially great companion to me while I was again at Tübingen University as the "Erwin von Bälz" Guest Professor, Institute for Japanese Studies, in the summer of 2001. I appreciate Professor Roger Griffin, British scholar of European intellectual history, for reading my chapter on Hozumi Yatsuki and offering me valuable comments and insights on European fascism. His early work *The Nature of Fascism* drew my interest and made me rethink and situate Japanese Shintō nationalism in a broader comparative context of fascism. His newest work, *Modernism and Fascism* (2007), came just barely in time for me to incorporate more of his ideas into this manuscript. I also want to thank him for sending me a chapter of *Modernism and Fascism* before it was published.

Finally, it is only proper and fitting that I pay tribute to those who got me intimately involved in Japan and Japanese culture in the first place at a very young age. In this regard, two individuals have been very special to me. One is Mr. Fred Sato, history teacher and terrific judo coach at Rainier Beach High School in Seattle, Washington. It was Fred Sato who inspired me and rigorously trained me to achieve my first dream—being one of the few American high school students to have been awarded a first degree black belt in judo from the Kōdōkan, the center of world judo, while still in high school. Thanks to him and his coaching, I went on to win numerous trophies in major judo tournaments in the Pacific Northwest and Canada, and finally progressed to the point that I was recognized as a promising judo athlete by United States Olympic judo coach Yosh Uchida, who invited me to join his group of judokas in San Jose, California. Fred opened so many doors for me that I cannot thank this wonderful human being enough for all he did for me during my formative high school years. The second person who has been a precious friend over the years is Taky Kimura, who encouraged me to join the Jun Fan Gung Fu Institute of Chinese martial artist Bruce Lee, an unknown at the time, but who would subsequently go on to become one of the most famous actors and martial artists in the world. It was a great honor to have actually had the opportunity to practice Gung Fu for a short time under Bruce Lee and with Taky for many years after. In short, if it had not been for these two individuals, Fred Sato and Taky Kimura, I would have never gone off to college to enroll in the East Asian Studies Program in what is now the University of Washington's Henry M. Jackson School of International Studies.

I have confronted setbacks and stumbled more than once in my career, but I never in my life have given up. I would like to thank the members of my family for putting up with me for so long to pursue my academic quest: my wife, Mariko; son, Mark; daughter, Amy; and mother, Mary. And, I pay tribute to the late Robert Joyce, husband of Rita, my sister, for teaching me all that I know about computers.

Introduction

To understand Japan and the inner forces that shape her and the problems with which she wrestles within her own borders it is essential to know something of the ramifications of Shinto in the thought and practices of the people. Support for such a statement can be found in the fact that from childhood the Japanese are taught that attitudes and usages connected with the shrines of Shinto are vitally related to good citizenship. To be a worthy subject of the realm requires loyalty to certain great interests for which the shrines are made to stand. These attitudes are deliberately fostered on a large scale by the government. The shrines and their ceremonies are magnified in the state educational system as foremost among recognized agencies for the promotion of what is commonly designated *kokumin dōtoku*, or national morality. They are thus accorded a place of chief distinction among the approved means for representing to the people the values of good citizenship and for firmly uniting the nation about the Imperial Throne.—DANIEL C. HOLTOM, *The National Faith of Japan*, 3–4

"To understand Japan and the inner forces that shape her . . . it is essential to know something of the ramifications of Shintō in the thought and practices of the people."[1] In his classic *The National Faith of Japan* (1938), Daniel Holtom identified the Shintō religion as the defining characteristic of a distinctly Japanese civilization. Shintō literally means the "Way of the *Kami*," or the "Way of the Gods." The *kami* were the objects of worship of the Japanese people prior to the introduction of divinities derived from foreign religions originating on the Eurasian continent. At the center of this kami worship were the divine beings that created the universe and their descendants, the divine ancestors of the Japanese people.

Holtom held the view that Shintō was inherently political and linked to particular notions of state and society that gave the Japanese a *Weltanschauung*, a comprehensive philosophy of the world and human life. It was this indigenous Japanese religion that provided the ideological foundations underpinning the modern Japanese nation-state and the Japanese empire from the late Meiji period until 1945.

Today, few scholars of prewar Japan would take issue with Holtom's claim that the Shintō religion was central to the prewar Japanese state. Nevertheless, despite the importance of Shintō in modern Japanese political history, the study of the ideology of State Shintō in the prewar period has received almost no attention from American scholars. The reason for this is unclear. Perhaps a liberal scholarly bias in the United States has stymied the study of Japan's prewar and wartime ideology. Maybe it has to do more with postwar politics.[2] Or, perhaps it seems incomprehensible or unbelievable to us. In the introduction to *The Crisis of German Ideology: The Intellectual Origins of the Third Reich*, George L. Mosse notes that historians have not given much serious attention to the study of Nazi ideology, "for they have regarded this ideology as a species of subintellectual rather than intellectual history."[3] He elaborates on this point, stating,

> The history of Germany in the past century has been discussed at great length by historians and laymen alike. All have wondered whether men of intelligence and education could really have believed the ideas put forward during the Nazi period. To many, the ideological bases of National Socialism were the product of a handful of unbalanced minds. To others, the Nazi ideology was a mere propaganda tactic, designed to win support of the masses but by no means the world view of the leaders themselves. Still others have found these ideas so nebulous and incomprehensible that they have dismissed them as unimportant.[4]

Similar things have often been said about Japan's prewar ideology of State Shintō.

Since the collapse of the Soviet Union and the end of the Cold War, a number of books have appeared identifying new sources of global conflict. One is Samuel P. Huntington's *The Clash of Civilizations and the Remaking of World Order* (1996).[5] Huntington predicted that the end of the ideological rivalry in the latter part of the twentieth century between the two superpowers, the Soviet Union and the United States, would in the twenty-first century give way to a clash among world civilizations. He tried to demonstrate where and how clashes and confrontations among civilizations might emerge as the greatest threat to world peace in the future. The book has caused much controversy and much criticism, especially since the terrorist attacks on New York and Washington, D.C., on September 11, 2001. Thinking in terms of the conflicts among civilizations, moreover, now suddenly seems to be frighteningly very real and dangerous. We are constantly reminded that this is Osama bin Laden's type of thinking, as Yossef Bodansky pointed out in *Bin Laden: The Man Who Declared War on America* (2001): "Ultimately, . . . bin Laden, his colleagues, and the states sponsoring them are all key components of the dominant megatrend in the Muslim world—the rise and spread of radical militant Islamism. They are all theologically motivated and driven, killing and dying in pursuit of an Islamist jihad against the rest of the world. To comprehend Islamist terrorism, one must address its theological-ideological roots."[6]

Huntington, however, went further with this analysis and insisted that the problem was not just radical militant Islamism or Islamic fundamentalism. "Fourteen hundred years of history demonstrate otherwise,"[7] he said. Further, he argued,

> The underlying problem for the West is not Islamic fundamentalism. It is Islam, a different civilization whose people are convinced of the superiority of their culture and are obsessed with the inferiority of their power. The problem for Islam is not the CIA or the U.S. Department of Defense. It is the West, a different civilization whose people are convinced of the universality of their culture and believe that their superior, if declining, power imposes on them the obligation to extend that culture throughout the world. These are the basic ingredients that fuel conflict between Islam and the West.[8]

Interestingly, Huntington's clash-of-civilizations thesis does fit quite well the ideology and worldview of Japanese radical Shintō ultranationalists of the 1920s and 1930s. They, too, viewed major conflicts in the world as conflicts among civilizations, the main clash being between the Western world and Japanese Shintō civilization.

An alternative approach to understanding the primary source of political upheaval in the post–Cold War world is given by the sociologist Mark Juergensmeyer.[9] He paints a provocative picture of a future world conflict between ethnic-religious nationalisms and Western-style secularized nationalisms:

The longing for an indigenous form of religious politics free from the taint of Western culture has been expressed by many in countries that have become independent in this century: not only by Egyptians, but by Central Asians and other Muslims from Algeria to Indonesia, and by Ukrainians, Sri Lankans, Indians, Israelis, Mongolians, and intensely religious persons of a variety of faiths throughout the globe. In fact, what happened to be an anomaly when the Islamic revolution in Iran challenged the supremacy of Western culture and its secular politics in 1979 has become a major theme in international politics in the 1990s. The new world order that is replacing the bipolar powers of the Cold War is characterized not only by the rise of new economic forces, a crumbling of old empires, and the discrediting of communism, but also by the resurgence of parochial identities based on ethnic and religious allegiances. Although Francis Fukuyama, among others, has asserted that the ending of the old Cold War has led to an "end of history" and a world-wide ideological consensus in favor of secular liberal democracy, the rise of new religious and ethnic nationalism belies that assertion.[10]

Juergensmeyer's idea that the source of future world conflict is fundamentally a conflict between religious nationalisms and secular nationalisms is another very useful conceptualization in understanding the origins of the conflict between Japan and the Western world in the first half of the twentieth century. He could very well have added Japan to the list of countries that had had a "longing for an indigenous form of religious politics free from the taint of Western culture . . . in this century." Japan was the first non-Western nation to challenge the Western world for global power in modern times. And as the reader will discover in this study, Shintō ultranationalist ideologues theorized that secularized Western civilization was Japan's mortal enemy. The only way for Japan to free itself spiritually and physically from the clutches of Western civilization was to destroy the Western secular democratic international world order and replace it with an emperor-centered hierarchical world order ruled by Japan's divine emperor. This work analyzes why radical Shintō ultranationalists were convinced of the necessity of waging, to borrow the words of Benjamin R. Barber, an "ethnic and religious jihad" against secularized Western civilization much like that proclaimed by many radical Islamic fundamentalists today.[11] The sources of conflict that Huntington and Juergensmeyer identified for understanding wars of the twenty-first century—civilizations versus civilizations, religious nationalisms versus secular nationalisms, and religious extremism versus mainstream religious moderation—were also at the heart of a conflict between Japan and the Western world in the first half of the twentieth century.

In addition to the fact that there has been no systematic and comprehensive analysis of the development of the ideology of State Shintō in prewar Japan, Western scholars of modern Japanese history have subscribed to the erroneous view that there had been no significant change in the ideology of State Shintō between the late Meiji period and the end of the Second World War, a viewpoint first popularized by the renowned Japanese political theorist Maruyama Masao, whose writings in *Thought and Behavior in Modern Japanese Politics* (1969) have played a powerful role in molding American scholars' perceptions of Japan's prewar ideology of extreme nationalism. In his essay "The Ideology and Dynamics of Japanese Fascism," Maruyama, discussing the distinctive characteristics of the ideology of State Shintō, noted that "the basic characteristic of the Japanese state structure is that it is always considered as an extension of the family,"[12] as Meiji ideologues such as Hozumi Yatsuka and Inoue Tetsujirō had theorized. Maruyama went on to say that this notion "is maintained [by fascists], not as an abstract idea but as an actual historical fact, that the Japanese nation preserves unaltered its ancient social structure based on blood relationship."[13] He further noted that this emphasis on the idea of the family was so important that it defined the social context of Japanese fascism, and he concluded his statement on this particular point by saying, "The insistence on the family system therefore may be termed a distinctive characteristic of the Japanese fascist ideology; and it is connected with the failure of Japanese fascism as a mass movement."[14]

Ishida Takeshi, another well-known early postwar scholar, took up the issue of the ideology of State Shintō in *Meiji Seiji Shisō Shi Kenkyū* (A Study of the History of Meiji Political Thought).[15] He sought to explain the intellectual structure of State Shintō by linking German organic state theory and Confucian family ideology. Although Ishida's formulation of State Shintō differed from Maruyama's, a point in common was that both saw the family-state concept as fundamental to the ideology of State Shintō. More recently, Irokawa Daikichi challenged both Maruyama's and Ishida's analysis of the intellectual structure of State Shintō. While Irokawa, too, considered the family-state concept essential to State Shintō, his chief concern was the validity of the ideological mechanism connecting the family and the emperor in the intellectual structure of State Shintō constructed by both Maruyama and Ishida.

Although for Irokawa, as well as for Maruyama and Ishida, the family-state concept was a core component of State Shintō ideology, Irokawa raised the following objection to Maruyama's and Ishida's theory:[16]

> What . . . was the link that allowed two such disparate elements [the family and the emperor] to be joined? Ishida proposes imported organic theory as the bonding agent, whereas his teacher, Maruyama, invoked the whole indigenous tradition since the Jomon period to account for it. Neither approach, it seems to me, satisfactorily explains the connection established between the family and the state under the emperor system.[17]

For Irokawa, neither Maruyama's nor Ishida's explanation of the mechanism linking the family and the emperor satisfactorily accounts for the reason the Japanese people would be so willing to risk their lives for the emperor in the same way that they would for their families. Irokawa insisted that there must be something else that allows the powerful emotional attachment the individual naturally has for his family to be transferred to the emperor. In short, Irokawa proposed four ideological intermediaries to join the family or the household to the state in the Meiji period: the imperial myth, the religious tradition of ancestor worship, the social structure of the family system, and the heritage of a *völkisch* morality. But again, what Maruyama, Ishida, and Irokawa all had in common was that they assumed the family-state concept to be an essential component of the intellectual structure of State Shintō throughout the prewar period. American scholars seem to have followed their Japanese counterparts and, for the most part, accepted their arguments at face value.

This work challenges the accuracy of this interpretation of Shintō nationalist ideology of the prewar Japanese state, raising a number of important questions that have not been adequately addressed by scholars of prewar Japanese political thought. First, how could a premodern theory of absolute monarchy constructed by Hozumi Yatsuka (whom Maruyama cited as the chief architect of the family-state concept) in the late Meiji period have served as an effective ideological force in mobilizing the Japanese masses for total war in Asia and the Pacific in the 1930s and the 1940s? Oddly, neither Maruyama nor Irokawa referred in depth to the ideological formulations of any of the Shintō ultranationalist state theorists in the Taishō or Shōwa periods. Second, how did State Shintō ideologues initially respond to the challenges posed by the popularity of Minobe Tatsukichi's emperor-as-organ theory of the state in support of political-party government and by the increasing politicization of the

Japanese masses in the first decades of the twentieth century? In other words, how did State Shintō ideology develop in ideological contestation with liberal democracy and socialism in the 1920s and re-create its own theoretical and practical relevance to meet the concerns of Japanese already involved with the affairs of state, as well as to encourage support for Japan's empire building in Asia and the Pacific War in the 1930s and the 1940s?

Third, I felt strongly that the traditional patriarchal family-state concept of State Shintō ideology could not account for the powerful element of fanatical behavior spectacularly displayed by Japanese Shintō ultra-nationalists in the 1930s and 1940s. And what about the suicidal behavior of the Japanese fighting man during the Pacific war? I had always been fascinated by the kamikaze, the pilots of the Tokkōtai, the Special Attack Force, who crashed their planes into enemy ships, and by the suicide charges of Japanese soldiers on the battleground. What motivated the Japanese soldier to seek death on the battlefield rather than surrender, even when the battle clearly had already been lost? Such behavior on the battlefield was a stark contrast to that of the American forces, who did everything they could possibly do to minimize the loss of human life among their own forces. Was this behavior sponsored and perpetrated by mentally deranged or obsessed people who were utterly indifferent to the sanctity of life? Or were they seeking martyrdom? I knew very well that such behavior had deep roots in Japanese tradition. I had studied for almost ten years in Japan, a number of those years in the late 1970s in the Ethics Department at the University of Tokyo with Professor Sagara Tōru, a scholar of Tokugawa intellectual history whose favorite book was *Hagakure*, the eighteenth-century treatise on the way of the *bushi*, Japan's traditional military aristocracy. Nearly every Japanese person at that time knew the famous first lines of this work: "The Way of the Warrior is to seek death."[18] I also was well aware of the fact that the spirit of the *Senjinkun* (Field Service Code) issued by Minister of War General Tōjō Hideki in January 1941 was close to that of *Hagakure*. However, suicidal behavior was not confined to the Japanese military. What motivated a Japanese mother to throw her infant son or daughter off a cliff and then plunge to her death rather than be captured by the Allied army? Could it be possible that this type of behavior had some connection to a radicalized form of State Shintō ideology? Were there extremist offshoots of mainstream State Shintō ideology of the Meiji period that encouraged such behavior?

Spectacular acts of terrorism and widespread public sympathy toward terrorists and political assassins were also conspicuous characteristics of political behavior in Japan of the 1930s. Take, for example, the "May 15 [1932] Incident," the terrorist plot by militant ultranationalists to assassinate top political, bureaucratic, and business leaders in Japan to force a military takeover of the government, which they believed would then lead to direct imperial rule at home and unlimited expansionism overseas. Navy Lieutenant Mikami Taku, one member of the group of military officers who killed Prime Minister Inukai, later testified in court: "Our revolution is intended to bring about direct Imperial rule and harmony between ruler and ruled."[19] Another participant in the plot, Lieutenant Itō Kameshiro, explained to the court a similar notion: "My life's desire will be fulfilled if a state is established on the principle that the Emperor and his subjects are one."[20] Still another terrorist told the court: "The Imperial Way should be spread through the world, the Asiatic nations being first consolidated into a unit and thereafter the rest of the world. . . . We demand direct rule by the Emperor."[21] Could acts of terrorism to bring about a political revolution and usher in a worldwide holy war possibly be justified or even encouraged by radical Shintō ultranationalist thought? Had religious political activism entered into a new phase? Or was this a perversion of Meiji State Shintō ideology? Still more, in view of the positive public response to the perpetrators of such acts of terrorism, I wondered whether political assassination had become an acceptable form of political behavior in the minds of the Japanese people. The fact that the counsel for the terrorists presented over one hundred thousand letters appealing for clemency and that "thirty thousand holders of the Golden Kite, the highest military decoration, signed a petition" says something very significant about the mood of the Japanese masses at the time.[22] Where was the public outrage over the killing of a prime minister? Extremists usually represent a tiny minority of the society in which they live, but the statistics revolving around the May 15 Incident seem, at least on the surface, to indicate mass public sympathy for them. Were there, by the 1930s, widely accepted doctrinal developments in Shintō ultranationalist ideology that would have condoned the overthrow of the government? I did not know the answers to these questions at the time, but I wanted to try to make sense out of things that did not make sense to me from what I had already learned about modern Japanese history and modern Japanese political thought. However, in my quest for answers, I was quite certain about one thing: these kinds of issues could neither be satisfactorily explained nor condoned by the traditional authoritarian, patriarchal family-state Shintō ideology constructed in the Meiji period. In short, I began this study out of a sense of frustration with the conventional wisdom among leading American scholars that the prewar Japanese state was fundamentally a traditional, conservative, authoritarian state to the bitter end.

My initial goal in this project was to examine the writings of Shintō nationalists from the 1910s to the 1940s to find out whether they, too, had followed their Meiji predecessors in conceptualizing the Japanese state in terms of a traditional patriarchal family-state. It did not take me long after I had begun my research to find out that this was certainly not the case. Although hardly any research had been done on this important topic, I discovered that a wealth of information on it existed if one was willing to try to pry it out of obscurity from Japanese libraries. In fact, when I really got deep into this research, I felt as if I had stumbled on an intellectual gold mine, a wealth of information and documents about a very important part of prewar Japanese intellectual history—a history almost totally untouched by, and virtually unknown to, Western scholars of modern Japanese history and political thought.

This book, then, focuses on a much neglected area of scholarly study by Western scholars. But it is not only among Western scholars that this topic had been neglected. The serious study of radical Shintō ultra-nationalist ideology in the Taishō and Shōwa periods has, for the most part, been shunned by Japanese scholars, as well. It is still somewhat of a taboo subject in Japan, for the story of the ideology of radical Shintō ultranationalism is connected with a prewar past that most Japanese would rather forget. Many Japanese still have difficulty coming to terms with their prewar and wartime history and do not seem to be comfort-able investigating the radical Shintō ultranationalist ideology that once glorified Japanese imperialism and mobilized the Japanese masses to wage total war in Asia and the Pacific in the 1930s and the 1940s. In other words, today's Japan is still very much in the business of trying to keep a tight lid on the ideology of its wartime past.

Since the death of Emperor Hirohito, a number of studies have been done on his life and his role in the wartime period. Herbert Bix's *Hirohito and the Making of Modern Japan* (2000) immediately comes to mind.[23] The question of Emperor Hirohito's personal decision-making role in the war is no doubt an important one. But even deeper and more fundamental issues need to be addressed and examined, for the crucial issue is not the question of the guilt of just one man, however important that one man may have been, but the ideology behind the man, the ideology that made the emperor the divine man that he was in the hearts and minds of millions of Japanese, the ideology that made for the fanatical loyalty of the Japanese people to their emperor, unshaken even after the dropping of two atomic bombs and the destruction of the Meiji state. Few men in history have commanded such total loyalty and devotion from the masses as did the Japanese emperor in prewar Japan. How else can one explain why on August 15, 1945, Japanese subjects prostrated themselves before the imperial palace to apologize to their sovereign for their inability to win the war? This work hopes to shed some light on the origins and the development of the powerful and pervasive emperor-centered ideology of radical Shintō ultranationalism in prewar Japan that, from the findings of this study, had achieved a "virtually totalitarian 'spiritual' control over the Japanese psyche" and led to the Second World War in Asia and the Pacific.[24]

This work is a study of the ideology of State Shintō from the promulgation of the Constitution of the Empire of Japan on February 11, 1889, to the publication of *Kokutai no Hongi* (Fundamentals of Our National Polity) and Japan's full-scale invasion of China in 1937. One of the significant discoveries of this study is that a transformation of the internal structure of the ideology of State Shintō did occur from a theory of constitutional monarchy inspired by Imperial Germany, established by Itō Hirobumi and his colleagues,[25] to a theory of absolute monarchy in the political thought of Hozumi Yatsuka in the late 1890s, and then to mass-based totalitarian ideologies in the constitutional theories of Uesugi Shinkichi and Kakehi Katsuhiko in the Taishō period. Further, it explains how this transformation of State Shintō ideology came about in contestation with liberal democracy and socialism and in response to the politicization of the masses in the first two decades of the twentieth century. Still more, for those who are interested in the relationship between religion and the political order, or in the global rise of political movements that base their claim to political legitimacy on religious orthodoxies, this study reveals another important transformation: the movement from a quasi-religious or quasi-secular state constructed by the Meiji oligarchs to Hozumi Yatsuka's traditional conservative theocratic state in the 1890s and, finally, to radicalized and militant forms of extreme religious nationalisms in the state theories of Uesugi Shinkichi and Kakehi Katsuhiko in the 1920s. This religious approach to understanding the evolution of State Shintō ideology is probably more relevant to understanding the conflict between ethnic-religious nationalisms and Western-style secular nationalisms that Juergensmeyer predicted would be the main source of global confrontation in the twenty-first century. From a religious perspective, we can raise our analysis to still another level by identifying two distinctive forms of radical religious nationalism. The theology of Kakehi Katsuhiko best represents one form of radical religious nationalism, and the ideology of Uesugi Shinkichi represents another. Kakehi's radical religious nationalism emerged in the 1910s in response to the growing politicization of the Japanese masses. However, radical religious nationalism in Japan began to take on an even more extreme form by the early 1920s and gave rise to terrorism. If one can define the term "terrorism" to describe the use of violence, or the threat of violence, to achieve certain political or religious ends, Uesugi's radical Shintō ultranationalism supplied a rationale for terrorism and a prism through which the perpetrators of terrorism could judge and condemn the actions of other people. The move to terrorism in the 1930s was not only due to the failure to achieve political goals by nonviolent methods. It was theologically motivated. Accordingly, this study gives an in-depth analysis of Uesugi's militant strand of radical Shintō ultranationalism that justified acts of terrorism and inspired one to seek death.

My analysis of this ideological transformation of the ideology of State Shintō in contestation with liberal democracy and socialism strongly suggests that creeping democracy and the secularization of the political order in Japan in the early twentieth century were the principal factors responsible for breeding terrorism and radicalism, a political trajectory from secularism to religious fundamentalism similar to that we have seen in the Islamic Revolution in Iran in 1979 and in the broader radicalization of much of the Islamic world.[26] Still more, it suggests that, with this rise of radical Shintō ultranationalist thought in the Taishō period and its subsequent diffusion in the early Shōwa period among the Japanese masses, who were increasingly susceptible to radical ideas, the preservation of a political environment in Japan free of extremism and violent threats to the domestic order proved virtually impossible—at least until the nation embarked on total war in Asia and the Pacific. Finally, this study gives a systematic analysis of the worldview of radical Shintō ultranationalists for whom the main source of conflict in the world was a civilizational and religious conflict between a divinely governed theocratic Japanese empire and a secular global order created and controlled by Western nations.

In short, this book offers a reinterpretation of the Japanese state from 1889 to 1945. In the epilogue of *Japan's Modern Myths: Ideology in the Late Meiji Period* (1985), Carol Gluck wrote:

In the three decades between the end of Meiji and the end of the Second World War, ideological effort did not flag. For from the viewpoint of later generations of ideologues, the task of influencing (*kyoka*) the people remained ever incomplete. And during the years of militarism and increasing state control of the 1930s the content and apparatus of ideology reached an intensity that required police enforcement and culminated in the "spiritual mobilization" for war. Thus the ideological process that had begun in the Meiji period continued. Yet it is also true that in the course of the prewar years few wholly new elements appeared.[27]

In a way, this work picks up the story of Japan's prewar ideology precisely from where Gluck left off at the end of the Meiji period. However, Gluck underestimated the nature and impact of ideological transformation that was about to take place in the immediate post-Meiji period when she stated, "Yet it is also true that in the course of the prewar years few wholly new elements appeared." The doctrinal developments transforming the nature of State Shintō ideology between the Meiji period and the Taishō period were fundamental because the difference between a traditional theory of absolute monarchy and totalitarian ideology is fundamental. Further, it is no exaggeration to say that the birth and spread of radical and militant strands of Shintō ultranationalist thought in the Taishō and Shōwa periods constituted a megatrend in State Shintō ideology, a mega-trend that has gone totally unnoticed by Western scholars. While the fundamental structures of the Meiji state remained largely intact, a hidden revolution in the realm of religious thought and state ideology had taken place. This study demonstrates that by the end of the 1930s, extreme nationalists had taken over the state by employing radical religious fundamentalist ideas to crush or sublimate the advocates of all competing ideologies.

This study examines in depth the state theories of several preeminent constitutional-law scholars and leading theoreticians of State Shintō ideology in the late nineteenth century and the early twentieth century. It is divided into three parts, which are organized in chronological order, and consists of a total of nine chapters, plus a concluding chapter. Part one, "Emperor Ideology and the Debate over State and Sovereignty in the Late Meiji Period," consists of four chapters. Chapter 1 discusses why the theory of absolute monarchy emerged to become a central state ideology in the late Meiji period. It suggests that political gridlock in government throughout the 1890s prompted the state theorists Hozumi Yatsuka and Minobe Tatsukichi to formulate and defend new visions of the Japanese state to serve as ideological foundations for a more stable and secure political system. Chapter 2 presents a detailed analysis of the family-state ideology of the constitutional-law scholar Hozumi Yatsuka and illustrates how his construction of the patriarchal state is structurally akin to European theories of absolute monarchy articulated by the French philosopher Jean Bodin and the English political writer Sir Robert Filmer. It also argues that Hozumi's State Shintō family-state ideology was a traditional authoritarian ideology that was out of touch with the prevailing political dynamics of the late Meiji period and that it was already being superseded by the beginning of the Taishō period by the new radical and revolutionary strands of Shintō ultranationalist thought. Chapter 3 is titled "Minobe Tatsukichi: The Secularization of Politics." It takes a fresh look at Minobe Tatsukichi's German-derived state-as-a-sovereign-person theory, or what is better known in literature on Japanese thought as the emperor-as-organ theory of the state, as a viable ideology in support of constitutional government and responsible political party government. It argues that Minobe's organ theory of the state represented a secular theory of the Japanese state and was accordingly vehemently attacked both by conservative and radical Shintō ultranationalists. Chapter 4 provides a detailed analysis of Kita Ikki's Meiji work *Kokutairon oyobi Junsei Shakaishugi* (On the Kokutai and Pure Socialism), a massive critique of Hozumi Yatsuka's patriarchal family-state. It shows how Kita sought to redefine the Meiji Restoration as a social democratic revolution. It also reveals how he argued that the doctrines of loyalty and filial piety actually worked against fostering allegiance to the emperor in the feudal period; that the emperor constructed by State Shintōists was neither the real emperor in Japan's history nor the emperor of the modern Japanese state. Further, it outlines Kita's theory that the Japanese state constructed by Shintō fundamentalists, who excluded ethnically and racially non-Japanese people, was against the wishes of the emperor and prevented the full development of the Japanese empire. Still more, it shows how Kita reasoned that black people as well as whites and other Asian peoples such as the Chinese should be welcomed as full-fledged members of the Japanese state. But most importantly, it argues that Kita, who is portrayed in Western writings on Japan as the most influential intellectual of radical ultranationalism, represented only one type of Japanese ultranationalism in the 1930s, a type of radical ultranationalism that was at odds with mainstream radical Shintō ultranationalist movements at the time.

Part two of this study, "Emperor Ideology and the Debate over State and Sovereignty in the Taishō Period," has three chapters. Chapter 5 briefly discusses the origins of political consciousness among the Japanese masses and the political milieu in which revolutionary mass-based ideologies of extreme nationalism emerged. It also deals with the theoretical issues regarding Japanese ideologies of extreme nationalism or ultranationalism in comparative context and the issue of Japanese fascism in terms of the wider global discourse on fascism, employing theories on fascism by recent scholars such as Stanley G. Payne, Roger Griffin, and Robert O. Paxton. Chapter 6 documents the ideological transformation of State Shintō between the late Meiji period and the Taishō period. It illustrates how, in *A New Thesis on the State* (1921), the constitutional-law scholar Uesugi Shinkichi formulated a theory of state based on very different sorts of human relationships from that of patriarchy.[28] In his metaphysical theory of the Japanese state based on the concept *hito no sōkan to renzoku* (human relationships in space and time), he linked people with one another in a horizontal social structure, not in a vertical, patriarchal structure, thus displacing the traditional patriarchal bonds of society that had been central to the concept of Hozumi Yatsuka's theory of absolute monarchy. It shows how Uesugi had worked out a totalitarian theory of the state that eliminated the authoritarian relationships between the emperor and the masses. It also claims that Uesugi's thought represented the most radical form of extreme religious nationalism in prewar Japan, a form of radical Shintō ultranationalist thought that both inspired and justified acts of political and religious terrorism that swept the country in the 1930s.

Chapter 7 introduces to the Western reader for the first time the state theory of Kakehi Katsuhiko, an intellectual leader among Japanese constitutional-law scholars and State Shintō theorists of the 1920s and the 1930s. Kakehi's thought had such influence among naval and army officers, as well as among civilian leaders and Shintō ultranationalists, that he was selected by the Japanese government to serve in Manchuria to tutor China's last emperor, Xuāntŏng (PǔYi), who had become the ruling figurehead of Japan's prewar state of Manchukuo, on the ideology and theology of State Shintō. This book examines how Kakehi articulated still another major reformulation of the concept of the patriarchal family-state established in the Meiji period. He constructed neither a traditional, patriarchal family state, as Hozumi Yatsuka had done in the Meiji period, nor a structureless state devoid of all institutions linking the masses to the emperor, as Uesugi had done in the Taishō period, but an emperor-centered theocratic state. Still more, I also show how Kakehi envisioned an orderly Japanese theocratic state situated at the center of a Shintō cosmology and a hierarchical world order. It was, I argue, Kakehi's theory of radical Shintō ultranationalism that most accurately represented the type of thinking of those who crushed the militant radical Shintōists involved in the February 26, 1936, Incident and who subsequently led Japan into a full-scale war with China in 1937 and with the Western world in the 1940s.

Part three, "Radical Shintō Ultranationalism and Its Triumph in the Early Showa Period," consists of two chapters. Chapter 8, "Terrorism in the Land of the Gods," discusses the ideological roots and movements behind a wave of ultranationalist terrorism that struck the Japanese state between 1930 and 1936, drawing on analyses of terrorism by noted contemporary Western writers on this subject, such as Walter Laqueur, Mark Juergensmeyer, Walter Reich, Bruce Hoffman, Ariel Merari, and Yossef Bodansky, as well as a Japanese analyst of right-wing terrorism who writes under the pseudonym Tendō Tadashi. It illustrates how ultranationalist terrorism evolved from the Meiji period to the Taishō and Shōwa periods. Ultranationalist terrorism under the rule of the authoritarian Meiji oligarchs, for instance, evolved into something distinctively different in the increasingly secular and more democratic Taishō period, which, in turn, evolved still more dramatically in the early Shōwa period.

Chapter 9 reexamines the famous prewar Japanese document *Fundamentals of Our National Polity* (*Kokutai no Hongi*), showing that it condemned the emperor-as-organ theory of the state, resulting in the establishment of an official ideological-religious orthodoxy. The chapter also re-situates the importance of this work in the general context of the great discourse over state and sovereignty as an ideological and religious blueprint for a holy war to destroy modern Western civilization—the roots of which go back to the European Enlightenment—as well as its ideological influences in the non-Western world. Still more, it contains a section on commentaries on *Fundamentals of Our National Polity* by some of its authors, such as Ijima Tadaō, Kōno Seizō, Yamada Yoshio, Ōgushi Toyō, and Hisamatsu Senichi.

The book ends with a lengthy conclusion.

Something should be said about methodology, the method of analysis used in this study. This book is concerned primarily with ideology and those who formulate state ideology. It is about the thinkers who articulated the ideologies that made political movements possible. As John Breuilly stated in *Nationalism and the State* (1993), "Ideology must, first and foremost, be understood as an intellectual phenomenon."[29] Only a set of ideas—an ideology—can bring people together to cooperate to achieve a common political purpose. The theories of each individual state theorist dealt with in this study are organized and analyzed around a central theme: the debate over state and sovereignty that began in the early Meiji period and continued throughout the Taishō and early Shōwa periods. This debate was arguably the most important political discourse in modern Japanese history. This work treats the ideas of individual state theorists not only on their own terms but, most important, on the basis of their function in the changing structure of the ideology of State Shintō. In each chapter, I analyze in detail at least one important work of a major constitutional-law scholar or state theorist and compare and contrast it with the writings of state theorists before and after that. Furthermore, whenever possible I situate the ideas or the works of each thinker in the context of the political and social milieu of the time. In other words, the formulations of ideologies by the intellectuals examined in this study are rooted in concrete concerns of the state and are analyzed in relation to the practical problems of managing government or organizing political movements in opposition to the government.

This approach differs from the approaches used by previous scholars and writers on this subject. First, works in the English language on Japanese ultranationalist state theorists and rightist Japanese ideology deal almost exclusively with the Meiji period. Gluck's *Japan's Modern Myths* is probably the most important book on this subject. In addition to Gluck's study, there is Richard Minear's biography of Hozumi Yatsuka, *Japanese Tradition and Western Law: Emperor, State, and the Law in the Thought of Hozumi Yatsuka* (1970). The only other study on a major nationalist state theorist of the Meiji, Taishō, and early Shōwa periods is George Wilson's biography of Kita Ikki, *Radical Nationalist in Japan: Kita Ikki 1883–1937* (1969).

Second, Minear and Wilson organized the state theories of these thinkers around the life of the individual. They did not connect the ideas of their individual thinkers extensively to the broader discourse over state and sovereignty throughout the prewar period. Moreover, their biographies tend to exaggerate the significance of the individual theorist in this debate over state and sovereignty. For example, Minear analyzed Hozumi's state theory within the framework of Hozumi's life history and intellectual development, but he said very little about Uesugi Shinkichi, Hozumi's disciple, who totally transformed Hozumi's theory.

Third, I use a highly comparative approach, discussing how the state theories of each Japanese state theorist are structurally related, or intellectually indebted, to the writings of Western political theorists. For instance, this study identifies Hozumi Yatsuka's theory of absolute monarchy with those of the sixteenth-century French political philosopher Jean Bodin and the seventeenth-century English defender of the theory of absolute monarchy Sir Robert Filmer. It also illustrates how Uesugi Shinkichi adapted to his reformulation of the ideology of State Shintō central concepts of the German state theorist G. W. F. Hegel.

In addition to the works on individual political theorists mentioned earlier and Gluck's study of Meiji ideology, there is one study of the relationship between the Japanese state and the Shintō religion written in the postwar period: Helen Hardacre's *Shinto and the State, 1868–1988*.[30] However, Hardacre's short work focuses on the problems involved in the establishment of a state religion during the so-called Great Promulgation Campaign between 1870 and 1884, the Shintō priesthood, Shintō shrines, shrine rites, and religious freedom under State Shintō. She deals with neither Shintō theology nor state theory.

The most important, and the only comprehensive, study in the English language on the ideology of State Shintō and Shintō nationalism thus far was actually done during the wartime period by Daniel C. Holtom. Holtom was an outstanding scholar who wrote two classic books on this topic: *The National Faith of Japan: A Study in Modern Shintō* (1938) and *Modern Japan and Shintō Nationalism: A Study of Present-Day Trends in Japanese Religions* (1947). *The National Faith of Japan* is a history of Shintō from the earliest times to the modern period. But nearly half of the book is devoted to an analysis of Sectarian Shintō, as opposed to State Shintō. As for State Shintō, through the meticulous analysis of the Shintō myth and the official interpretations of the Shintō creation story by Japanese state authorities and by leading Japanese scholars of the time, Holtom shows how the Shintō myths were utilized and carefully manipulated to "surround a doctrine of political absolutism with the final sanctions of religious belief."[31] He charged that Japanese state ideologues entrusted with the moral education of Japanese youth had distorted the original cosmological myth by assigning unwarranted importance to the deity Amaterasu Ōmikami, the Sun Goddess, while minimizing the importance of the deities Izanagi and Izanami, who were actually the primary deities of the myth, and by teaching that Amaterasu Ōmikami was an actual flesh-and-blood historical person or genuine ancestor of the reigning emperor instead of a solar deity.

Although *Modern Japan and Shinto Nationalism* was published in 1947, it was actually a revised edition of a work written in 1943 in the midst of the Pacific war. The content of the first six chapters appeared as originally published in 1943 and two chapters on Shintō in the postwar period were added, plus two important appendixes: the Directive for the Disestablishment of State Shintō and the Imperial Rescript on the Reconstruction of New Japan. In *Modern Japan and Shintō Nationalism*, Holtom argued that a state religion centering on Amaterasu Ōmikami and the emperor was reestablished in the Meiji period, and "from that time onward its influence has augmented with the passing years until it has become the strongest force in contemporary Japan and the chief inspiration of her purpose as she extends her cultural and political domination throughout the Far East."[32] He also dealt with the issues of "nationalism and universalism," "Japanese Christianity and Shintō Nationalism," "Buddhism and Japanese Nationalism," and "The Overseas Expansion of State Shintō."

My study of the development of radical Shintō ultranationalism differs from Holtom's in that Holtom never made an in-depth examination of any of the ideologies of the great state theorists; nor did he interpret their works in a comparative and developmental way. He also did not see the interactive way in which internal politics was driving ideological change, on the one hand, and how ideological change itself was driving political behavior, on the other. This study differs fundamentally from the works cited earlier and offers a radically new way to look at the nature of the prewar Japanese state.

Finally, there is an important work in the German language on Shintō and the Japanese state: Klaus Antoni's *Shintō und die Konzeption des japanischen Nationalwesens (kokutai): Der religiöse Traditionalismus in Neuzeit und Moderne Japans* (1998). In it, Antoni discusses the historical development of Shintō and national thought in premodern and modern Japan. He also investigates the function of Shintō as a religious system to legitimize political power and explores how this culminates in the concept of the *kokutai*. And, of interest to scholars writing in the English language, Antoni's work includes some very interesting sections on the prewar German–Japanese relationship, including a short discussion of fascism in Japan and Germany and "German admirers of the Japanese kokutai (*Deutsche Bewunderer des japanischen kokutai*)."[33]

Something, too, must be clarified with regard to definitions, classifications, and the terminology used in this study. It is important to mention here that there is still no commonly agreed-on name for the ideology of extreme nationalism that, in the opinion of this study, inspired the elite and mobilized the masses to wage war in East Asia and the Pacific. In this introduction, I have already used several terms in reference to this ideology, such as "State Shintō," "Japanese fascism," "Shintō ultranationalism," "emperor ideology," and "radical Shintō ultranationalism." Other words commonly used by writers discussing this movement of extreme nationalism in prewar Japan include "emperor-system fascism," "Japanism," "Shintōism," or just plain "militarism." None of them, it seems to me, will be satisfactory to everyone. Nevertheless, this study refers to the revolutionary, mass-based form of ethnic nationalism that had at the center of its ideology the Shintō creation story of the Japanese islands by Izanami and Izanagi, the divine origins of the imperial line, the divinity of the emperor, the ethnic divinity and superiority of the Japanese people, the belief in a divine world mission for the Japanese state, global imperial rule under the emperor, and so on, as "radical Shintō ultranationalism."

I use the word "ultranationalism," or "extreme nationalism," to distinguish this political phenomenon from another form of nationalism that one might identify with the rise of the nation-state and liberal nationalism. In further clarification of the use of this term, however, I have found the British historian John Breuilly's historical analysis of nationalism extremely useful. In his acclaimed *Nationalism and the State*,[34] a comprehensive and systematic historical comparison of nationalistic politics, Breuilly provided a definition of nationalism that focused on nationalism's political character and developed an elaborate typology of nationalism. He treats "nationalism primarily as a form of politics."[35] He further emphasized that "nationalism is, above and beyond all else, about politics and that politics is about power. Power, in the modern world, is principally about the control of the state. The central task is to relate nationalism to the objectives of obtaining and using state power."[36] He used the term "nationalism" to refer to political movements seeking or exercising state power and justifying such action with nationalist arguments built on the three following assertions:

(1) There exists a nation with an explicit and peculiar character.
(2) The interests and values of this nation take priority over all other interests and values.
(3) The nation must be as independent as possible. This usually requires at least the attainment of political sovereignty.[37]

With this broad definition, he went on to develop his theory of nationalism as principally a form of politics in opposition to the state. He categorized nationalist movements first on the basis of whether or not they were in opposition to "non-nation states" or "nation-states." Under opposition to "non-nation states,"[38] he constructed three subcategories of nationalist movements based on the relationship between the nationalist movement and the state, which are as follows: a nationalist opposition can seek to break away from the present state (separation), to reform it in a nationalist direction (reform), or to unite it with other states (unification).

Breuilly described the origins of Japanese nationalism as a type of "reformist nationalism."[39] This was a type of nationalism that emerged in states that, "although profoundly affected by contacts with the Western world, were never subjected to formal political control by western powers."[40] He explained that nationalist movements in such states had a "desire to reform indigenous society along modern lines; to reject various economic controls and Western pretensions to cultural superiority; and to link both a reformed and independent state and society to a sense of national identity."[41] He also noted that "the reform impulse usually originated within rather than outside the state itself. It tended to begin with a narrow focus on military reform which was seen as necessary in order to combat direct threats from Western powers. The obstacles to such narrow reforms soon became apparent and pushed reformers into the development of ever more radical objectives which could eventually envisage total transformation."[42] This was certainly true of the Japanese Meiji Restoration movement. Members of the lower-ranking samurai elite who led the revolt against the Tokugawa regime and the feudal system sought to take over the state to push through a national revolution from above. They wanted to transform state institutions to make the state effective in resisting demands from the West.

However, the important consequence of pushing through this nationalist revolution from above was that the Meiji Restoration movement itself was an elitist revolution in that it was carried out by members of the traditional elite ruling class. Breuilly noted this, too, saying that "continuity was as marked and as important as discontinuity."[43] One could well argue that the almost bloodless revolution was largely due to the powerful form of cultural nationalism that had emerged in Japan in the Tokugawa period through the Kokugaku (National Learning) Movement.[44] This Shintō revival provided for an ideological and institutional alternative within Japanese tradition. This opposition ideology, in tandem with other ideological currents of thought, had functioned to gradually undercut the legitimacy of the Tokugawa regime throughout the eighteenth century and nineteenth century. By the time Commodore Matthew C. Perry appeared in 1853, the regime was rapidly decaying from internal problems, and dissatisfied bushi (samurai) rallied behind the Shintō movement to restore the emperor to political power.

It was also an elite-controlled revolution in the sense that the Meiji reformers within the military aristocracy believed that they could, and should, control and restrict change from above. The elite themselves were united only in a very broad sense, agreeing only that the Tokugawa regime must be destroyed and that the emperor should be at the political center of the new state. Breuilly noted this, too:

> Very diverse elites ranging from reactionary samurai in the domains to enthusiastic Westernizers in the imperial court co-operated, at least for a time, in a common opposition to the Shōgunate. There was a clear institutional alternative for this opposition to form around within the state itself. Continuity, the confinement of political activity to elites, the diversity of elites involved, and existing institutional alternatives—all were reflected in the artificial, syncretic ideology of emperor loyalty and the restoration of Shintō religion which were used to justify the Meiji Restoration and the subsequent actions of the new regime.[45]

The key point to keep in mind was that the semi-Westernized military elite holding political power wanted to preserve control over the state, eventually opting for the Prussian-inspired Constitution of the Empire of Japan, which they thought would allow them to have the legal authority to do this as well as to permit some sort of political representation to organize mass support for their political purposes. Breuilly concluded his chapter "Reformist Nationalism Outside Europe" by stating, "Only the Japanese [he considered the cases of Turkey, China, and Japan in comparative context] can be regarded as a case of successful reform nationalism."[46] The only other noteworthy point in his analysis of Japanese nationalism in terms of this study was that, in chapter 13 ("Nation-Building and Nationalism in the New States") he mentioned that, "after some time, however, such nationalism, authoritarian from the outset, became increasingly conservative."[47] Breuilly ended his analysis of Japanese nationalism by concluding that the Japanese nationalism of the leaders who made the Meiji Restoration was constructed on the basis of a traditional authoritarian nationalist ideology, a conclusion offered by American and European scholars in the field of Japanese studies.

However, this study shows that the Meiji state was not a politically and ideologically static entity. It had a dynamic political system and was in a constant state of flux. It rapidly evolved in response to complex ideological pressures from within and to foreign pressures from without. One could well argue that the promulgation of the Constitution of the Empire of Japan, the supreme law of the land, by Emperor Meiji in 1889 did little to stabilize the regime. Political gridlock ensued year after year as the opposition in the parliament, using their legal powers to withhold approval of laws and the annual budget, sought to wrestle control of the government from the oligarchs. As chapter one in part one of this study suggests, it was in response to continued political instability in the last decade of the nineteenth century that alternative articulations of the Japanese nation-state and nationalism emerged.

The term "ultranationalism" as used in this study differs from the type of nationalism that Breuilly described and from popular notions of liberal nationalism in modern, secular democratic states such as the United States. Most important, ultranationalism here includes a powerful religious component. It is something close to what Juergensmeyer refers to as a "religious nationalism,"[48] a form of nationalism that merges fanatical religious faith and the nation-state. According to Juergensmeyer, religious nationalism shares the following characteristics: (1) it rejects secular nationalism; (2) it regards secular nationalism as Western and neocolonial; (3) its rejection is fundamental and hostile and violent; (4) it wages the struggle with religious rhetoric, ideology, and leadership; and (5) it offers a religious alternative to the secular nation-state.[49] He also warned that the "merger of the absolutism of nationalism with the absolutism of religion might create a rule so vaunted and potent that it could destroy itself and its neighbors as well."[50] Juergensmeyer further distinguished between types of religious nationalism: religious nationalism that we can live with and religious nationalism that we cannot live with. (Actually, he had a third category: one that we cannot live with easily but that we might have to coexist with.) Included among the characteristics of religious nationalism that we cannot live with are "the potential for demagoguery and dictatorship, the tendency to satanize the United States and to loathe Western civilization, and the potential to become violent and intolerant."[51] It might be further noted here that Juergensmeyer said, on the ideological level, that "there can ultimately be no true convergence between religious and secular political ideologies."[52] On the level of ideology, conflict between religious nationalism and secular nationalism would persist. Thus, this work uses the term "ultranationalism" mainly in conjunction with the Shintō religion—thus, Shintō ultranationalism.

This study shows that Shintō ultranationalism as an ideology emerged at the center of political discourse in the late Meiji period with Hozumi Yatsuka. However, Hozumi's brand of Shintō ultranationalism was married to a traditional authoritarian *völkisch* family-state ideology and thus differed fundamentally both from the ideology of the framers of the Constitution of the Empire of Japan as well as from the radical forms of Shintō ultranationalism what were to follow in the Taishō period. This study further makes a distinction among categories of Shintō ultranationalism as follows: "conservative Shintō ultranationalism" and "reactionary Shintō ultranationalism," or, perhaps, "counterrevolutionary ultranationalism," on the one hand, and "radical Shintō ultranationalism," on the other hand. Alarmed by the degree to which the new Meiji government was modeled after Western political institutions and the gradual evolution to political-party government in the first decade of politics under the Constitution of the Empire of Japan, Hozumi advocated a return to an absolute monarchy governed by the divine monarch. He was a religious ultranationalist who could not tolerate a semi-religious, semi-secular authoritarian constitutional regime giving way to a fully secularized democratic government consonant with the secularized Western world that had inspired democratic governments around the world. He was one of those religious nationalists who, as Juergensmeyer said, "loathed" Western civilization. His form of nationalism was religious and extremist, a type of nationalism not present among those such as Itō Hirobumi and Yamagata Aritomo who created the Meiji state.

However, Hozumi was not what this study refers to as a "radical Shintō ultranationalist." To further clarify this distinction, I have found again Breuilly's analysis particularly useful. He states, "It is essential to distinguish radical right nationalism (henceforth referred to as fascism) . . . from nationalist movements which might variously be described as traditional, conservative, reactionary or authoritarian."[53] Relying on the definition of fascism from Ian Kershaw's *The Nazi Dictatorship*, Breuilly defined radical right nationalism as "a radical, anti-bourgeois, anti-liberal, anti-Marxist movement of national-imperialist integration."[54] He then went on to expand on these key terms, noting, for example, that "unlike traditional right-wing movements, which may take a nationalist form, fascism does not work primarily as informal elite politics dependent upon the absence of popular participation. Rather, fascism comes into its own at times of intense popular involvement in politics and the breakdown of established political parties."[55] Radical-right nationalists are openly hostile to large-scale capitalism, in opposition to political pluralism and parliamentary government, and deny Marxist views of class conflict and materialism. In short, he states,

> In place of traditional conservativism, parliamentary politics or working-class victory fascists offer the vision of a strong and united nation whose heroic leaders pursue a glorious and expansive foreign policy. . . . The rejection of class, party and elite politics leads to the idea of the nation as a classless, partyless, permanently mobilized organism bound together by blood or language or intuition or some such entity whose values, in some mysterious and direct way, are made known to and expressed through extraordinary leaders.[56]

In this story of the rise of radical Shintō ultranationalism, Hozumi was a traditionalist in that he was adamantly opposed to the masses' participating in the political affairs of the state. Therefore, I have classified him as a "conservative Shintō ultranationalist" or "reactionary Shintō ultranationalist," as opposed to what Breuilly called "radical right nationalism" or what this study defined as "radical Shintō ultranationalism."

Radical Shintō ultranationalists in Japan began to emerge in the early twentieth century in response to a continued sense of crisis in government operating under the Constitution of the Empire of Japan, which, in their minds, was tantamount to a breakdown of the Meiji political system. But at the same time, they were also reacting to Hozumi's conservative or reactionary Shintō authoritarianism, correctly perceiving that the politicization of the masses was making his theory of state largely irrelevant.

Although this study relies in part on Breuilly's analysis to clarify radical Shintō ultranationalism, or what he called "radical-right nationalism"—his words for fascism—Breuilly's emphasis on the negative character of fascism does not give us much help in trying to understand its powerful appeal. He stated,

> Fascism, then, came to power in circumstances in which its negative response to class, parliamentary and elitist politics corresponded with a situation in which none of the three forms of politics could cope with a crisis facing a political system with a new, politically mobilized population. Much of this population was scared of threats from the left, unattached to

or subsequently detached from parliamentary parties and beyond the control of conservative elites. In a crisis fascism, the negation of those three forms of politics, could seem to be the only remaining solution.[57]

While it is absolutely true that the conditions for a powerful fascist movement existed in places where the leftist threat appeared dangerous to the political order and in places where parliamentary governments failed to govern effectively, it did have a very powerful ideology and a powerful ideological appeal. It was not only the vision of a strong and united nation pursuing an expansionist foreign policy that attracted people to fascism. Fascism had deep philosophical roots. In *Communism, Fascism and Democracy: The Theoretical Foundations* (1967), Carl Cohen explained that fascism drew on the long traditions of absolutism, organicism, and irrationalism in Western thought. He reasoned that a powerful leader was necessary to maintain and expand the state; that the organic theory of state had a powerful appeal for political unity of the nation; and that the popular attraction of a "deliberate irrationalism" can be seen in the use of the myths of "eternal Rome" and the "Aryan master race."[58]

The Japanese radical Shintō ultranationalists also drew on the powerful traditions of absolutism, organicism, and irrationalism in Japanese history, as well as in Western history. The Shintō doctrines of the "unbroken line of emperors from ages eternal," "eight corners under one roof," and "dying to the self and returning to the one" were all used to mobilize the nation. It was precisely this "deliberate irrationalism" that Cohen talked about as a key to understanding the appeals of European fascism and radical Shintō ultranationalism. This is something that George Mosse also strongly emphasized in *The Crisis of German Ideology: Intellectual Origins of the Third Reich*. In the concluding chapter, Mosse wrote, "Fascists everywhere spurned existing social and economic systems in favor of an irrational world view. . . . This irrational world view was itself objectified in the form of a new religion with its own mysticism and its own liturgical rites."[59] He further commented that "all these western fascisms exhibited a flight from reality into the realm of an emotional and mystical ideology."[60] To Breuilly, it may seem to be a crazy and an "absurd view of politics,"[61] but fascism's appeal is probably the oldest and the most powerful force known to man: religion. Politicized religion was something he totally overlooked in his analysis of fascism. In respect to the importance of myths, Roger Griffin's analysis of European fascism is insightful. In *The Nature of Fascism* (1993), Griffin established a conceptual framework for a "fascist minimum," a core or nucleus that all fascist states had in common. He argued that all fascist states had in common what he referred to as "palingenetic myth" and "populist ultra-nationalism," or just "palingenetic ultra-nationalism," although he did not equate this myth with genuine religion.

This study shows that radical Shintō ultranationalism was a revolutionary, mass-based religion of ethnic or völkisch nationalism that centered on the emperor nation-state and included the following characteristics: (1) deliberate irrationalism; (2) unlimited expansionism; (3) a tendency to pursue total destruction or global rule; (4) internal repression; and (5) total absorption of the individual into the collectivity. In summary, this work is the story of how the völkisch religion of radical Shintō ultranationalism emerged, how it ideologically came to dominate the Japanese state in the early Shōwa period, and how it was articulated to mobilize the masses for consolidating state power and enable radical Shintō ultranationalists to pursue their global ambitions.

It is also worth noting here that another reason no single ideological label readily comes to mind for many people who discuss the ideology of extreme nationalism in prewar Japan probably has much to do with the fact that, unlike in the case of the Nazi Party in Germany or the Fascist Party in Italy, no single extreme nationalist movement seized state power in Japan. Hundreds of Shintō ultranationalist groups sprouted up in the post-Meiji era that often engaged in violent struggle with one another and did not specifically refer to themselves in any obvious way as being Shintōists. They commonly referred to themselves as this or that society or this or that association. However, names like the Jimmu Association or the National Foundation Society are code names for radical Shintō ultranationalist groups. The nature of Japanese radical Shintō nationalism is extremely complex and its essence, I believe, is more difficult to comprehend than German Nazism or Italian Fascism.

In any case, if these definitions and classifications do not satisfy everyone, I do not think that this in itself should pose a particular problem for those of us trying to study the phenomenon of Japanese radical nationalism. As students of European fascism know all too well, despite the hundreds of books and thousands of writings on the theory of fascism, there seems to be still no agreement among scholars on any single definition. I would, in this case, therefore take refuge in the words of Walter Laqueur, author of *Fascism: Past, Present, Future* (1996): "There is the widespread misconception that one cannot begin to study a subject if it does not have an exact definition and a good theory. Unfortunately, however, the real world is very complicated and one usually must do research and describe events without the benefit of a theory, which, in any case, should come at the end rather than the beginning."[62] It is my hope, however, that the reader will have a good understanding of the essence of the ideology of extreme nationalism in prewar Japan after reading this book.

Still more, my study inevitably involves itself in the long-standing debate over whether Japan's behavior between 1931 and 1945 represented an aberration in the nation's modern development. In terms of the development of the radical Shintō ultranationalist ideology that gave the Japanese elite the vision and justification to seek the establishment of a new world order and that mobilized the Japanese masses to fight and die to achieve this aim, I lend support to the view that the Japanese wartime period from 1931 to 1945 was the logical outcome of the triumph of a long, slowly developing but deeply rooted Shintō ideology that goes back to the late Meiji period and, ultimately, back to the revival of *kokugaku* thought in the Tokugawa period. This is not to say or imply that this was simply a straight path from the Meiji period to the Second World War. Intense ideological struggles took place along the way. Indeed, this study documents the ongoing ideological struggle among the competing strains of Shintō thought, showing how radical Shintō ultranationalism emerged as the dominant national ideology in contestation with liberalism and, to some extent, socialism, and how it spread to the masses by the early 1930s.

Finally, the findings of this study present a direct challenge to those who would argue that State Shintō had no systematic ideology and to those who would argue that Japan's prewar leaders lacked ideas and ideological principles on which to base their prewar foreign policy. This was an issue that frustrated even Holtom when he wrote *The National Faith of Japan* in the late 1930s. On this topic, he quoted an article by Yamashita Yoshitarō, a former counselor in the Imperial Japanese Consulate in London, titled "The Influence of Shintō and Buddhism in Japan" that appeared in *Transactions and Proceedings of the Japan Society of London*: "Students of this religion [Shintō] have been struck with the simplicity of its doctrine. It enforces no special moral code, embraces no philosophical ideas, and, moreover, it has no authoritative books to guide believers."[63] Holtom responded to this argument by remarking, "All of the statements in the above quotation require careful examination and it is to such a study that the following pages are dedicated."[64] At the end of his book, Holtom returned to the statement by Yamashita Yoshitarō, stating, "It is to overlook the most important aspects of official Shintō to say that it has no doctrinal beliefs and no ethical teachings and that it is without sacred scriptures."[65] It seems that Holtom was motivated by trying to expose what Ivan P. Hall referred to as the "manipulated dialogue,"[66] the way in which many Japanese intellectuals and spokesmen for Japan manipulate their dialogue with the outside world to "deflect scrutiny, put down criticism, and raise false hopes of intellectual decartelization."[67]

My study also leads to the conclusion that Japan's decision to go to war was as much motivated by internal ideological and religious factors as it was the result of external factors, something that has been given surprising scant attention by writers on Japanese history. Those who do focus on the internal factors that led Japan to war in Asia tend to concentrate on economic factors or the idea of some kind of quest for economic security. Almost totally neglected are the origins, development, and diffusion of the radical, religious ultranationalism that came to grip the Japanese nation in the 1930s and early 1940s. So little has been written about the relationship between the Shintō religion and Japanese ultranationalism in postwar scholarship on Japan that one is tempted to seriously question whether there has been a concerted effort or campaign to de-link them. This has not gone unnoticed by scholars outside Japanese studies. Again, Juergensmeyer, who has done such significant work on religious nationalism around the world, lamented the lack of data on this topic in the case of prewar Japan: "Germany's ally, Japan, also engaged in the war with a religious zeal. Among the neglected aspects of the war were Japanese religious concerns related to the honor of the emperor, who was regarded as both a political and a spiritual leader."[68] Juergensmeyer's observation that the religious dimension to Japan's war in Asia and its neglect in analyses of Japanese nationalism is certainly astute.

The overall orientation and focus of my analysis of Japanese radical Shintō ultranationalism is conceptually very close to Mosse's analysis of German National Socialism. Mosse, who saw National Socialism as a völkisch religious movement that went back to the German Romantic movement of the nineteenth century, stated:

> The Volkish movement triumphed in Germany because it had penetrated deeply into the national fabric. Rather than trying to explain away this fact, it would seem more profitable to ask how this could have been accomplished. This book will argue that the triumph grew out of a historical development, helped along by concrete causes, which resulted in an

attitude of mind that was receptive to the solutions offered by Volkish thought; that January 1933 was not an accident of history, but was prepared long beforehand; and that if National Socialism had not taken the lead, other Volk-oriented parties stood ready to do so, for by that time Volkish ideas had captured almost the entire powerful German right.[69]

This book should be of interest to those who are interested in the intellectual history of extreme nationalism in a broad comparative context. A debate has been going on for the past several decades among academics whose specialty is Japan as to whether fascism is a valid label to define the phenomenon of Japanese ultranationalism.[70] There are also well-known scholars of European fascism (German Nazism and Italian Fascism) who have commented on the case of prewar Japan in regard to fascism. One example here should suffice. In a chapter titled "Fascism outside Europe?" in his book *A History of Fascism, 1914–1945*, Stanley Payne notes that scholars of Japan who hold the opinion that the term "fascism" does not apply to the Japanese case give as their reasons one or more of the following: (1) continuation of a traditional authoritarianism; (2) similarities between Japan and other Third World and developmental dictatorships, (3) the fact that the Japanese system was an emergency wartime expedient; and (4) a radical nominalism that defines the Japanese system as uniquely Japanese or Japanese rightist authoritarianism.[71] Commenting on Japanese ultranationalist thought, Payne cites Kita Ikki as the most prominent theorist of Japanese right-wing fascism. I do not want to jump into this particular debate. I merely observe that when non-Japanese specialists such as Payne ponder the case of prewar Japan and try to apply their theoretical frameworks of fascist ideology outside Europe, it is clear that they have very little literature available in English. Kita Ikki is not the best example of Japanese right-wing fascism because Kita's secular nationalist thought was not representative of the mainstream of Japanese Shintō ultranationalist thought in the prewar period. Why does Payne fail to cite the thought of radical Shintō ultranationalist thinkers of the 1920s through the 1940s? What about the thought of Uesugi Shinkichi, Kakehi Katsuhiko, Yamada Yoshio, Minoda Muneki, Satō Tsūji, or anyone else among the dozens of major radical Shintō ultranationalist thinkers? The reason for this, of course, is quite simple: Virtually nothing is available in English-language works on the thought of these radical ultranationalist thinkers.

Eugen Weber claimed, "Because neither Fascism nor National Socialism has been thoroughly analyzed, we lack sound definitions of either and frequently confuse the two."[72] Weber made that statement in 1964. More than thirty years later, in 1996, Laqueur wrote: "The question of what fascism is has been debated for many decades but frequently has produced more heat than light."[73] It seems to me that if people are still confused about what German National Socialism or Italian Fascism is despite the large number of books on the subject, it should not be at all surprising that there is even more misunderstanding about the nature of Japanese extreme nationalism in the prewar and wartime period. It is my hope that this book, by its analysis of the State Shintō theorists and other intellectuals in prewar Japan, will contribute to a better understanding of the nature of extreme nationalism in prewar Japan. The purpose of this study is to give a historical interpretation of the development of the radical, mass-based, emperor-centered religion of extreme ethnic nationalism in prewar Japan and elucidate the type of arguments that have been used by ultranationalist ideologues to win converts in support of their cause in prewar Japan.

Throughout this book, Japanese proper names are given in Japanese order—family name followed by the given name. Unless otherwise indicated, translations from the Japanese are mine.

I

EMPEROR IDEOLOGY
AND THE DEBATE OVER STATE
AND SOVEREIGNTY IN THE LATE
MEIJI PERIOD

1

From Constitutional Monarchy

to Absolutist Theory

The Meiji political system both in theory and practice was a mixture of authoritarianism and constitutionalism, a hybrid "absolute constitutional monarchy." — JOSEPH PITTAU, *Political Thought in Early Meiji Japan, 1868–1889*, 201

"So Japan is a family-state!" I thought. Even as a child I thought there was something phony about the idea. Had it meant that all Japanese were to join together *as if* in a family-state, I might have understood. But there was nothing I could see in the world around me that suggested a "familial harmony unparalleled in the world." And while they filled us with this at school our parents, on this subject anyway, held their tongues. In the early years of the Showa period, when fascism began to gain ground in Japan, it is said that even the German fascists envied the Japanese *kokutai* its status as a "family-state." But who invented the term in the first place?"

After the defeat I found out: it appeared to have been created for the Meiji government by ideologues like Hozumi Yatsuka, Kato Hiroyuki and Inoue Tetsujiro for the purpose of solidifying the emperor system. — IROKAWA DAIKICHI, "The Emperor System as a Spiritual Structure," 280

Emperor Ideology and Early Meiji Politics

As Irokawa Daikichi suggested in the epigraph, new ideological perspectives do not appear out of the blue. They are rooted in concrete political and social concerns. According to Irokawa, the family-state concept was invented to solidify the emperor system against the increasing power of Western liberal thought. This is certainly true. But what is important to bear in mind is that it was not until the late Meiji period that the Meiji government began aggressively to promote the family-state ideology through ideologues such as Hozumi Yatsuka, Katō Hiroyuki, and Inoue Tetsujirō. This in itself represented a fundamental shift from early Meiji thought, for in the initial phases of the Meiji period, members of the ruling oligarchy proposed ideas of the state that were astonishingly liberal. The first well-known political statement by the new leadership that overthrew the Tokugawa government was the so-called Five-Point Charter Oath of 1868. Article 1 stated: "Deliberative assemblies shall be widely established and all matters decided by public discussion," a clear illustration of this liberal-mindedness and openness of the new Meiji leaders in 1868.[1]

Regardless of whether the Charter Oath was to be interpreted as a quickly drawn-up statement issued by the new leadership as a calculated political action to gain support among the daimyo for the new regime, there is no question that the promise of deliberate assemblies turned out to haunt the ruling oligarchs in subsequent years. The companion document to the Charter Oath, the "Constitution of 1868," showed that the new leaders were also thinking in terms of representative government and the separation of powers of government. Article 3 of that document states in part that "the legislative organ [of the Council of State] shall not be permitted to perform executive functions, nor shall the executive organ be permitted to perform legislative functions."[2] The idea of a separation of powers, according to legislative and executive branches of government under a monarchy, brings to mind such political notions as Montesquieu's concept of a monarchical system tempered by competing intermediary governmental powers.

Still more, the first constitutional drafts drawn up by leading oligarchs such as Kido Kōin, Ōkubo Toshimichi, and even Iwakura Tomomi in the early days of the Meiji regime contained surprisingly strong democratic ideas. All of them presented differing proposals on how state power ought to be shared. For example, we find in a constitutional draft drawn up under instructions from Kido Kōin, who had once been a radical from the domain of Chōshū and a student of Yoshida Shōin, statements such as, "All the articles of the constitution are rules agreed upon between the emperor and the people."[3] Ōkubo Toshimichi expressed similar constitutional ideals. In his "Opinion on Constitutional Government," submitted to Itō Hirobumi in 1873, he stated: "Constitutional monarchy is a joint government of the ruler and the people; it is a limited monarchy."[4] In short, these key members of the ruling oligarchy appeared to have envisioned some kind of constitutional monarchy with representative institutions and clearly defined limitations on the powers of the government and the emperor. Few of the oligarchs or higher-echelon bureaucrats at the center of state power seem to have been in favor of arbitrary or absolute imperial rule.

However, ideological contestation among the ruling oligarchs broke out into the open in 1873. A split occurred in the heart of the collective leadership in the ruling Council of State in that year over the issue of whether or not to invade Korea. Many of those who resigned from government in the wake of this real crisis in the leadership, such as Itagaki Taisuke, Gotō Shōjirō, Etō Shimpei, and Soejima Taneomi, together submitted a memorial to those remaining in the ruling oligarchy calling for the establishment of a national assembly. This memorial marked the beginning of the freedom and popular rights movement and stimulated support for parliamentary government among journalists and intellectuals of the time. Initially, Itagaki and his followers constituted the core of the freedom and popular rights movement. At the same time, those who remained at the center of power in the oligarchy tended to become more conservative in their political outlook and less inclined to entertain thoughts of sharing any real political power.

The central issue of this political struggle between those in government and those former oligarchs who left the government was not an issue of whether to adopt a constitutional monarchy. That, too, was almost a foregone conclusion, given the political circumstances surrounding the Meiji Restoration. The legitimizing authority for the overthrow of the Tokugawa feudal regime had always been recognized, implicitly or explicitly, as the emperor. Thus, this fact insured that the emperor was to be the focus of political power. Moreover, most of the key members of the collective leadership long before the coup d'état in 1868 were aware that almost all of the powerful Western states had constitutions and were convinced that this was a key element contributing to their state power. The oligarchs for the most part had resigned themselves to granting limited popular participation in the affairs of government in the hope of obtaining broad public support from educated subjects for government policies and the long-range goals of the state. In other words, the government oligarchs sought to use liberal institutions for conservative ends. An equally important factor ensuring the adoption of a constitutional government was that the oligarchs were fully aware that constitutional government was a minimal requirement to gain acceptance by the Western powers and rectify the unequal treaties imposed by them. And the demands for representative government by the former oligarchs and other intellectual elites were of course the overriding factor that contributed to the establishment of constitutional government.

Such political circumstances out of which the Meiji Constitution of 1889 eventually emerged virtually ensured that the modern Japanese state would have both monarchical government and constitutional government. In short, it would be a constitutional monarchy. Thus, the real ideological cleavage among the political elite was not over the inevitability of a constitutional monarchy, but over the type of monarchy and the timing of the constitution to be granted.

On one side of this debate, we tend to find the oligarchs in government who subscribed to the Prussian model of constitutional monarchy, which, in line with Hegel's ideas of state organization, represented a rejection of Montesquieu's principle of the separation of powers. It was a system of constitutional monarchy in which the ministers of state were to be responsible to the emperor and whose function it was to serve him as advisers. In this Prussian system of constitutional monarchy, the parliament was designed to function not as a real legislative organ of the government but as a kind of mediating organ between the executive and its bureaucracy, on the one side, and the masses of people outside government, on the other side. It was seen as a useful representative organization to channel potential organized opposition to the state into an acceptable form of participation in government. Still more, the popularly elected parliament was regarded as a potentially powerful vehicle for mobilizing broad support among the population in support of state policy.

On the other side of this debate, we tend to find the former oligarchs who demanded variations of English and French popular-sovereignty theories of state. In general, they held the notion that political authority derives ultimately from the people, and they envisioned a type of constitutional monarchy in which sovereignty resided jointly in the emperor and in the people, something very close to the English tradition of the "King-in-Parliament." Under this kind of government, the cabinet was to be responsible to a popularly elected parliament, which held real legislative power in the state.

Repercussions from this debate among oligarchs and former oligarchs over whether to adopt a Prussian system of constitutional monarchy or an English style of constitutional monarchy were felt well into the next decade. As time passed, an increasingly broad segment of the educated elite became involved in this debate, and the positions taken by people in the debate tended to become increasingly polarized. Opinion makers such as the editorial staff of the *Kōchi Shimbun*, for example, went far beyond the English style of constitutional monarchy, expressing ideas close to republicanism. An editorial in *Kōchi Shimbun* on October 7, 1881, said,

> In the words of Rousseau, society is built upon a social contract. This is not completely according to historical data, and, therefore, we cannot easily agree with him. However, we firmly believe that society should not exist without a social contract. Thus, we are convinced that sovereignty must reside in the people. Since the people are the nucleus of the state, without the people the state cannot exist. If there are the people, even without a king, society can exist.[5]

Still more striking during the early Meiji period is that, in the early 1870s, we find intellectuals such as Katō Hiroyuki who not only argued for liberal democracy but were not in the least afraid to openly declare that the emperor was a man just like any other man. In *Kokutai Shinron* (A New Theory on the Kokutai), published in 1874, he stated:

> It has been taught that the true "Way of the Subject" is to submit, without questioning whether it is good or evil, true or false, to the Imperial Will and to follow its directives. . . . This type of behavior has been characteristic of our national polity. It has been said that for this reason Japan's national polity is superior to that of any other country. This viewpoint is a base and vulgar one! . . . Our national polity is characterized by the mean and vulgar tradition of servility, the land held to be the private property of the Emperor alone. The Emperor and the people are not different in kind: the Emperor is a man; the people too are men.[6]

Joseph Pittau noted that in this context Katō was aiming his attack not at the ruling oligarchy so much as at the Kokugaku scholars of the time who, despite their small numbers, were a political force to be reckoned with and whose political view was that "people born in Japan exist only to serve the imperial will."[7] Pittau further noted that it was Katō's opinion that under such a system of thought, which demanded that people be subservient to the will of the emperor, "the people of Japan will become as cattle and horses."[8]

Katō's attack on *Kokugaku* ideology in the passage from *A New Theory on the Kokutai* reveals the existence of a state Shintōist movement advocating absolute monarchy. They were certainly actively, although not centrally, involved in this debate over the state at that time. The fact that we find the Office of Shintō Worship above the Council of State in the first reorganization of government after 1868 is proof enough that the state Shintōists held, though for a very brief period, considerable clout in the highest circles of government. In the extreme, some Shintō fundamentalists believed in direct emperor rule in some kind of religious mystical sense. One might liken them to political romantics who imagined some kind of a direct relationship between the emperor and a communal collectivity.

Accordingly, these Shintō fundamentalists "could not project the principles on which to erect a state apparatus capable of ensuring order and security."[9] They failed to propose concrete institutions and structures of government because their vision of a restoration of emperor rule was "too radical for the present and bordered upon utopia."[10] Quickly pushed aside by the practical oligarchs attempting to establish a powerful centralized state, they became, as H. D. Harootunian eloquently put it, mere "accomplices of restoration."[11] Although relegated at this juncture in history to the fringes of politics, their involvement in modern Japanese politics did not end, for they would gradually reemerge at the center of state politics in the twentieth century. In the meantime, however, the masses had yet to be politicized, and the Japanese state did not have the industrial and technological capabilities to project massive power on a global scale. Political realists were left with the task of working out a system of government in which the emperor and the emperor system would be legally and institutionally linked to some form of bureaucratic state structures.

To reiterate, the central debate over the state in the pre-constitutional period was over the adoption of two different systems of constitutional monarchy. Indeed, Iwakura Tomomi, one of the most powerful oligarchs in the early years of the Meiji Restoration, stated that the essence of this constitutional debate boiled down to whether Japan should adopt a system of constitutional monarchy close to that of England or one close to that of Prussia:

> If we plan to establish a constitutional government in our country and open a parliament, we will be creating something new. The problem is: shall we follow the English model and establish a party government, making the parliamentary majority responsible for the administration?

Or shall we, following the principle of gradualism, grant only legislative power and reserve the executive power to the Emperor, according to the Prussian model? Today's decision between these two alternatives will establish a permanent foundation and determine the interests of the country for a hundred years.[12]

Iwakura's remark about the high stakes involved in the outcome of this debate was quite perceptive. Subsequent history would show that this pre-Meiji Constitution debate over the state was the beginning stage of an ideological dynamic driving the nation in two opposite directions.

This pre-constitutional debate ended with the defeat of those who held to English and French theories of the state, theories of the state based on the conception of the contract origins of government, and individualistic rationalism that formed the intellectual backdrop for popular sovereignty theories of state. This victory for the establishment of a Prussian-style of constitutional monarchy therefore eliminated the possibility—at least theoretically, although not in actual political practice—of Japan evolving into a classical Western European liberal-democratic state based on the theoretical concept of popular sovereignty. The intellectual legacy of the outcome of this pre-constitutional debate in favor of German constitutionalism was that Japan was then left without an ideology or a solid theoretical basis on which to build a liberal-democratic state.

An "Absolute Constitutional Monarchy"

A constitution is, of course, the supreme law of a nation. It is the fundamental law that forges the way people come together and function as a community. However, as Paul Brest once stated, "A document cannot achieve the status of law, let alone supreme law, merely by its one assertion. . . . The authority of a constitution derives from the consent of its adoption."[13] Likewise, if government is to function smoothly, the intellectual foundations supporting the constitution must be based on homogenous notions of government and a commonly agreed on political ideology.

The Constitution of the Empire of Japan, however, neither functioned to bring people together as a community nor provided a legal framework for the smooth functioning of government. On the contrary, it crystallized in legal form the existing, fundamental ideological cleavages among the political elite and created the political structures within which the ruling oligarchy and the opposition members of parliament could wage a long, drawn-out battle for hegemony that would cause chronic gridlock in the first decade of constitutional government. In other words, it appears that the drafters of the Constitution of the Empire of Japan did not aim to end the crippling power struggle the ruling oligarchs had been engaged in with their former colleagues and opponents in the parliament. The final version of the Constitution of the Empire of Japan was not a compromise of original drafts drawn up by the collective leadership and the alternative drafts prepared by those in the opposition. Instead, the oligarchs sought to establish a kind of constitution that was most favorable to ensure their own control of the state.

Although the drafting of the Constitution of the Empire of Japan had been a long process, starting in the mid-1880s and stretching throughout the rest of the decade, in the final stage, Itō Hirobumi, Inoue Kowashi, Itō Miyoji, Kaneko Kentarō, and the German legal scholar Karl Friedrich Hermann Roessler deliberated on and drafted the constitution in secret on a little island in Tokyo Bay in late 1888. On February 11, 1889, they had the emperor announce the constitution as a gift from the emperor to the people of Japan. There was no constitutional convention; no ratification was needed by a constituent assembly, to say nothing of a popular referendum. Consequently, the Constitution of the Empire of Japan failed to represent an agreed on power-sharing arrangement among the political elite. It did not, in other words, resolve the fundamental ideological cleavages dividing the elites in and out of government originating in the pre-constitutional debate over the state.

Contradictions and ambiguities inherent in the Constitution of the Empire of Japan were to lead eventually to a political crisis. It established structures of government that provided neither for a smoothly functioning parliamentary democracy nor for an unassailable absolute monarchy. But at the same time, it left open the possibility of interpretation favorable to both absolutism and constitutionalism. Many scholars have argued that the Constitution of the Empire of Japan had given legitimacy to irreconcilable notions of absolute monarchy and constitutionalism. For example, Pittau characterized the new Japanese state as an "absolute constitutional monarchy."[14] Robert Scalapino stated that "the Meiji Constitution was essentially an attempt to unite two concepts which when viewed in the abstract were irreconcilable: Imperial absolutism and popular government."[15] Trying to account for the failure of democracy in prewar Japan, Scalapino noted that one of the prime obstacles to the success of democracy in prewar Japan was the institutional structure within which it had to operate. By "institutional structure" he meant a whole set of political institutions set up in the decades of the 1880s and 1890s, including, of course, the Constitution of the Empire of Japan and other state documents such as the Imperial Rescript on Education and the Imperial Rescript to the Armed Forces. Scalapino observed, and I think correctly, that in these institutions the cards were stacked heavily against the democratic elements.

But just where can we find the constitutional justification for absolutism? This is not as apparent as it might seem from studying the articles of the Constitution of the Empire of Japan. According to the constitution, both the executive and legislative powers of government were concentrated in the executive branch. The executive branch of government consisted of the emperor, the emperor's ministers of state, and the Privy Council. But the emperor alone had the right to appoint and dismiss the ministers of state, and the Privy Council was his private advisory body. So the emperor in theory *was* the executive power, and his constitutional prerogatives were indeed overwhelming. For there to be constitutionalism, however, the oligarchs were compelled to give the parliament some powers in the Constitution of the Empire of Japan. They gave the most minimal concessions without which a parliament would have no legislative purpose whatsoever: the responsibility to *approve* laws and to *approve* the annual budget. In this respect, the most important power was to approve the annual budget. As it turned out, this was a great power given to the parliament, and it was through this power that the parliament was able to paralyze the functioning of government. Lacking real legislative power to propose and make laws, the parliament could block the passage of the annual budget and force the ruling oligarchy to share power. The parliamentarians wanted parliamentary rule under the formality of a constitutional monarchy in which the monarch was the titular head of state but without real political power.

The ruling oligarchy, however, insisted on control of the state. Itō and the other members of the ruling oligarchy who put together the constitution saw the parliament's function as service to the emperor, contributing to the smooth workings of the state. When the parliament did in fact exercise its power of vetoing a proposed budget, the oligarchs were forced to come to terms. When attempts at compromise between the oligarchs and the parliamentarians failed, it led to gridlock in government that threatened to destabilize the country. The Constitution of the

Empire of Japan merely crystallized in legal form the fundamental ideological cleavages among the political elite and gave both sides the political weapons to engage each other.

Because of the parliament's legislative power to approve proposed laws, the Constitution of the Empire of Japan did not establish an absolute monarchy. Nor did Itō Hirobumi construe the state to be an absolute monarchy. He made this quite clear on more than one occasion. For example, in his *Commentaries on the Constitution of the Empire of Japan,* he emphasized that "a constitution allots the proper share of work to each and every part of the organism of the State, and thus maintains a proper connection between the different parts. . . . It will thus be seen that the theory of absolute power, which once prevailed in Rome, cannot be accepted as a constitutional principle."[16] When challenged, however about the ambiguities inherent in the Constitution of the Empire of Japan, Ito evaded the issue. Mikiso Hane notes that during the discussions on the various drafts of the constitution held in 1887,

> Two contradictory positions were simultaneously upheld by Itō. First, when it was suggested that the Diet should be given the right to appeal to the Throne regarding illegal actions by government officials, Itō objected saying, "this constitution was drafted to strengthen the authority of the ruler and make it 'weightier.'" Second, when Mori Arinori suggested replacing the term "rights of the subject" with "status of the subject," Itō held that "the spirit behind the constitution is to limit the authority of the ruler and protect the subject's rights."[17]

Apart from this issue of absolutism in the Constitution of the Empire of Japan, one must keep in mind that the former oligarchs who dominated the parliamentary opposition held no illusions as to who actually controlled state power. They knew very well that the powers delegated to the emperor in the constitution formalized decision making by the government oligarchs. Even granting the fact that all major policy decisions involving the affairs of state were to be discussed with the emperor, and that all state actions were taken in his name, the emperor was regarded by few, if any, as the real decision maker. The oligarchs were constantly accused, and rightly so, of having created a system of government in which they could preserve their own powers behind the facade of the authority of the emperor. In other words, Itō and the other framers of the constitution had assigned extensive authority to an emperor who was perceived to be removed from any real decision-making power.

The constitution was clearly the product of an internally divided oligarchy. Ignoring practical political realities, Itō and the other framers had legalized ambiguous rule among multiple sources of power at the highest levels of government. Nakae Chōmin, the chief Liberal Party ideologue and spiritual founder of the radical intellectual faction of the democratic movement, aptly characterized the Meiji Constitution as a "strange creature with one body and many heads."[18]

Karl van Wolferen, another astute analyst of modern Japanese political behavior, characterized the whole process of state institution building by the Meiji oligarchs in the 1880s as "institutionalizing irresponsibility." He observed that those "who partake in the sharing of power are unremittingly ambivalent about who among them should have the right to rule," a problem that "is essentially and by definition a problem of political legitimacy."[19] Given the tacit understanding that the emperor could not constantly be directly involved in the nitty-gritty politics in ruling the state, the ministers' formal accountability to the emperor and not to the parliament meant in fact that they were accountable to no one but themselves. Masataka Kosaka, a scholar of international politics in the Department of Law at Kyoto University, claimed that the fragmented prewar Japanese political structure was a relic of the Meiji Constitution and that it was part of the reason Japan was able to plunge into the Second World War. He, too, concluded from an analysis of the constitution that the way the executive structure was set up pointed to a divided oligarchy:

> According to the constitution, the emperor entrusted the handling of state affairs to the Cabinet. However, the prime minister was merely the head of the Cabinet and had no right to dismiss any of the ministers under him. His rights and responsibilities were limited. To make matters worse, the military was accorded independent status. The powers of government in prewar Japan were fragmented; the prime minister was weak; the military was independent.[20]

The constitution made reference neither to a Cabinet nor to a prime minister. Apparently reflecting on the origins of the prime ministership in England under Sir Robert Walpole, the oligarchs openly argued during the drafting of the constitution that should the prime minister have the right to dismiss ministers of state, that would usurp the prerogatives of the emperor and in effect leave the door open to the evolution to a British system of constitutional government. But for Itō and his colleagues, who were well aware where real power lay, the more plausible reason for limiting the role of the prime minister was that none of them was willing to grant real control of the state to any one person.

In addition, Yamagata Aritomo sought to ensure that the military would be independent of the cabinet by making the emperor supreme commander of the armed forces. The head of the General Staff was the direct subordinate of the emperor and had the power to organize and lead the armed forces without governmental restrictions. The prerogative of supreme command and other imperial prerogatives apart from and independent of the cabinet gave military leaders the power to overturn civilian-controlled governments. And once the original oligarchs had passed from the political scene, there was no individual or cohesive group of individuals who had the political influences to effectively control the state or restrain the military.

Given such pluralization of power, where in the Constitution of the Empire of Japan does one find legal justification for the notion of monarchical absolutism? In a nutshell, the theoretical basis for absolute monarchy was brought into the Constitution of the Empire of Japan with Article 1, which stipulates: "The Empire of Japan shall be reigned over and governed by a line of Emperors unbroken for ages eternal." Article 1 is a proclamation of the main tenet of State Shintō doctrine in legal form: that Japan has always been reigned over and governed by an unbroken line of emperors descended from the divine deity Amaterasu Ōmikami in the Shintō religious doctrine of creation.

It is difficult to judge the extent and depth of Itō Hirobumi's religious convictions, but we can state with certainty that he was convinced that religion and religious values were essential to the ultimate success in creating a unified state. In a speech delivered before the Privy Council prior to beginning deliberations on the constitutional draft, Itō said: "In Europe, religion is the foundation of the state. The feeling of the people is deeply penetrated by and rooted in religion. In our country, however, the religions represent no important force. In our country what alone can be the foundation is the Imperial House."[21] In connection with deliberations on Article 1 of the constitution, Pittau noted that Roessler, Itō's close German constitutional adviser, was opposed to the religious implications of this article and instead proposed that it read, "The Japanese Empire is one indivisible constitutional monarchy."[22] Pittau further noted that the inclusion of this Shintō doctrine of faith "went against [Roessler's] scientific convictions to accept the myth of an eternal progenitor as the founder of the imperial family as the fundamental article of the constitution."[23] Also, Article 3, stating, "The Emperor is sacred and inviolable," implicated the religious nature of the Japanese state. Elaborating on this article in *Commentaries on the Constitution of the Empire of Japan*, Itō states: "The Sacred Throne was established at the time when the heavens and the earth became separated (*Kojiki*). The Emperor is Heaven-descended, divine and sacred."[24] Thus, we can lay the blame squarely on Itō Hirobumi for opening the door to the legal mystification of the emperor.

For the ruling oligarchs and the opposition leaders at the top of the power structure, as well as for secular political realists, such articles in the Constitution of the Empire of Japan meant little beyond acknowledgment that the emperor was to be the nominal head of state. But for State Shintō fundamentalists such as Hozumi Yatsuka, Articles 1 and 3 carried with them the entire weight of the Shintō religious tradition. The inclusion of the Shintō doctrine in the Constitution of the Empire of Japan also gave the religious nationalists powerful political and legal positions from which to wage an ideological battle for the establishment of an absolute monarchy. On the legal basis of the Constitution of the Empire of Japan and its companion state document, the Imperial Rescript on Education, the masses would be taught that the emperor who reigned and governed their state was a deity.

In conclusion, the Constitution of the Empire of Japan set the stage for national disaster. The problem was not ambiguity. The first seventeen articles of the constitution clearly spelled out the overwhelming powers of the emperor. The supreme irony is that the emperor, divine being that he was, could not in fact carry out his constitutional prerogatives and be held responsible. That would have quickly destroyed the Meiji system of government. Johannes Siemes summed up the crux of the problem nicely:

> The myth which made the Emperor a quasi-divine being prevented his carrying out the supreme political decision-making which the constitution clearly assigned to him. If the Emperor was to retain the halo of superhuman wisdom and sanctity, he could not be allowed to be dragged down into politics, into the arena of party strife and fallible decision. Therefore, the Japanese avoided asking political decisions from him and kept him away from governmental affairs. In this vacuum of decision-making in the constitutional system stepped anonymous rulers, those who in reality dominated the throne and made the will of the Emperor by deciding for him the selection of ministers and the policy of the Cabinet.

Under Emperor Meiji it was the Genrō of the Restoration, in the final phase it was the military clique. Those real decision-makers behind the throne were men and power groups which stood outside the constitution and were, in the last resort, responsible to nobody. So the way was open to an abuse of the imperial power, and this abuse of the imperial power by uncontrolled power cliques perverted the whole structure of the Meiji Constitution.[25]

Political Gridlock and the Search
for Alternative Systems of Government

Politics under the Constitution of the Empire of Japan began with the first parliamentary elections held on July 1, 1890. The problem of political gridlock in government in the 1890s under the constitution is well documented. Kenneth Pyle identified several distinct phases of the development of the dispute between the oligarchs in power and parliamentary opposition:

> The first phase, from the opening of the Diet in 1890 to the beginning of the Sino-Japanese War in 1894, was characterized by implacable hostilities between the oligarchy and the parties. The latter posed repeated obstacles to the passage of government budgets, and the oligarchy responded by frequently dissolving the Diet. During the second phase, from 1895 to 1900, tentative short-lived alliances were struck between the cabinet and elements in the House. This was a time of rapid expansionism of armaments, and the oligarchs were willing to make limited concessions to the parties in order to gain the passage of budgets. Those alliances, however, tended to break down once the oligarchs had won their way.[26]

Pyle noted that a third phase of accommodation between the oligarchs and the parliament ensued, but the dynamics of the fundamental problem remained. And it must be noted that even Emperor Meiji began to have reservations about his granting of the constitution and the establishment of a parliament:

> The emperor had reached the same conclusion as Itō—no matter how many times debates might be suspended, there was unlikely to be any change of attitude. Not long afterward he confided to Sasaki Takayuki that he felt such collisions between the government and the House of Representatives were caused by the excessive haste with which the Diet

had been established. From this point on, the emperor's political views seem to have become more conservative. He had begun to think that the granting of the constitution and establishment of the Diet, in which he had taken pride, had been premature.[27]

Meanwhile, the political parties in the 1890s continued to push for what they thought was real constitutional government in which the political parties controlled the cabinet. In 1898, the Jiyū Tō (Liberal Party) and the Shimpō Tō (Progressive Party) joined to form the Kensei Tō (Constitutional Government Party). The reasons given by Ōkuma Shigenobu of the Progressive Party and Itagaki Taisuke of the Liberal Party for forming the new Constitutional Government Party were as follows:

> It will soon be ten years since the promulgation of the constitution and the opening of the Diet. During this period the Diet has been dissolved no fewer than five times, and constitutional government has yet to bear fruit. The political parties likewise have made no progress, and as a consequence, the lingering evils of the domain cliques are still frozen solidly. This has shattered the harmony between the government and the people and delayed matters of state, something that all men who love their country deeply deplore. We, in consideration of the situation at home and abroad, have dissolved the Jiyū and Shimpō parties in order to organize one large political party, rallying men of like mind. We hope that renewal and renovation will create a fully constitutional government.[28]

While the political parties continued to work for parliamentary government, the oligarchs sought to prevent that from happening. Yamagata was very concerned about such a development. He expressed this when asked about supporting Itō's idea of a political party: "To allow a political party to form a cabinet would be to destroy the history of the Meiji government and to violate the imperial constitution. If this is done, we shall undoubtedly share the fate of countries like Spain and Greece."[29] Other oligarchs also expressed strong reservations about the idea of political parties controlling the cabinet. Katsura Tarō even went so far as to suggest that, "if the Diet continued to oppose the government, it could be dissolved, and if necessary, the constitution could also be suspended."[30]

One finds a polarization emerging between those who wanted to maintain rule by the oligarchs in the name of the emperor and those who wanted parliamentary government. Of course, politics was not that simple. The political problems Japan faced were much more complex than the struggle between the ruling oligarchs and the parties in opposition.

For instance, there were powerful cleavages among the oligarchs and between the political parties. And after the formation of the Constitutional Government Party, factions within the party contributed much to destroying the first party cabinet of Ōkuma and Itagaki in 1898. Emperor Meiji was terribly upset with the way in which the parties were handling the affairs of state and expressed his dissatisfaction to Sasaki Takayuki a few weeks after the Ōkuma cabinet was formed:

> The present major change in the cabinet, like a tidal wave that sweeps in a moment over the shore, was of irresistible force. It had been brought about by the times, and that is why I listened to Ito's recommendation and commanded Ōkuma and Itagaki to form a cabinet. I believed at first that because Ōkuma was the head of the Shimpō-tō and Itagaki the president of the Jiyū-tō, the two of them would lead and guide the Kensei-tō and select cabinet appointees. This was definitely not the case. Their strength within their party is nil, and their wishes are paid not the slightest attention. The selection of members of the cabinet was made at party headquarters. Moreover, the Jiyū and the Shimpō factions have yet to resolve their differences. If the Jiyū faction recommends something, the Shimpō faction disapproves, and if the Shimpō faction advocates something, the Jiyū faction is against it. Ōkuma and Itagaki can do nothing about it. They are constantly being manipulated by party members and harassed by their demands. As long as the two of them are at cabinet sessions, everything is peaceful, but once they return to their residences, dozens of party members, relying on their numbers, are there to ask for various favors, and their demands never stop. At first I thought that if I entrusted the situation to Ōkuma and Itagaki, they would suitably reorganize general affairs and would be able to carry out the administration, but I was completely mistaken.[31]

Nevertheless, Itō "had become convinced that there was no way to prevent the majority party in the Diet from appointing the cabinet."[32] Political forces were beginning to polarize between those who were either actively promoting parliamentary government or resigned to it as an inevitable consequence, on one side, and, on the other, those who were adamantly opposed to allowing political parties to take control of the Japanese government.

The Constitution of the Empire of Japan, flawed in theory, proved cumbersome to work with in practice, and gridlock in government resulted. It was during this first decade of politics under the Constitution of the Empire of Japan that we begin to hear of mounting fears among the intellectual and political elite that the country was steadily descending into political chaos. Critics of the system began searching for a stable and workable form of government to break the political impasses brought on by a parliament bent on trying to force the ruling oligarchs to relinquish power, and an oligarchy equally determined to retain control of the state. But the critics of the political system, regardless of their ideological differences, were nearly all in agreement on one thing: if government was to function smoothly, the intellectual foundations supporting the constitution must be based on homogenous notions of government and a commonly agreed on political ideology.

Japanese leaders were finding out the hard way what others had been saying about government hundreds of years earlier. As far back as the sixteenth century, Jean Bodin had claimed that sovereignty is indivisible and that a "mixed state" is in fact impossible.[33] No matter how many organs of government a state may contain, Bodin said, sovereignty or supreme power must rest in a monarchy, an aristocracy, or a democracy. Astute Japanese politicians and political observers well understood that the Constitution of the Empire of Japan did not create this type of unified sovereignty; it had merely intensified the pre-constitutional conflict between those who wanted a parliamentary system of government and a divisive collective leadership who insisted on total control of state power. To make matters worse, the passing of the oligarchs, the architects who designed and supervised the construction of the Meiji state, exacerbated the problem, for their departure from active participation in positions of leadership began to produce a political vacuum at the center of state power. Who could possibly have the political clout of an Itō Hirobumi or a Yamagata Aritomo necessary to assist the emperor in maintaining even a semblance of political unity? Who should replace the oligarchy? Virtually all critics of the system felt the need for full unity and concentration of governmental powers. If political power is divided, there is no real, single sovereign power, and without a single sovereign power, there could be no stable state. Who had the ultimate right to rule the state? This was the fundamental issue around which the post-constitutional debate over state and sovereignty would take place.

This study suggests that there is a direct link between this problem of political pluralism under the Constitution of the Empire of Japan in the last decade of the nineteenth century and the formulations of state theories by thinkers such as Hozumi Yatsuka, Minobe Tatsukichi, and

Kita Ikki in the 1890s and in the first decade of the 1900s. This linkage of statist thinkers to the concrete political and social concerns of government has been largely overlooked. Meiji thinkers and their ideas are usually introduced in a way that is divorced from the concrete political realities with which they were coping. Take, for instance, Edwin O. Reischauer's *East Asia: Tradition and Transformation* (1965), co-written with John K. Fairbank and Albert Craig. It has been the standard text in university courses on East Asia across the country for more than three decades. In the section "The Orthodox Philosophies of the Japanese State," in chapter 7, Reischauer discusses at some length the ideas of several state theorists, including Hozumi Yatsuka, Minobe Tatsukichi and Uesugi Shinkichi:

> It would be wrong to say that Japan's leaders consciously set to work after 1890 to create an orthodox philosophy. . . . But having written a constitution, Japanese leaders and thinkers had to say what it meant in relation to Japanese tradition and to define how it would function legally. The result of their efforts produced a number of interrelated philosophies of state.[34]

It is quite misleading to state that Japanese thinkers were not consciously seeking to create a state orthodoxy and that they were just trying to figure out what the constitution meant in relation to tradition. In such an explanation of the emergence of these state theories, there is a total disconnection between the concrete political actions and the social realities in which they emerged. Furthermore, although I am not quite sure what Reischauer meant in saying that these Japanese state theorists were motivated to devise their state theories in order to understand the Meiji Constitution in relation to Japanese tradition, at least on the surface it strikes me as ridiculously incongruous. Minobe, Hozumi, and other state theorists of the time were devoting their energy to finding a viable solution to the problem of political gridlock under the Constitution of the Empire of Japan and establishing an orthodox state ideology that would serve as a solid foundation for their respective constitutional interpretations designed to establish a stable political system and a smoothly running constitutional government.

What were the alternative forms of government articulated in place of an authoritarian oligarchic monarchy that was forced to share power with a recalcitrant parliament? What were the solutions to the problem of the "hermaphroditic creature" that Itō and his colleagues had created when they made the Constitution of the Empire of Japan?[35] Theoretically, there are at least two possibilities. The first is to place all legislative as well as executive power in the emperor and deny the parliament the right to challenge laws and budgets originating in the cabinet. In other words, reduce the national parliament to a rubber-stamp parliament. Such theorists began to advocate absolute monarchy as the sole alternative to what they perceived as an increasingly corrupt and morally bankrupt state system of secular democracy. Hozumi Yatsuka, a scholar of constitutional law and a Shintō fundamentalist, was the chief political theorist justifying the absolute authority of the emperor as indispensable to social and political unity. According to the Shintō scriptures, was not the Japanese state created to be ruled over by a divine emperor descended from a line of god-emperors going back to the origins of the universe? How, then, could the emperor's authority be limited by a popular assembly or by man-made law? The second option is to place all political and legislative power under the control of the parliament and reduce the status of the emperor to that of a figurehead. Those who opted for this course saw no alternative to parliamentary rule under an English-style constitutional monarchy.

The supreme irony of all this is that, within the first decade of politics under the Constitution of the Empire of Japan, political realities had been driving the Japanese political system into the very system of government that the Prussian-style of constitutional monarchy set up by Itō and his colleagues was specifically designed to prevent: British-style parliamentary rule. But interpreting the Constitution of the Empire of Japan in such a way that one could justify parliamentary control of the government would be difficult. How could parliamentary control over the executive branch of government be justified theoretically under the Constitution of the Empire of Japan? It was in response to this fundamental question that Minobe Tatsukichi would reinterpret the Constitution of the Empire of Japan, placing the entire document within the theoretical framework of German organic state theory, thus presenting his famous emperor-as-organ theory of the state in defense of parliamentary government.

Still other political theorists entered the debate over state and sovereignty from a decidedly different set of priorities: socialism. Advocating not parliamentary democracy but social democracy, Kita Ikki sought to implant a redefined emperor system into his own evolutionary theory of socialism. In his massive *Kokutairon oyobi Junsei Shakaishugi* (On the Kokutai and Pure Socialism [1906]), Kita, while reinterpreting Japanese history and defining a new course for Japan, launched a scathing attack on both Hozomi's orthodox emperor-as-sovereign theory of the Japanese state and Minobe's emperor-as-organ theory of the state.

Ideologies and ideological contestation are rooted in a historically defined environment of political concerns. This study suggests that the explosion of ideological contestation in the last decade of the nineteenth century and in the first decade or so of the twentieth century was the result, by and large, of the contradictions inherent in the Constitution of the Empire of Japan and the subsequent political problems of operating within the framework of that constitution. One may argue over the extent to which ideological justifications for any form of state or governmental institutions have practical influence on politics, but few would argue that any political institution can endure for long without the support of those willing to defend it. In this ideological contestation for the hearts and minds of the Japanese people in the early twentieth century, both liberal democracy and socialism would eventually lose out to the emperor-centered ideology of Shintō ultranationalism, which first began to emerge at the center of Japanese political discourse with Hozumi Yatsuka in the last decade of the nineteenth century. But why? How could a state theory of absolute monarchy, which was a thing of the past in Europe and elsewhere in the world because of the onslaught of Westernization, emerge in Japan in the twentieth century as the most powerful political ideology? What was the nature of this ideology? I will now turn to Hozumi Yatsuka's theory of absolute monarchy and try to find some answers to these important questions.

2

Hozumi Yatsuka:

The Religious, *Völkisch* Family-State

For as Kingly power is by the law of God, so it hath no inferior law to limit it. The Father of a family governs by no other law than by his own will, not by the laws or wills of his son or servants. There is no nation that allows children any action or remedy for being unjustly governed. And yet for all this every Father is bound by the law of nature to do his best for the preservation of his family. But much more is a King always tied by the same law of nature to keep this general ground, that the safety of his kingdom be his chief law.— SIR ROBERT FILMER, *Patriarcha*, 35

A Traditional Theory of Absolute Monarchy

To understand the late Meiji formulation of State Shintō ideology, there is no better place to start than with Hozumi Yatsuka. Of the three Meiji theorists of State Shintō mentioned by Irokawa, Hozumi Yatsuka (1860– 1912) is probably the most important, for it was Hozumi who first welded the fundamental Shintō doctrines to the family concept of the state into a comprehensive theory of monarchical absolutism.

Hozumi's doctrine of the absolute authority of the emperor was a theory of state not unlike European theories of absolute monarchy in such works as Jean Bodin's sixteenth-century *Six Books of the Common- wealth* or Sir Robert Filmer's seventeenth-century *Patriarcha*. In fact, as we shall discover, Hozumi linked the Shintō dogma of the "unbroken line of Emperors from ages eternal" with his family-state concept much in the same way that Filmer, John Locke's ideological rival in England's debate over state and sovereignty in the seventeenth century, formulated his theory of absolute monarchy on the basis of divine grace and the patriarchal construction of society.

Hozumi's life spanned the entire Meiji period. He was born in 1860 in what came to be called Ehime Prefecture after the Meiji Restoration. He excelled academically and entered Tokyo Imperial University in 1879, graduating from the Faculty of Letters four years later, in 1883. Hozumi's early writings while still a student at Tokyo Imperial University show a strong hostility toward democracy. Richard H. Minear noted that Hozumi attacked the "radical concepts" at the time: "first, that the people have the right to participate in the enactment of the constitution; and second, that the constitution is more important than the sovereign."[1] Hozumi argued: "If one says that we have a right to participate in the enactment of the constitution, this is to assert that sovereignty resides in us."[2] This he vehemently denied was the case: "In a democracy it is possible to say this, but it is clear that in a monarchy this is an inexcusable statement. As subjects of the empire we can only hope for the honor of being consulted."[3] Further, he held the opinion that there could be no limitations on the powers of the emperor: "If the constitution is determined by the sovereign, then we as subjects cannot use the constitution to restrict the sovereign."[4]

Hozumi abhorred socialism, too. In response to the formation of the Tōyō Shakai Tō (Eastern Socialist Party) in 1882, he wrote:

If these fanatics are already steeped in socialism, wandering about in heresy, and beyond morality, then it is useless to dispute with them about right and wrong by appealing to the judgment of logic. Yet if, now when people's hearts are immoderate, there should be many who with fearfully clever arguments seek to give free reign to private desires, then it is to be expected that unhappy results will follow. In accordance with the maxim to seal the shutters before it becomes dark and rainy, it is most urgent directly to destroy their socialist delusion and indirectly to hope that their compatriots will not be deceived by their heresy.[5]

Such were the political opinions held by Hozumi in the early 1880s during his undergraduate university years.

In 1884, shortly after graduation, Hozumi went to Germany, where he would spend the next four years. According to Nagao Ryūichi, Hozumi was in Heidelberg from October 1884 to April 1885; in Berlin from April 1885 to March 1886; and in Strasbourg from March 1886 to the winter of the same year.[6] He studied at the University of Heidelberg briefly under

Hermann Schulze; at the University of Berlin under Rudolf Gneist; and at the University of Strasbourg under the famous scholar Paul Laband (1841–1917). However, whatever he learned about German state theory in Germany from Laband, Schulze, and Gneist, he subsequently applied this knowledge in a very different way in his own writings on the Japanese state. For example, Hozumi's state theory contained practically nothing from the school of legal positivism, for which Laband was noted. Hozumi returned to Japan from Germany on January 29, 1889, less than two weeks before Emperor Meiji promulgated the Constitution of the Empire of Japan on February 11, 1889. Soon after that, he became a professor of constitutional law at Tokyo Imperial University, a post he held from 1889 to 1912 (serving as chairman of the Faculty of Law from 1897 to 1911). During his tenure at Tokyo Imperial University, Hozumi was actively engaged in the important political and legal issues of his times. Minear noted that it was sometime between the mid-1880s and 1890 that Hozumi's political views changed significantly:

> The political thinking of Hozumi Yatsuka in 1882 is conservative, but his conservatism is well within the limits of Western constitutional and political thought of the late nineteenth century. At this time Hozumi is committed to a science of politics transcending national and racial boundaries. There is no trace now of compelling concern with what is uniquely Japanese; there is no linking of government with religion; there is no worship of the emperor. These are all characteristics of Hozumi's later thinking, but they are not present in 1882.[7]

After 1890, influenced profoundly by the way politics had operated under the Constitution of the Empire of Japan, Hozumi became adamantly opposed to the idea of giving the political parties control over legislation and the administration of government, and he rejected popular participation in the affairs of government. For instance, he rose in opposition to broadening suffrage, rejecting a bill for universal manhood suffrage that came before the House of Peers in 1911. His anti-liberal political tendencies were also revealed when he criticized the original draft (1890) of the Civil Code, based on a French civil code strongly influenced by Enlightenment ideas of individual property rights and the doctrine of individual liberty. He claimed that the adoption of such a civil code would destroy Japan's unique *völkisch* state and mean the death of the values of loyalty and filial piety. Still more, he was one of the influential members of a government committee charged with revising the state's moral-education textbooks from 1908 to 1911. In short, he was an important member of the Japanese elite dedicated to blocking Japan's slide toward political-party government and liberal democracy.[8] Thus, by the early 1890s he had become what this study refers to as a "conservative Shintō ultranationalist" or a "reactionary Shintō ultranationalist." Let us take a look at his theory of state.

The Japanese Völkisch Family-State

"The foundation of our nation's unique kokutai and national morality is ancestor religion."[9] This is the opening line of Hozumi's *Kokumin Kyōiku: Aikokushin* (National Education: Patriotism), a work written in 1897 to awaken the Japanese masses to the distinguishing characteristics of the Japanese Shintō patriarchal family-state. Although a polemical work, it contained the essence of his theory of the Japanese state. In this opening statement, Hozumi immediately introduced the reader to a concept that is central to his theory of the Japanese state: the *kokutai*. "Kokutai" is a term that is difficult to render into English. Various translations, such as "national polity," "national essence," "body politic" and "state structure" have appeared in scholarly literature, but none seems to adequately convey the whole meaning for the users of this word in all cases. Part of the problem is that the term has been defined historically in different ways. If kokutai were to be translated at all in the writings of Hozumi Yatsuka, however, "form of state" would probably be most fitting. But what did Hozumi mean by Japan's unique kokutai? In its simplest terms, this involves two propositions: (1) that the Japanese state has always been and shall always be reigned over and governed by one unbroken line of emperors of divine origin; and (2) that the Japanese state is a völkisch, or ethnic, state, and the emperor is the father of all Japanese. These two propositions functioned to support and maintain two inextricably linked aims of his conservative Shintō ultranationalist ideology: that sovereignty shall always reside in the emperor, and that the Japanese state shall always remain a single, völkisch state.

In *National Education*, Hozumi defined the state as follows: "the state is a völkisch group (*minzoku no dantai*) protected by the sovereign power."[10] A völkisch or ethnic group consisted of "blood relatives of the same womb."[11] The "same womb" referred to here was the originator of the line of descent of the unbroken line of emperors, Amaterasu Ōmikami. The sovereign power, of course, was the emperor, who was "Amaterasu Ōmikami existing in the present."[12] In other words, Hozumi was adhering to a Shintō doctrine that the emperor was Amaterasu Ōmikami reincarnated in human form.

Ethnicity was the fundamental principle that was to determine who could qualify as a member of the Japanese state. In other words, the Japanese concept of minzoku here involved blood as well as culture. Only one who was "Japanese" by ethnic blood descent was entitled to be a member of the Japanese state. A person of non-Japanese origins could not become a member of the Japanese nation merely by cultural assimilation. Hozumi, in fact, took great pride in the fact that ethnicity and the purity of ethnic blood as the principle of the Japanese state had remained unchanged since antiquity. His frequent use of the word "blood" to denote ethnicity gives the reader a strong impression that, for Hozumi, "blood" carried with it a certain religiosity and mysticism. We find the Chinese character for the word "blood" used in a rich variety of ideographic compounds, such as *ketsuzoku*, *kettō*, and *ketsumyaku*,[13] the last word meaning literally "blood vessels." "Blood" in the West also has had a long history as a poetic metaphor. But Hozumi, as in the case of Nazi völkisch ideology, extended the concept of "blood" to encircle the whole state, thus advocating the concept of the union of "blood" and "state" and of "blood" and "ethnicity." Hozumi at one place in *National Education* referred to the Japanese völkisch state as a *kokuminzoku*,[14] an unusual combination of three Chinese characters that literally means "state ethnic nation," presumably a translation of the German word *Volksstaat*, but is probably better translated into English as "ethnic nation-state" or "völkisch nation-state." This idea that the Japanese state must be a pure ethnic state would be a constant political principle among Shintō ultranationalists from the late Meiji period to the end of the Second World War. Thus, Hozumi's definition of the state as a *minzoku dantai*, which consisted of "blood relatives of the same womb," clearly indicated that he was conflating ethnicity with blood lineage, the direct descendants of a common ancestor considered to be the founder of the line.

To put this linkage of ethnicity and lineage in perspective, we might note that the amalgamation of these two concepts has parallels with what happened to the völkisch movement in Germany in the late nineteenth century. George Mosse has noted that, if the völkisch movement in Germany can be said to have had a founder, it was a scholar named Paul Bottischer, who had his name changed to Paul de Lagarde (1827–91). Lagarde was born in 1827 and wrote throughout the second half of the nineteenth century. According to Mosse, he argued that the political unity of Germany was a unity in form only and that the German people needed an inner, spiritual unity to achieve real unification. This could come about only through the consciousness of the people as a nation and a Volk. In a collection of essays in *Deutsche Schriften* (German Writings) in 1878, Lagarde stressed that true unity of the German state could be achieved only "through the preservation and vitalization of the life force to be found in the genuine nation and Volk."[15] However, it interesting to point out that Lagarde's concept of the Volk, or what the Japanese would refer to as *minzoku*, was not based on blood. Mosse stated that Lagarde coined a saying that was to "echo and re-echo in all völkisch writings: 'Germanism lies not within the blood but in the character.' "[16] In other words, the ideal of the German Volk had not yet been tied to racial thought. It was not until Julius Langbehn (b. 1851) that German völkisch thought was linked to race. In this regard, Mosse wrote

> Ideas of race played a greater role in Langbehn's theology than in Lagarde's. Race and the vitality of nature were viewed as equivalent forces. Consequently, if nature and race are identical, then the Germanic life spirit must perforce be racial. All *völkisch* virtues, the physical as well as spiritual, were considered nature's eternal gifts transmitted through blood inheritance. Race was a pervasive and decisive force. The outward appearance of the Volk, as expressed in its physical and spiritual culture, was seen as bearing the imprint of the inner qualities, as the signature of the soul. Langbehn even told his readers that investigations into human facial characteristics were a valid part of historical research. Gone was the possibility that as long as only cultural differences prevented assimilation into the Volk, all who lived in Germany, Jews excepted, could become true Germans. The essentially non-racial anti-Semitism of Lagarde had been superseded; emphasis upon racial incompatibility had become an indelible part of *völkisch* ideology.[17]

An important point of Mosse's statement is that the concept of the Volk had become identical to race in the völkisch thought of Langbehn. One could well argue that a similar shift had occurred with Hozumi's Shintō ultranationalism—a shift from a concept of ethnicity not totally connected to bloodlines to one that was based exclusively on "blood descent."

Hozumi's publication of *National Education* came just at a time when Japan had begun to acquire an empire. Japan had gained the territory of Taiwan two years earlier as a result of its victory over the Chinese empire in the Qing Dynasty–Japan War of 1894–95 and soon would incorporate ethnic Chinese into the Japanese state, thus making them "imperial subjects." Hozumi's ethnic theory of the Japanese state as outlined in *Na-*

tional Education subsequently came under attack from several sources. Nagao Ryūichi has an interesting discussion about this in *Hozumi Yatsuka Shū*.[18] He noted that after Hozumi published the article "Kempō no Seishin [The Spirit of the Constitution]" in the journal *Meigi* in 1900, one of his colleagues at Tokyo Imperial University, Tomizu Hirondo, ridiculed him in an article titled "Hozumi Yatsuka and Robert Filmer" in *Hōgaku Kyōkai Zasshi* (Law Society Journal). Tomizu pointed out that Hozumi's theory of the Japanese state based on ancestor worship going back to Amaterasu Ōmikami structurally resembled Sir Robert Filmer's theory of absolute monarchy in which the English monarchs derived their powers from their succession from the sons of Noah and, ultimately, back to the biblical Adam. And just as Filmer's theory of state had caused a backlash against the English monarchy and was eventually destroyed by John Locke, so, too, predicted Tomizu, would Hozumi's imperial restoration theory, which was intended to strengthen the Imperial Throne, have the opposite effect and trigger a revolution.

Hozumi's völkisch theory of state also came under heavy criticism from other sources, but the gist of the attacks focused on the contradiction between Japan's foreign policy of imperialism and Hozumi's "isolationist (*sakoku teki*)" theory of state: "The unity of church and state theory is a theory of isolationism; it is a theory of 'expel the barbarian.' "[19] Critics charged that building the Japanese state on the basis of "blood ties (*ketsuzoku dantai*)" was definitely faulty.[20] They argued that it would be tantamount to saying that the Japanese government's policy of expansionism was essentially a policy to incorporate barbarians (*yabanjin*) into the pure ethnic state,[21] which ultimately would weaken and destroy the Japanese nation-state, and they pointed to that fact. Hozumi's "blood-family state theory (*ketsuzoku kokka ron*)" was also attacked by Minobe Tatsukichi and Kita Ikki on similar grounds.[22] As we shall find out in chapter 4, Kita also led a massive attack on Hozumi's reactionary Shintō ultranationalism.

In a similar fashion, Hozumi came out against the Japanese government's policy of assimilation of ethnic Koreans into the Japanese nation after Japan's annexation of Korea in August 1910. Although he recommended no alternative policy in this regard, he sought support for his position by noting at the time that Europeans such as the British in India had no similar policy of assimilation. For Hozumi, the relationship between the Japanese Volk and the Korean Volk was inherently a relationship between an "inferior ethnic group (*rettō minzoku*)" and a "superior ethnic group (*yūtō minzoku*)."[23] In Hozumi's opinion, this relationship would always remain this way regardless of any assimilation policy of the two nations by the Japanese government. Nagao Ryūichi included an interesting section on this subject titled "Korean Education" in his edited work on Hozumi. Nagao quotes a document in which Hozumi stated that the policy to assimilate the Koreans into the Japanese nation would result not in the formation of a "single ethnic nation (*ichi minzoku*)," but only in the "idea [intellectual project or dream] of a single ethnic nation (*kannen no ichi minzoku*)."[24] In other words, Hozumi was a purist as far as blood ties of ethnicity were concerned. This assimilation policy of the Japanese government would eventually result in a policy of "cultural obliteration" of the inferior Korean ethnic group by the superior Japanese ethnic group. I seriously doubt whether Hozumi was genuinely concerned in any real sense about the prospect that Korean ethnicity and culture would eventually disappear under the Japanese government's position of incorporating Korea into its body politic. More likely, he was primarily concerned about the impact on the Japanese state should Korea be subsumed by the empire of Japan. At any rate, Hozumi was deeply involved in an intense debate on the nature of Japanese nationalism at the time. Kevin Doak informs us that the "annexation of Korea in 1910 renewed and sharpened the debate on whether Japan should be a homogenous ethnic nation-state and whether the concept of *minzoku* was flexible enough to incorporate Koreans in the Japanese *minzoku*."[25]

The second essential characteristic of Hozumi's state that needs to be clarified was Japan's unique "form of state," the kokutai. Japan's kokutai posited that the Japanese state is inherently a hierarchically organized state because the originator of the line of emperors, Amaterasu Ōmikami, gave her descendants the authority to rule over everyone who came after them. In other words, all Japanese were born under the rule of the emperor and were therefore to remain eternally subject to the authority of the emperor. As a Shintō fundamentalist, Hozumi believed that the living emperor was in fact a direct descendant of an unbroken line of emperors literally going back to the supernatural deity Amaterasu Ōmikami, and that this unbroken line of emperors had ruled the Japanese state from its origins up to the present. It necessarily follows that for Shintō ultranationalists, the minzoku, or the ethnic nation, came *after* the emperor—that is, the state, if one assumes that the emperor, in theory, is the state, as Hozumi had argued. As Harry Harootunian eloquently stated, "With the conception of kingship derived from the *Ise* myth, this was an emperor whose deity was guaranteed by his descent from the sun goddess and whose authority was therefore prior to the people and even the land."[26]

Article 1 of the Constitution of the Empire of Japan, which stated, "The Empire of Japan shall be reigned over and governed by a line of Emperors unbroken for ages eternal (*Dai Nihon Teikoku wa Bansei Ikkei no Tennō Kore o Tōchis*)" was, for Hozumi, the legal recognition of this Shintō religious doctrine of the kokutai in the Meiji Constitution. In more specific legal terms, the kokutai was the "location of sovereignty in the state." Sovereignty resided in the hereditary emperor; it could reside neither in the people nor in the state. In Hozumi's ideology, this relationship between rule by emperors of this unbroken line and Japanese subjects was a structural relationship that had never changed from antiquity, and it was this fact that, in his mind, made the Japanese kokutai unique in the world.

Tomizu's reference to the striking similarity between Hozumi's Shintō religious theory for the justification of absolute monarchy and Sir Robert Filmer's Christian theory for the justification of absolute powers of the English monarch is instructive. Filmer's *Patriarcha* was also an essay on the political obligation of subjects to obey the king and on the historical origins of political power. His prime assumption was that the Bible contained the truth about the origins and nature of the world, including the nature of the state and society. In his interpretation of the Bible, human society originated with Adam; before the creation of Eve, Adam had owned everything—all the land and the living creatures on it. According to Peter Laslett, "Filmer inferred that God's meaning was to show that all other human beings were to be subordinated to this first human being, Adam."[27]

This absolute principle of "an unbroken line of rulers" is found not only in the writings of Filmer. It is also clear, for example, from the writings of the nineteenth-century English scholar J. Neville Figgis, who, in the 1890s, wrote in *The Theory of the Divine Right of Kings*:

> The succession to monarchy is regulated by the law of primogeniture. The right acquired by birth cannot be forfeited through any acts of usurpation, of however long continuance, by any incapacity in the heir, or by any act of deposition. So long as the heir lives, he is king by hereditary right, even though the usurping dynasty has reigned for a thousand years.[28]

No doubt Hozumi would have agreed wholeheartedly with Figgis's position because the Japanese emperor system was defined in terms of absolute adherence to the hereditary principle of sovereignty. Only by birth could one succeed to the throne in Japanese history. This meant that a medieval Shōgun in Japanese history, for example, could not have deposed a Japanese emperor and declared himself emperor; nor by the same token could one have been elected emperor. This hereditary principle of the "unbroken line of emperors (*bansei ikkei no tennō*)" was something sacred. In Hozumi's political theology, the present emperor was not really an independent individual but "*Amaterasu Ōmikami* living in the present."[29] Hozumi stated: "The [Imperial] Throne is the throne of *Amaterasu Ōmikami*; the throne is the *Amaterasu Ōmikami* of this world. Thus, to worship the throne is to worship *Amaterasu Ōmikami*. The throne is the source of state law and state religion."[30] However, he also stressed the notion of divine parentage for all Japanese: "The ancestor of our [all Japanese] ancestors . . . is *Amaterasu Ōmikami*."[31] This notion of divine parentage meant of course that each and every Japanese subject was ultimately divine, too. Thus, the Japanese ethnic group was a divine ethnic group, and the Japanese state was a divine state, since ethnicity was identical to the state and nationality. This notion worked positively to strengthen the political order by making everyone in the state a community of worshipers.

According to Hozumi, these two characteristics of the Japanese state, which were interdependent and worked to reinforce each other, were the natural properties of the original Japanese state. But he argued Japan was not totally unique in this respect. For him, the original nature of all states in the primitive age had similar characteristics. What made the Japanese state with this original organizational structure unique among all the states of the world, however, was that Japan alone had retained this kokutai since antiquity. The key point here is that once in the course of historical events the "unbroken line of emperors" is broken—that is, the monarchy physically destroyed—it is gone from history forever and cannot be revived in the original form. From that point on in history, the state becomes naturally and inherently an egalitarian state and at the same time loses its foundation of being a purely ethnic state.

Hozumi stated that there were basically only two forms of kokutai, or two organizational principles underlying the origins of government. One, of course, was the principle of this monarchical, ethnic state in which all were born subject to authority and always remained politically dependent and unequal. The other one was the contract theory of the origins of government, systematically best articulated first by John Locke, in which autonomous and independent individuals agree to form a compact to guarantee their interests and mutual well-being. This latter theory of the origins of government he considered an invention and therefore unnatural and against the nature of man. On this matter, too, Hozumi's opinion paralleled that of Sir Robert Filmer. Filmer also thought that God, by creating Adam first, gave Adam absolute authority over everyone who came after him. Filmer, however, without the Shintō tradition of "the unbroken line of emperors" from ancient texts that Hozumi could readily use in his theory of state, had the impossible task of trying to prove that the English king and the heads of other states derived their powers from their succession to the sons of Noah and ultimately back to the first father, Adam, who was the first head of the "human race."

Going back to Hozumi's definition of the Japanese state, we already noted that he defined that state in *National Education* as an ethnic or völkisch group protected by a sovereign power. But he also defined the state in a slightly different way on the first page of his monumental *Kempō Teiyō* (A Handbook of the Constitution of the Empire of Japan), published in 1910 toward the end of his career: "A state is an organization formed by a specific ethnic nation governing a specific territory by means of an independent sovereignty."[32] In part 1 of this text, Hozumi discussed in great detail the nature of the state (*kokka*). It contains chapters 1–4, titled "The State," "The *Kokutai*," "The *Seitai*," and "The Constitution," respectively. Discussing the "structure of the state (*kokka no taisei*)," Hozumi stated that "the structure of the state is determined by the location of sovereignty and the form of its [governmental] operations."[33] "The former is referred to as the *kokutai* and the latter is referred to as the *seitai*."[34] That is to say, in Hozumi's conceptualization of the types of states that exist, the kokutai refers to the "location of sovereignty" in the state, and the seitai denotes a specific type of governance under a particular kokutai. Elaborating still further on the relationship between the kokutai, or "form of state," and the seitai, the variations in the institutions of governance, or the "form of government," he argued again that there are fundamentally two "forms of state" that are of particular concern at the present time: monarchical and democratic. He did, however, acknowledge that the German "state sovereignty theory (*kokka shuken setsu*)" was an attempt to harmonize the heretofore fundamental distinction between the historical monarchical kokutai (*kunshu kokutai*) and the democratic kokutai (*minshu kokutai*). As for the Japanese state, sovereignty resides in the emperor in terms of his legal definition of the general concept of the kokutai. However, if we dig deeper into

Hozumi's theory of sovereignty, the Japanese state is unique in that sovereignty resides not just in the current emperor but, more importantly and specifically, in the imperial throne, the (*kuni*).[35] The distinction here between the present reigning emperor existing in human form and the imperial throne is important. The *kuni* denotes the unbroken "hereditary succession (*seshū keishō*)" of emperors traced back to the age of the Gods who existed prior to the origins of the earth and who created the universe.[36] In all other states, dynasties can be said to have begun and ended at some identifiable points in historical time.

To complicate matters with regard to his definition of the Japanese state, however, Hozumi also stated that "the emperor is the state."[37] Accordingly, he asserted that "without the emperor, there is no state."[38] That is to say, he defined the Japanese state in two different ways: (1) the state was an ethnic corporation protected by the sovereign power as discussed earlier; and (2) the state was the emperor. The distinction here may seem meaningless, but, as we shall find out in the next chapter, it was on this particular point that Hozumi's ideological rivals viciously attacked him. They accused him of stubbornly holding two contradictory theories of state and believing in them both at the same time.

A third characteristic of Hozumi's Japanese state was that it was a family-state. That is to say, Hozumi connected the individual household to the emperor through the theory of the patriarchal construction of society, or what has been referred to as Hozumi's "family concept of the state." Like Filmer, he characterized the Japanese state as a government of households:

> In the household, the head of the house, representing the authority of his ancestors, exercises his patriarchal authority over the family. In the state, the emperor, representing the authority of Amaterasu Ōmikami, exercises sovereign power over the state. Both patriarchal authority and sovereign authority are powers by which the emperor-father, with the authority to act for the ancestors, protects his children beloved of their ancestors.[39]

As we find in this passage, the state for Hozumi was literally one gigantic extended family system composed of interlocking related families. It is also important to remember that patriarchalism is based on the notion that parental authority is identical or equivalent to political authority. It was on this point that Locke, in *Two Treatises*, devoted much effort to refute Sir Robert Filmer's theory of absolute monarchy. For Hozumi, the household was the smallest social unit and a miniature state: "The family is a small state. The state is a large family."[40]

Hozumi also argued that the state based on patriarchalism was the only natural construction of state and society. Hozumi actually employed two modes of argument in support of the patriarchal construction of society. Alongside his Shintō religious justification for it, he claimed that the patriarchal social organization of the Japanese state was in accordance with the teachings of nature. He stressed in a number of passages that the group based on mutual blood relations was the only natural form of group solidarity and that the formation of the state under the authority and spirit of the same progenitor was the only natural solidarity. Hozumi, in fact, argued that the state evolved through the natural development of the family lineage group: the family grew into the village community, which in turn developed into the state. The head of the state was really an extension of the father's rights over the family. Hozumi came to the conclusion that the Japanese state was thus the most natural state because the imperial family was literally the head family of the nation. The people were the emperor's children. While the state grew over the centuries, the ethnic organizational principle of state and society remained the same: the extension of the blood lineage group.

I have tried to illustrate that Hozumi's theory of state in support of monarchical absolutism was characteristic of some early modern Western theories of state. Hozumi employed essentially the same mix of elements—that is, divine revelation and the theory of naturalness of the patriarchal construction of society in defense of rule by an absolute monarch. And like his European counterparts, such as Filmer in the seventeenth century, Hozumi argued against the Lockian theory of popular sovereignty and the contract theory of the origins of government. He maintained that the Constitution of the Empire of Japan was a decree issued on the sole authority of the emperor as absolute monarch; it was not, he said, "a contract between the monarch and his subjects."[41] In this quote, Hozumi was referring to Locke's contract theory of the origins of government. Circumstantial evidence, then, points to Hozumi making use of the theories of these Western absolute monarchists such as Filmer, who, as the subtitle of *Patriarcha—A Defense of the Natural Powers of Kings against the Unnatural Liberty of the People*—suggested, believed that the liberal view of state and society and the notion of absolutely autonomous and independent individuals joining to form the original state were not only groundless, but also contrary to the laws of nature.

The term traditionally used by Hozumi and other Japanese political philosophers to express the idea of the Japanese state as one large family was the ideographic compound *chūkō*.[42] In direct translation, this means "loyalty-filial piety," but it actually means "loyalty and filial piety as one." The key characteristic here is an identity of the concepts of loyalty to the emperor and filial piety to one's father. Because the vocabulary used to express this Japanese völkisch or ethnic patriarchal state may have been originally of Chinese origin associated with the Chinese Confucian tradition, the essence of the Japanese state is often characterized in scholarly literature as a synthesis of nativist Shintō religion and Confucian morality. This, however, is a mistaken view, because State Shintō has its own morality that is in direct conflict with morality in the Chinese Confucian tradition.

In broad terms, one must clearly distinguish between Hozumi's concept of the Japanese kokutai and the Japanese ethnic, hierarchical state, on the one hand, and the Confucian political theory of the state, on the other hand. First, the Chinese state was not articulated in Chinese political theory as an ethnic group or a state formed on the basis of ethnicity. On the contrary, Confucian political theory presupposes universal values above and beyond ethnicity and the principle of hereditary rule. Whether or not the ruler who ruled the empire was of Han Chinese ancestry was largely irrelevant as long as he received the "mandate of heaven" and ruled in compliance with the proper Confucian "way." Other than realizing heaven's virtue, he needed no specific qualifications. In other words, neither ethnicity nor heredity was a primary factor in Chinese political theory. On the contrary, Chinese Confucian political theory posed a direct challenge to the principle of heredity as the ultimate principle of legitimate power. It was therefore a direct ideological threat to Hozumi's theory of the Japanese ethnic family state. This is not to suggest that Confucianism questioned the hereditary right of the emperors to govern, but it did insist that it was their duty to rule in a virtuous way. This was in direct challenge to the theoretical principle of hereditary rule of the "unbroken line of emperors from ages eternal" because of the primacy of virtue and knowledge over heredity as the ultimate basis of political legitimacy.

The Confucian notion that only a virtuous emperor was entitled to rule of course went back to the mythical sage emperors Yao and Shun, who broke with the monarchical principle of hereditary rule and passed their thrones to their most worthy ministers of state. The central Confucian concept used to justify political legitimacy was the "mandate of heaven." If the ruler were to lose his mandate of heaven, he could be legitimately opposed and overthrown, the so-called right of revolution. The mandate of heaven manifested itself through the acceptance of the emperor by his people. If the people killed or deposed an emperor, it was a sure sign that the emperor had lost the mandate of heaven. It was Mencius, the second great Confucian philosopher, who had turned the argument that Chou had used to justify the overthrow of the Shang into a general theory of revolution. In other words, behind this Confucian theory of legitimate political rule was the assumption of accountability of the emperor to Heaven (*Tian*). This idea of the accountability of the Chinese ruler was diametrically opposed to the concept of the Japanese Shintō-based ethnic patriarchal state or the Japanese Shintō kokutai theory.

Second, Chinese Confucian political thought presumed a clear distinction between parental authority and political authority. It was for this reason that Hozumi repeatedly stressed that "loyalty and filial piety as one" was unique to the Japanese ethnic state. For Chinese political theorists, loyalty and filial piety were a matter not of identity but of choice. In a conflict between loyalty to the Chinese emperor or to one's father, loyalty to one's father was the supreme value. In other words, a fundamental tenet of Confucian political thought was the primacy of the value of filial piety over loyalty to the emperor, while the potential conflict between the values of loyalty to emperor and filial piety did not exist for Hozumi. Chinese Confucian political thought places restrictions on patriarchalism, and there is a clear distinction between parental authority and political authority embedded in Chinese Confucian thought. Many studies inadvertently may have placed too much stress on Chinese-style patriarchalism, which has its limits in fostering absolute obedience to a hereditary ruler. It would make better sense for Hozumi to have drawn on Western theories of patriarchalism, such as those expounded by Jean Bodin and Sir Robert Filmer, which ultimately are far more akin to the Shintō ideal of the unbroken line of emperors. That is to say, traditional Western theories of the family principle to bolster political stability and unqualified allegiance to the monarchy were certainly more useful to Japanese nationalists than the traditional Chinese family ideology. Thus, if Japanese Shintō ultranationalists such as Hozumi had adhered to the Chinese concepts of loyalty and filial piety, their ideas might very well have functioned to weaken the emperor's power, not strengthen it. Ultimately, however, it is important also to keep in mind that Hozumi's state theory is unique and only has parallels and affinities with Western cultural models of absolutism and what Max Weber calls "traditional" or dynastic power systems.

Hozumi's ideas with regard to the incompatibility of core Chinese

Confucian principles and the Japanese Shintō political ideal of the unbroken line of emperors would later be molded and adapted to meet the needs of Japanese thinkers engaged in similar discourses at the beginning of the twentieth century. For instance, Stefan Tanaka, talking about a discussion of a 1911 article written by Inoue Tetsujirō, "Waga Kokutai to Kazoku no Seido (Our Kokutai and the Family System)," stated:

> To establish emperor worship as the Japanese national ethic, Inoue distinguished between two types of family systems: the nuclear (*kobetsu*) family and the national (*sōgō*) family system. This distinction of social structures enabled him to merge loyalty (*chū*)—which implied the object of that loyalty, the head of the moral family (*kazoku dōtoku no kunshu*)—with the Confucian concept of filial piety (*kō*), a combination that facilitated the connection between Confucianism and the emperor, head of the family-state of Japan.[43]

Tanaka went on to note that Inoue's interpretation also separated China from Japan: "Japan alone, he argued, possessed both national and nuclear family systems; China had only nuclear families. Thus, while Chinese possessed the virtue of filial piety, its moral system did not encompass loyalty to their emperor."[44]

In the second section of *National Education*, Hozumi abruptly switched focus to the Western discourse over state and society. It is at this point in the text that Hozumi began to focus on the concept of patriotism— literally "love of country (*aikoku*)"[45]—that, unlike the ideas of loyalty and filial piety, was a concept that grew out of modern Western history. Interestingly, however, under this general section of patriotism, he talks not about the state per se, but about the individual, the society, and the relation between the individual and the society. This discussion is important to keep in mind because, as we shall discover, his aim in this discourse was to show that the concepts of state and society were identical if applied to the Japanese state, a position in contradiction to his patriarchal construction of state and society. At the very start of this section, he noted that a great debate was going on in the West between the doctrine of individualism, which makes the individual the ultimate value, and the doctrine of socialism, which makes the society the ultimate value. He further noted that those who adhered to the doctrine of individualism asserted that "society exists for the individual," while those in opposition who supported the doctrine of socialism maintained that the "individual exists for the society." In Hozumi's opinion, however, the mere fact that this clash existed was proof enough that the concept of individualism had become irrevocably embedded in the consciousness of Westerners and that, in the end, individualism was at the root of all occidental ideologies: not just of liberalism and democracy, but also of socialism and, by implication, communism. That is to say, socialism also was a derivation of liberalism and the thought of the Enlightenment. Both individualism and socialism were premised on atomistic and mechanistic assumptions of state and society that were antithetical to his organic doctrine of sociality.

According to Hozumi's social theory, the individual was born into society and exists only in society. The individual exists in society and society in the individual; thus, the individual exists for the society and society for the individual. The Western clash between individualism and socialism is brought to rest by his concept of *gōdō seizon* (literally, fusion or amalgamated existence),[46] by which he meant the merging of the individual into the society. Society was thus composed of the existence of merged individuals. The individual, in other words, was an element, or *bunshi*, of society.[47] The individual thus became an irreducible constituent of a composite entity called society.

The ideal person was one who had this desire for total assimilation into the society, which was a higher organic totality. Hozumi had a special term for this: *kōdōshin*, the desire for two or more independent elements to become one.[48] It is in the realization of kōdōshin that we find the identity of individual and society. The purpose of all ethics and morality in the society was to direct the individual to kōdōshin—that is, to acquire the desire to submerge the self totally into the social totality. There could be no ethics or morality accepted or excluded from this consideration of this desire for total integration into the society. Hozumi clarified this by citing the relationship of kōdōshin to Confucian moral values. According to Confucian morality, the organization of human society is constituted by what are called the "five human relationships." A superior man is one who has virtue (*jin*), a term that embraces all those moral qualities that should govern a person in his or her relations with others: emperor and subject, father and son, husband and wife, younger brother and older brother, and friend and friend. But for Hozumi, these Confucian relationships and their corresponding virtues were only important insofar as they functioned to facilitate the total assimilation of the individual into the society. They were not important in themselves, as in the case of the Chinese Confucian value system, where the individual was not totally eliminated—that is, not totally merged into society— but merely regulated by specified proper social relationships. Hozumi thought that without this desire for total assimilation of the individual into society—or kōdōshin—Japan's unique social structure would eventually collapse. Hozumi's ideas here on state and society were totalistic; he considered any theory of state and society that did not advocate the total integration of the individual into society as within the orbit of liberal thought.

In the final analysis, it appears that Hozumi's organic theory is at best a kind of overlapping addition to his ethnic, patriarchal concept of state. It was this kind of organic theory in Hozumi's thought that Ishida Takeshi said was the mechanism used to forge the link between the family and the emperor in the family-state concept of the state. Irokawa Daikichi disagreed about how effective this link was: "The theoretical analogy of familism and the organic theory of society can never adequately explain the conjunction of two utterly opposite values."[49] What Hozumi did was to first set up his theory of absolute monarchy based on Shintō religious doctrine and the concept of the patriarchal construction of society, then to claim that this was somehow one great organic totality. The key point for our analysis of Shintō ultranationalism in this study, however, is that within Hozumi's organic totality, the structure of state and society was hierarchical. Nevertheless, Hozumi's organic theory of the relationship between the individual and society was a small piece of the greater puzzle in his overall theory of the Japanese state in which all human activities—political, economic, social, and cultural—were to be directed to a single purpose: the preservation of the ethnic national purity of the Japanese emperor-centered family state.

History and the Völkisch Family-State

Hozumi's emperor ideology was not just a theory of the state. Like all other ideologies, it had its own distinctive *Weltanschauung* and a theory of history. In antiquity, accordingly to Hozumi, various ethnic groups emerged, scattered about in virtual isolation on the globe. Each ethnic group naturally formed into an ethnic nation. Originating in this global segregation, consciousness of a "human race" did not exist. In other words, "mankind" had not been conceived of as a community, nor had there been the idea that all mankind had a common origin. That is to say, Hozumi rejected the monogenetic theory of the origins of man, the idea that there was unity of mankind in the beginning.

Hozumi theorized that the ethnic states in antiquity were theocratic states and that the internal structures of these original ethnic states were naturally and inherently hierarchical, although it appears that he was baffled by the pre-Christian Germanic tribes, which, according to his understanding, had no kings. Nevertheless, at the apex of the ethnic state was the patriarchal monarch, who was the direct descendant of the progenitor of the ethnic nation. Sovereignty resided in the patriarch, and there was no distinction between the religious and the secular. The patriarch's will was the law. Thus, in the Japanese state, "Law is the word of the emperor."[50] Law was the word of Amaterasu Ōmikami, and law continued to be the word of Amaterasu Ōmikami even after she had entrusted her descendants to rule in her place: "In our family-state, which is constructed on the basis of ancestor worship, sovereignty is the authority of *Amaterasu Ōmikami*."[51] Since state law was the command of Amaterasu Ōmikami through the body of the emperor, "state law [was] sacred"[52] because "the emperor is *Amaterasu Ōmikami* existing in the present."[53] Obedience, therefore, was not just mere obedience to the will of the emperor in the usual sense of the term. The very act of obedience itself was religious in quality. "In our kokutai sovereignty is sacred," Hozumi wrote. "The people not only obey the sovereign, they worship the sovereign."[54] Law—that is, divine governance—was the central force that maintained the order of the entire patriarchal structural of the state.

In short, ancestral religion, which meant worship of the patriarchal monarch and his ancestors, was the very foundation of this ethnic state. It was the political and moral force that cemented everything together. Morality and law were therefore identical. Since law was the word of the emperor, morality, too, was the will of the emperor, which in turn was the will of Amaterasu Ōmikami. A crucial point here in Hozumi's conceptualization of primordial ethnic groupings is the total absence of universal norms of morality that applied equally to everyone in the state and in society. Herein lay the key to understanding the preservation of the original völkisch state: law and morality were not defined in terms of obedience or disobedience to a supreme law above the state, whether that be the law of a supreme being as in the Christian tradition; the natural-law theory, which holds that individuals are "endowed by their creator with certain inalienable rights"; popularly adopted laws written down in statutes or constitutions, commonly referred to as "positive law"; or, indeed, the Chinese concept of "Tien," which is essential to the theory of the mandate of heaven. In the ethnic state, law, morality, and the definition of the Good were defined in terms of integration of the self totally into the hierarchical society, which was accomplished by identification with the monarch. In practice, this meant that knowing what was required of one was to know one's place in the hierarchical structure and to do what one's role required.

If we follow Hozumi's line of historical reasoning, however, at some point in time we arrive at what we might refer to as the "fall of man," to borrow a concept from Christian theology. Certain individuals appeared who grasped the idea of "mankind" as a community. They concocted universal religions with their own internal systems of morality that applied to all individuals, ruler and subject alike, above and beyond the ethnic community. It was precisely at this point that we find the existence of the "individual" for the first time. This very recognition of the existence of the individual was a Pandora's box, because it led necessarily to a series of consequences that in the final stage was the destruction of the ethnic patriarchal state. These universal religions provided ontological grounds for the moral existence of the individual outside the ethnic state or ethnic community. Society then would consist of real individuals. Once the individual and the individual's moral justification for existence outside the ethnic community is postulated, the existence of a "private morality" necessarily follows. In Hozumi's theory, the introduction of private morality created for the first time the distinction between state law (*kokuhō*) and religious doctrine (*kyōgi*).[55] This separation of state law and morality meant the separation of morality from the emperor and imperial rule, since the emperor was the state, and law was the word of the imperial ancestors.

As a consequence, state sovereignty would no longer be obeyed and worshipped with total devotion. Instead, the individual was given an independence of spirit, or a sense of inner freedom to defy authority. The notion of private morality translates into the idea of moral equality, and once the idea of moral equality permeates society, the foundations for social and legal equality are in place. After that, it is only a matter of time until the demise of the ethnic state with its patriarchal monarchy. Hozumi cited what had happened in the Western world as evidence to support this ethnic theory of history and as a lesson of history for the Japanese: "The ancient organizations of the European states—Greek, Roman and Germanic—were no different from that of our state in that they were all built on the basis of ancestor worship and on the unity of state and religion."[56] But what subsequently happened in the Western world was that the original ethnic states were eventually destroyed by Christianity. With the introduction of Christianity, the worship of the patriarchal king in the ethnic state was displaced by the worship of the transcendental God of all humanity. The primary moral obligation of the people became that required by God, because they had to obey God's laws first if they were to be destined for eternal salvation in heaven. This effectively stripped the ethnic state of its sacredness and left it with only secondary loyalties. Richard Minear, also quoting Hozumi, pointed out Hozumi's hostility toward Christianity in this regard: "Ever since Christianity arose, preached the equality and brotherly love of all mankind, and in addition to believing in only one God abolished the doctrines of ancestor worship, the European ethnic nations have lost entirely this ancient belief."[57] Doak also observed the deeply ingrained hostility on the part of Japanese Shintōists toward Christianity. For example, he noted that in 1897, the same year Hozumi wrote *National Education*, Kimura Takatarō, Inoue Tetsujirō, and Takayama Chogyū joined together to form the Great Japan Society. The very first article of its founding charter boldly declared: "We worship the founder of our country."[58] Doak further informs us that the Great Japan Society's journal *Nipponshugi* took a leading role in publishing attacks on Christianity. This should not be surprising, however, if one understands the inner logic of Shintō ultranationalist thought.

This existence of a private morality provided to the individual by a universal religion or any system of thought that had at its core universal principles as opposed to ethnic religion constituted a rebellion against the state. Once this private morality takes hold among a significant number of people, the whole völkisch state starts to falter and begins a process of decline that eventually ends in its demise. Recalling the opening statement of Hozumi's essay—"The foundation of the Japanese ethnic state's unique kokutai and national morality is ancestor worship"— the reason ancestor worship is the foundation is that it guarantees this unity of state law and religious doctrine. It guarantees that the individual as an independent moral being does not come into existence. In the völkisch or ethnic state, the purpose of all morality and of all culture is to maintain and enhance the ethnic state. Christianity had been the mortal enemy of the völkisch state in the European world; Confucianism and Buddhism had once served the same function of destroying the völkisch or ethnic states in the Asian world because Confucianism and Buddhism also postulated the individual with an ontological basis of his or her own outside the völkisch state. The triumph of Confucianism resulted in the demise of the völkisch state in China. The spread of Buddhism was the cause of its downfall elsewhere in Asia. In other words, all of these universal systems—Christianity with its God of the human race and its commandments, Confucianism with its transcendental *Ten* and its personal moral relationships, and Buddhism with its moral precepts and individual salvation—all in one form or another postulated the individual as a moral being with a raison d'être outside the völkisch state. And by the extension of this reasoning, the triumph of Islam in the Middle East and elsewhere caused the demise of völkisch religions in those parts of the world.

Hozumi inferred that only the Japanese state had managed to escape this fate and had preserved its original kokutai—that is, the patriarchal völkisch state—through the centuries and into the present. Japan had been able to do this despite the introduction of the doctrines of Confucianism and Buddhism. This was the reason for the uniqueness of Japan's ethnic kokutai. Once the emperor is contested, the monarchy is deposed, and the "unbroken line of emperors" from divine antiquity is broken, it is lost forever. It cannot be brought back, and from that point onward the society becomes a naturally egalitarian society. Japan's kokutai is unique because it has been preserved in its original natural form since antiquity. Why has the Japanese ethnic state been successful in warding off the universalistic doctrines of Confucianism and Buddhism, and why has it escaped the historical tragedy that befell ethnic states elsewhere? Hozumi found his answer to this question in the continued vitality of ancestor religion in Japan's emperor state. To cite an example, he stated: "Although Buddhism was practiced widely in the Middle Ages, it was not able to destroy this unique belief [ancestor worship]. Its subtle doctrines were practiced by but only a fraction of society, and the majority of the population continued to worship our ancestors in the name of Buddha."[59] The vitality of ancestor worship, in other words, had effectively neutralized Buddhism and successfully prevented it from permeating the essential core of the völkisch family-state.

But the challenge to the Japanese ethnic state by Buddhism and Confucianism was all in the distant past. What Hozumi was now concerned about was the present and the future of the Japanese state. The magnitude of the threat to the Japanese ethnic state from the modern Western powers was unprecedented. Not only was the West able to dominate the world physically with its military, political, and economic power; it also dominated the world culturally. Modern Western thought had unleashed tremendous revolutionary forces in the lands with which it had come into contact, revolutionary forces that were sweeping away traditional political, social, and religious institutions. In Hozumi's theory of history, the modern secular state based on the philosophy of the Enlightenment represented the logical development of a historical trend away from the principles of the original völkisch states that had begun with the introduction of Christianity centuries earlier. He urged the Japanese not to succumb to the fads of the decadent West because, in so doing, he was sure, they would destroy the Japanese völkisch family-state:

> If we are to contaminate the purity of the blood of our ancestors and destroy the wholeness of their customs and religion unwittingly in the name of social change, we shall have in this divine land and paradise the peoples of different ethnicities and races (*ishu*), and the customs and religions of different ethnicities and races, and find ourselves at war with one another. This [scenario] would be the demise of our nation's völkisch or ethnic community.[60]

In other words, Hozumi was warning the Japanese people not only against those who adopted foreign ways outright but also against those who he thought were unwittingly contributing to the annihilation of the Japanese ethnic state, with its unique political and social structure. The ultimate disaster for the Japanese völkisch state would, of course, have been the immigration of foreigners, which would result in the jumbling together of a heterogeneous mass of humanity in which all beliefs and customs of the ethnic group eventually would be lost. Hozumi could not tolerate a multiethnic state or a multiracial state. It is interesting to note that Japanese Shintō ultranationalists and Japanese Christians had vastly different notions on the makeup of the Japanese state in this respect. Doak wrote: "Japanese Christians generally welcomed the incorporation of Koreans into the empire since they hoped the relatively larger number of Korean Christians would strengthen the voice of Christianity within the empire and counter the rising Shintōist nationalism at home."[61] This position taken by Japanese Christians might have been expected of Japanese imbued with universal Christian values.

In contrast to Hozumi's ideal state, the modern Western state, of course, rested on the thinking of the Enlightenment, which was based on rationalism and universalism. Enlightenment thinkers had hoped that reason would replace authority and tradition. They thought of themselves not as French or European, but as members of the human race. They assumed that rational principles were universal and therefore independent of national, social, or cultural particularities. They also represented the trend toward the secularization of politics. Religion was pushed to the background. Did not men create their own state by agreement among themselves? The political Enlightenment was a revolt against patriarchalism and the theoretical justifications on which it was based. The divine right of kings theory was strongly challenged, and individualism displaced patriarchalism as the foundation of the natural order of state and society in the Western world.

For Hozumi, the Enlightenment thought of Western liberal democracy was the ultimate ideological threat to the Japanese ethnic state. Thus, Hozumi bitterly attacked Enlightenment thought with every theoretical weapon at his disposal; for him, this war with Western civilization was a holy war. His work contains statements such as "The individual does not exist in isolation" and "It is already a mistake to think that society is made up of isolated self-supporting individuals."[62] Such statements were made within the context of his attack on the contract theory of the origins of government and in defense of patriarchalism and the State Shintō version of the origins of government. Just as Sir Robert Filmer once argued against Locke, Hozumi rejected any theory of state and society that started with independent and equal individuals. But there was more to it than that. These statements suggest that Hozumi was under the impression that political theorists such as Locke did not acknowledge any communal values whatsoever. He also attacked the secular liberal state on the grounds that it guaranteed freedom for a few at the cost of ignoring the weak and inarticulate members of society, and that the latter would be devoured because liberalism was essentially a system for the survival of the fittest, a doctrine that life is a struggle in which the strong survive and the weak perish. He charged that in this fight, the "weak become food for the strong."[63] Still more, he seems to have been convinced that a state formed by equal and independent individuals was inherently unstable, and such a state could not guarantee permanent order:

> A blood relationship: one receives it from one's ancestors and passes it on to one's descendents. This bond is eternal. It cannot be severed and joined, or continued and discontinued according to advantages and disadvantages. Therefore, this bond is rock solid. What unites it is the authority of the ancestors. The authority of the ancestors does not rest on a contract among equals. Therefore, the feeling of respect and love is strong and the concept of loyalty and obedience deep.[64]

The "contract among equals" in this passage was, of course, a reference to the contract theory of the origins of government.

A Constitution Stripped of Constitutionalism

Hozumi Yatsuka's passionate faith in Shintō supplied him with an understanding of reality. The State Shintō version of Genesis announced a central point: Amaterasu Ōmikami was the originator of the unique Japanese form of state. This idea became a powerful tool for Hozumi. The inclusion of this religious truth in Article 1 of the Constitution of the Empire of Japan, "The Empire of Japan shall be reigned over and governed by a line of Emperors unbroken for ages eternal," made it possible for Hozumi to justify his constitutional interpretation in terms of this ultimate religious-fundamentalist meaning. The emperor as the original framer of the Constitution of the Empire of Japan was the living representative of the founding deity of the state.

It was the creator's law that the scheme of government for the Japanese state was to be structurally hierarchical. This was behind Hozumi's theory of the immutable kokutai: that Japan should always be reigned over and governed by a line of emperors descended from Amaterasu Ōmikami, the founder of the state. Under no circumstances could the possibility exist of a radical restructuring of the fundamental political relationship between the emperor and his subjects in the Japanese state. The sacred kokutai categorically rejected it. Sovereignty resided in the emperor, which had remained and should remain unchanged throughout history. What had changed throughout Japanese history was not the kokutai, the "form of state," but the *seitai*, the "form of government."[65]

From this assumption of the religious origins of the sovereignty of the emperor naturally flows a methodology and a grand frame of reference for constitutional interpretation. Imperial sovereignty, for example, precluded the notion of the separation of powers between a divine emperor and his subjects. Perhaps the most effective way in which Hozumi applied this to constitutional interpretation was in his discussion of Article 5, which states, "The Emperor exercises the legislative power with the consent of the Imperial Diet." Hozumi claimed that under no circumstances could "consent of the Imperial Diet" be somehow construed as a limitation of the emperor's powers. Nor could this constitutional provision imply a sharing of power between the emperor and a legislative branch of government that had independent authority to control legislation. He charged that anyone whose interpretation of the Constitution of the Empire of Japan was premised on the fallacious notion of the separation of powers of government was reading into the constitutional provisions a totally alien political ideology—that is, liberal democracy. It was under the political philosophy of liberal democracy that independent political institutions were designed to avoid the concentration of power in any one person or agency. Behind liberal democracy, too, was a secular notion of the state and the political order.

Hozumi stressed that Article 5 did not mean the emperor shared legislative powers with the parliament. The parliament had no independent legislative powers whatsoever. It had no "legal will (*hōritsu ishi*) " of its own.[66] He stated categorically, "The subject exercising legislative power is the emperor (*rippōken o okonau no shutai wa kunshu ni shite*)," while the "parliament is the constitutional organ that consents to this (*gikai wa kore ni kyōsan suru no hōritsujo no kikan taru*)."[67] It is clear that Hozumi was not merely urging the parliament to cooperate for effective government. He was far more concerned with the notion that parliament was an independent power with legislative powers of its own. Parliamentarians were supposed to comply with the provisions of the Constitution of the Empire of Japan from the perspective of his Shintō-based theory of absolute monarchy and *approve* laws, and to do so without objection. In short, the parliament was to be a rubber-stamp legislature.

In a section of *Handbook of the Constitution of the Empire of Japan* titled "*Yosan no Hiketsu* (Rejection of the Budget),"[68] Hozumi applied the same kind of argument in regard to the issue of parliament's constitutional role of approving the annual budget, which at times had paralyzed the government and brought on constitutional crises. For the parliament not to pass the budget this would constitute a "constitutional violation (*kempō ihan*)."[69] Hozumi stated that the "parliament is without authority to reject the budget (*gikai wa yosan o hiketsu suru no kennō nashi*)."[70] The ministers of state were also responsible to the emperor and not to the parliament. This, of course, included the prime minister, a position not specifically mentioned in the constitution. In regard to Article 55, which read in part, "The respective Ministers of State shall give their advice to the Emperor, and be responsible for it," Hozumi clarified the latter part of the sentence, saying that it was "the emperor and not the members of parliament who question this responsibility."[71] These are just some of the many examples of the ways in which Hozumi interpreted the Constitution of the Empire of Japan according to his ideology of absolute monarchy. The aim of Hozumi's constitutional interpretation, however, is unmistakable: a constitution stripped of constitutionalism.

How does one assess the political thought of Hozumi Yatsuka? Where did it fit into the discourse over state and sovereignty in prewar Japan? First, it was one solution to the difficult problem of operating under the Constitution of the Empire of Japan. If all political control was placed in the emperor, and the parliament was left without any real legislative power, the problem of gridlock in government could be solved. Theoretically, this was certainly a viable alternative form of government. In the political context of the times, however, it represented the beginning of a trajectory away from constitutional government in prewar Japan. Hozumi had turned his back on the nascent parliamentary and democratic institutions and the value of individual liberty on which they were ultimately based. His ideas were collectivist, authoritarian, anti-parliamentary, antidemocratic, and a form of religious-fundamentalist ultranationalism.

In conclusion, I have argued that Hozumi's formulation of the Japanese state was a theory of state much like those one finds in the European world in the seventeenth-century writings of Sir Robert Filmer, which were used to justify absolute monarchy against the rising tide of liberal thought and representative government. Such a theory of state, of course, does not allow for the participation of the masses in government. In Hozumi's patriarchal state, as in all patriarchies, the people were treated politically as children. Hozumi showed this when he came out against expanding the franchise in the 1910s. He wanted filial loyalty and obedience from the people, but this did not really involve the emperor's subjects in the political decision making of the emperor's state. His thought was representative of the thinking of the religious Shintō ultranationalist movement of the late Meiji period, which might be best characterized as a kind of "conservative Shintō ultranationalism." However, for anyone interested in further comparative studies of monarchical absolutism from a slightly different perspective, Hozumi's thought in this debate over state and sovereignty may perhaps be similar to what Roger Griffin would refer to as a form of "futural counter-revolutionary" reaction to the rise of modernity. That is to say, Griffin would sort out the distinction between reactionary absolutism and counter-revolutionary absolutism. In short, reactionary absolutism seeks to resist modernity and the rise of democracy and re-create the past, while counter-revolutionary absolutism is futural—positing an alternative modernity under which Japan could modernize with a strengthened imperial tradition retooled and reasserted to provide the basis for the emergence of Japan as a strong nation.

Griffin, a well-known scholar of the history of ideas and European fascism, offered me the following assessment of Hozumi's thought as outlined in this chapter:

In terms of my own theories of absolutism and modernity, I would suggest that [Hozumi] Yatsuka's assertion of absolutism has at least three phenomena familiar in the history of Western absolutism: one is the counter-Reformation absolutism of the Papacy that arises when its legitimacy is challenged in early modern Europe by Protestantism; another is the Filmer-type monarchical absolutism asserted in the face of millenarian, Protestant and early rationalist ideas of sovereignty that eventually, when secularized, transmuted into Enlightenment ideas of popular sovereignty; and the third is nineteenth century and twentieth century conservative ideas of organic nationhood and royalism associated with such figures as [Joseph] de Maistre, [Louis Gabriel Ambriose] de Bonald, and [Charles] Maurras.[72]

There is much food for thought here for anyone interested in further comparative studies of Japanese and European theorists of monarchical absolutism from a variety of perspectives. Joseph de Maistre (1753–1821) argued for a restoration of the French monarchy and was one of the most influential thinkers of counter-revolutionary and authoritarian conservatism following the French Revolution. Louis Gabriel Ambroise de Bonald (1754–1840) was another French counter-revolutionary philosopher who constructed a system of political absolutism. And Charles Maurras (1868–1952) was a French writer and principal founder and thinker of the reactionary Action Francaise (founded by Maurras in 1899), a political movement that was monarchist and opposed to parliamentary government. Pondering an explanation for the combination of these elements in Hozumi's thought, Griffin reasoned that perhaps it was "because modernity in a globalizing sense hit Japan so late while it was still a feudal theocracy all its reactions to modernity assume elements of Renaissance, Enlightenment, and 19th and 20th century Europe simultaneously."

At any rate, when Hozumi wrote *National Education* in 1897, the common people in Japan still had not fully begun to feel that they should have a voice in the political affairs of the state. But times were rapidly changing. The movement toward parliamentary government was gaining momentum, and this was something that worried and distressed Hozumi. I hope to demonstrate in the next several chapters that Hozumi's theory of state was a transitional theory of state, because the type of Shintō ultranationalist ideology that would appear in the next few years would be something radically different. Meanwhile, his theory of state and his interpretation of the constitution was subsequently challenged by his junior colleague Minobe Tatsukichi, who adopted the theory, prevalent among German state theorists in the nineteenth century, that sovereignty resided in the state, of which the emperor was but one organ. It would also come under vicious attack by those who were converted to an ideology that saw things from a decidedly different worldview: socialism. The religious foundations of Hozumi's religious Shintō ultranationalist state theory prompted one sharp critic, Kita Ikki, to refer to it as a "mirage-like theological state theory."[73]

It is to the state theorists who articulated theories in support of parliamentary rule in the late Meiji period that we now turn our attention.

3

Minobe Tatsukichi:

The Secularization of Politics

Sovereignty is at its simplest when there exists a State in which a multitude of individuals is subordinated to the sovereign power of a single prince. . . . The moment that a greater complexity makes its appearance either in the political or in the social structure of the community, the simple concept of sovereignty ceases to have any but the most tortured application. There can be no question that a full measure of complexity was part of the German State after 1871. Even before that date the sovereign princes had been forced to share their power with the representatives of the people and the Stände . . . Only by means of a fiction which would hide the fact that there existed an essential division of power and function could the concept which had fitted the States of Louis XIV and Frederick the Great be used in relation to the modern German federal State. . . . A scheme of things which rested on the view that all power resided in the hands of the sovereign, who disposed of the public affairs of his subjects, could result only in a pathetic travesty of the new social and political reality.— RUPERT EMERSON, *State and Sovereignty in Modern Germany*, 127–28

The nineteenth-century German doctrine of the personality of the state is important because it was in part a polemical antithesis to the personality of the absolute prince, and in part to a state considered as a higher third with the aim of evading the dilemma of monarchical or popular sovereignty.— CARL SCHMITT, *The Concept of the Political*, 42–43

Hozumi Yatsuka's main political and ideological rival in finding a solution to the problem of political gridlock under the Constitution of the Empire of Japan and in facilitating the smooth functioning of government was the constitutional-law scholar Minobe Tatsukichi (1873–1948). Unlike the religious Shintō ultranationalists, who found constitutional government utterly distasteful and sought to thwart its growth, Minobe inclined toward liberalism. He was convinced that constitutionalism was irrevocably established and thought it desirable for Japan to move ahead with the strengthening of parliamentary institutions. He would devote most of his academic career to trying to achieve this, working out the most powerful ideology in prewar Japan in support of responsible parliamentary government. However, in his later years he would fall victim to militant radical Shintō ultranationalists, who tried to kill him as well as his ideas.

Minobe was born on May 7, 1873, five years after the Meiji Restoration. Immediately after he graduated from Tokyo's First District Higher Middle School in 1894, a preparatory school for entrance into Tokyo Imperial University, he was admitted to the Law School of Tokyo Imperial University. He attended lectures on the Constitution of the Empire of Japan taught by Hozumi Yatsuka and Ikichi Kitokurō (1867–1944), but it was the lectures and writings of Ichiki that made a deep and lasting impression. According to Ienaga Saburō, Minobe had thoroughly read Ichiki's *Nihon Hōrei Yosan Ron*, a book on Japanese law and the national budget, before he attended Tokyo Imperial University.[1] Minobe was intellectually predisposed to Ichiki's broader constitutional ideas well before he attended his lectures. Ichiki, who had expounded an emperor-as-organ theory of the state, had become professor of state law at the Tokyo Imperial University Law School in 1894 following the death of Sueoka Seiichi,[2] still another early advocate of the emperor-as-organ theory.

In contrast, Minobe found Hozumi to be too opinionated and complained that his ideas were founded on an "illogical dogmatism (*hironri teki na dokudan*)."[3] Hozumi failed to impress Minobe even as a young, immature first-year student. After graduating from Tokyo Imperial University in 1897, Minobe found employment as a government clerk in the Home Ministry. However, life as a bureaucrat did not appeal to him, so he resigned his position in 1898 and, with an important recommendation from Ichiki, was admitted to graduate school at Tokyo Imperial University in preparation for a professorship position in comparative legal history (*hikaku hōsei shi*).[4] In 1899, he traveled to Europe to study comparative legal history on a commission from the Ministry of Education. After three years of study in Europe, Minobe returned to Tokyo, in 1902, and began teaching comparative legal history at the Tokyo Imperial University Law School.[5]

Minobe was one among the hundreds of Japanese students who flocked to famous German universities in the late nineteenth century and early twentieth century. As did many Japanese students studying in Germany, he absorbed German methods of academic research and German thought, which had been dominated by the concept of the state pioneered by G. W. F. Hegel (1770–1831), the intellectual giant of German state theorists, beginning in the first two decades of the nineteenth century.[6] Hegel asserted that the state was not a contractual relationship among individuals; rather, "It was itself an Individuality, independent of and superior to all other individuals: A Person taking all other persons into itself and bringing to them that universality and fullness which otherwise they must lack."[7] Accordingly, he wrote, "Sovereignty . . . is the right or power not of any individual or sum of individuals but of the whole conceived as an organic unity with a real personality of its own."[8] That is, according to Hegel's theory of the state as a real, organic, independent personality, sovereignty rested not in the monarch or in the people but in the state itself. As an individual organism, the state consisted of different organs with separate functions. Further, the constitution was "the organization of the State and the process of its organic life in reference to its own self."[9] Hegel's concept of the state as a person and the emperor as an organ of the state became the dogmas in mainstream German scholarship on the state throughout the rest of the nineteenth century and into the first two decades of the twentieth century. Nagao Ryūichi noted that "such doctrines (the doctrines of state sovereignty and of the monarch as an organ of the state) were the *communis opinio* in German *Staatslehre*."[10] Japanese students in Germany from the 1880s to the 1910s studied under a generation of German scholars of jurisprudence who drew heavily on these very basic Hegelian concepts. Perhaps the most influential were Johann Bluntschli (1808–81), Paul Laband (1838–1918), Gerhard Anschutz (1867–1948), and Georg Jellinek (1851–1911). Also, one must not forget that the ideas of the German scholars Lorenz von Stein (1815–90) and Rudolf von Gneist (1816–95) had a lasting impact among students at Tokyo Imperial University.

Minobe's thinking was particularly influenced by Jellinek—so much so that Minobe was described by one of his own students as "the Jellinek of Japan."[11] There is no question about the overwhelming influence of Jellinek's writings on Minobe's state thought. Nevertheless, Minobe was no clone of Jellinek. In fact, in *Nihon Kempō Shisō Shi* (The History of Japanese Constitutional Thought), Nagao Ryūichi pointed out that it is not the similarities but the differences between Minobe's thought and that of Jellenik that are striking.[12] According to Nagao, one thing that influenced Minobe deeply about Jellinek's theory of the state was that Jellenik's state-legal theory was underpinned by certain psychological, historical, and sociological assumptions. Moreover, in Nagao's opinion, Minobe went well beyond Jellenik in emphasizing the force of socio-psychologicalism (*shakai shinrishugi*) in transforming the state from what the state is (*sonzai*) in its imperfect present form to what the state should strive for in its ideal form (*toi*),[13] or to the ends to which public efforts should be directed. Nagao also noted that Minobe rejected Jellenik's "two-sided theory of the state (*kokka sōmensetsu*)" and instead stressed the essential sameness of the legal nature of the state and the sociological and political natures of the state.[14]

Nevertheless, Minobe was convinced that the German state-sovereignty theory was the most advanced system of thought in the world to explain the nature of the modern state, and he used it to serve as the ideological underpinning of his interpretation of the Constitution of the Empire of Japan. The state-sovereignty theory would commonly be referred to in Japan in the ideological debates between constitutional-law scholars such as Hozumi Yatsuka, who advocated absolute monarchy, and those who advocated responsible parliamentary government as the "emperor-as-organ theory (*tennō kikansetsu*)" of the state. In contrast, the theory of the state that supported absolute monarchy was referred to as the "emperor-as-sovereign theory (*tennō shukensetsu*)." It was within this overarching German state-sovereignty theory or emperor-as-organ theory of the state that Minobe worked out his own theory of the nature of the Japanese state.

Frank Miller has noted that Jellinek, together with Paul Laband and Gerhard Anschutz, "were most influential in providing the methodology and suggesting the content of the theories of the 'liberal school' of constitutional interpretation in Japan."[15] Miller summed up the fundamental ideas of this Japanese school of German constitutionalism:

> The principle of constitutionalism, despite the restrictive definition attached to it, had the effect of reducing the monarch, along with other

elements in the constitutional structure, to a status subordinate to a superior entity, the state. In the Hegelian tradition, high ethical and cultural value was ascribed to the state, which, in the form first of the Prussian state and later the empire, was viewed throughout the nineteenth century as the instrument of German national liberation and unification. The superiority of the monarch became a relative matter, not fundamental to the nature of the state, resting on social and political tradition and on sundry more-or-less utilitarian arguments which might vary from place to place and from time to time. This idea of the state had rich and far-ranging implications in conjunction with organic and corporate theories concerning its nature, and ethical, cultural, and racial theories regarding its purpose and destiny.[16]

It is no exaggeration to say that this idea of state had "rich and far-ranging implications" in the Japanese context, too. It would be at the center of arguably the greatest debate in modern Japanese history—a debate over state and sovereignty that raged from the beginning of the Meiji period through the Taishō and early Shōwa periods.

Minobe's general theory of law and state can be found in his major works *Kempō Kōwa* (Lectures on the Constitution, 1912), *Nihon Kempō* (The Constitution of Japan, 1921), *Kempō Satsuyō* (Essentials of the Constitution, 1923), and *Kempō Seigi* (Commentary of the Constitution, 1927).[17] Miller said that Minobe's *The Constitution of Japan* was virtually *Allgemeine Staatslehre* (The Theory of the State in General), Georg Jellinek's work on state law written in 1900. In *The Constitution of Japan*, Minobe's "discussion of the nature of law and of the state was to establish the definition of the state as a corporate entity, possessed of legal personality and thus of a capacity for rights and duties, and distinguished from other such legal personalities by its possession of governmental power and sovereignty."[18] In the development of this definition, he defined law as "a rule of will in social life, which is recognized in the social mind as being for human advantage and therefore inviolable."[19] The state was also a "governing corporation (*tōchi dantai*)."[20] He further refined his definition of the state as a human corporation, "an organized collectivity of persons having a common aim and possessing its own ends and its own vitality."[21] Miller summed up Minobe's characteristics of the state this way:

1) The state has its own ends, different from but not unrelated to ends of its constituents, and its own vitality or life. 2) The state has a will, for ends are understandable only as the ends of a will. . . . All that the law deter-

mines is who, as an organ (*kikan*) of the state, occupies the position of making the will of the state, and also how that will is made. 3) The state is a unity. 4) In the case of a monarchy, the monarch, as well as his subjects, is contained within the state.[22]

The state was distinguishable from other corporate entities in that it had a fixed territory and governmental power. Therefore, it follows that the state is a "supreme territorial, governmental corporation."[23] Finally, Miller stated that Minobe had added a fifth purpose of the state: "maintaining world peace and contributing to world culture."[24]

A corollary to this human, corporate definition of the state was that the state had a personality of its own and that the will of the state was expressed through the actions of the organs of which it was composed. The nature of the state in terms of classifications such as absolute monarchy, constitutional monarchy, or republic was determined by the arrangement and jurisdiction of the organs within the state. In other words, the configuration of the organs in the state determined the form of government. Each organ had its proper function in the inner workings of the state. Minobe distinguished between "direct organs" and "indirect organs" of the state.[25] The direct organs of the state were the important ones in that they "constituted the basic governmental organization."[26] A change in the nature of direct organs constituted a fundamental change in the form of government. For example, if the monarch was the sole direct organ of the state, the state was an absolute monarchy. But when there were other direct organs of the state in addition to the monarch, there was a limited monarchy. A limited monarchy by definition was a constitutional monarchy. In his interpretation of the Constitution of the Empire of Japan, the parliament was also a direct organ of the state—that is, the popularly elected parliament constituted one of the direct organs of the Japanese state. However, it must be noted that Minobe did not regard the parliament as a direct organ of state equal to the emperor, who also, of course, was a direct organ of the state. According to Miller, Minobe "further classified direct organs functionally as ruling organs (the emperor), participating organs (the diet), and electoral organs (the electorate). The Imperial Diet was thus assigned a restricted and subordinate role in relation to the emperor. But, on the other hand, it enjoyed a status superior to that of the privy council, the cabinet, the courts, or other indirect organs whose existence and competence derive from the other organs by delegation."[27]

Minobe further asserted that "when the monarch and the people jointly exercise state authority true constitutional monarchy exists."[28] In this sense, Minobe's emperor-as-organ theory of the state, which was consistent with nineteenth-century Hegelian German state theory, theoretically supported neither liberal democracy, in which sovereignty theoretically resided in the people as a whole, nor absolute monarchy, in which sovereignty resided in the monarch, who possessed the state as though it were his own personal property. Minobe's emperor-as-organ theory justified Japan's constitutional monarchy as a form of shared rule by the emperor and the people. His distinctions among organs of the state was, of course, derived and adapted from German theorists. Jellenik, for example, divided the organs of the state into "independent" organs and "dependent" organs. In his theory of related organs within the state, the monarch was the "independent" and "highest" organ of the state, while the Volk, or people, "were understood as a body whose will was represented in the secondary and dependent organ of the Parliament."[29]

As has been discussed, the paramount task that preoccupied the minds of constitutional-law scholars in the late Meiji period was to find a solution to the contradictions inherent in the imperial constitution. Miller was well aware of this overriding issue, as he indicated in his discussion of Minobe's interpretation of the constitution. He wrote: "Interpretative analysis of the Japanese constitutional system tended to support one of the other of two formulas contending within that system: strong imperial rule operating through a centralized despotic bureaucracy or constitutional government emphasizing the role of the diet. Minobe was conscious of his part as a state-law specialist in the resolution of this conflict."[30] It was from this general emperor-as-organ theory of the state that Minobe tried to interpret the Constitution of the Empire of Japan to legally justify and support parliamentary rule and majority-party government. This was no easy assignment: "To make a persuasive case that the parliamentary cabinet system and, ultimately, party government was in harmony with the letter and spirit of the constitution required no little ingenuity."[31] The project would entail the enormous task of constructing a constitutionally supportive line of reasoning that essentially would result in the removal of the emperor from all important governmental decision-making responsibilities and make the cabinet responsible to the parliament. To accomplish this aim, Minobe had to reject categorically Itō Hirobumi's interpretation of Article 55 of the Constitution of the Empire of Japan, which said that "the respective Ministers of State shall give their advice to the emperor and be responsible for it." In *Commentaries on the Constitution of the Empire of Japan*, Itō clearly stated that the parliament had no power to hold ministers of state responsible:

> When a Minister of State errs in the discharge of his functions, the power of deciding upon his responsibility belongs to the Sovereign of the State: He alone can dismiss a Minister, who has appointed him. Who then is it, except the Sovereign, that can appoint, dismiss and punish a Minister of State? The appointment and dismissal of them having been included by the Constitution in the sovereign power of the Emperor, it is only a legitimate consequence, that the power of deciding as to the responsibility of Ministers, is withheld from the Diet.[32]

How could Minobe possibly argue against Itō, the father of the Constitution of the Empire of Japan? But he did just that. In brief, Minobe defined "constitution" in its "essential meaning as the basic law of organization and processes of the state."[33] Although constitutional government dated back to 1890 in Japan, he argued, there was a "historical constitution," or a basic law, that dated back to the founding of the Japanese state in ancient times.[34] That "historical constitution" was "self-established and self-modified as a matter of historical phenomena."[35] It "was not established by an autocratic legislature."[36] The promulgation of the written constitution in 1889 made the historical constitution into an authoritative legal document. For the first time, said Minobe, "It became possible and necessary to distinguish between the constitution in its essential form sense and in its formal sense, between the basic law of the state, whether laid down in the text of the constitution or not, and the constitution as set forth in the 76 articles of the Imperial Constitution."[37]

Minobe then proceeded to argue that the Constitution of the Empire of Japan was supposed to have established the fundamental law of the Japanese state in a formal legal document. However, for him, the Constitution of the Empire of Japan did not accurately reflect this "essential" law of the Japanese state and the historical conditions of the times. It contained flaws that needed to be corrected. Minobe asserted that the constitution had flaws because "the men who established the Meiji constitutional system were ignorant or careless of the principles of constitutionalism."[38] In other words, Minobe said that, although the founders of the constitution sought to establish constitutional government, they did not fully comprehend the idea of constitutional government, which had resulted in an imperfect constitution. Thus, the task of constitutional-law scholars was to identify the errors in the Constitution of the Empire of Japan and overcome the practical problems associated with them by correctly interpreting the constitution according to the spirit of constitutional government. For Minobe, constitutional government meant responsible parliamentary government. That is, responsible government meant that the cabinet had to be responsible to the elected parliament for its actions. Other constitutional problems that blocked the smooth running of responsible parliamentary government included the independent counseling powers of the Privy Council, matters of military command and organization, and the makeup and function of the House of Peers.

To support his interpretation that the emperor was an organ of the state, Minobe made full use of the second paragraph of the preamble to the constitution, which stated, "The rights of sovereignty of the State, We have inherited from Our Ancestors, and We shall bequeath them to Our descendants. Neither We nor they shall in future fail to wield them, in accordance with the provisions of the Constitution hereby granted."[39] He read this in conjunction with Article 4, which stated, "The Emperor is the head of the Empire, combining in Himself the rights of sovereignty, and exercises them, according to the provisions of the present Constitution."[40]

Minobe accepted the position that the "emperor is sacred and inviolable,"[41] but he maintained:

> There is an idea current that the imperial prerogative is sacred and inviolable—that because it is executed by imperial will there can be no discussion of it nor can anyone debate its merits in any particular instance of its exercise. This idea is asserted with special vigor and breath against academic theory, so that anything may be construed as "discussion of the imperial prerogative" or "interference with the imperial prerogative" and thus as lese majesty. . . . [T]his is a gross error contrary to the spirit of the constitution. Constitutional government is responsible government. All exercise of the prerogative is made on the responsibility of state ministers and their responsibility can be debated. . . . The principle of sacred inviolability extends only to the person of the emperor.[42]

Minobe claimed that the person of the emperor was sacred and inviolable, but the prerogatives or commands of the emperor relative to the state were not. He interpreted Article 55, which stated, "The respective Ministers of State shall give their advice to the Emperor, and be responsible for it. All laws, Imperial Ordinances and Imperial Rescripts of whatever kind, that relate to the affairs of State, require the countersignature of a Minister of State,"[43] with this to assert that the emperor could exercise the imperial prerogative only on the ministers' advice, thereby protecting him from political or legal accountability for his actions regarding affairs of state. The ministers alone must be held responsible, because the emperor could do no wrong. Since he discarded as "unreasonable" the contention that the emperor in fact exercised this prerogative personally,[44] the ministers of state had to be responsible to someone, and that someone ultimately had to be the parliament. In effect, Minobe was saying not only that the council and consent of the ministers of state were necessary, but that the emperor had no legislative power by himself.

In a nutshell, this was the essence of Minobe's theory of state and constitutional interpretation.

The Emperor-as-Organ Theory in Crisis

Minobe Tatsukichi first began expounding his theory of the emperor as an organ of the state in the early 1900s. He was not the first to embrace this theory of state. Minobe assumed his position as chair of administrative law at Tokyo Imperial University in 1908, filling a position vacated by Ichiki Kitokurō (1867–1944). Ichiki had been a "professor-bureaucrat" for many years,[45] dividing his time between his teaching duties at Tokyo Imperial University and the Japanese Home Ministry. Through the influence of Ichiki's and Minobe's constitutional-law theories, the emperor-as-organ theory gained wide acceptance among legal scholars as the basis for understanding the nature of the modern Japanese state and interpreting the Constitution of the Empire of Japan. The influence of the theory probably reached a high point in the 1920s but is said to have continued to dominate the ideological landscape into the early 1930s. Miller noted that "the ministry of education's classification of the thirty leading academic lecturers and publicists in public law active in 1935 described twelve as adherents of the *tennō shutai setsu* (theory of the emperor as sovereign of the state) and eighteen as advocates of the *tennō kikan setsu* (theory of the emperor as organ of the state)."[46]

Judging from these statistics, one might be likely to conclude that the emperor-as-organ theory was *the* hegemonic state ideology during this period of Japanese history. By 1935, however, it was in crisis. Minobe's emperor-as-organ theory was bitterly and emotionally denounced by adherents to the emperor-as-sovereign theory of the state in both houses of the parliament in February–March 1935, and in April of the same year the Home Ministry banned three of Minobe's books. Minobe soon resigned his seat in the House of Peers and barely escaped an assassination attempt. He was not the only proponent of the emperor-as-organ theory to be attacked. For instance, Ichiki, who for decades had held a number of high-profile positions in the Japanese government, including vice minister of the Home Ministry, president of the Privy Council, and Imperial Household minister, was forced to resign as Privy Council president after he was attacked by radical Shintō ultranationalist groups.

The attack on Minobe and the emperor-as-organ theory of the state in 1935, which led to a movement to "clarify the national polity" that culminated in the Japanese government publication *Kokutai no Hongi* (Fundamentals of Our National Polity) in 1937, came to be referred to in Japanese writings as the "*tennō kikan setsu jiken* (emperor-as-organ theory incident)."[47] The important question to answer is: what happened? How can one account for the seemingly sudden demise of the emperor-as-organ theory, which Japanese constitutional-law scholars had begun to apply to the Japanese state as early as the 1880s? Can such a major shift in the ideological landscape come about in such very short time? Or were the Japanese government statistics cited earlier on the relative influence of the two theoretical positions misleading? One way to approach these issues and get deeper insight into the cause of the demise of support for parliamentary government in prewar Japan would be to take a closer look at how the debate between the emperor-as-organ theory of the state and the emperor-as-sovereign theory of the state has been construed.

In a chapter titled "The Minobe Affair," Miller characterized the emperor-as-organ theory incident as a contestation between the "liberal school" of constitutional thought and the authoritarian "orthodox-historical" school of constitutional thought.[48] He noted that while the liberal school of constitutional thought supported political-party rule and a cabinet responsible to the parliament, the "orthodox-historical" school sought to establish direct imperial rule.

Miller identified the roots of the opposition to the emperor-as-organ theory of the state as coming from three important sectors of Japanese society: academics, government bureaucrats, and the military establishment. First, he acknowledged that there had always been a core of dedicated supporters of the emperor-as-sovereign theory of state and that Kakehi Katsuhiko carried the burden of "imperial orthodoxy" at Tokyo Imperial University into the 1930s,[49] along with Satō Ushijirō at Tōhoko Imperial University and Shimizu Tōru at Chūō University. He also discussed a number of organizations established by Uesugi Shinkichi and others in support of nationalistic political movements. Second, Miller stated that it was "more in character for civil bureaucrats as a class to feel hostile, or at least unenthusiastic, towards the liberal school, whose emphasis on responsible representative government threatened bureaucratic influence."[50] Third, he reasoned that "many of the senior military officers had never been reconciled to the *Taishō Seihen* [a political change of government]; they continued to cherish authoritarian, elitist, hyper-loyalist concepts of the state as idealized in the golden era of the Satchō oligarchy, when the civil and military arms of the empire were the common and exclusive preserve of the post-Restoration nobility and when capitalistic-parliamentary politics had not yet cracked the citadel of military and bureaucratic autonomy erected by the *genro* Yamagata."[51] In short, it was in the context of ideological sympathy for the emperor-as-sovereign theory of state among conservative academics, bureaucrats, and military officers that the emperor-as-organ theory incident took place. The upshot was the understanding that a highly political environment of conservatism had existed in Japanese society that was strongly supportive of the emperor-as-sovereign theory of state within which the Minobe affair was enacted.

I am indebted to Miller for his pioneering English-language study of Minobe and his emperor-as-organ theory of the state. However, the overarching conceptual framework within which Miller situates the debate and his analysis of the Minobe affair must be reexamined. To clarify, it is not Miller's account of Minobe's theory of state and constitutional interpretation that need to be reconsidered but, rather, his portrayal of Minobe's opponents—those who argued for imperial sovereignty, which is the focus of this study. First, it is inaccurate to portray or characterize all of the emperor-as-sovereign theorists who opposed Minobe's emperor-as-organ theory of the state as belonging to an authoritarian, "orthodox-historical" school of constitutional thought.[52] As this study has suggested, before the official publication of *Fundamentals of Our National Polity* in 1937, which was the outcome of the Japanese government's effort to clarify the fundamental nature of the Japanese state, no political or ideological consensus existed on a state orthodoxy, which was precisely why the debate raged for several decades. Miller seems to have accepted the opinion of conservative postwar Japanese scholars who have tried to assert that there was indeed a state orthodoxy prior to the clarification campaign where none, in fact, could actually have existed.

In *Nihon Kindai Kempō Shisō Shi Kenkyu* (A Study of Japanese Modern Constitutional Thought, 1967),[53] Ienaga Saburō also expressed serious reservations about the assertion by some Japanese scholars that there had been an orthodox interpretation of the Constitution of the Empire of Japan. For instance, in an interesting section of that book titled "Tennō Kikan Setsu Gakuha no Kempō Shisō (The Emperor-as-Organ School of Constitutional Thought),"[54] Ienaga singled out Suzuki Yasuzō, an early postwar Japanese scholar who, we are told, wrote the first major comprehensive history of prewar Japanese constitutional thought, as the one who first popularized the notion that the constitutional thought of Hozumi Yatsuka and others who held the emperor-as-sovereign theory of state position in this debate as the "orthodox constitutional theory (*seitōteki kempō gakusetsu*)."[55] Ienaga countered this assertion by reasoning that if there had been any such orthodox interpretation of the Constitution of the Empire of Japan, it would have been Itō Hirobumi's *Kempō Gikai* (Commentaries on the Constitution of the Empire of Japan, 1906). Ienaga also noted that "Yatsuka criticized points in the argument of [Itō's] *Commentaries on the Constitution of the Empire of Japan* in his own writings."[56] That being the case, he argued, Hozumi's constitutional thought certainly could not be considered the "orthodox (*seitō*)" interpretation of the constitution. On the contrary, Ienaga asserted, if anyone were to be considered the "orthodox" scholar of the Constitution of the Empire of Japan, it would have to be Sueoka Seiichi, the sole scholar of public law who participated in the final drafting of Itō's *Commentaries on the Constitution of the Empire of Japan*.

Second, it is critically important to understand that, for the most part, it was not those who held traditional, absolutist views of the Japanese state who were ultimately responsible for destroying the emperor-as-organ theory of the state. Miller did not sort out and make clear distinctions among Minobe's ideological opponents. He was unable to distinguish among more pragmatic, moderate nationalists who established the Meiji state such as Itō Hirobumi and Yamagata Aritomo, ultraconservative or reactionary Shintō ultranationalists such as Hozumi Yatsuka, and radical Shintō ultranationalists such as Uesugi Shinkichi and Shintō terrorists, who were to emerge at the center of Japanese politics in the late Taishō and early Shōwa periods. As we shall see in the coming chapters, the emperor-as-organ theory of the state was destroyed primarily by radical Shintō ultranationalists and radical Shintō terrorists, who were also often in direct and violent confrontation with the moderate nationalists and conservative Shintō nationalists that we find in the Meiji period. It is also important to keep in mind that attempts were made on Minobe's life more than once, and the terrorists who tried to assassinate him and those who were sympathetic to using terrorist methods to gain political aims were certainly not "conservative," in any sense of the term. One must not forget that conservative, authoritarian Meiji leaders such as Yamagata came under attack from extreme nationalists in the Taishō period. Indeed, had Minobe's opponents been confined to traditional, authoritarian Meiji leaders or even reactionary Shintō ultranationalists such as Hozumi, his emperor-as-organ theory of the state very likely would have survived and eventually emerged victorious in the ideological battle to determine the direction of Japanese nationalism.

Third, one must make crystal clear the nature of Minobe's "liberal" school of constitutional thought. Minobe's emperor-as-organ theory of the state and his interpretation of the constitution certainly brought liberalizing tendencies to Japanese politics, and his theory was certainly liberal in contrast to the absolutist views of the conservative or reactionary Shintō ultranationalists. But his liberalism should not be confused with classical liberal political thought and democratic state theory in support of democratic government, as one finds, for example, in the American Declaration of Independence. Ultimately, behind the emperor-as-organ theory of the state and all of Minobe's constitutional interpretation lay the nineteenth-century German idea of "the State," which had nothing to do with the fundamental concepts of "self-evident truths," the doctrine of the "inalienable rights" of man, "social contracts," and "government based on consent" that underpin the basis of governmental authority in a democratic society. English-language writings on Minobe's emperor-as-organ theory tend to blur this distinction.[57] State sovereignty theory was devised and used by German state theorists and political authorities to obtain popular support for authoritarian rule. It was not a disguised or watered-down form of democracy; rather, it ideologically and legally justified a limited participatory form of authoritarianism.

Fourth, in Miller's discussion of the debate between Minobe's secular conceptualization of the Japanese state, on the one hand, and Hozumi's and Uesugi's religious characterization of the Japanese state, on the other hand, Miller seems to have underestimated or misunderstood the powerful attraction of the ideology of the Shintō ultranationalists, referring to it in one place as an ideology built on the "obscure doctrines of the *kaminagara* tradition."[58] There was nothing obscure about the radical Shintō ultranationalist ideology constructed on the "*kaminagara* tradition." As will be shown later in this study, a radical militant Shintō ultranationalism alone proved to be the most powerful ideology in the debate over state and sovereignty and the one used by those who would take over the Japanese state in the 1930s and mobilize the Japanese people for total war. The chief constitutional-law scholar who wove the *kaminagara* tradition into a systematic theory of state was Kakehi Katsuhiko. However, Miller seems to make conflicting statements that bear on this issue. In another passage, he does acknowledge the importance of Kakehi's thought:

> The burden of imperial orthodoxy was even more evident in the case of Tō-Dai Professor Emeritus Kakehi Masahiko [*sic*; Kakehi Katsuhiko], who in 1935 was teaching concurrently at the Tokyo University of Commerce, Hōse University, and the Kokugaku-in. Kakehi had begun teaching at Tō-Dai the same year that Minobe did; he taught jurisprudence and administrative law, sharing the latter field with Minobe. Kakehi was opposed to the [emperor-as-]organ theory from the beginning, but his participation in the Uesugi–Minobe debate had been marginal since the argument was primarily in the realm of legal theory while his objections were raised from theological considerations. Indeed, Kakehi was known chiefly for his writing on the moral basis of the Japanese state, in which he was strongly influenced by Shintō doctrines. The peak of his activities, professionally and in the conservative political movement, had passed before 1935, but his works still commanded great respect and were frequently cited as authority against Minobe.[59]

To reiterate, the theological arguments of Kakehi and other radical Shintō ultranationalists would win out over Minobe's formal legalistic arguments.

Miyazawa Toshiyoshi on the Minobe Affair

Miyazawa Toshiyoshi, the man who succeeded Minobe as professor of constitutional law at Tokyo Imperial University, wrote one of the most insightful and authoritative accounts of the meaning of the Minobe affair. Miyazawa was able to do this because he was close to Minobe personally and very familiar with his professional writings on Japanese constitutional law; he also had been involved in the ideological struggle at the time. Minobe retired from Tokyo Imperial University following the winter academic semester in 1934. Miyazawa started lecturing in the summer semester of the same year. Still more, he knew Minobe's opponents well and shared many of Minobe's concerns. He "had been deeply worrying about the end of party government in Japan by the assassination of [Prime Minister] Inukai in 1932 and the Nazi seizure of power in Germany in 1933."[60] Influenced by Hans Kelsen, whose theories Minobe opposed, Miyazawa nevertheless shared with Minobe a similar threat from the rightists. According to Nagao, "For not only 'Japan's Jellinek' Minobe, but for 'Kelsen students,' the monarch-organ theory had been accepted theory, which many scholars had written in their textbooks. Jellinekians and Kelsenians faced a common front against nationalist fanaticism."[61] Nagao further noted that, when the Minobe affair occurred, "dark clouds hovered over Miyazawa's academic future. He was constantly watched by the right-wing intellectuals and students who were influenced by them, scrutinizing what Minobe's successor spoke on the emperor and the emperor-organ theory. He was repeatedly attacked for his article on relativism."[62] Nagao and other Japanese historians of the history of modern Japanese constitutional thought still consider Miyazawa's two-volume *Tennō Kikan Setsu Jiken* (The Emperor-as-Organ Theory Affair) one of the most authoritative accounts of the emperor-as-organ theory incident written in the postwar period.[63] It is thus instructive to summarize Miyazawa's analysis of the nature and significance of the ideological struggle between the emperor-as-organ theory of the state and the emperor-as-sovereign theory of the state.

Miyazawa argued that there were three distinctly different, although often overlapping, levels of understanding of the meaning of the emperor-as-organ theory of the state in prewar Japan. First, there was what he defined as the "emperor-as-organ theory proper," which was the core of the emperor-as-organ theory within a strictly limited sense.[64] This essential core meaning was derived from the concept that the Japanese state was a legal or "juristic" person (*hōjin*) and that the corollary from this definition of the state as a legal person was that the emperor was an "organ (*kikan*)"[65] of the state. This was the most basic meaning of the emperor-as-organ theory. Minobe was persuaded that the emperor-as-organ theory proper was the most modern, "scientifically" valid doctrine explaining the nature of the state, which certainly illustrates the prestige accorded by Minobe and like-minded Japanese intellectuals to German constitutional-law thinkers and their thought.

Second, there was what Miyazawa referred to as the "interpretive meaning (*kaishaku no imi*)" or the "broader sense of the [emperor-as-] organ theory (*kōgi no kikan setsu*)."[66] According to this wide interpretation, the emperor-as-organ theory was an interpretation of the Constitution of the Empire of Japan based on constitutionalism and liberalism.

More specifically, it was a constitutional interpretation of the Meiji Constitution that placed great importance on the authority of the popularly elected Diet (*kōsen gikai*) in opposition to the "divine-right type of absolutism (*shinken teki zettaishugi*)" expounded by Hozumi Yatsuka and like-minded Shintō ultranationalists.[67]

Third, there was what Miyazawa labeled the "popular [emperor-as-] organ theory of the state (*zokuryū kikan setsu*)."[68] This was not a legal theory of state law. Rather, it was a view widely held by the public that the emperor-as-organ theory meant that the emperor was used and controlled by his close advisers and was unable to act and make decisions on his own free will. According to this notion, the emperor had become a "robot" and was "emperor in name only (*tennō no kyoki*)."[69] This popular view of the emperor-as-organ theory is also referred to as the "emperor-as-puppet" organ theory.[70] According to this understanding, the emperor's will was determined by the will of others.

These are distinctions with great differences. Expanding on these three understandings of the emperor-as-organ theory in Japan, Miyazawa emphasized that for Minobe the core meaning of the emperor-as-organ theory was a purely science-based constitutional or legal state theory that enabled the recognition of the legal existence of the state and the emperor. It merely explained a legal phenomenon and was not an interpretation of the law. Miyazawa stressed that this scientific theory must be clearly distinguished from the interpretive theory. Elaborating on this point, he asserted that the scientific core of the emperor-as-organ theory had nothing to do with such issues as the sacredness of the emperor or the kokutai, just as the fact that the scientific theory of evolution (*shinkaron*) and the "Copernican theory that the earth and other planets revolve around the sun (*chidōsetsu*)" had nothing to do with morality and religion. Miyazawa claimed that Minobe never believed even in his wildest dreams that expounding this core emperor-as-organ theory of the state, which was arrived at as a conclusion through the latest German scientific research, had in any way violated the moral norms of the kokutai that loyal Japanese subjects should obey. For Minobe, the core emperor-as-organ theory changed nothing with regard to the Japanese subject's ultimate loyalty and devotion to the emperor. Neither did it alter the fundamental nature of the Japanese state. He asserted that the emperor was an organ of the state before as well as after the promulgation of the Constitution of the Empire of Japan.

Elaborating still further on these distinctions with regard to the political characteristics of foreign states, Miyazawa explained that regardless of whether a state was an absolute monarchy, a constitutional monarchy, or a state with a president (as in a republic), as long as the state was conceptualized as a legal person, it necessarily followed that the ruler was an organ of the state. He lambasted Japanese criminal-investigation authorities for having made the erroneous judgment that expounding the core emperor-as-organ theory was a criminal act in violation of the state's Publication Law, a judgment that was as faulty as making the evocation of the Copernican theory or the theory of evolution an illegal act.

In defense of Minobe's case, Miyazawa claimed that, during the ongoing investigations and trial over the emperor-as-organ theory, Minobe had argued mainly in support of recognizing the core emperor-as-organ theory as an accurate scientific theory, while attacks from his adversaries were leveled not against the core emperor-as-organ theory per se but primarily against the interpretive meaning and popular understanding of the emperor-as-organ theory. In other words, they were talking at cross purposes, misunderstanding each other's purposes as well as colliding in a medley of contradictions. Miyazawa believed that the attacks on Minobe had been made from a confused position, driven largely by a "moral resentment and a righteousness indignation (*hifun kōgai chō*)" reminiscent of the patriotic *shishi* during the Meiji Restoration movement at the end of the Tokugawa regime.[71] Miyazawa also accused Minobe's critics of trying to manipulate science to achieve political and religious objectives.

Miyazawa insisted that the broader meaning of the emperor-as-organ theory was not a scientific theory. It was an interpretive theory that heavily supported liberal leanings sanctioned by, or permissible according to, the Meiji Constitution. In more concrete terms, this meant applying a very narrow interpretation of the absolutist powers (*kennō*) of the emperor while giving the broadest possible interpretation to the powers of the ministers of state (*kokumu daijin*),[72] who served the emperor by giving him advice on matters pertaining to the affairs of state. Miyazawa berated those individuals in the camps of "militarism" and "fascism" for having taken full advantage of the controversy over the emperor-as-organ theory to launch an all-out attack on constitutionalism and liberal politics.[73] In an apparent analogy to feared heavy hitters in baseball, such as Babe Ruth and his teammate Lou Gehrig in the late 1920s and early 1930s, Miyazawa identified Minoda Muneki, who will be discussed in more detail in part 2 of this study, as the king of the sluggers on the team of "militarism" and "fascism" attacking Minobe throughout the course of the emperor-as-organ theory affair.[74]

Miyazawa accused Minoda of attacking Minobe and the emperor-as-organ theory primarily on the basis of the interpretive emperor-as-organ theory and from an intolerable standpoint of a "fanatical absolutism (*kyōshinteki zettaishugi*)."[75] Miyazawa further added that when Baron Kikuchi Takeo took the floor in the House of Peers to denounce Minobe's theory in 1934–35, he also did so from the basis of the broader emperor-as-organ theory. In the emperor-as-organ theory affair, Miyazawa contended, the core of the emperor-as-organ theory proper was wrongly attacked as an interpretive theory.

In spite of Miyazawa's effort to draw a clear distinction between the emperor-as-organ theory proper and the interpretive emperor-as-organ theory, he did clearly acknowledge that there was a historical linkage. He noted that the theory emerged in Germany as a purely scientific discovery, but in reality it was employed primarily as a "function to oppose the theory of popular sovereignty and parliamentarianism in order to defend the [ruling] status of the monarch, which was under siege by the onslaught of [government by] a national assembly elected by the people."[76] This meant that the state-as-a-legal-person theory was not originally devised to support democratic government.

Miyazawa's analysis of the emperor-as-organ theory affair becomes much more complicated with the inclusion of the *zokuryū*, or popular emperor-as-organ theory. To reiterate, this was the popular notion that the emperor was emperor in name only and that his behavior was wrongfully determined by the will of others. Miyazawa noted that the words "organ" and "legal person" with regard to the emperor-as-organ theory proper and the interpretive emperor-as-organ theory discussed earlier had become widely known and used in discourse by legal scholars by the end of the Meiji period, but that was certainly not the case outside academia. Among those outside the profession, the emperor-as-organ theory was mentioned only with reference to this popular meaning of the emperor-as-organ theory. Still more, during Meiji times references to the emperor-as-organ theory did not necessarily conjure up feelings of displeasure or moral indignation even among the authoritarian Meiji political leaders. For instance, Miyazawa pointed out that senior Meiji statesmen such as Itō Hirobumi tacitly supported the theory: "The senior Meiji statesmen, though they would not admit it verbally, were emperor-as-organ theory advocates."[77] Further, in the Shōwa period, he noted, even the emperor was not immune from getting drawn into the controversy over the emperor-as-organ theory. Miyazawa wrote that the emperor had a favorable opinion regarding the emperor-as-organ theory, but, displeased when the military failed to carry out his wishes, he grilled his chief aide-de-camp, charging, "Isn't it because they deal with me [on the basis of] the [emperor-as-]organ theory that they carry out their actions on their own against my wishes?"[78] The key point in citing these cases here is that it was this popular notion of the meaning of the emperor-as-organ theory was at the center of political contestation.

Conflicting Japanese "Imagined Political Communities"

From a long-term perspective, the debate over state and sovereignty from 1890 to 1937 might be seen as a gigantic brawl in Japanese politics and society that took place shortly after the formal establishment of the modern Japanese state with the promulgation of the Constitution of the Empire of Japan. The fact that the fight was waged with intensity and violence for several decades was a clear indication that a genuine national consensus in Japanese society had not been achieved with regard to the fundamental structures of the state and the ideological underpinnings on which they rested. It was a bitter fight that was to determine the future course of the new Japanese state and Japanese nationalism.

A powerful argument can be made that, ultimately, this clash stemmed from the antagonisms between conceptions of Japanese civilization based on Shintō religious doctrine and modern Western civilization. As discussed, Minobe Tatsukichi's theory of state that asserted that the state was a sovereign legal person and that the emperor was an organ of the state was pirated from European thought, while Hozumi Yatsuka's patriarchal, theocratic family-state drew heavily on the native Shintō religious tradition in conjunction with the idea of the nation.

A global perspective on this Japanese debate over state and sovereignty can be gleaned from Benedict Anderson's excellent analysis of the origins of the nation-state in Western civilization and the spread of the idea of nationalism to other civilizations. In what is probably one of the most widely read books on nationalism, *Imagined Communities: Reflections on the Origins and Spread of Nationalism*, Anderson defined the nation as an "imagined political community."[79] He further argued that this political community was imagined in the following ways: first, as "*limited* because even the largest of [nations], encompassing perhaps a billion living human beings, has finite, if elastic boundaries";[80] second, as "*sovereign* because the concept was born in an age in which Enlightenment and Revolution were destroying the legitimacy of the divinely-ordained, hierarchical dynastic realm";[81] and third, as a *"community,* because, regardless of the actual inequality and exploitation that may prevail in each, the nation is always conceived as a deep, horizontal comradeship."[82] Anderson was careful to point out that the idea of the nation was a new way of organization in human history, quoting Ernest Gellner that "nationalism is not the awakening of nations to self-consciousness: it invents them where they do not exist."[83]

Anderson's imagined nation was, of course, in stark contrast to the imagined community from which the idea of the nation-state originally emerged in the American and Western European experiences. "Nation-states, republican institutions, common citizenship, popular sovereignty, national flags and anthems, etc.," had liquidated "their conceptual opposites: dynastic empires, monarchical institutions, absolutisms, subjecthoods, inherited nobilities, serfdoms, ghettoes, and so forth."[84] For most people now living in the Western world, where ruling monarchs have long since vanished and where religion, for the most part, has been relegated to the periphery of daily life, he wrote, "It is perhaps difficult to put oneself empathetically into a world in which the dynastic realm appeared for most men as the only imaginable 'political' system."[85] Anderson devoted significant sections of his work to firmly implanting in our minds that the historical process in the Western world of going from large sacred communities ruled by dynasties based on the notion of divine right, on the one hand, to individual, secular nation-states governed on the theoretical basis that governmental authority derives ultimately from the people, on the other hand, took a very long time, indeed—not years or even decades, but centuries. He presented a brief outline of the interacting processes that had led to the breakdown of the traditional sacred Western world order and to the establishment of the nation-state in the Western world. For instance, Anderson noted that it was during the seventeenth century that the "automatic legitimacy of the sacred monarchy began its slow decline."[86] Other phases of this process of decline of the sacred community started much earlier, even as early as the thirteenth century. He noted that, "for all the grandeur and power of the great religiously imagined communities, their *unselfconscious* coherence waned steadily after the late Middle Ages."[87] He emphasized two reasons for this: the effects of the exploration of the non-European world, which, as he put it, "abruptly widened the cultural and geographical horizon and hence also man's conception of possible forms of human life,"[88] and the "gradual demotion of the sacred language,"[89] which, of course, was Latin. A revolution in the written language had occurred in the sixteenth century.

From this origin of the nation-state in Western Europe and the Americas, the concept of nationalism gradually spread to Central Europe and Eastern Europe and the non-Western world, where it would function to undermine the existing sacred communities, as it had done in the Western world, "creating increasing cultural, and therefore political, difficulties for many dynasties."[90] He had set forth the proposition that before modern times, all the "great sacred cultures" of the world such as Christendom, the Muslim world, and the Chinese Middle Kingdom for the most part had shared certain characteristics and institutions: "All the great classical communities conceived of themselves as cosmically central, through the medium of a sacred language linked to a superterrestrial order of power."[91] Politically, these traditional civilizations were dynastic realms, where rulers derived their legitimacy from divine sanction.

Anderson claimed that, "by the second decade of the nineteenth century, if not earlier, a 'model' of 'the' independent national state was available for pirating."[92] Western colonialism enabled the transmission of the idea of the nation-state and nationalism to the non-Western world. However, wherever the concept of nationalism was consciously adopted by non-Western elites or leaders to create a nation-state, reform a state, gain independence, or preserve the independence of threatened states— that is, when the nationalism model already made available from the Western experience was deliberately pirated—Anderson referred to it as "official nationalism."[93] A key point that Anderson made with regard to "official nationalism" was that it was the "willed merger of nation and dynastic empire."[94] That is, it was the "conscious welding of two opposing political orders, one ancient, one quite new."[95] What this meant was that the elites were attempting to combine inherently contradictory worldviews and systems of government, which resulted in various problems, depending on the state and the particular internal and external conditions it faced. He presented examples and analysis of the consequences of "official nationalism" for several states, including the Austro-Hungarian Empire, czarist Russia, British "India," feudal Japan, the Kingdom of Thailand, and the territory of Indochina.

In the case of Japan, Anderson stated, "One of the basic means adopted for consolidating the oligarchy's domestic position was . . . a variant of mid-century 'official nationalism,' rather consciously modeled on Hohenzollern Prussia-Germany."[96] Based on the Prussian-German model of nationalism, the changes enacted by the former samurai elite enabled Japan to successfully modernize. "That the gamble paid off, in spite of the terrible sufferings imposed on the peasantry by the ruthless fiscal exactions required to pay for a munitions-based programme of industrialization, was certainly due in part to the single-minded determination of the oligarchs themselves."[97] The samurai elite had been successful in creating a strong, powerful nation-state based not on the original "popular model," but on the "official model" of nationalism. He stressed this point by stating: "Spectacular successes by Japan's conscript army against China in 1894–5, and by her navy against Czardom in 1905, plus the annexation of Taiwan (1895) and Korea (1910), all consciously propagandized through schools and print, were extremely valuable in creating the general impression that the conservative oligarchy was an authentic representative of the nation of which Japanese were coming to imagine themselves members."[98] Anderson added that there were two reasons that Japanese nationalism took on an imperialist policy: the legacy of Japan's long period of isolationism and the power of "official nationalism" on the one hand and the fact that the new Japanese oligarchy's prime models were the "self-naturalizing dynasties of Europe on the other hand."[99]

What I find particularly fascinating and useful about *Imagined Communities* is Anderson's concept of "official nationalism" versus "popular nationalism" and his corollary thesis that official nationalism was the conscious welding of two opposing political orders. If one follows his logic, Anderson brilliantly set up a conceptual framework that can explain the outbreak of the contestation over state and sovereignty in the late Meiji period after the formal establishment of the modern Japanese state with the promulgation of the Constitution of the Empire of Japan. As this study has argued, Itō and his colleagues set up a political structure that combined two inherently contradictory theories of state: a state that was theoretically ruled over and governed by an absolute monarch on the basis of divine descent in combination with elective representative bodies of government, which were, of course, institutional expressions of secular popular sovereignty. This combination of conflicting state elements had produced almost constant gridlock in government but did not have a calcifying effect on the political system. Quite the opposite: it generated new political dynamics. The Meiji reforms had unleashed tremendous latent energies in the population that could not be easily contained. In response, constitutional interpreters such as Hozumi and Minobe stretched the meaning of the Constitution of the Empire of

Japan to its outer limits to try to accommodate yet contain and channel political dissent into manageable patterns.

Thus, while Anderson offered extraordinary insightful analysis, his lack of detailed knowledge of Japanese history led him to portray the Meiji state as an unqualified success. While Japan was indeed exceedingly successful in defeating two of the world's largest empires—the Qing Dynasty in the Qing Dynasty–Japan War of 1894–95 and Imperial Russia in the Japan–Russia War of 1904–1905—from an internal perspective this was an erroneous perception of reality. For the Japanese state, as we shall see in parts 2 and 3 of this study, it was to be the beginning of political and ideological trajectories that would lead to the splintering of state power among many contentious groups, waves of terrorism, and uncontrolled expansionism abroad.

It is no exaggeration to say that the Japanese state was beginning to unravel. Itō's ill-conceived imagined community could not possibly have been sustained in the long run. In response to this constitutional crisis, Hozumi Yatsuka's imagined community was designed to revert back to the absolute monarchy of a traditional Japanese sacred order. Minobe's proposed imagined community was a half-baked theory of state that the Germans came up with when faced with what I believe was a similar dilemma. In other words, the oligarchs did not create the "general impression that the conservative oligarchs were an authentic representation of the nation of which the Japanese were coming to imagine themselves members." Itō's "official nationalism" was already coming apart at the seams, and Japan was heading down the road to national disaster.

Religious Nationalism Confronts the Secular State

The root nature of the debate over state and sovereignty was much more than just a debate about whether the emperor was the state or just one of several organs constituting the Japanese state. On the most fundamental level, it was arguably a clash between ethnic-religious nationalism and Western-style secular nationalism. Miyazawa's analysis of the emperor-as-organ theory affair corroborates the fundamental underlying argument of this study that this affair was ultimately a contestation between those who adhered to extreme forms of religious nationalism and others who were, more or less, in favor of constructing a strong, viable, democratically organized secular state, regardless of the fact that the emperor-as-organ theory was not based on democratic ideals. In other words, the Japanese people were ideologically divided between two fundamentally opposing systems of state and society, as also outlined in *Imagined Communities*. In this regard, Miyazawa's point that the assault on Minobe by Hozumi, Uesugi, Minoda, and Kikuchi and others in the "militarist" and "fascist" camps was not an attack on the emperor-as-organ theory per se is particularly insightful: Shintō ultranationalists were not particularly interested in debunking the emperor-as-organ theory of the state from a purely academic standpoint or by employing a supposedly value-free scientific method of analysis.[100] Kikuchi Takeo's denunciation of Minobe's theory in the House of Peers in 1935 is a powerful case in point. Defending himself against Kikuchi's accusations, Minobe noted that Kikuchi vigorously criticized the fact that his textbook *Essentials of the Constitution*, which had been used widely in the Law School at Tokyo Imperial University, "emphasizes the influence of actual circumstances and vigorously expounds logic and the law of reason."[101] This is a remarkable statement by Kikuchi. What is so disturbing about it is not so much that it was one manifestation of his attack on Minobe's emperor-as-organ theory, but, more important, that it was an assault on rational discourse itself. Minobe was being attacked by people who had no use for reasoning things out in a rational discussion. As Miyazawa indicated, expounding logic and adhering to the law of reason had become unacceptable (and dangerous) in Japan of the 1930s.

This event is so disturbing for another reason: this denunciation of the use of reason and rational debate took place in the chamber of the Japanese parliament. Although it was in the House of Peers and not in the House of Representatives, it was still the parliament, the supreme institutional manifestation of democratic government. What had become of democratic institutions in Japan by the 1930s? One thing is quite certain: despite Japan's thin veneer of democratic institutions, many individuals wished to destroy the last vestiges of democracy. Miyazawa's analysis of the Minobe affair fell short, however. Where did this religious fanaticism come from? This critically important issue was never discussed by Miyazawa as thoroughly as it should have been. It was stated, but without elaboration.

Minobe's life was threatened more than once. Those who tried to kill him cannot by any stretch of the imagination be considered "conservative." They were terrorists, and their actions were supported by such "intellectuals" as Minoda Muneki, a radical Shintō ultranationalist scholar and self-proclaimed successor to Uesugi Shinkichi. He is said to have shouted with joy at Keiō University after learning of the assassination attempt on Prime Minister Hamaguchi Osachi by Tomeo Sagoya in 1929. Such men had little in common with conservatives of the Meiji period such as Yamagata Aritomo.

Many ironies surround the Meiji debate over state and sovereignty. As Miyazawa pointed out, the emperor-as-organ theory as a theory of state that supported full parliamentary government in Japan suffered from its historical association with the governmental institutions and state ideals of imperial Germany. The state-sovereignty theory itself, of course, emerged in Germany *in opposition* to the theory of popular sovereignty. As a result, it retained a highly authoritative character. The coming of the constitutional era in Germany might have brought about the theoretical substitution of the state for the monarch as the subject of sovereignty, but that amounted to little more than a type of reformist monarchism, not popular sovereignty. Minobe was well aware of this historical tradition of the state-sovereignty theory and the type of state it was designed to support, but he still stubbornly argued for it even after he had witnessed the actual transformation of the political process in Japan to a more modern, English type of constitutional monarchy with the rise of party cabinets in the 1920s. Moreover, he was certainly aware of the fact that the emperor-as-organ theory of the state had passed into history in Germany, too, with the establishment of a government that was appointed by a National Assembly, popularly elected in 1919, after the demise of the Hohenzollerns. Political realities in Weimar Germany and Japan's evolution toward democratic government were running ahead of Minobe's outdated state-sovereignty theory, but this de facto transformation to an awkward, hybrid semi-democratic, semi-authoritarian regime did not encourage him to make any fundamental change in his theory of sovereignty. This does not mean, of course, that a mere recognition of the democratic ideal that sovereignty resides in the people would have been sufficient to ensure the triumph of parliamentary democracy that did emerge from party cabinets, but it did clearly demonstrate that Minobe lacked commitment to the most fundamental theoretical idea of liberal democracy: that political power emanates from the people. Also, one must remember that German state-sovereignty theorists in the nineteenth century never recognized the "basic proposition that 'all human beings are born free and equal in dignity and rights.'"[102] In the German state-sovereignty theory, the rights of individuals were "understood as particular 'concessions' made to the individual by a state constrained by law,"[103] not natural rights or God-given inalienable rights attached to the individual.

The supreme irony is that Minobe sought to support Western liberal-democratic institutions that had evolved in Japan through intense internal political struggles with a philosophy and theory of state designed in Germany specifically to prevent the spread of popular sovereignty. The consequences of his theory of state were clear: It satisfied neither the Shintō ultranationalists such as Hozumi nor the true democrats, if, indeed, there were any. While the true Shintō ultranationalist believers in the divinity of the emperor were followers of the emperor-as-sovereign theorists, the de facto or institutional democrats had no prominent theoreticians to plant the seeds of democratic ideals in the minds and hearts of the people.

Yet the ultimate effectiveness of Minobe's emperor-as-organ theory of the state as a viable ideological force in opposition to the Shintō ultranationalists is another question. In the final analysis, the nineteenth-century German state-sovereignty theory should not be equated with the great ideologies of liberal democracy, socialism, and fascism of the twentieth century. It was the product of the sophisticated authoritarian elite and may have influenced some of the minds of the politically important groups educated in the faculty of law and political science at Tokyo Imperial University, but it could not attract broad support from the masses. Like other modern ideologies, the emperor-as-organ theory of the state was created by intellectuals, but to triumph it had to have the support of the bourgeoisie—that is, the manufacturers, the merchants, and a broad sector of the expanding middle class. Further, the masses could never have come to identify themselves in any real personal or emotional sense with such a formalistic and arid theory. When the chips were down and the real test came to decide who would rule Japan, Minobe's emperor-as-organ theory of the state attracted little emotional commitment and produced no martyrs. People did not take to the streets and expose themselves to danger to defend the ideals of the emperor-as-organ theory of the state. The theory offered no real basis for rallying the public against the military and civilian radical Shintō militants to keep the popularly elected civilian officials in control of state policy in the 1930s.

In conclusion, the fundamental problem with the Constitution of the Empire of Japan was that it established in legal terms a system in which state power was shared between a divine emperor and secular human beings. The outcome of this national debate would decide if Japan would be driven by secular nationalism or religious nationalism. From Minobe's position, tremendous power was assigned to a divine emperor through the first seventeen articles of the constitution. His task was to remove the divine emperor from the actual workings of government, thus separating the religious element of the constitution from the state. In a nutshell, the formula he worked out for this was as follows. First, the meaning of Article 1 of the constitution, which was the Shintō doctrine, had to be adjusted to convey merely the idea of the monarchy "as the perpetual form of government in Japan."[104] He brushed off the idea that the words "The Empire of Japan shall be reigned over and governed by a line of Emperors unbroken for ages eternal" had anything to do with the Shintō religion. Second, he interpreted Article 3, which says, "The Emperor is sacred and inviolable," in conjunction with Article 55, which states, "The respective Ministers of State shall give their advice to the Emperor, and be responsible for it. All laws, Imperial Ordinances and Imperial Rescripts of whatever kind, that relate to the affairs of State, require the countersignature of a Minister of State," to mean that the "principle of inviolability applied only to the person of the emperor and not to imperial commands relative to matters of state, all of which were subject to criticism as to the legality or prudence of the advice of the countersigning ministers."[105] Miller stated, "This interpretation of imperial inviolability was but the first proposition in a formula by which Minobe sought to demonstrate the constitutional necessity and propriety of the political accountability of ministers of state to the diet."[106] That is, the prerogatives given to the emperor in the first seventeen articles of the Constitution of the Empire of Japan would then have to be turned over to the ministers of state, who would be accountable to the parliament. Minobe's ultimate constitutional project was to remove the sacred emperor from both the legislative and executive powers of the Japanese state.

Quite expectedly, Minobe's interpretation of the Constitution of the Empire of the Japan, which, if widely adopted, would have lead to the secularization of the Japanese state, was bitterly attacked by conservative Shintō ultranationalists and radical Shintō ultranationalists in the mid-1930s during the so-called Minobe affair. "On April 6, 1935, Superintendent of Military Education General Mazaki [Jinzaburō], a member of Hiranuma [Kiichirō]'s *Kokuhonsha* and a dispenser of secret army funds to right-wing newspapers, had issued an instruction to the army on 'clarifying the *kokutai*.' In it Mazaki reminded one and all that Japan was a holy land ruled over by sacred emperors who were living deities."[107] Mazaki and other the radical Shintō ultranationalists vehemently denounced Minobe, who had argued that "imperial rescripts issued in matters of state were not 'sacred and inviolable' but could be criticized by the Diet and the nation."[108] That is, they rejected Minobe's secularization of politics. Likewise, when Uesugi Shinkichi, Hozumi's protégé, explained that Article 3 of the constitution meant that

[our] emperor is the direct descendent of the Gods and rules the state as a living God. He originally dwelt with the gods and was inherently different from his subjects. . . . That being so, it is obvious indeed that Article 3 of our constitution has a nature completely different from the same article in the constitutions of other countries.[109]

Uesugi was not just giving a legal interpretation and making a political statement. He was challenging the supremacy of Western culture and secular politics. It was proof of the resurgence of völkisch and religious nationalism over Western secular liberalism. To underscore the unique nature of the Japanese religious state, he stressed that Article 3 of the Constitution of the Empire of Japan ("The Emperor is sacred and inviolable") meant something quite different from such statements in Western constitutions, such as those in Germany and Italy. For example, Article 43 of the Constitution of the Kingdom of Prussia of 1850 stated, "The person of the king shall be inviolable," and Article 44 said, "The king's ministers shall be responsible. All official acts of the king shall require for their validity the counter-signature of a minister, who shall thereby assume responsibility for them."[110] Article 4 of the Constitution of Italy of 1848, which stated, "The person of the King is sacred and inviolable,"[111] is like Article 3 of the Constitution of the Empire of Japan. The one difference is that the Italian constitution and the German constitution specify that it is "the person" of the emperor that is sacred, which is somewhat different from saying that "the emperor" is sacred. In the Japanese case, the Shintō ultranationalists would argue that divinity was not specifically limited to the emperor's body but extended to his actions.

In the long run, however, neither Hozumi Yatsuka's Shintō family-state ideology nor Minobe Tatsukichi's emperor-as-organ theory of the state would survive the ideological battles of the Taishō and Shōwa periods. The reason for this is that neither ideology was mass-based and thus designed to capture the hearts and minds of the masses. The political realities of radical religious mass politics would make Hozumi's conservative Shintō family-state ideology irrelevant and ensure the destruction of Minobe's emperor-as-organ theory of the state. We will return to this debate in later chapters, but let us turn our attention now to another theory of state in the late Meiji period that competed with both conservative religious Shintō ultranationalism and the supporters of a secular nationalist state such as Minobe, a conflict that would enter a more intense and violent phase in the Taishō and Shōwa periods and finally lead to a global disaster—the greatest war in the history of the human race.

4

Kita Ikki: A Social-Democratic Critique

of Absolute Monarchy

> What I fear is that the higher religions may be replaced by lower
> religions. I mean religions that agree with the higher religions in telling
> us to overcome self-centeredness, but do not agree with them in telling
> us to love all our fellow men and to love the presence behind the
> universe. The lower religions tell us to love nothing beyond our own
> tribe's power, and to my mind this is an evil form of religion.
> —A. J. TOYNBEE, *Life and Death*, 16–17

Another powerful critique of Hozumi Yatsuka's theory of absolute monarchy in the first decade of the twentieth century was produced by a
young writer named Kita Terujirō, who is better known as Kita Ikki.[1] Kita
detested State Shintō ideology with an intensity and a passion found in
few Japanese thinkers in modern history. Accordingly, he wrote one of
the most massive and systematic critiques of the ideology of State Shintō
in modern times. The aim of this section is to present the essence of
Kita's argument against Hozumi Yatsuka's ideology of the Shintō völkisch
family-state in the late Meiji period.

In his 1906 work *Kokutairon oyobi Junsei Shakaishugi* (On the Kokutai
and Pure Socialism), Kita Ikki launched a devastating attack on Hozumi
Yatsuka's theory of the Japanese state and the ideology of the conservative ruling elite. It was published during the administration of Saionji
Kimmochi, one of the most liberal prime ministers of the modern Japanese state up to that period. Nonetheless, retribution from on high came
quickly. Within a matter of days, the Home Ministry banned Kita's book
from sale or further distribution. His writings also caused consternation
in the academic community. One scholar from Niigata, Kita's native

prefecture, noted with alarm: "Kita Terujirō is the [most] dangerous thinker since the founding of Japan [the Japanese state]."[2] But just what was it about Kita Ikki's thought that so frightened even men with real state power?

Kita began *On the Kokutai and Pure Socialism* on a note of concern about the fate of socialist thought in Japan. He charged that Japanese socialist thinkers had been too willing to abandon the fundamental principles of socialism out of fear of contradicting the state "orthodox theory" of the kokutai.[3] Japanese socialists, however, were not alone in their reluctance to confront the official ideology of the state. Japanese intellectuals had a long history of not doing so. In fact, he noted that whenever foreign systems of thought or foreign religions entered Japan, they inevitably became subject to what might be referred to as a process of intellectual distortion. In the past, Buddhism had been introduced from the Asian continent and Christianity from Europe. However, their universal doctrines were scrutinized with great care by Japanese thinkers at the time to determine just how they violated the fundamental tenets of the kokutai. By the time they had gone through a process of indigenization, anti-kokutai ideas had been eradicated from their doctrines. Kita referred to this as the Japanese equivalent of the Inquisition established by the Roman papacy for the examination and punishment of heretical ideas in Medieval Europe. Consequently, Buddhism and Christianity had been reduced to comparative insignificance in Japanese history in terms of changing the fundamental thought patterns of the Japanese. In short, Kita asserted that throughout Japanese history, foreign ideologies found to be in conflict with the kokutai were either completely strangled or stripped of their original essence.

Concerned that socialism, too, was in danger of being absorbed into State Shintō ideology and sapped of its vigor, Kita charged that many of those who advocated national socialism had made the fatal mistake of trying to graft socialism onto the state orthodox kokutai ideology rather than directly confronting it.[4] He was strongly critical of such people, accusing them of acting as "assassins of socialism (*shakaishugi no ansatsusha*)."[5] What advocates of socialism in Japan lacked, he asserted, was a historical consciousness independent of Japanese state ideology. That is, they had to free themselves from the shackles of the ruling kokutai ideology. They had to reassert the principles of "pure socialism (*junsei shakaishugi*),"[6] critique the orthodox kokutai ideology on the basis of unadulterated socialist principles, and rearticulate the notion of kokutai in conformity with socialist doctrine rather than redefining socialism to fit the official state ideology. Failure to do so was a recipe for disaster. In other words, Kita was concerned that in the same way that the official kokutai ideology had digested Buddhism and Christianity, as well as Confucianism and other rival systems of thought in earlier periods of Japanese history, the Meiji period would also absorb useful elements of socialist thought while eliminating its fundamental tenets.

Kita attributed the rise of socialism in Europe to the political and social unrest brought on by the Industrial Revolution. Consequently, the main function of socialism in Europe was to create the institutions needed to abolish economic and social inequality among people that had developed out of the great bourgeois revolution. However, socialism in Japan was to have a role different from that in Europe. Kita claimed that conditions in the Japanese state showed that industrial capitalism was well developed and that Japan had already progressed into a mature industrial society. He believed that the Meiji Revolution of 1868 had, in fact, established the institutional framework for winning full political and social democracy.

However, he expressed profound disappointment in the fact that the Japanese people had been unable to reap the full benefits of political and social equality opened for them by the Meiji Revolution because of their ignorance regarding the true essence of the modern Japanese state and the principles of state law as set down in the Constitution of the Empire of Japan. Accordingly, for him, the role of socialist thought in Japan was to give the Japanese people a new socialist consciousness. This socialist consciousness had to be spread to the masses so they would have the intellectual tools to begin to liberate themselves from the stranglehold of the ruling kokutai ideology, which Kita said was constructed on the basis of "Shintō superstition," a "slave morality," and a "false interpretation of history."[7] Interestingly, Kita maintained that the responsibility for this state of affairs was not the fault of the emperor himself. Rather, he accused the collective Meiji leadership of treachery in sabotaging the cause of the revolution. To obscure the real nature of the state, Kita argued, the oligarchs, in their construction of the modern Japanese state, had transformed the emperor into an object of blind devotion and worship, a "clay figure," as he put it.[8] Thus, Kita was convinced that only through a solid understanding of socialist evolutionary theory could the Japanese people hope to comprehend the real historical significance of the Meiji Restoration, the essence of modern statehood, and the principles of the Constitution of the Empire of Japan.

Kita asserted that, for the Japanese people even to begin to realize the ideals of the Meiji Revolution, they had to understand the fact that a real revolution had indeed taken place. He accused the state propaganda machine of working frantically to deny this fundamental fact. Kita referred to the official interpretation of the Meiji Restoration as "restorationist revolutionism (*fukkōteki kakumeishugi*)."[9] It was this notion of "restorationist revolutionism" that had permeated the minds of the Japanese people to such an extent that they could not reason correctly to comprehend the true nature of this epoch-making event in Japanese history. He called for the destruction of "restorationist revolutionism" thought for the sake of understanding the real Japanese kokutai and Japanese history. With this introduction, he proceeded to reinterpret the significance of the Meiji Ishin, the nature of the modern Japanese state, and Japanese history.

Kita argued that the modern Japanese state was fundamentally a social democracy (*shakai minshushugi*).[10] He reasoned that regardless of the particular type of political system of the modern state, be it a monarchy or a republic, sovereignty necessarily resided in the state, which he defined as a society with legally recognized geographic boundaries. For him, the very notion of the modern state included the idea that the state was composed of citizens, people who were actively involved in the political affairs of the state. Accordingly, he conflated the concepts of state and society and argued that the state was socialist because sovereignty resided in the state. The state (*kokka*) equaled society (*shakai*), which in turn was identical to the nation (*kokumin*). At the same time, the state was a democracy because the new institutions and structures of state had placed the administration of government in the hands of the representatives of the people. Still more, for Kita, socialism was not only a system of thought with a theory of politics, economics, society, and history. It also contained a theory of jurisprudence as well as a theory of the state. Socialism, legally, was "statism (*kokkashugi*)."[11] In this way, he identified socialism with nationalism as he had equated state with society.

Kita reasoned that sovereignty could lie neither in the monarch, as the official orthodox state theorists maintained, nor in the people, as Western scholars who supported liberal democracy had articulated. Both positions were based on a theory of jurisprudence in the age of individualism of an earlier period of history in man's evolution. The placement of sovereignty in either the monarch or the people was based on the premise of individualism, an ideology that regards individual rights as taking precedence over the collective entity of the state. Classical liberals such as John Locke and Jean-Jacques Rousseau had articulated political society in terms of contracts. But in Kita's conceptualization of the modern state, the rights and obligations that the people had within the state, including the rights and duties of the emperor, were not derived from contracts among individuals. Rather, they were inherent in the nature of the state itself. Viewed from a metaphysical position, Kita's description of the state closely matched those of nineteenth-century German organic state theorists. He said that the existence of the state was a "biological fact" and that the state was a product of "biological evolution." Ultimately, then, the state was a large organic body consisting not of independent human beings but of "elements (*bunshi*)" separated spatially in an organic totality who cannot survive apart from the body.[12] The state, in other words, was a gigantic organism that existed and evolved according to its own biological purposes.

Moving back from the metaphysical notion of the state to a more concrete examination of the development and the inner workings of the state through Japanese history, Kita argued that the state had gone through several evolutionary stages in its history. For instance, like many constitutional-law scholars of his day, he made the distinction between kokutai as "form of state" and seitai as "form of government." He challenged Hozumi Yatsuka and other State Shintōists by insisting that the Japanese state had undergone a historical change in the kokutai with the Meiji Revolution of 1868. In its premodern period, Japan had a patriarchal kokutai (*kachō kokutai*).[13] Furthermore, he argued, the seitai, or "form of government," had changed twice. Originally, Japan had had a monarchical form of government under the emperor, as his ideological nemesis Hozumi Yatsuka had claimed. But, Kita argued, as time passed, political power shifted to other political groups, and an aristocratic form of government evolved out of the monarchical form of government. In the process of this change in the seitai, the emperor then became what Kita called the "Roman Pope of Shintō (*shintō no rōmahō*)," and the Shōgun became the "Holy Roman Emperor of Kamakura (*kamakura no shinsei kōtei*)."[14] Despite this change in the form of government, however, there was no change in the kokutai. The *kokutai* remained patriarchal throughout the premodern period of Japanese history.

The Meiji Revolution of 1868 was a momentous event in Japanese history. In Kita's evolutionary theory of the Japanese state, it constituted a revolution and therefore represented a fundamental change in the kokutai as well as in the seitai. It gave birth to the "nation-state (*kōmin kokka*)."[15] The kokutai had changed from a patriarchal kokutai to a nation-state kokutai (*kōmin kokka no kokutai*), and the aristocratic seitai became the "democratic seitai (*minshuteki seitai*)."[16] Kita was convinced that the Meiji Revolution was successful in overthrowing the Tokugawa feudal system due to the collaboration of the emperor and the people to overthrow the military aristocracy. By the "people," Kita meant those who had participated in the countless peasant uprisings at the end of the Tokugawa period, as well as members of the lower-ranking military aristocracy. The fact that the emperor was involved on the side of the revolutionaries to overthrow the military class may have made it appear as if the new state were a monarchical state. But this was not the case. Kita maintained that the emperor and the people had acted together as constituent elements of the state on the basis of absolute equality to overthrow the old regime and establish a social democracy.[17]

To distinguish his conceptualization of the Meiji Restoration as a social-democratic revolution from the official interpretation of the event—which, as noted earlier, Kita referred to as the "restorationist revolutionism"—he called it the "*Ishin Kakumei*."[18] For Kita, the Ishin Kakumei, or "reform revolution," signified a truly revolutionary event. It left little room for the idea maintained by Hozumi and other Shintō ultranationalist legal scholars that absolute power had been restored to the emperor. To reiterate, in Kita's evolutionary scheme of Japanese history, the year 1868 marked the beginning of a completely new era: the birth of a social democracy.

The Politics of Family Lineages and Filial Piety

Throughout *On the Kokutai and Pure Socialism*, Kita hammered away from almost every conceivable angle at Hozumi's orthodox theory of the kokutai and his constitutional interpretation derived from his Shintō fundamentalist beliefs. Deconstructing Hozumi's ideology of State Shintō, Kita claimed that the essence of his state kokutai ideology was constructed on two core principles: *keitōshugi* and *chūkōshugi*.[19] Keitōshugi is the "doctrine of [the worship of] family lineage." The notion of common ancestry here was also linked to a theory of origins, a theory of ethnic genesis. In Hozumi's Shintō theology, the birth of the Japanese state originated with the deities Izanami and Izanagi and in the person of Amaterasu Ōmikami, the deity from which the unbroken line of divine emperors originated. Accordingly, the Japanese völkisch, or ethnic, group came from one divine progenitor, and accepting this as historical fact was to accept the principle of keitōshugi. Chūkōshugi is the "doctrine of loyalty and filial piety." What this meant was that the Japanese state was a patriarchal state—literally, a gigantic family. Accordingly, the internal construction of the state was inherently hierarchical. In this patriarchal family state, the emperor ruled over his subjects as a father would rule a family. The Shintō doctrine of chūkōshugi also meant that there could be no contradiction between the doctrine of loyalty to the emperor and the doctrine of filial piety to one's father. In fact, loyalty to the emperor itself constituted a fulfillment of filial piety. In short, it was through keitōshugi and chūkōshugi that Hozumi had linked the god-emperor to the Japanese subjects. Both doctrines, then, constituted the core of State Shintō. According to Hozumi, ethnic national unity could be achieved through the theocratic conception of the Japanese state. Religion was the glue that held together the nation. In this context, Kita quoted Hozumi as stating:

> Our ethnic nation sprang from one progenitor. Some say that to worship the Imperial Family as the [nation's] founding family is wrong, but their argument is insufficient to refute my theory. The source of solidarity among Christians lies in their belief in God. The argument whether or not God exists cannot break their solidarity. Faith is first; knowledge is second. People are moved by faith, not by reason. This also applies to the nation. National unity is achieved through religion.[20]

Such statements by Hozumi were proof enough for Kita that "Hozumi Yatsuka's constitutional theory rested totally on his [Shintō] faith."[21] Kita, however, questioned the constitutionality of an officially sponsored state religion. He asserted that interpreting the Constitution of the Empire of Japan on the basis of religion was itself a "violation of the constitution."[22] In this contention, he referred to Article 27, which states that "Japanese subjects shall, within the limits not prejudicial to peace and order, and not antagonistic to their duties as subjects, enjoy freedom of religious belief,"[23] interpreting it as a guarantee of freedom of religion to all Japanese. This served as proof that the empire of Japan was not founded on the basis of any particular religious belief. From Kita's viewpoint, jurisprudence had to be anchored in positive law, not in religious faith.

Striking still another blow at the very heart of the State Shintōists' version of the kokutai, Kita reinterpreted the origins of Japanese history and the Japanese state on the basis of his biological theory of historical evolution. His aim was to refute the belief that the morality of keitōshugi and chūkōshugi was present at the origin of the Japanese state. Reasoning from his evolutionary approach to the origins of human society, he claimed that social stratification did not exist in primitive society. Primitive society was not a hierarchically structured society of vertical relationships. On the contrary, it rested on horizontal social relationships. Primitive society was essentially "republican" and "egalitarian." This was the universal human experience of primitive society. He referred to the morality of man in its original state as a "primitive type of republican equality."[24] Primitive human organization enjoyed a "republican kokutai [based on] primitive egalitarianism."[25] He claimed that in a primitive society, wherever it appeared, political and social control were informal and unstructured; members of the group reacted spontaneously.

From this line of reasoning, Kita concluded that the origins of political society were not patriarchal, an assertion that constituted a devastating critique of the Shintō theological explanation of the cosmological origins of the Japanese state. From his standpoint, a monarch could not have been the head of the state in primitive Japanese society, and he reasoned that consciousness of a structured political order did not, in fact, exist. Therefore, human society in its original state was fundamentally egalitarian. Kita referred to Hozumi a number of times as a superstitious person who believed in myths, a person who had made the *Kojiki* and the *Nihon Shoki* his "bibles."[26]

While Kita argued that the doctrines of keitōshugi and chūkōshugi could not have served as the basis of morality of primitive Japanese society, as Hozumi Yatsuka, Inoue Tetsujiro, and other spokesmen for "national morality" had claimed, he did acknowledge that keitōshugi and chūkōshugi became the morality of society under the post-primitive stage of man's social and biological evolutionary development, which in Japan, he argued, was from the ancient period up through the Middle Ages. In other words, it was in the second stage of human social development that hierarchical relationships emerged in man's social organization. Hierarchical political and social order evolved from primitive human groups. Accordingly, this morality of keitōshugi and chūkōshugi emerged with the patriarchal system. Morality in the evolution of human groups was said to have emerged with the consciousness of being under a patriarch.

The key point of Kita's discussion of primitive society is that is was an ideological weapon to attack the Shintō ultranationalist religious theory of the patriarchal origins of state and society. In comparative context, Kita seems to have attacked Hozumi's ideological justification for absolute monarchy in much the same way that modern European secular thinkers from the seventeenth century to the nineteenth century did to destroy the argument for the religious basis of absolute monarchy in Europe. Interestingly, Kita equated Hozumi's Shintō-based emperor-as-sovereign theory of the state with the state theory of the late-nineteenth-century German state theorist Max von Seydel,[27] who also argued that sovereignty resided in the emperor rather than in the state, as most post-Hegelian German state theorists had argued.

Kita argued that contrary to official kokutai ideology, it was precisely because of the strength of keitōshugi and chūkōshugi that the emperor system had been weak throughout Japan's history. Interpreting Japanese history from his universal evolutionary perspective, Kita claimed that in the patriarchal stage of man's evolution, keitōshugi and chūkōshugi served as the moral basis for all men in the patriarchal stages of development. This morality fostered a "social consciousness" that was tied to blood-related kin relationships.[28] This social consciousness had originated in the immediate family between the mother and the child, then gradually extended to other members of the primary family group, and finally moved outward to more distant relatives. It was from this very basic level in man's primary social group that the patriarchal system emerged. In the early stages of the patriarchal system, people worshipped the common ancestor whose soul was believed to be immortal and who communicated to the group through the living patriarch. In other words, the Japanese practiced a form of totemism.

However, he argued, as the kinship group expanded, kinship ties loosened. Branch families developed and, gradually, members of the branch families came to recognize not the head of the main family branch of the clan—that is, the emperor—but the head of the branch family. Ancestor worship itself became the bond of cohesion among family members of each branch family. Kita noted that the introduction of Buddhism and Confucianism greatly facilitated this shift of social consciousness from the emperor to the patriarch of one's own branch. But this was not all. There was still another important outcome of this historical process of kinship development: as this process of branching developed, the strength of keitōshugi and chūkōshugi worked to create a sense of equality among branch families of the emperor. This sense of equality vis-à-vis the emperor generated fierce competition among the patriarchs for positions of power around the emperor. The clash between the Taira and the Minamoto clans in the twelfth century, for example, was but one manifestation of this. The leaders of the two great clans believed that they had an equal right to share in political power since they were of the same origin as the emperor.

In short, Kita sought to prove that it was precisely because of keitō-shugi and chūkōshugi that people developed strong ties of loyalty to their own lineage group rather than to the imperial line. He noted that the intensity of this loyalty to clan-group superiors culminated in the bushi class with the practice of *junshi*,[29] a willingness of a vassal to follow his lord in death. Accordingly, for the vassal bushi, there could have been no consciousness of any loyalty to the emperor. As far as Kita was concerned, this bushi loyalty was the product of a type of "slave morality" that developed to an extreme in Japan,[30] but it nevertheless illustrated the point for the purpose of his argument that the values of keitōshugi and chūkōshugi served to undermine, rather than support, the existence and the strength of the imperial line. To suggest otherwise, he said, was a false reading of history.

Kita's Critique of the State Theories of Hozumi Yatsuka and Minobe Tatsukichi

Kita also denounced Hozumi for mixing fundamentally contradictory notions in his theory of the nature of the Japanese state for his own ideological purposes. For instance, he noted that Hozumi, in defining the state, took the position that "the emperor is the state."[31] By this definition, the emperor constituted the state, or the emperor was identical to the state. This was the position taken by the Shintō ultranationalists, which the leading, German-influenced emperor-as-organ theorists attacked. Kita mentioned that the state-sovereignty theorists, in attacking the Shintōists, raised the argument that if the emperor constituted the state in its literal sense, as Hozumi and other Shintō fundamentalists had claimed, then one must come to the logical conclusion that the "state should perish along with the death of the emperor."[32] But Hozumi had an answer to this seemingly illogical position of the State Shintōists. He retorted by saying that "the emperor is not one who dies; as an extension in the unbroken line of emperors for ages eternal, he is the life of Amaterasu Ōmikami."[33] Hozumi did indeed—as Kita pointed out—take the position that the present emperor was really the earthly manifestation of the deity Amaterasu Ōmikami.[34] Kita felt that it was difficult, using logic and reason from a secular point of view, to convince Hozumi and other Shintō fundamentalists of the fallacy of their ideology and state doctrine.

Kita charged that Hozumi also found it convenient to employ the modern organic definition of the state whenever he had found it useful to bolster the deficiencies of his premodern-patriarchal-state theory. Hozumi had also defined the state as follows: "The state is a specific ethnic corporation (*minzoku dantai*) on a fixed territory and governed by means of an independent sovereign."[35] This definition of the state implied, of course, that the state consisted of more than just the person of the emperor. How could one possibly hold two contradictory positions and believe in them both at the same time? Such inconsistencies in the thought of Hozumi and other orthodox theorists of the Japanese state were enough to convince Kita of the inherent fallacies of State Shintō fundamentalist doctrines.

But it was more than just the mere contradictions of Hozumi's state theory that mattered here. The organic theory of the state placed sovereignty in the state. It is a state theory in which the people are considered citizens of the nation-state. Accordingly, in the organic idea of the state, the "emperor is situated within the state."[36] The organic definition of the state was one in which the sovereign–subject relationship was superseded by the political thinking of a state–citizen relationship. This change was not merely one of words or polemical argument, because it had been accompanied by changed ideas of sovereignty and political obligation. The relationship between the emperor and the subject in the patriarchal conception of the state was one of command and obedience, while that between state and citizen was one of mutual obligation. The sovereign, too, in the modern state was included as part of the interdependent relationships of all parts of the whole state, and the emperor also had to operate according to the laws of the state. Constitutional rights were shared by the emperor and the people, who were represented by the parliament.

It might be noted here that in *On the Kokutai and Pure Socialism*, Kita did not spare from criticism the leading ideological rival to Hozumi Yatsuka and other orthodox state theorists: Minobe Tatsukichi. According to Minobe, sovereignty lay in the state, and the emperor was the highest organ of the state. But the Constitution of the Empire of Japan and the Meiji Ishin had different meanings for Kita and Minobe. For Kita, the Constitution of the Empire of Japan was an embodiment of the aspirations of the people for social democracy. He argued that Minobe had distorted this meaning and that this distortion was reflected in Minobe's assertion that the emperor was the highest organ in the state. Kita said that Minobe's interpretation of the emperor's role in the state was irreconcilable with the structures and institutional relationships established by the Constitution of the Empire of Japan. He insisted that the emperor and the parliament together constitute the highest organ of the state. To support his assertion of the dual role of the emperor and the parliament, he cited Article 5, which states, "The emperor exercises legislative power with the consent of the Imperial Diet," and Article 73, which states, "When it has become necessary in the future to amend the provisions of the present Constitution, a project to that effect shall be submitted to the Imperial Diet by Imperial Order."

The Emperor as Enemy of the Völkisch Family-State

Kita developed his notion of the social-democratic state based on a conceptualization of organic unity, but it was an organic unity not premised on ethnic or racial identity. He sought to brand Hozumi's ethnic conceptualization of the Japanese state as dangerous and an outright fabrication of Japanese history. Racialism or ethnicity had absolutely no part in his theory of the modern Japanese state. On the contrary, Kita tried to discredit the common assumption that the Japanese state had always been an ethnic nation and argued that people who were not ethnically Japanese should be allowed to become full members of the Japanese state. That is to say, ethnicity or racialism was not to be an essential element of national identity. To take this position, of course, was to attack the core doctrine of Shintō ultranationalism.

Kita argued that State Shintōism offered no grounds for national cohesion for the expanding modern Japanese state. The Shintō state theory of the kokutai, which made the Japanese state into a patriarchy whereby the people were literally regarded as children of the emperor, and the emperor the parent of the people, posed a dilemma for a multiethnic and multiracial state. He noted that under the present law, foreigners who acquired Japanese citizenship were under the same obligations as ethnic Japanese subjects. But under Hozumi's ethnic family theory of the state, "naturalized citizens (kikajin)" who were not ethnically Japanese could never hope to be full-fledged members of the state.[37] Furthermore, he argued that to equate ethnicity or race with nation was contrary to the wishes of the emperor himself. To support this claim, he referred to the fact that it was in the name of the emperor that treaties were signed with the Qing Dynasty following the Qing Dynasty–Japan War of 1894–95, incorporating ethnic Chinese into the Japanese empire and granting them citizenship. More recently, following the Russo-Japanese War of 1904–1905, the Japanese state had incorporated ethnic Russians into the Japanese empire and also granted some of them Japanese citizenship.

Thus, for Kita, ethnicity or racial considerations had to be excluded from the concept of the modern Japanese nation. Since the Japanese state was expanding through conquest and incorporating peoples of other ethnic groups and races, the only way non-Japanese could be absorbed into the body politic was to separate ethnicity or race from the concept of the nation. For instance, he said that while it would be virtually impossible for anyone to consider a red-bearded, blue-eyed European who had been given Japanese citizenship (*kokuseki*) a child of the emperor, there should be no problem in treating him as a citizen of the Japanese state.[38] Likewise, black people or people of African descent also should be allowed to become Japanese citizens, although it would be inconceivable that Japanese would be willing to regard the emperor as the parent or ancestor of a black slave (*kurombo*).[39] Kita claimed that under Hozumi's idea of the pure ethnic state, the state would be left with two options regarding non-Japanese people: either it would be obliged to exempt them from their obligations as citizens or it would have to expel them from the empire.

To further discredit Hozumi's conception of the nation as a super-ethnic family-state, Kita accused the Shintō state ideologues of covering up the fact that, historically, Japan had never been an ethnically homogeneous state. For instance, he noted that during the regency of Empress Jingū (AD 201–269), the empress had dispatched troops to the Korean Peninsula, where the three Han states of Korea (Mahan, Byeonhan, Jinhan) were located, and then incorporated ethnic Koreans into the Japanese state.[40] In ancient times, Emperor Ōjin also had introduced Chinese culture into Japan and naturalized large numbers of Chinese.[41] So according to Kita's logic, Empress Jingū and Emperor Ōjin, as well as the present Meiji Emperor, must be considered as themselves embracing the opposite of Hozumi's ethnic state ideology. For Hozumi, the ultimate disaster for the ethnic national state would be the incorporation of people of different ethnic and racial groups. This would result in the jumbling together of a heterogeneous mass of humanity in which all beliefs and customs of the ethnic group would be lost.

Kita continued his attack on the ethnic conception of the state by further noting that Ainu and other groups of ethnically non-Japanese people had been living in the Japanese state for centuries. He wondered how any rational person could really believe in the Shintō ultranationalist doctrine that, on the one hand, maintained that the Japanese people were a divine ethnic group because they descended from the deities Izanami and Izanagi via Amaterasu Ōmikami while, on the other hand, foreigners or ethnically non-Japanese were considered less than human —"monkeys."[42]

This Shintō "orthodox" kokutai ideology of the state was indoctrinated into the Japanese masses through a national educational system. At the center of this system was the Imperial Rescript on Education, a document that was distributed to every school in Japan and hung alongside a portrait of the emperor. Moral education in the schools was based on this document, which "remained until it was finally withdrawn from the curriculum by government order in October 1946."[43] One of the central figures in interpreting the Imperial Rescript on Education and promoting moral education in the Meiji period was Inoue Tetsujirō.[44] Kita made a scathing condemnation of the Rescript and Inoue, its principal spokesman. He based his argument against the Rescript fundamentally on two grounds. First, he claimed that the emperor did not have the legal authority to legislate morality under the Constitution of the Empire of Japan, stating: "The Japanese emperor is not the Roman Pope. The Emperor is not the state organ that establishes scientific principles."[45] Although Kita acknowledged that the emperor made law with the consent of the Imperial Diet, and that he did indeed have the authority to issue Imperial Ordinances under the constitution, he was not the state organ that authorized national doctrines. Second, Kita objected to the actual contents of the Imperial Rescript on Education. He specifically cited the section that stated, "Our subjects ever united in loyalty and filial piety," and denounced the phrase "and thus guard and maintain the prosperity of Our Imperial Throne coeval with heaven and earth." Still more, he found repugnant the notion that the way set forth was indeed the teaching "bequeathed by Our Imperial Ancestors," claiming that the authors of those words were yearning for the "despotism of Louis XIV."[46] In short, he maintained that it was not to the emperor or to the Imperial Household that Japanese owed their loyalty but to the Japanese nation as a whole.

Kita felt isolated for his unorthodox ideas and equated his situation with that of Galileo Galilei, the Italian astronomer who was ordered to appear before the Inquisition for disputing the Ptolemaic theory that the earth was at the center of the universe and that all the heavenly bodies revolved around the earth.[47] For Kita, the historical importance of Galileo lay in the fact that he became an inspiration to others who opposed authority in order to seek the freedom to oppose accepted doctrine. He also noted that the church unwisely took a position on a scientific theory that later proved to be totally wrong, and exercised its power to suppress the search for truth by prosecuting those who sought the truth. He claimed that for the State Shintōists to force the nation to accept as truth the false doctrine of the rule of the "line of emperors unbroken for ages eternal" and to brand as heretical any opposing theories was tantamount to the Roman pope's support of the Ptolemaic system and the persecution by the Inquisition of people like Galileo who challenged it.

Kita ended *On the Kokutai and Pure Socialism* with the following remarks:

The philosophy of history which examines the evolution of the Japanese people embraces a character different from a history of the Imperial Household written for itself. The Imperial Household is not the backbone of Japanese history. All peoples have branched off and evolved from a single common human origin and share a common historical evolution.

To regard contemporary Japan as a patriarchal state releases non-Shintōists and peoples of other races and ethnic groups from their obligations as citizens. . . .

To acknowledge that the Japanese nation owes its loyalty to the imperial lineage of the unbroken line of emperors for ages eternal is the Ptolemaic theory of the Roman Pope. It is an admission that the Japanese nation has persecuted the Imperial Household during the class states of the ancient period and the Middle Ages on the basis [of the doctrines] of keitōshugi and chūkōshugi.

As for the "line of Emperors unbroken for ages eternal," the Imperial Household rested at the top of a historical pyramid of treachery and rebellion that eventually drove them to total despair because the Japanese people were faithful so long to the aristocratic [military] class and severely persecuted it.

Japanese history leaves out a one-thousand-year-long primitive age, which existed fourteen or fifteen hundred years ago, prior to the appearances of the *Kojiki* (The Records of Ancient Matters) and the *Nihonki* (The Chronicle of Japan), when historical life started with recorded history. The ancient period should be characterized as the monarchical state because one patriarchal monarch was the ruler of all Japan from a legal standpoint. The Middle Ages should be characterized as the period of the aristocratic state because many patriarchal monarchies were rulers in their own territories. Moreover, during this lengthy period, we find a distinct kokutai (form of state) called a "patriarchal state" because the people lacked a consciousness of the purpose of national survival and evolution.

In our own era, we have a nation-state kokutai in which sovereignty resides in the state. We have a democratic seitai (form of government) in which all parts of the state are organs that act for the purpose of the survival and evolution of the state as a whole. Accordingly, both the advocates of the monarchical sovereignty theory and the state sovereignty theory are blindly conjecturing in vain. From a strictly legal point of view, since the [Meiji] Ishin, Japan has been a social democracy.

Still more, the literal meaning of the word tennō has evolved historically. The tennō, a title ridiculously given in later ages to the position in the primitive age, struggled with heads of other small kinship groups as the head of a small region and a small number of people, who based on their belief in a primitive religion. Until the Fujiwara period, "emperor" essentially referred to the strongest authority who possessed the land and the people of Japan in its entirety. In the period of the aristocratic state after the establishment of the Kamakura regime, the emperor, as the "Roman Pope of Shintō," struggled constantly with the "Holy Roman Emperor of Kamakura" as well as with the patriarchal monarchs in his own region, just as all other patriarchal monarchs did. After the Ishin Kakumei, the emperor became the highest organ, representing national sovereignty in a democratic nation acting under the ultimate purpose of the state. Finally, the meaning of tennō has evolved greatly in the last twenty-three years, and now the emperor is significant as an element that with the Imperial Diet constitutes the highest organ of the state.

In short, the emperor of the so-called kokutairon is a clay figure of a village community and regards the present emperor as its enemy.[48]

Kita referred to the socialism that incorporated the idea of the patriarchal conception of the state from the ancient period and the Middle Ages as "henkyokuteki shakaishugi," or, literally, "one-sided socialism."[49] It was a socialism tainted with State Shintō ideology. It was, of course, in contrast to this type of socialism that Kita proposed his own concept of "pure socialism," which in his revolutionary scheme of historical evolution was social democracy. According to his own state theory, Japan was a social democracy. However, Kita's theory of socialism was not the socialism of Karl Marx, which he specifically stated in the preface of *On the Kokutai and Pure Socialism*. He also stated that his idea of democracy was not the idea of democracy of Jean-Jacques Rousseau. He did not believe in the contract theory of the origins of government. His theory of evolutionary socialism was his own. In the final analysis, his ideas, as he expressed them in *On the Kokutai and Pure Socialism*, represented one of the most massive and thoroughgoing attacks on the ideology of State Shintō in modern Japanese history.

II

EMPEROR IDEOLOGY
AND THE DEBATE OVER STATE
AND SOVEREIGNTY IN THE
TAISHŌ PERIOD

5

The Rise of Mass Nationalism

There is one fact which, whether for good or ill, is of utmost importance in the public life of Europe at the present moment. This fact is the accession of the masses to complete social power. As the masses, by definition, neither should nor can direct their own personal existence, and still less rule society in general, this fact means that actually Europe is suffering from the greatest crisis that can afflict peoples, nations, and civilizations. Such a crisis has occurred more than once in history. Its characteristics and its consequences are well known. So also is its name. It is called the rebellion of the masses.
—JOSE ORTEGA Y GASSET, *The Revolt of the Masses*, 11

My life's desire will be fulfilled if a state is established on the principle that the Emperor and his subjects are one. . . . The Imperial Way should be spread throughout the world, the Asiatic nations being first consolidated into a unit and thereafter the rest of the world.
—RADICAL SHINTŌ ULTRANATIONALIST, as quoted in Hugh Byas, *Government by Assassination*, 46–47

The Masses and a New Political Consciousness

To restate the general argument of the chapters in part 1, the fundamental internal political problem facing the Japanese state in the Meiji period stemmed from the fact that the original architects of the modern Japanese nation had constructed a political system based on two inherently contradictory ideologies: sacred monarchical absolutism and secular representative democracy. Flawed in theory, the Constitution of the Empire of Japan proved unworkable in practice. As the founding-father oligarchs passed from the political scene, a second generation of oligarchs proved incapable of keeping together the particular brand of "official nationalism," to use Benedict Anderson's term again, that their predecessors had tried to impose on the nation. As a result, by the end of the Meiji period the Japanese state was rapidly losing its integrative power and starting to weaken internally. Something had to be done to strengthen the state. Hozumi Yatsuka's patriarchal family-state theory in support of absolute monarchy and Minobe Tatsukichi's emperor-as-organ theory of the state to justify parliamentary government were the two main solutions offered to solve the problem of governing the nation and strengthening state power. And, of course, socialism was beginning to make an impact, so one can also include as a third alternative Kita Ikki's particular brand of socialism.

Other problems were soon to emerge that would exacerbate the problem of governability. The end of the Meiji era and the beginning of the Taishō period signaled more than just the passing of one emperor and the beginning of the reign of another in July 1912. The changeover to a new imperial era coincided with new challenges to the Meiji state and conjured up in the minds of other farsighted intellectuals that a crisis was looming and that new conceptions of state and society and new visions for the future were needed as the Meiji debate over state and sovereignty continued to rage. It is important to note that Hozumi Yatsuka also died in 1912, only two months after Emperor Meiji. Uesugi Shinkichi, Hozumi's able protégé, who by that time had already become Minobe's chief ideological opponent to the emperor-as-organ theory of the state, would fundamentally change the nature of this debate. For Minobe, however, it seemed as if the new political developments were heading in the direction that he had predicted: the rise in power of the political parties and a party system of constitutional government. Nagao Ryūichi noted that after the death of Hozumi, Minobe, who taught constitutional law at Tokyo Imperial University from 1919 to 1934, came to be regarded as the highest authority in constitutional law and "became a symbolic figure of Japanese constitutionalism and rational science of constitutional law. His textbooks and commentaries were the most authoritative for scholars as well as for law students."[1] Nevertheless, in spite of Minobe's increasing popularity as the chief ideologue in support of parliamentary rule, the Meiji political system was beginning to unravel, and this unraveling would soon accelerate and spread from the intellectual and political elites to the rising middle class and finally to the masses.

The Japanese philosopher and activist Kuno Osamu provided a somewhat different perspective on the problem of the Meiji political system that is instructive to address before analyzing the political and ideological contestation in the Taishō period. In the essay "The Meiji State, *Minponshugi*, and Ultranationalism,"[2] Kuno also acknowledged that the Meiji political system was a mixture of the sacred emperor, who as "Tennō, . . . was not only the equivalent of emperor and Pope, but also wore the mantle of Jesus, the son of God in Japan's national religion,"[3] and secular government of popular participation by elective representatives of the people. In his opinion, it was a very intricately and delicately crafted system of government that Itō and his colleagues had created. Everything depended on precisely the right set of circumstances and conditions if the machinery of government was to function properly and operate smoothly. In theory, the many complexly arranged elements of the state, such as the *genrō*, the *jūshin*, the cabinet, the military, the Privy Council, and the national parliament were to interact harmoniously and mutually support one another in an elaborate framework to give assistance and advice o the emperor, although all persons who occupied these organs of the state knew that the emperor was merely a ceremonial ruler. This was called the "esoteric" or secret theory of the state. At the same time, the common people were taught that they "could not really be called . . . loyal Japanese citizen[s] unless [they] held the emperor's authority in utmost regard and [gave] it highest priority even in [their] inner conscious and subconscious impulses."[4] Kuno referred to this conception as the "exoteric" theory of state for the masses, who were thoroughly indoctrinated in the view that the emperor was an absolute monarch with unlimited authority and political-religious power. Kuno stressed that the "esoteric belief remained persuasive only in the upper echelons of the society and never captured the minds of the people."[5]

It is important to note that this explanation of the prewar Japanese state system continues to be accepted by many Japanese intellectuals and foreign scholars of Japan. For Kuno and others who adopted this theory, the crux of the problem came when the military, alone among the groups at the top of state power still clinging to the exoteric view of state, began to clash with the House of Representatives, which began to overstep its supposedly advisory rule to assist imperial rule and started to dominate the national government.

If one examines the logic of Kuno's esoteric-exoteric state ideology, however, one finds that it depended largely on deception and falsehood to function efficiently and effectively. The masses were inculcated into believing that their beloved and infallible god-emperor had "absolute authority and autonomy,"[6] but when they discovered that this was a big lie as the state started to unravel, their beliefs were shattered and they became angry for feeling duped. As the theory goes, their response was to demand direct imperial rule. At the top of the power structure, however, the political, bureaucratic, and intellectual elites, who knew that the emperor did not actually rule the state, made state policy and ruled in the name of the emperor. Theoretically, of course, they acted as advisory organs to the emperor. If this were indeed political reality, in a sense, the relationship between the emperor and the political and bureaucratic elites surrounding him was all a masquerade, a false outward show. And consistent with the theory, when the emperor was formally involved in decision making, it was a charade, a political game in which the words and phrases of the emperor were often represented in pantomime.

A clever component of Kuno's esoteric-exoteric emperor system theory included the recruitment process into government and positions of responsibility in the state. The masses were educated in the exoteric belief that the emperor ruled the state, a belief that was inculcated in them in the elementary and secondary schools and, of course, in the military. However, "Should one succeed in attaining a university education or passing a higher civil service examination, he would, for the first time, be allowed to share the tacit understanding" that the emperor's advisers were the true rulers of Japan.[7] In other words, those who had believed in the ruling divine emperor all their lives were suddenly let in on the big secret and from then on were supposed to be included in the real decision making and share in the management of the state, which, in essence, had developed into a very awkward kind of secular, hybrid bureaucratic-parliamentary government.

Although this esoteric-exoteric emperor system theory has served many Japanese intellectuals well for more than half a century, it has major flaws. First, to have expected Itō's elaborately devised political system in which all of the diverse political players—from the transcendental cabinet ministers and military leaders, who theoretically were under the command of the emperor, to popularly elected members of parliament and the political parties—to cooperate harmoniously to advise the emperor was an idea built on sheer political fantasy. Itō and his colleagues constructed a fundamentally flawed political and legal system of state. When they chose as their model the constitution of Germany of the Second Reich, it was like the blind following the blind. One need only recall Max Weber's warning to the German people in 1917, in the midst of the Great War (the First World War) about the legacy of the German constitutional setup with regard to the future of the German nation: "Our primary task at home consists in making it possible for the returning soldiers to rebuild that Germany which they have saved—with the ballot in their hands and through their elected representatives."[8] Weber admonished those who for decades had sought to discredit the German parliament without ever seriously trying to understand the preconditions for effective parliamentary rule, which for him was the only way for Germany to achieve peace and prosperity. He also blamed Germans for placing authoritarian government above the nation's political interests. "The present condition of our [pathetic] parliamentary life is the legacy of Prince Bismarck's long domination and of the nation's attitude toward him since the last decade of his chancellorship," Weber stated in the summer of 1917.[9] "He left behind him a nation *without any political sophistication*, [and] *a completely powerless parliament* was the purely negative result of his tremendous prestige."[10] Although no Japanese political figure had attained the stature of a Bismarck, there were striking parallels between the popular political attitudes of Germans and Japanese in that period.

Second, the emperor's actual historical role in national decision making is conveniently sidestepped. As Kuno's theory has it, in the minds of the ruling elites the emperor was a non-ruling constitutional monarch, as in the case of the English model of constitutional monarchy. But this was certainly not the case, as Herbert Bix has clearly demonstrated.[11] The Constitution of the Empire of Japan was a Prussian German style of constitutional monarchy, which was a dual structure of authority between the emperor and the parliament. As such, it necessitated the active participation of the emperor in an extremely cumbersome political decision-making process. To understand the fundamental difference between these two models of constitutional monarchy is critically important. Furthermore, the Japanese constitutional setup was even more bizarre than the German one because a supreme Shintō deity, shielded from any political accountability, was placed at the center of the Japanese nation's legal and political system.

Third, Kuno's theory conveniently diverts one from engaging in any serious discussion of the nation's elite intellectuals and their role as fostering and promoting radical ultranationalist ideologies. Kuno stated:

"In spite of all the pains taken by Itō, the military and the House of Representatives frequently stood out as disharmonious elements in the symphony of advice and assistance to the emperor. Among the groups at the top of the power structure, only the military continued to cling to the exoteric belief system concerning the emperor."[12] This is a disingenuous statement. It was not in the military academies but at Tokyo Imperial University and other leading state and private universities where the fundamental ideas of radical Shintō ultranationalism were generated in the first place and then subsequently, and relentlessly, promoted to mobilize the masses to eventually destroy Itō's Meiji "work of art." Maruyama Masao is equally responsible for perpetuating this fallacious notion that most of Japan's intelligentsia was not supportive of what he referred to as the fascist movement. For instance, in his essay "The Ideology and Dynamics of Japanese Fascism,"[13] he stated that it was primarily the "pseudo-intellectuals"[14] who provided the social foundation for fascism because the true Japanese intellectual was "essentially European in culture and, unlike its counterpart in Germany, could not find enough in traditional Japanese culture to appeal to its level of sophistication."[15] Finally, the esoteric-exoteric theory is a type of blame-the-gullible-masses theory. One would think that the Japanese people deserve more credit for their political savvy than that assigned to them by this simplistic theory of politics.

To return to the idea of a sense of crisis felt by many intellectuals at the beginning of the Taishō period and the need to construct new conceptions of state and society, however, the central problem the intellectuals wrestled with was how to devise a way to control and guide the behavior of the politicized masses that were becoming increasingly susceptible to an "unmediated individualism as a basic unit of social action," as H. D. Harootunian has put it.[16] That is to say, the intellectuals felt it was necessary to foster a new political consciousness for the masses, because they were well aware that the politics of the Meiji period and the ideological foundations on which they were based extended, for the most part, only to the lower echelons of the former samurai class. For many in power and for the socially conservative, the emergence of the "claims of mass culture—consumption and consumerism, and the feared 'secularization' and democratization of cultural life" must indeed have been a frightening development.[17]

Another, related concern of both those who supported a multiparty parliamentary system of government and the oligarchs and bureaucrats around them was a resurgence of a viable socialist movement. The nascent Meiji socialist movement, which originated around the turn of the century, was crippled by a Japanese government frightened by the conspiracy to assassinate Emperor Meiji. The potential for the rebirth of a much more powerful socialist movement, however, was certainly a real possibility, considering what had been occurring in the Taishō period. In the 1910s, for example, we find a dramatic increase in union membership and in the number of organized labor unions. The rice riots of 1918, which toppled the Terauchi government and brought to power Hara Takashi, certainly shook the oligarchs and drove home the recognition that dire political consequences would result if government were not more responsive to the needs of the masses. Still more unsettling to the liberals, the conservative oligarchs, and Shintō ultranationalists was the impact of the Russian Revolution, which no doubt gave a profound psychological boost to the socialists and anarchists in Japan.

In short, for many intellectuals the problems of the Taishō period demanded a new political consciousness and a rearticulation of existing ideologies to give meaning to the real concerns of a new era, for ideologies, too, no matter how abstract they may appear, are inseparable from practical social and political concerns. To make the kind of "adjustment of politics" required by the new age, to quote the words of one writer of the Taishō period, "we must open up a politics of democratism which is founded on the idea of the Emperor."[18] This idea of democracy founded on the idea of the emperor was exactly what was in the mind of a leading political theorist of the Taishō period: Yoshino Sakuzō.

Yoshino Sakuzō was highly conscious of the dawn of a new era. "It cannot be doubted," he wrote, "that from the late Meiji and early Taishō, a new trend has begun to emerge in conspicuous fashion."[19] He, in fact, identified the emergence of the Japanese masses on the political stage as far back as the Hibiya riots of 1905. Tetsuo Najita, writing on the political thought of Yoshino, stated,

> Yoshino observed unprecedented numbers of people taking to the streets in movements and demonstrations of protest such as in riots against the Portsmouth Treaty of 1905, the Movement for Constitutional Government in 1912–1913, the protest against naval corruption in 1914, and the rallies against high consumption taxes throughout these years. And he felt the momentous transformation of political consciousness among the people to be the central theme of these demonstrations. Thus, in his essays of 1914–1916, his first and in many respects most important, he heralded the demonstrations as marking the dawn of a new era.[20]

The intense ideological rivalry between Hozumi Yatsuka's conservative or counter-revolutionary Shintō ultranationalist ideology and Minobe Tatsukichi's emperor-as-organ theory of the state in support of party government continued unabated into the Taishō era. However, Uesugi Shinkichi had replaced Hozumi as the leading theorist of Shintō ultra-nationalist ideology, while Yoshino Sakuzō had entered the political arena alongside Minobe in support of parliamentary government. Faced with having to deal with the newly politicized masses, we find, inter-estingly enough, both Yoshino and Uesugi attracted to the same political concept of *minponshugi*, "the principle of the people as the end of gov-ernment."[21] Although the core of Yoshino's political theory rests on the concept of minponshugi, he was initially inspired by his ideological rival Uesugi to revive the concept and bring it to the center of political discourse in the early Taishō period. This has been noted by Irwin Scheiner:

> Interestingly and ironically, Yoshino had borrowed the word *minponshugi* from Uesugi Shinkichi . . . who argued that Japan had always been a country with a "monarchical sovereign [*kunshu*]" but had never been a "monarch-centered [*kunpon*] polity" like France of Louis XIV. Rather, it had been a "people-centered [*minpon*] polity" responsive to the needs and welfare of all the people, and the basic moral imperative of the imperial family had always been *minponshugi*.[22]

Scheiner goes on to say that "Uesugi was clearly stating that the Japanese monarchy was benevolent and that imperial sovereignty was compatible with popular welfare."[23] Although he did not identify the actual docu-ment in which Uesugi's concept of minponshugi appears, it can be assumed he was referring to Uesugi's essay *Minponshugi to Minshushugi* (1913),[24] which was actually a part of a series of essays on that subject published throughout that same year. In that particular essay, Uesugi noted that Inoue Tetsujirō used that term in his work *Tōa no Hikari* (Light of the East). The usage of the notion of minponshugi among extreme Shintō nationalists such as Uesugi was to underscore the fact that the emperor, divine being that he was, was responsive to the needs and the welfare of all of the Japanese people, even though his gov-ernmental prerogatives were theoretically unlimited. Uesugi, and Inoue earlier, derived this notion of minponshugi from the European tradition, referring at times to enlightened monarchs such as Frederick the Great of Prussia (1740–86) and Catherine the Great of Russia (1762–96). Affected by the impact of the philosophers of the Enlightenment, enlightened European monarchs, although they still held on to the theory of the divine justification of their rule as absolute monarchs, were nevertheless convinced that the purpose of their rule was to benefit the people.

No less immune than anyone else from the new political consciousness of the masses sweeping the country around the beginning of the Taishō era, Uesugi found this concept of minponshugi very useful. He was at this point already beginning to distance himself from the state theory of his mentor, Hozumi, who had passed away the previous year. Uesugi was aware that a new set of political dynamics determining the politics of the new era was rapidly making Hozumi's patriarchal theory of state largely irrelevant. In Uesugi's mind, there was no question that the authoritarian, "monarch-centered polity" of Hozumi, who had always liked to quote Louis XIV, had to be rearticulated. In terms of the evolution of Shintō ultranationalist ideology, Uesugi's use of the concept of minponshugi signaled the beginning stages of this rearticulation of Shintō ultranationalism, which ultimately would constitute a massive reorientation of that ideology. That task, however, would take Uesugi almost a decade to complete; it was not until 1921 that Uesugi would publish his *Kokka Shinron* (A New Thesis on the State). In the meantime, however, it was not Uesugi but his ideological rival Yoshino Sakuzō who would take up the idea of minponshugi and within a few years make it the central concept of his theory of state in support of parliamentary government.

Yoshino's liberal thinking can be traced to his early years. While still a teenager, he began to attend a Bible study class run by an American missionary named Anna Buzzell and converted to Christianity in 1898 at the age of twenty. In 1900, Yoshino entered the Law School of Tokyo Imperial University and shortly after became an active member of the Hongō Church, with Ebina Danjō as its pastor. Yoshino had frequent contact with Ebina, who had believed in "the development of democracy, the realization of true internationalism, the liberation of the individual and human dignity in society."[25]

In 1905, Yoshino had become the chief editor of *Shinjin* (The New Man), a magazine started by Ebina, and contributed articles to it. It was as a journalist that he came to believe passionately that the Japanese masses should be politically informed and enlightened. From 1906 to 1909, Yoshino was working in the Qing Imperial Court as a tutor to Yuan Keming, Yuan Shikai's eldest son, and became interested in Chinese politics and Japan's activities on the Asian continent, particularly in Korea, which he strongly criticized. Yoshino then went to study abroad in Europe from 1910 to 1913.

Yoshino returned to Japan to become a professor at Tokyo Imperial University. He wrote an article titled "On the Meaning of the Mass Demonstration," which appeared in the April 1914 issue of *Chūō Kōron* (Central Review), a monthly magazine aimed at the educated Japanese middle class. He wrote this article after having been influenced by the mass demonstrations that helped topple the Katsura cabinet in February 1913. The purpose of the article was to discuss the meaning of such demonstrations and, more important, the meaning of the involvement of the masses in the political affairs of the Japanese state.

He began his essay by saying that the first significant mass demonstrations occurred in 1905, the year of large demonstrations in Tokyo against the Treaty of Portsmouth, which ended the Russo-Japanese War. The Japanese public was angry over the treaty because they had expected much more from the settlement. Yoshino welcomed these demonstrations because he thought that they signified the importance of public opinion in the workings of Japanese politics. He criticized the oligarchy and asserted that the mass demonstrations emerged as a natural result of the closed nature of Japanese politics and that this should be interpreted as an indication of an increased political consciousness among the masses. He also argued that although democratic government is not without its faults, it was definitely preferable to oligarchic politics. Moreover, he maintained that the idea of democracy does not contradict the theory of the *kokutai*, Japan's unique structure of state:

> Although sovereignty resides in the emperor, it does not mean that he is the only person who engages in politics. He has to consult others. It is therefore not wrong to consult the opinions of the public instead of a small select group of people. If sovereignty should stay strictly only with the emperor, and no one else, the oligarchy also has to be looked at as being unconstitutional. Also, the party cabinet does not intervene with the emperor's right to appoint the ministers because, again, in the process of selection, the emperor has to consult others, and thus such consultation can be made with the political parties as well.[26]

Accordingly, he argued for the importance of popular suffrage. In rebuttal to those who claimed that it is dangerous to grant suffrage to the ignorant masses, he said that there is nobody who is truly knowledgeable enough about politics and competent to lead the country:

Even among existing politicians, there are many who do not understand the philosophy of politics. If one argues that only truly competent people should participate in politics, politics would become something only for philosophers. In a democracy, it is important that the general public has the ability to choose the representatives who are trustworthy as the leaders of a country. Such ability does not have anything to do with one's understanding of political philosophies, thus one cannot say that the Japanese people do not have the ability to participate in politics. Generally speaking, the general public is not restricted by obligations which result from a variety of business interests held by a small group of people. When it comes to state matters, therefore, it is better to consult public opinions which can be expressed from a totally neutral position.[27]

However, Yoshino asserted that the people must give meaning to their participation. They must have informed opinions, and they must have goals. A voluntary and active force, the people must not be led blindly by others for political gain. He further stated:

If the public movement becomes nothing but a mere riot without a purpose, it loses its meaning. Moreover, if the movement does not arise from within, it will be easily exploited by the people who seek to use it to their political advantage. Although the rise of the mass demonstration is a favorable advancement in Japanese politics, when one considers its passiveness, it cannot be said that it is showing a healthy development.[28]

Yoshino claimed that behind the rise of the mass demonstration was the failure of constitutional government. In the last section of his essay, he discussed the future of the people's movement. He suggested two directions for reform. One of them concerned constitutional government; the other concerned the enlightenment of the public. He first argued that, for the successful application of constitutional government, it is important to expand suffrage and redefine the existing constituencies. It is also necessary to establish party cabinets based on the two-party system. As far as the enlightenment of the public is concerned, he said that more attention must be paid to economic and social developments. He believed that the public should be made aware of the course of Japanese politics. For this purpose, it is important that each political party make its policies on various issues transparent to the public. In a concluding statement, he asserted that the most important thing of all for the development of democracy was the spiritual education of the public, because a moral spirit forms the basis of democracy.

Yoshino published another important article in the January 1916 issue of *Chūō Kōron* titled "On the Meaning of Constitutional Government and the Methods by Which It Can Be Perfected." It was in this article that he introduced his concept of minponshugi. In "On the Meaning of the Mass Demonstration," he never used the word "minponshugi." In this article, Yoshino not only distinguished minponshugi from *minshushugi*; he also demonstrated and explained how minponshugi could be applied successfully within the existing Japanese political structure.

Yoshino adamantly held to the position that sovereignty resided in the emperor not merely because he felt that it was the proper interpretation of the Constitution of the Empire of Japan, but also because he thought that the placement of sovereignty somewhere other than in the emperor, particularly in the people, would be a threat to the continued existence of the imperial institution: "Of course, I, too, am agreed that in order to protect the imperial institution we should reject the dangerous theory of popular sovereignty."[29] According to Bernard Silberman, Yoshino did not advocate popular sovereignty because "he rejected the idea of replacing the Meiji constitution with another that would specifically place sovereignty in the hands of the people. His reasoning seemed to be that the Japanese people had not fought to establish this principle and therefore could not claim sovereignty as a historical right."[30]

Silberman goes on to note that Yoshino further reasoned that "the validity of the English and French constitutions rested on the fact that the people had brought them into existence to insure their rights against any incursions from a powerful elite," but that in Japan "a constitution based on popular sovereignty was unacceptable because it did not fit the historical experience of Japan."[31] This seems to indicate an inherent conservatism underlying at least one aspect of Yoshino's thought. At any rate, one wonders why Yoshino did place such weight on this aspect of Japan's historical experience, for if one follows the same line of reasoning, it is not difficult to arrive at the conclusion that multiparty parliamentary government would also inevitably be unacceptable because it, too, would not fit the historical experience of Japan. As we have already seen, Kita Ikki argued that the "people" did overthrow the Tokugawa feudal regime. At any rate, Yoshino was equally committed to formulating a theory of state that would make the cabinet responsible to the parliament. This was precisely his dilemma: trying to reconcile in his state theory "two disparate intellectual legacies from the Meiji period."[32]

To reconcile these two fundamentally irreconcilable views of imperial sovereignty and popular sovereignty, Yoshino had to alter the commonly accepted definition of one of them. This is exactly what he did. Unwilling to deny imperial sovereignty, he instead redefined the concept of democracy, severing it from its theoretical tenet that "sovereignty resides in the people." He stated: "Democracy is not contingent upon where legal theory locates sovereignty. It merely implies that in the exercise of this sovereignty, the sovereign should always make it his policy to value the well-being and opinions of the people."[33] In other words, Yoshino had redefined the meaning of democracy so as not to equate it with the concept of popular sovereignty, the idea that ultimate power in the state resided in the people. It was in this context of his argument that he found very useful Uesugi's concept of minponshugi, the people-centered (*minpon*) polity (in contrast to the *kunpon*, or emperor-centered, polity) in which the monarch is responsive to the needs and the welfare of the people. Once this theoretical linkage between democracy and popular sovereignty was severed, Yoshino could theoretically make emperor sovereignty compatible with democracy. From this departure point, Yoshino was able, through a roundabout line of reasoning, to work out a justification for ultimate control of the government by the parliament. In short, the ideological justification of a multiparty parliamentary government with a cabinet fully responsible to popularly elected officials was the ultimate goal of Yoshino's state theory. This was, of course, the original aim of Minobe's emperor-as-organ theory formulated in the Meiji period.

In his preface to "On the Meaning of Constitutional Government and the Methods by Which It Can Be Established," Yoshino again discussed the importance of educating the general public for the successful development and achievement of constitutional government. Drawing on examples from the comparison between the United States and Mexico, he argued how differences in the level of people's knowledge and virtue could affect the successful development of constitutional government. His emphasis on this idea clearly demonstrated his belief that, if the level of knowledge and virtue of the public were low, minponshugi could not be fully developed.

What was the essence of such constitutional government? In addressing this issue, Yoshino stated that constitutional government is government based on a constitution. However, constitutional government must include two very important factors. First, the constitution has to be assigned greater weight than ordinary laws, for the constitution is the supreme law of the land. Second, a constitution has to include three main features: the guarantee of civil liberties, the principle of the separation of the three branches of government, and a popularly elected legislature. His definition of what is true constitutional government is significant because he was indirectly criticizing the existing political system created by the oligarchs. Yoshino criticized the oligarchy for being a plutocracy. He further pointed out that Japanese politics, which was exercised by a small group of people, had come to neglect public opinion. He therefore asserted the involvement of the masses under minponshugi, because the ultimate end of political power was to be the people's welfare. Political power, therefore, should not be used for the benefits and the interests of a small group of people. It is also important to note here that Yoshino was careful not to criticize the emperor. He did not believe that minponshugi created a contradiction between imperial sovereignty and the involvement of the people in politics because, according to the concept of minponshugi, the emperor's sovereign power, by definition, was always to be exercised with the welfare of the people in mind. In other words, the privileged classes between the people and the emperor were the source of the problem. It was for this reason that he approved of demonstrations as a physical expression of the contempt of the masses toward the oligarchic system of politics. The rise of the mass demonstration was therefore looked on as the means for advancing minponshugi, or democracy as he defined it, something that was completely compatible with the emperor's sovereignty. In theory, minponshugi advocated the direct involvement of the people in politics.

At the end of his essay, Yoshino made several suggestions to advance the involvement of the masses in politics. The most important was representative government, of which he singled out two essential features. One had to do with the relationship between the people and the legislators; the other had to do with the relationship between the parliament and the government. With regard to the first relationship, he argued for the extension of the franchise and the strict enforcement of electoral laws. As for the second relationship, between the parliament and the government, he argued that, for the healthy functioning of government, it was essential that the executive branch of government be under the control of the parliament—that is, cabinets responsible to the parliament.

Within the context of this debate over state and sovereignty, how do we assess the success of Yoshino's theory of imperial democracy as a viable ideology in contestation with Shintō ultranationalist ideology in support of monarchical absolutism and Minobe's emperor-as-organ theory of the state? One could well argue that Yoshino's attempt to reconcile two disparate ideas—imperial sovereignty and popular sovereignty—by severing the concept of popular sovereignty from the definition of democracy and redefining democracy to mean that the sovereign emperor governed for the good of the people was a manifestation of an idealism almost totally divorced from the weight of history of democratic ideals and democratic thought. His willingness to sacrifice the fundamental principle of democracy that sovereignty resided in the people for the sake of the fundamental principle of the kokutai (that sovereignty resided in the line of unbroken emperors descended from the deity Amaterasu Ōmikami) illustrates a lack of bold commitment to democratic ideals. In terms of this ideological contestation with Shintō ultranationalist ideology, he had already conceded victory to the opposition on this key principle. His ideological underpinning for party government, which was ultimately based on the principle that, "in the exercise of his sovereignty, the emperor should always make it his policy to value the well-being of the people" had something of an unreal quality about it. In short, Yoshino had conceded too many points to the Shintō ultranationalists for his minponshugi to have been a viable opposition force. In fact, this study suggests that Yoshino's minponshugi was a much weaker ideology in support of multiparty parliamentary government than Minobe's emperor-as-organ theory of state. It should be noted here, however, that Yoshino never sided with the Shintō ultranationalists, and he remained a Christian and an opponent of Shintō ultranationalism until his death in 1933.

Yoshino's minponshugi as a powerful ideological force was short-lived. Irwin Scheiner notes that, "by the end of 1918, neologisms like *minponshugi* were gradually abandoned in favor of a more straightforward term like *minshushugi* or simply *demokurashii*."[34] Furthermore, with the revival of the socialist movement in the late 1910s and the early 1920s, Yoshino's ideology of minponshugi came under severe attack from the more radical thinkers in the socialist movement. Scheiner stated that the socialist Yamakawa Hitoshi "dismissed Yoshino's distinction between *minshushugi* and *minponshugi* as a sophistry equivalent to saying that pork consisted of two unrelated concepts—meat and fat."[35] Still more, early supporters of minponshugi such as Oyama Ikuo soon abandoned their defense of it and moved on to more solid socialist thought.

Meanwhile, the secularization of Japanese politics gained momentum with the universal suffrage movement, which began to spread rapidly throughout Japan by the end of the second decade of the twentieth century, culminating with the passage of the Universal Manhood Suffrage Act of 1925 during the administration of Katō Takaaki. As Kuno Osamu also admitted, by that time Yoshino's minponshugi had become "an idea devoid of support."[36]

Kita Ikki: Anti-Shintō Fascist?

Although this study of Kita Ikki has focused on Kita's ideas in *On the Kokutai and Pure Socialism* in the late Meiji period, something must be said about his ideas in the Taishō period. In writings by American and Japanese scholars, Kita is almost always cited as one of the most influential radical ultranationalist thinkers in the prewar period. This view of Kita is based largely on his *Nihon Kaizō Hōan Taikō* (An Outline Plan for the Reorganization of Japan; 1919) and the common understanding that his ideas inspired those who carried out the February 26, 1936, Incident.[37] This leads us to an important question: Was Kita another Benito Mussolini—a man who started out as a socialist but ended up as a fascist?

There is no question that Kita expounded radical revolutionary ideas in *An Outline Plan for the Reorganization of Japan*. However, the ideas Kita set forth in this work had little to do with the radical Shintō ultranationalism that was at the core of radical ultranationalist movements in the prewar period. For instance, Kita's conceptualization of the emperor as the "people's emperor (*kokumin no Tennō*),"[38] which is the title of the first section of the book, is in direct conflict with the idea of the emperor as a living deity in Shintō ultranationalist theology and ideology. From the perspective of radical Shintō ultranationalists, this was lese majesty. His reference to the emperor as the "people's emperor" was just as blasphemous as Minobe saying that the emperor was an organ of the state. Further, Kita's position that the kokutai had evolved through three stages, which was the same argument he had put forth in *On the Kokutai and Pure Socialism*, was a direct violation of the fundamental State Shintō doctrine that Japan had always been ruled over by the unbroken line of emperors from Jimmū, who was descended from Amaterasu Ōmikami. Still more, even though Kita referred to the emperor in *An Outline Plan for the Reorganization of Japan* as a "divine person (*shinkakusha*),"[39] he was referring to the fact that the emperor was a divine person in the eyes of the Japanese people and therefore thought that a true restoration revolution, if ordered by the emperor, could be accomplished with little bloodshed and disorder, unlike in the case of the French Revolution.

That is, Kita was not in love with the emperor and therefore was not pining to die for the emperor. Kita, in fact, attacked the radical Shintō ultranationalists, saying that it was "laughable" for them to try to argue the kokutai on the basis of the Takamagahara (Plain of High Heaven).[40]

Kita's ideological influence on the terrorists who carried out the February 26, 1936, Incident has also been oversimplified. Although "Kita himself had ties with some young officers whose concern over Japan's China policy played such an important role in the military putsches of the 1930s,"[41] and even though he allegedly was involved with the Kōdō Ha (Imperial Way Faction), he was not truly one of them in terms of fundamental ideology. What attracted some radical Shintō ultranationalists to Kita was the fact that he had worked out a plan for the reorganization of Japan. The point that Kita did not believe that the emperor was "sacred and inviolable," as Article 3 of the Constitution of the Empire of Great Japan proclaimed, was actually an issue that came up during preliminary court hearings conducted for those who were indicted in the February 26, 1936, Incident. One of the military officers connected with the insurrection was Kurosaki Sadaaki. He was implicated in the plot at the time and faced charges before the Special Military Court but was eventually acquitted for lack of evidence. However, at a preliminary hearing he admitted that he was a follower of Kita and had read Kita's *An Outline Plan for the Reorganization of Japan* and *Shina Kakumei Gaishi* (An Unofficial History of the Chinese Revolution). He was asked point blank by the presiding judge: "Does not Kita's [conceptualization of the] emperor as a representative of the people violate the Constitution of the Empire of Great Japan, which states that the emperor is sacred and inviolable?"[42] Kurosaki then gave a rather convoluted explanation of his understanding of Kita's idea of the people's emperor, but in the end he stated that the essence of his own belief was expressed in the two-character word "*renketsu*," which meant love of country and love of emperor.[43] Also noteworthy is that he then emphasized to the judge in this preliminary hearing that Kita's *An Outline Plan for the Reorganization of Japan* was merely one "reference book" consulted by the radical ultranationalist junior officers.[44] Although radical Shintō ultranationalist junior officers may have found much of what Kita had written useful for their purposes, they selectively took what they wanted and either ignored the rest of his ideas or reinterpreted them to fit what they wanted to hear. Contrary to the mission of radical Shintō ultranationalists, Kita's mission, as Christopher Szpilman pointed out, was to "lead a world federation of nations by spreading the divine way of Buddha to the four corners of the world."[45] He further noted that Kita "desperately tried to prevent the February 26 Incident."[46]

As this study will illustrate, it was Uesugi Shinkichi and Kakehi Katsuhiko rather than Kita Ikki who articulated the ideas that best represented the true beliefs of those who participated in the February 26, 1936, Incident. In a way, Kita might be considered a fascist in the European sense—particularly Italian Fascism. But in the case of Kita, one must straddle the fence between socialism and fascism. At any rate, he was not a radical Shintō ultranationalist.

Kita eventually paid the ultimate price for his unorthodox views. Some thirty years after he wrote *On the Kokutai and Pure Socialism*, the army "decided to put him out of the way because he was an anti-*Kokutai* radical."[47] He was executed in 1936 along with the military insurrectionists who staged the February 26, 1936, Incident.

We must conclude from this analysis that of the two main ideological formulations in support of liberal democracy—the emperor-as-organ theory of the state represented by Minobe Tatsukichi in the Meiji period and minponshugi, articulated best by Yoshino Sakuzō, in the Taishō period—Minobe's theory was the more formidable opponent to Shintō ultranationalist ideology. While minponshugi had been relegated to obscurity by end of the 1920s, there were still many adherents of the emperor-as-organ theory well into the 1930s. To restate what was happening in terms of the ideological dynamics of this debate over state and sovereignty, ideological articulations in defense of parliamentary government steadily continued to weaken as Japan moved from the Meiji period to the Taishō period. Still more, we find no major ideological rearticulation in support of liberal-democratic government after the end of the 1910s. In other words, the supreme irony is that, as party government became more politically entrenched, ideological support for it became increasingly weaker. But contrary to the conventional wisdom that "Taishō era [democracy] could not successfully assault the fortress of traditional nationalism built during the Meiji era,"[48] what has gone almost totally unnoticed was that Hozumi's reactionary Shintō ultranationalism was also coming under heavy attack and rapidly losing its ideological relevance. It was at this particular time that we find a major rearticulation of Shintō ultranationalist ideology that was designed to win over the support of the masses. It would be Uesugi Shinkichi, Hozumi's protégé, who would become the chief theorist (along with Kakehi Katsuhiko) of emperor ideology in the Taishō period and go down in history as one of the greatest theoreticians of the modern Japanese state. Uesugi, the man who initially set the tone for the debate over state and sovereignty in the early 1910s by reviving the concept of minponshugi, would by the end of the Taishō period formulate the most powerful state ideology. By the time of the publication of his *A New Thesis on the State* in 1921, radical Shintō ultranationalism was well on its way to becoming the dominant political ideology.

Preconditions for the Success of Radical Shintō Ultranationalism

A question often asked by scholars of modern Japanese history is whether or not the liberal trends characteristic of the 1920s represented a fundamental break with the oligarchic rule of the Meiji period before it and the period of militarism and ultranationalism that followed. This issue is difficult to grapple with, because we find both significant changes and striking continuities during those years. Those who tend to emphasize the sociopolitical changes leading Japan toward democratic government stress the importance of developments such as the rise to power of the political parties, the introduction of universal male suffrage, and Japan's active cooperation with the Western democratic nations and its participation in the League of Nations. Others who see the continuities of Meiji authoritarianism as key to understanding Japan's drift toward war in Asia focus on the unchanging institutional structures of the state, the Constitution of the Empire of Japan, and the attack on Pearl Harbor as the final extension of Meiji imperialism. In "Taisho Democracy as the Pre-Stage for Japanese Militarism," Katō Shūichi stated the conflicting positions on this issue as follows:

> Was this [shift from liberalism and "Taishō Democracy" to militarism and "super-nationalism"] a conversion of a nation or did it merely indicate a new stage of that Japanese imperialism which had its origins in the Meiji period? Those who emphasize the contrast are inclined to idealize the term "Taishō Democracy" and consider the war years from 1931 to 1945 a national conversion or rather an unfortunate accident or nightmare which had best be forgotten. Hence, the success story of Japanese modernization. Those who underline the continuity of the Meiji oligarchy throughout the Taishō and Shōwa eras until 1945 are inclined to minimize the extent of liberalization which did take place in the 1920s within the tradi-

tional framework of the state and society. In doing so, they obscure, in part, the origins of militarism insofar as it was a reaction to Taishō liberalism, and underestimate the heritage from the Taishō era evident in the post-Second World War period.[49]

In Katō's opinion, the crucially important point in understanding modern Japanese history was to fully recognize *both* fundamental changes and continuities. While he did acknowledge that a significant degree of democratization and secularization had occurred in Japanese society, he also stressed that it was in reaction to a partially democratized society that we find the origins of "militarism." In other words, a precondition for the success of "militarism" in taking over the Japanese state was a "relatively developed but structurally weak liberal political culture" and "a limited consensus to democracy and liberalism."[50]

Roger Griffin argued:

> Fascism can only break out of its marginalized position . . . if it operates in a secularizing and pluralistic society struck by crisis. It will only stand a chance of carrying out a successful revolution in a liberal democracy caught in a particularly delicate stage of its evolution: mature enough institutionally to preclude the threat of a direct military or monarchical coup, yet too immature to be able to rely on a substantial consensus in the general population that liberal political procedures and the values which underpin them are the sole valid basis for a healthy society.[51]

Griffin wrote this in his discussion of the conditions for fascism as an ideology to succeed in dominating the state, as in the cases of Fascist Italy and Nazi Germany. If we apply this theory to the Japanese case, Japan in the 1920s does indeed fit these conditions. Clearly, the movement toward parliamentary rule was irreversible in the sense that Japan at that point in time could not revert to feudalism or to a premodern system of absolute monarchy. As Katō indicated, the trend toward democratic liberalism was closely linked with Japan's rapid industrialization, urbanization, and new middle class: "Taishō Japan created an urban mass society, with a relatively high level of education and with a quickly developing system of modern mass communications media, thus preparing the ground for the participation of the masses in politics, but at the same time opening the way for the manipulated mass society of the future."[51]

But who would succeed in manipulating the Japanese masses to determine the society of the future? The only conceivable alternatives to democratic government were other mass-based movements with underpinning ideologies that could effectively harness the emerging forces of popular nationalism. Meiji authoritarian oligarchic rule was in crisis and the democratic movement stymied due to its own inability to secure a critical mass base. Katō wrote:

> The participation of the masses in politics still rested largely on votes in elections which were not much more than mere formalities. In the first place, the membership of Japanese political parties was extremely limited in number, even in the case of the party having a majority in the House. Functional in elections, perhaps efficient in intra-parliamentary maneuvers, political parties were merely organizations of the representatives without involvement of the mass.[53]

Similarly, parties on the ideological left could not effectively organize the Japanese masses to make a bid for state power. Communists, for example, challenged the whole Meiji state in ideas, but not in actions. "They were too isolated to exert an important influence on the course of political events in the country," according to Katō.[54] Kita Ikki and his particularistic brand of national socialism also would not survive the ideological confrontation of the 1930s.

We have learned from Katō and many other scholars that the Japanese state would finally be taken over by militarists and "super-nationalists" and succeed in mobilizing the masses for war in Asia and the Pacific. But from where did they emerge in this ideological contestation? It is critically important to understand that the militarization or radicalization of the masses did not occur automatically. The masses had to have been led and inspired for this to have occurred. Jose Ortega y Gasset once reminded us that the politicization of the masses also was *not* a naturally occurring process:

> In the XVIIIth Century, certain minority groups discovered that every human being, by the mere fact of birth, and without requiring any special qualification whatsoever, possessed certain fundamental political rights, the so-called rights of man and the citizen. . . . Every other right attached to special gifts was condemned as being a privilege. This was at first a mere theory, the idea of a few men; then those few began to put the idea into practice, to impose it and insist upon it. Nevertheless, during the whole of the XIXth Century, the mass, while gradually becoming enthusiastic for those rights as an ideal, did not feel them as rights, did not exercise them or attempt to make them prevail, but, in fact, under democratic legislation, continued to feel itself just as under the old regime.[55]

Likewise, the radicalization of the masses did not occur spontaneously. What made possible "radical change?" As Ortega suggests, there must be a theory for it to happen—a theory of radicalization that starts in the minds of a few individuals who impose it and insist on it. It was the intellectual elites at the top of Japanese society who would radicalize the Japanese masses in the Taishō period. This radicalization would emerge out of Hozumi's traditional conservative or counter-revolutionary Shintō ultranationalism. As we saw in chapter 2, Hozumi's Shintō ultranationalism was a traditional, patriarchal family-state ideology of monarchical absolutism. It was a premodern theory of state in which the people were considered passive political objects to be acted on. It was not a theory of state designed to appeal to the politicized masses. Thus, it would have to be rearticulated to appeal to the politicized masses or face falling into irrelevance. Interestingly, all of the ideologies discussed thus far— Hozumi's traditional monarchist ultranationalism, Minobe's emperor-as-organ theory of the state, Yoshino's minponshugi, and Kita's nationalist socialism—would not survive the political and ideological contestation of the Taishō and prewar Shōwa periods. They would be swept aside and destroyed by radical ultranationalist ideologies, "both radically populist and anti-conservative,"[56] that would appear in the Taishō period and advance to center stage of Japanese politics. Just as the politicization of the masses did not come about automatically, as Ortega showed, neither did the radicalization of the masses occur spontaneously. A revolutionary ideology had to exist. This study suggests that a fundamental transformation in the ideology of Shintō ultranationalism took place in the Taishō period, an ideology that this study refers to as "radical Shintō ultranationalism."

We will now turn to the state theorists who would transform Hozumi Yatsuka's conservative, völkisch state ideology into the ideology of radical Shintō ultranationalism, the ideology that would come to dominate the ideological space in Japan until the end of the Second World War.

6

Uesugi Shinkichi:

The Emperor and the Masses

The state is the actuality of the ethical Ideal.
—G. W. F. HEGEL, *Philosophy of Right*, 155

The state is ultimate morality.
—UESUGI SHINKICHI, *A New Thesis on the State*, 1

The Radicalization of a Shintō Ultranationalist

Louis Napoleon once proclaimed that "the reign of castes is over; one can govern only with the masses. It is necessary, therefore, to organize them so that they can formulate their wishes and to discipline them so that they can be guided and enlightened concerning their own interests."[1] He went on to say that to govern no longer meant to dominate the masses by force but to appeal to their hearts and reason. The awakening of the masses was undoubtedly the most important political development in Europe in the nineteenth century. In recognition that a new era had begun in politics—and, indeed, in the history of mankind—with the politicization of the masses, Napoleon, who sought to revive the system of monarchy, clearly understood that a government could endure only if it was based on mass support. No longer could it be based on the support of a privileged minority and on the nostalgia of a glorious past while ignoring the problems of the masses. For that reason, he was convinced that a Bonapartist doctrine and a Bonapartist movement were needed to adapt the system of monarchy to a modern, mass-based society. The monarchists, no less than the liberal democrats and the socialists, were vying for the allegiance of the masses in the nineteenth century.

While the politicization of the masses had changed the nature of politics, it had also changed the nature of warfare among states. In his famous treatise *On War (Vom Kriege)*, the Prussian military officer Carl von Clausewitz stated that warfare was no longer the business of just governments and armies; it was also the business of the masses. He understood that Napoleon's victories in battle had as much to do with the support and enthusiasm of the French people as with his own military skills. The mobilization of the masses was at least as important as the mobilization of the armed forces. It had become not only the key element in political competition within the state, but also the major factor in competition among states.

The politicization of the masses that occurred in Europe in the nineteenth century would not come about in Japan until the dawn of the twentieth century. The politics of the nineteenth century in Japan were still largely the politics of the military aristocratic class. The revolutionary movement of the Meiji period in the late nineteenth century extended for the most part only to the lowest ranks of the samurai class. But by the end of the first decade of the twentieth century, the Japanese masses had begun to reveal their power in various demonstrations, which caused concern within the Meiji leadership. As Kenneth Pyle has noted:

> The period after World War I witnessed a succession of crises in Japanese society, and the problem of maintaining a stable political community sorely tried Japanese leadership. During the preceding fifty years the Japanese masses had slowly been awakened to political experience. By the first decades of the twentieth century it was becoming clear that they could no longer be kept out of political life. Industrialization and universal education contributed to this end; by the turn of the century there was a large number of newspapers and magazines designed for a mass audience. The increasing involvement of the populace in the issues of the day caused the leadership growing concern.[2]

This was evident even to observers closer to those times. For instance, Yoshino Sakuzō wrote that the Hibiya Riot (1905) signaled the emergence of the Japanese masses on the political stage. And, as Andrew Gordon has demonstrated, 1905 was the beginning of a series of mass disturbances that would culminate in the rice riots of 1918:

In the first two decades of the twentieth century, crowds of city-dwellers took to the streets of Tokyo and launched the most vigorous urban protests yet seen in Japan. At least nine times from the Hibiya riot of 1905 to the rice riots of 1918, angry Tokyoites attacked policemen, police stations, and national government offices, smashed streetcar windows and beat the drivers, marched on the Diet, and stormed the offices of major newspapers. They destroyed public and private property, launching both symbolic and substantive attacks on the institutions of the established order of imperial Japan.[3]

Other historians also saw the importance of the Hibiya Riot in terms of the beginning of mass participation in politics. For example, Okamoto Shumpei defined its historical significance as "participants in the mass protest movements . . . unwittingly exposed a grave conflict that had been hidden within the Meiji political system. They touched on the contradiction between the public facade of an absolute emperor's personal rule and the actual role of the emperor as a constitutional monarch to be exploited by the ruling oligarchies."[4]

Okamoto's observation about seeing the Hibiya Riot as a clear manifestation of the newly awakened masses was certainly correct. But it is somewhat misleading to say that this conflict exposed a grave conflict that was "hidden" in the Meiji political system. There was nothing at all hidden about the contradiction of the Meiji political system. It was clearly evident from its inception, as many Japanese historians and political theorists have noted. Joseph Pittau pointed this contradiction out by aptly characterizing the Meiji political system as an "absolute constitutional monarchy."[5] The crux of the problem of the prewar Japanese state was that elements of both absolute monarchy and constitutional (limited) monarchy were inherent in the Meiji political system. This contradiction was the source of constant political gridlock between the oligarchs in power and the parliamentarians in opposition in the first decades of government under the Constitution of the Empire of Japan. It was also the central problem to which each political and state theorist directed his attention, which soon crystallized into a debate that centered on the issue of whether the emperor constituted the whole state or was merely an organ of the state. As I have discussed, while Shintō ultranationalists such as Hozumi Yatsuka sought to eradicate the elements of constitutionalism from the system and theoretically place all political power in the hands of the emperor, advocates of parliamentary government such as Minobe Tatsukichi did the reverse, trying to displace the absolute elements from the political system and place political power in the hands of the elected parliament.

For Uesugi Shinkichi (1878–1929), however, the problem was not that simple. It was more than just that of the contradictory nature of the Meiji political system to which those on both sides of the debate had offered solutions. The era of rule by imperial bureaucracy was rapidly coming to an end.[6] As he saw it, the newly politicized masses not only posed a threat to the state established by the Meiji oligarchs; they had by their actions in the streets negated the fundamental assumptions on which Shintō ultranationalist ideology in support of absolute monarchy had rested. He was convinced that the dissatisfaction of the masses had exposed a serious flaw inherent in the conservative Shintō ultranationalist theory of state formulated by Hozumi Yatsuka in the latter part of the nineteenth century.

We might restate the problem of the politicized masses with respect to Hozumi's theory of absolute monarchy in another way. In the Hibiya Riot incident, the masses did not blame the emperor for their problems. Rather, they had made a conscious distinction between the desire of the emperor, on the one hand, and that of the ministers of state and, indeed, that of all other organs of government, on the other hand. The masses, in other words, had their own knowledge of the emperor's "true desires," independent of the government authorities mediating between them and the emperor. In Hegelian terms, the Hibiya Riot was the outward manifestation of a nascent form of "subjective freedom."[7]

The actions of the masses were clear signs that the hierarchical and authoritarian patriarchal construction of society imagined as a fundamental characteristic of Japanese society by Hozumi and other Meiji state theorists was in the process of rapidly breaking down and that it could no longer serve as a viable ideology for "direct imperial rule." Treating the whole state as literally one gigantic family, thus making no distinction between parental authority and political authority, Hozumi had in theory treated the Japanese people politically as children. This was no oversight on the part of Hozumi. He had mistrusted the masses, as already indicated. In a debate over the extension of the franchise in the early 1910s, he preferred to keep the franchise restricted, in effect rejecting the participation of the masses in politics. In other words, he wanted to keep the masses depoliticized.

Hozumi's theory of the patriarchal Japanese state was much like the nature of state and society characteristic of the Oriental world that Hegel referred to in *The Philosophy of History*. In Hegel's Oriental world, the political form was "despotism." It was a world in which only one person —the emperor—was free to determine law and morality for all others. In his image of the Oriental states, no individual had a moral existence separate from the ruler. People lacked what he called subjective freedom, the idea that the individual, reflecting on his own consciousness, was a law unto himself. It was this unreflective consciousness that character- ized the Oriental world. Without this "subjective freedom," subjects were "like children, who obey their parents without will or insight of their own."[8] If a ruler's subject does not obey the command of the ruler, "he thus virtually separates himself from the substance of his being."[9]

The politicization of the masses in Japan in the first decade of the twentieth century had prompted Shintō ultranationalists such as Uesugi to search for a new theory of state in an attempt to enlist the masses to actively support imperial rule. The central issue for them was to prove that Shintō ultranationalism was capable of adapting itself to modern society and convince the politically awakened masses that Shintō ultra- nationalism, just like liberal democracy and socialism, had a program relevant for them.

Uesugi was born in Fukui Prefecture in 1878. He graduated from the Law School of Tokyo Imperial University, where he studied under Ho- zumi Yatsuka. When Hozumi retired from Tokyo Imperial University in 1910 due to bad health, Uesugi, who had joined the faculty there in 1903, succeeded him. He was promoted to full professor in 1912 and taught there until his death in 1929. It is important to note that he also lectured at the army and naval academies for many years.

Like his teacher Hozumi, Uesugi in his early days was influenced heavily by Western state theories. He was once an adherent to the emperor-as-organ theory of the state, believing that sovereignty resided in the state and that the emperor was the highest organ of the state. However, it was apparently during his stay in Europe from 1906 to 1909, studying under George Jellenik (1851–1911), that he turned decidedly away from the state-sovereignty theory and Western thought. Ida Teruto- shi, writing about Uesugi's life in Germany, noted that Uesugi had a very close personal relationship with Jellenik in Heidelberg, not only attend- ing his lectures, but also living at Jellenik's home. Ironically, however, it was precisely because of Jellenik and his European experience that Uesugi finally turned away from the German state theory: "He was not one who denied the state-as-a-legal-person theory or emperor-as-organ theory in spite of the fact that he studied under Jellenik, but [precisely] because he studied under Jellenik."[10] In other words, it was Uesugi's personal exposure to Western civilization as a student in Germany that turned him against the Western world.

Uesugi was a political activist as well as an intellectual, a man with an evangelical spirit who preached in the guise of teaching. His theoretical and ideological struggle with Minobe Tatsukichi's emperor-as-organ theory of the state, which began in the first decade of the twentieth century when Minobe began writing on constitutional issues, took on a new political dimension in 1911. In the summer of that year, under the auspices of the Ministry of Education, Minobe give a series of lectures on the Constitution of the Empire of Japan in a summer course organized for middle-school teachers. Later that same year, Minobe's lectures were compiled and subsequently published in *Kempō Kōwa* (Lectures on the Constitution). This publication also included a severe criticism of Uesugi's *Kokumin Kyōiku Teikoku Kempō Kōgi* (Lectures on National Education and the Imperial Constitution). Uesugi was enraged by this and launched a vicious attack on what he regarded as Minobe's heresy against the kokutai, Japan's unique form of state. He charged that Minobe had violated the principle of the kokutai by saying that the state was a corporate body possessing a legal personality in which the emperor exercised governmental power as an organ of the state. For Uesugi, sovereignty resided in the emperor, and the emperor's sovereignty, as he understood it in the Constitution of the Empire of Japan, was absolute, indivisible, and subject to no law. Furthermore, he was particularly troubled by the fact that the Japanese government had sponsored Minobe's lectures. He was concerned that the emperor-as-organ theory would gain a following among teachers in Japan's public education system and through the education system spread to the next generation of Japanese.

As early as 1913, Uesugi formed a group called the Tōkagakkai (Paulownia Flower Society) to defend the kokutai against Minobe's emperor-as-organ theory of the state and to work for the eradication of the political parties.[11] The Paulownia Flower Society expanded to include more than two hundred members, including radical Shintō ultranationalist scholars (including Kakehi Katsuhiko), military officers, and bureaucrats. The opening ceremony in celebration of the founding of the Paulownia Flower Society was held on the campus of Tokyo Imperial University in that year.

The nineteen-tens were a deeply disturbing decade for Uesugi. Japan seemed to be sliding irreversibly into rule by the political parties. Farsighted thinkers and astute politicians began to realize that nothing could prevent the steady extension of political democracy. The death of Emperor Meiji and the start of the Taishō period marked the beginning of an era of thought and culture of the masses. While the elite may have felt a sense of ending, the masses looked on the new era as the beginning of liberation and freedom. Yoshino Sakuzō, who in 1912 had returned to Japan after studying for three years in Europe and the United States, began formulating his concept of minponshugi (government for the people). Yoshino had been inspired by the memorable words "government of the people, by the people, for the people (*jinmin no, jinmin ni yori, jinmin no tame no seiji*)" spoken by U.S. President Abraham Lincoln at Gettysburg in 1863.[12] Of course, it was the idea expressed in the last part of this phrase, or "government for the people," that Yoshino was interested in incorporating into his theory of government for the Japanese state. Discussions centering on the concepts of "mass government (*minshūseiji*)" and "popularism (*minshūshugi*)" were also very much in the air,[13] and, as mentioned, Uesugi was a major participant in this discussion.

International trends of the 1910s were no less troubling for Uesugi. The victory of the democratic nations in World War One contributed heavily to the advancement of the democratic movement everywhere. Monarchies seemed to be collapsing around the world: the Romanovs in Russia, the Hohenzollerns in Germany, the Hapsburgs in Austria-Hungary, the Ottomans in Turkey, and the Qing Dynasty in China. Equally disturbing was the Bolsheviks' seizure of power in Russia in 1917. Uesugi lashed out against these trends in numerous articles in the late 1910s, attacking both Minobe Tatsukichi and Yoshino Sakuzō. For example, he asserted that "the spirit of the Constitution excluded parliamentary government. . . . It is therefore regrettable that so many have taken parliamentary government to be the ultimate virtue of constitutional government."[14]

Under Uesugi's sponsorship, the Kōkoku Dōshikai (Association of Those Devoted to the Advancement of the State) was organized among law-school students at Tokyo Imperial University in 1920.[15] The purpose of the organization was to counter democratic and socialist ideas, which were very much in vogue at the time. One of the members of the Kōkoku Dōshikai was Minoda Muneki, an activist who became an extremist even within the radical Shintō ultranationalist movement.[16] He landed a teaching position at Keiō University in 1922 and started the journal *Genri Nihon* (True Japan) in 1925. In 1932, he transferred to Kokushikan University. Following in the footsteps of Uesugi, Minoda led the attack on "liberal" scholars throughout the 1930s, arguing that the fundamental root of Japan's problems, both internally and externally, was Japan's infatuation with European and American thought, which had dominated the imperial universities intellectually since the beginning of the Meiji period. He claimed that the Western-derived "materialistic individualism (*yūibutsu teki kojinshugi*)" was responsible for destroying the Japanese kokutai.[17] According to Minoda, "One who is not a devout believer in the emperor as a religion is not a Japanese."[18]

In 1923, Uesugi joined forces with Takabatake Motoyuki and his national-socialist movement to found the radical Shintō ultranationalist organization Keirin Gakumei (Society for the Study of Statesmanship or Statecraft Study Association). The purpose of their society was to inspire their followers with the idealism and fanaticism to defend the "pure spirit of the Japanese ethnic nation (*Nihon minzoku no shinseishin*)" against the corrupting influences of Western thought and institutions of government and to utilize the genius and capabilities of the Japanese people to benefit the world.[19] Uesugi saw himself as an ideological pioneer in initiating a new movement in world history that was striving to overcome Western liberalism and materialism.

The Society for the Study of Statesmanship was short-lived, owing apparently to a rift that developed between Uesugi and Takabatake. This falling out between Uesugi and Takabatake is often seen as the result of a conflict of views between traditional nationalists and radical nationalists. For example, in his study of postwar trends in right-wing movements in Japan, Ivan Morris quoted Richard Storry as saying:

> The disagreement between the two men exemplified a split that was to run right through the nationalist movement before the Pacific War. On the one side were those, like Uesugi, who preached Nippon-shugi ("Japanism"), a fundamentally nostalgic, conservative *mystique*. On the other were radical nationalists, such as Takabetake, the advocates of revolutionary reconstruction, of national socialism.[20]

Morris, in agreement with Storry's interpretation, then noted that this dispute between Uesugi and Takabatake was "essentially the split between reactionary traditionalism and modern Fascism."[21] Both Storry's and Morris's portrayal of Uesugi as a leader of a reactionary, traditionalist nationalist movement is incorrect. It is at odds with the analysis of this study on Uesugi's thought and with Japanese scholars who have written extensively on Uesugi, such as Ida Terutoshi and Nagao Ryūichi. On the contrary, Uesugi was arguably one of the most radical Shintō ultranationalist theorists in prewar Japan. And if there had been a dispute between Uesugi and Takabatake, it was undoubtedly a dispute between two extreme revolutionary nationalists with very strong convictions.

The Society for the Study of Statesmanship, despite its brief existence from 1923 to 1926, had a tremendous influence on the organization and thought of subsequent ultranationalist movements in prewar Japan. With the exception of two ultranationalist movements with roots extending back to the nineteenth century in the Meiji period—the Genyōsha (Dark Ocean Society), a terrorist organization that was established in 1881 in Kyūshū following the crushing of Saigō Takamori's revolt and led by Hiraoka Kotarō, Tōyama Mitsuru, and Uchida Ryōhei; and the Amur River Society, also known as the Kokuryūkai (Black Dragon Society), formed in 1901 by Uchida Ryōhei—the Society for the Study of Statesmanship can be considered the progenitor of the main grouping of subsequent ultranationalist movements originating in the Taishō and Shōwa periods. This is clearly illustrated in appendix 4, a chart of leading ultranationalist societies in the prewar period, in Storry's *The Double Patriots*.[22] The Society for the Study of Statesmanship differed from the two earlier ultranationalist organizations in important ways. Most important, unlike the Dark Ocean Society and the Amur River Society, which remained relatively small organizations that attempted to influence governmental policy either by allying with, or engaging in terrorist activities against, political elites,[23] Uesugi's Society for the Study of Statesmanship aimed toward mobilizing the Japanese masses. Uesugi's six-point agenda for the Society for the Study of Statesmanship was clearly modern and fascist: (1) realization of the ideal of "the whole nation beating as one heart" through ideology; (2) the enhancement of national glory through the mobilization of the entire nation; (3) the resolute enforcement of national militarization based on the premise that each and every individual in the nation is a soldier; (4) the creation of a national economy through the control of capital and labor; (5) the establishment of a nation of one people through administration of a public welfare system and the preservation of the national characteristics of the nation; (6) the adoption of a nationwide system of elections.[24] Uesugi considered these measures as indispensable for the advancement of the essence of the kokutai. Ida Terutoshi notes that Uesugi's six points were the main tenets of "Japanese-style fascism (*wasei fashizumi*)."[25]

There is documentary evidence to show that Uesugi was considered a radical revolutionary ultranationalist by his contemporaries and that many of his followers and associates were personally involved in terrorist activities. For instance, according to a secret document of the Criminal

Investigation Bureau of the Ministry of Justice, the Society for the Study of Statesmanship—along with the Yūzonsha (Society of Those Who Yet Remain), whose members included people who are better known by Western scholars, such as Ōkawa Shūmei and Kita Ikki—was regarded as one of the "two great wellsprings of recent radical national revolutionary movements in our country."[26] Radical nationalist groups had been placed under police surveillance, and Japanese law-enforcement authorities had arrived at the conclusion that Uesugi was one of the intellectual giants among Japanese radical ultranationalists. This is not to suggest that Kita Ikki's ideas were not important. His manifesto *An Outline Plan for the Reorganization of Japan* had an impact on Japanese radical ultranationalists. However, American and European scholars have almost unanimously identified Kita as the most influential intellectual ultranationalist thinker, while Uesugi Shinkichi is not even mentioned. On the contrary, if his name does appear at all in scholarly writings in the English language, is portrayed as a "conservative."[27]

Although Uesugi died in 1929, before the wave of terrorism struck the Japanese political world in the 1930s, this study argues that he represented a movement that ideologically justified terrorism, not merely a particular group of terrorists. His thought represented a type of thinking that inspired the mainstream of radical Shintō ultranationalists to the end of the Second World War. Nevertheless, Uesugi is acknowledged by Japanese scholars as having directly mentored people who would engage in terrorist activities. For instance, in 1925 Uesugi formed still another group called the Shichishō Sha (Seven Lives Society).[28] Ivan Morris noted that the Seven Lives Society was created "largely due to combat the influence of the left-wing Association of New Men,"[29] which was formed by Yoshino Sakuzō. But there was much more to it than that. It aimed not only to stem the flood of liberal-democratic thought in Japan, but also to promote Japanese expansionism on a global scale. "In extraordinary times, one must do extraordinary things."[30] This was Uesugi's idea, an idea that was very much a part of the Seven Lives Society. It is interesting to note that members of the Seven Lives Society met every Thursday at 3 P.M. in the society's headquarters to study ideas, talk about current events, and engage in round-table discussions. Monthly proceedings of the society were recorded and saved. The proceedings from July 4, 1926, for example, show that the American Declaration of Independence was a topic of the group's discussion.[31] During the discussions on that day it is recorded that Uesugi remarked that war between Japan and the United States was inevitable. The reason he gave for predicting a clash between the two nations was that the United States, which he thought was potentially the most powerful Western state and the largest liberal democracy in the world, had tremendous energy and vitality and was bound to continue to expand its influence overseas. Of course, in Uesugi's mind Japan was destined to purge the world of Western culture and Western domination and establish a new world order led by Japan. Thus, during the high point of the democratic period in Japan, Uesugi predicted the Japan-U.S. war more than fifteen years before the outbreak of the Pacific War in 1941. But most interesting are the linkages between members of Uesugi's Seven Lives Society and the Ketsumeidan (League of Blood), which planned the murders of Inoue Junnosuke, former minister of finance, in February 1932, and Dan Takuma, director of the Mitsui holding company, in March 1932. Although Uesugi died in 1929, leading members of his Seven Lives Society, such as Yotsumoto Yoshitaka, Ikebukuro Seihachirō, Kukida Sukehiro, and Tanaka Kunio, were deeply involved in the Ketsumeidan Incidents, which first exploded in February 1932.[32]

Uesugi also maintained a very close relationship with the notorious Akao Bin (1899–1990), whom many considered one of the most militant radical Shintō ultranationalist thinkers of the times. In 1926, Akao, along with Tsukui Tatsuno and Atsumi Masaru, established the Kenkokukai (National Foundation Association), one of the main ultranationalist organizations of the 1920s. Uesugi was a key figure (president) in this ultranationalist organization together with Akao, an anarchist turned radical Shintō ultranationalist and a supporter of terrorist activities. Morris wrote the following brief description of Akao Bin:

> Akao Bin (b. 1899). Professional agitator and one of the most vociferous anti-communists in the pre-war ultra-rightist movement. His fury has always been directed primarily against Soviet Russia. Mr. Akao headed the National Founding Association and in 1942 was elected to the Diet. He is still active in rightist circles as president of the Great Japan Patriot's Party (*Dai Nihon Aikoku Tō*) and was an influence on the young assassin who in October 1960 killed Mr. Asanuma Inejirō, the Chairman of the Socialist Party.[33]

Hiranuma Kiichirō and Tōyama Mitsuru were also leading figures in the National Foundation Association. It is instructive to note that Akao openly advocated the use of terrorism to further the group's ends and was actually involved in terrorist acts himself. For instance, in 1928 he was involved in a bomb attack on the Soviet Embassy in Tokyo. Akao's open support for terrorist activities even alienated Hiranuma and Tō-yama, who, according to Storry, "were not averse to a discreet use of terrorist methods."[34] After Hiranuma, Tōyama, and other powerful members withdrew from the National Foundation Association, the organization's financial situation worsened to the point that it could not even pay the rent to maintain its headquarters. Nevertheless, Uesugi continued to support Akao and the National Foundation Association to the end, even to the point of allowing Akao to set up headquarters for the association in his own home. This continued support for Akao when every other prominent figure had abandoned him tells us a lot about where Uesugi's sympathies lay. It is noteworthy that Akao continued his radical Shintō ultranationalist activities after the war. Morris also noted that after the Second World War, Akao founded a new Shintō sect in the Asakusa area of Tokyo.[35]

In short, these are just some examples of the ultranationalist organizations that Uesugi either helped to start or was actively involved in. It is no exaggeration to say that Uesugi had extensive contacts with nearly every major radical Shintō ultranationalist organization that flourished in the 1910s and the 1920s. Moreover, it was also during the 1910s that we find a major transformation in Uesugi's own Shintō ultranationalist thought. No longer was he defending and promoting the premodern authoritarian family-state of Hozumi Yatsuka and other conservative nationalists. He came to the realization that the pressures for political democracy were irresistible and the extension of the franchise inevitable. Meiji-era conservative Shintō ultranationalists such as Hozumi were suited neither temperamentally nor ideologically to engaging in ideological competition with those, like Minobe, who wanted responsible party government. Hozumi had mistrusted the masses and preferred to keep the franchise restricted to the propertied and educated classes. But this was no longer possible. Politics were rapidly becoming mass politics. Japan was experiencing the arrival of the masses in history that most Europeans had experienced in the nineteenth century. As Carl Schmitt had said:

> The history of political and state theory in the nineteenth century could be summarized with a single phrase: the triumphal march of democracy. No state in the Western European cultural world withstood the extension of democratic ideas and institutions. Even where powerful social forces

defended themselves, such as in the Prussian monarchy, no intellectual force that could have defeated democratic beliefs reached outside its own circle of adherents. Progress and the extension of democracy were equated, and the antidemocratic resistance was considered an empty defense, the protection of historically outmoded things and a struggle of the old with the new.[36]

Much the same could have been said of Japan of the 1910s. Japan was moving toward modern mass democracy. It was this crisis situation in which Uesugi and other Shintō ultranationalists found themselves and that drove them to extreme radicalism. Furthermore, Uesugi began contemplating another motive for a new theory of monarchy that would have mass support: mass mobilization for total war. In *The Inevitability of a Japan-U.S. Collision and National Preparedness*, he predicted war with the United States and urged his countrymen to prepare for it. He sought to mobilize his nation into mass armies—armies of politically conscious people ready and eager to fight for the emperor. Uesugi responded to this historical challenge with a new theory of the Japanese state.

Finally, it is instructive to mention at this point that many politically savvy people in Japan had somehow perceived that a radicalization had occurred in the nature of nationalist groups and their aims. Ida Terutoshi, who has done extensive research on radical nationalist thought and ultranationalist movements in prewar Japan, noted this and referred to Uesugi's Society for the Study of Statesmanship as a Japanese version of Mussolini's Blackshirts.[37] The Blackshirts, of course, were members of the Italian Fascist Party who wore black shirts as part of their uniform; the black shirt was adopted by Mussolini in 1919 when he founded the first of the political groups known as the *fasci di combattimento*. Mussolini had employed this private paramilitary group when he seized power in October 1922. Although the Italian Fascist Party had just appeared on the political scene in Italy, the Blackshirts were already known by 1922 to the politically aware Japanese. It is interesting to note that by 1923 the Shihōshō Keijikyoku (Criminal Investigation Bureau of the Japanese Ministry of Justice) was said to have stated in a secret report that Uesugi's Society for the Study of Statesmanship was seen by many Japanese as a "fascist group."[38] If this is accurate, it was an extraordinary insight. If these people had not read Uesugi's 1921 theory of the Japanese state, they must intuitively have sensed that the nature of Japanese politics was rapidly changing into something like extreme rightist movements that had just begun to emerge in Europe.

"Kokka wa saikō dōtoku nari (The state is ultimate morality)."[39] These are the first words of Uesugi's *A New Thesis on the State* (Kokka Shinron). Written in 1921, the work set forth the theoretical framework of a theory of state that had a profound influence on Shintō ultranationalist thought in the prewar Shōwa period. The idea that the state is ultimate morality was at the heart and the center of Uesugi's theory of state. But what did he mean by asserting that the state was ultimate morality?

Uesugi's theory of state was built on a moral philosophy that rested on his theory of metaphysics. A prerequisite for the knowledge of ultimate morality was the possibility of knowledge of the ultimate nature of being. If we were to deconstruct his theory of being into its constituent elements and discern its special characteristics, we would come up with something like the following. First, in Uesugi's ontology—that is, his theory of the nature and relations of being—being in its totality could not be defined in terms of the self as a complete entity in distinction or differentiation from other selves. It could not be conceived of in its entirety as an entity existing independently of the existence of other selves. The self thus was merely a part of a greater "being as a totality." Being was being only insofar as it formed an organic part of an irreducible aggregate of Beings. To put it another way, the affirmation of the existence of the self, one's own being, was possible only in the recognition of the interdependent existence of the self with other selves as an organic totality.

Second, in Uesugi's ontology, being did not simply denote what might be referred to as static given being. One's individual being, as a constituent element of "being as a totality," had movement. This movement of being related in a cause-and-effect relationship to the movement of other beings in a spatial environment was what Uesugi called man's *sōkan*.[40] Being's movement, however, involved not only this spatial relationship. It also involved this interrelationship with other beings in a spatial totality in time, which he called man's *renzoku*.[41] The movement of being in this spatial-temporal relationship was not generated by the type of dialectic found in Hegel's ontological category of negativity. We do not find in Uesugi's ontology the idea of conflicting forces resolved in a dialectic synthesis. Instead, we find being as becoming being in terms of a continual and never-ending process of development. Each being, as part of "being as a totality" mutually and interdependently developing and perfecting the self in relation to other selves in a definite spatial-temporal matrix, was what Uesugi called *hito no sōkan to renzoku*.[42] The mutual development and perfection of beings in this spatial-temporal matrix was what Uesugi defined as morality.

Uesugi's concept of being was not limited to the physical living self interacting with other living beings, each as part of "being as a totality," in this spatial-temporal totality. It also included "spiritual" beings. That is to say, it included the spirits of those who had come before us as our ancestors and those who would come after us as our descendants. According to this logic, all of the people and events from the origins of the state exist at this very moment. In short, what Uesugi imagined was a community of moral beings, both physical and spiritual, which as an aggregate made up being in its totality, harmoniously striving for perfection.

Third, this perfection, or the object of being's becoming, was what he called man's "essential being (*honsei*)."[43] Man's essential being constituted the real being, which inherently contained in it a moral nature that was to be perfected. It was the purpose of moral man to work toward a moral end. Thus, Uesugi's conception of being rested also on a teleological thinking as well as the union of being and morality in an imagined metaphysical order. That is to say, the essence of man's being constituted at the same time the end or goal of being itself. The supreme goal of morality accordingly was this: realize your own essential being, which at the same time, of course, was your innate nature. This teleological conception of essential being was therefore the basis of the essential unity of being and ultimate morality.

The full realization of being's essential nature was the goal of man's being. The closer one progressed to one's essential being, the closer one came to the fulfillment of being and the closer to ultimate morality. It was the motivation for action and the ultimate purpose of existence. The problem was to determine which actions correspond to man's essential being. Uesugi's ontology presupposed that man's being is essentially social and that man's Being is perfected in society. This society of beings interacting in an organic totality leading toward essential being was what constituted the state. In other words, state and society were theoretically identical. Therefore, being reached its fulfillment only in the state; the ideal of man could be perfected only in the state. Man was a part of state, just as the state was a part of man. Uesugi, echoing Aristotle's dictum that "man is a political animal," stated that "man is a statist animal."[44] The state is what leads man to his ideal that originated in his essential being: "If there were no state, one could not develop and perfect one's essential being."[45] The ideal state was, of course, the state of ultimate morality.

The state of ultimate morality would encompass the totality of man's life and embrace it in its entirety.

Uesugi's metaphysics of being was very much a theory of holism—a philosophical theory in which the determining factors in nature are wholes (as organisms), which are irreducible to the sum of their parts; the history of the universe was a history of the activity and perfecting of those wholes. States were like organisms that developed and responded to laws of organic functional relationships between parts and wholes. This holistic theory was a state theory that denied that the state was a logical construction of the sum total of individual people who made up the state.

Uesugi denounced the idea that the society could be disconnected from the state. He observed that the problem with China, to which he had traveled and that had disintegrated after the failure of the republican revolution in 1911, was that the concept of society was separate from the concept of state: "Probably the most striking thing about present-day China is the separation of state and society. It is in a situation where there is almost all society and no state."[46] But in Uesugi's understanding of Chinese political thought, Chinese society and culture would continue intact even without the state because the family, not the state, was at the core of society. Uesugi noted that the Japanese, in contrast to the Chinese, had never conceptualized Japanese society and the Japanese state as separate entities. When a Japanese spoke of Japan, he spoke of one state, one society, and one ethnic group.

A key concept Uesugi used to clarify the nature of the Japanese state was "organizational will (*taisei ishi*)."[47] This organizational will was the source of state cohesion and national solidarity. It was the will that organized each individual into the state. It was a mode of thought, a consciousness of what one should do and not do. However, this organizational will was not the will of each individual; nor was it the sum total of all wills. It was the will existing in an irreducible totality, the will of one power. But it was also inherent in the essential being of the individual as well as in the founding of the state. Organizational will included man's sōkan and renzoku, that spatial-temporal matrix of social solidarity and man's essential being, that inner force drawing man to his perfection. Organizational will was a moral force, since sōkan and renzoku constituted moral bonds and essential being a teleological moral vision. Organizational will was the moral force that drove man to cooperate with his fellow man, to continuously progress and develop, to strive to moral perfection. In this metaphysical conception of being, where the

individual being was an organ of "being in its totality," the moral development of the self automatically translated into the moral development of
all the other selves in the totality of the state.

What constituted moral action corresponding to man's essential being
was that which contributed to the collective "being as a totality." The
result was the elimination of contradictions between the individual self
and all other selves. Thus, sacrifice of the self for the good of "being as a
totality" was not really sacrifice in the sense of giving up something in
order to attain something else, but it was tantamount to the realization of
one's own essential being.

Ultimately, the emperor was the source of organizational will. He
alone possessed the ideal and perfect qualifications for the embodiment
of the organizational will. The emperor was the state; the emperor's will
was the organizational will in man's spatial-temporal matrix. To obey the
emperor's will was the highest realization of the self, the realization of
one's "essential being." To absorb the self into the emperor, to become a
part of the emperor, was to accomplish man's essential being. In other
words, organizational will was the emperor, man's essential being, ultimate morality. This was the special characteristic of the Japanese state,
the essence of the kokutai.

Opposed to Uesugi's emperor-centered organic organizational theory
of state was a conception of the state built on what he called "mechanistic organization (kikaiteki soshiki)."[48] The mechanistic organizational
theory of the state rested on a metaphysics that perceived the individual
as a self-sufficient and complete entity in itself. He charged that from this
mechanistic theory of state organization, individuals were isolated from
each other and from the whole and that this was the source of aggressive
selfishness and vanity, personal advantage seeking at the expense of the
state at large. It was a theory of organization in which the whole of
society was sacrificed to the personal profit of a part of the whole in some
form or another. It was a theory created by those who assumed that
conflict was at the basis of society. And it was a theory in which the very
spiritual root of sociality was denied and thus contradicted the whole
meaning of human nature. It was a theory of organization that contradicted the belief that man had a natural inclination toward mutual help
and cooperation.

Uesugi attacked the mechanistic theory of organization as a theory of
social Darwinism, the "struggle for existence" that Darwin had found in
nature, applied to man's social life, as well. According to social Darwinism, man, too, was engaged in a constant struggle against his fellow men

from which only the fittest emerged victorious. It was a theory in which free economic competition, laissez-faire at its most extreme, performed the same function in society that natural selection performed in nature. For Uesugi, social conflict was artificial and transitory, while social harmony was the natural condition of man. It is noteworthy that in connection with his criticism of the mechanistic theory of organization Uesugi chastised Katō Hiroyuki and even his own teacher Hozumi Yatsuka for incorporating ideas of social Darwinism into their state theories. According to Uesugi, social Darwinism, a Western concept introduced into Japan in Meiji times, was not consistent with Japanese tradition in which social organization was based on mutual cooperation.

Uesugi did not reject all Western political ideology and was much in debt to anarchism for his idea that society was based on social harmony and mutual cooperation. His idea of man's sōkan and renzoku was very similar to the anarchist idea that society should be run by means of a network of voluntary agreements among individuals and groups associating freely on the basis of equality. What Uesugi objected to was the anarchist claim that the society they sought to create was completely different from the state in that it did not recognize voluntary authority.

Uesugi maintained that a union of people could not be accomplished without authority, and he urged anarchists to rethink their idea that the fundamental source of state cohesiveness or state unity was coercive power. He charged that anarchists (and socialists) placed too much emphasis on the state as a mere pseudonym for power and oppression. The anarchists, he thought, represented an extreme solution in reaction to another extreme. On one side was the idea of state based on power alone; Hobbes's theory of the state would be an example of this. Uesugi totally rejected such ideas, which denied that man had any inclination toward mutual help and love. The other extreme was the anarchist idea that a union or association can be made on the basis of feelings or emotions without authority. He claimed that the extreme radical ideologies of anarchism in Western civilization grew out of disgust with the theories of state based on profit alone or theories of state that saw the state as an instrument of the struggle over survival. He argued that the Japanese had never been under the notion that the Japanese state, formed in ancient times and continuing to exist in the same form in the present, was based on physical force. Uesugi claimed that in ancient times the Japanese had never felt oppressed. And even when the military aristocracy had control of government in the feudal period, when there was admittedly extensive oppression, the Japanese people did not feel that it was the state—that is, the emperor—that was the oppressor. In other words, even if the Japanese had experienced oppression in the feudal period, which he willingly acknowledged, the problem was not the state per se. Rather, it was a perversion of the true concept of state, which was a part of man's essential being.

He charged that anarchism was unthinkable for most Japanese. In the state of sōkan and renzoku, there was undeniable authority, but it was only moral authority under the founding gods of the nation. It was for this reason that he felt there could never be a serious anarchist movement in Japan. He claimed that anarchism was only a scheme to deny the existing Western state; it was not a universal theory that denied or rejected all states and certainly not the Japanese state. The anarchist discourse should therefore be shifted from the question of whether or not a state can exist without force or authority to the question of under what kind of authority it should exist. Uesugi argued that the kind of authority he was talking about in the state was moral authority, which, in his mind, was the authority based on man's essential being. Uesugi's state of mutual aid and mutual cooperation was precisely what the anarchists denied was a state. In short, Uesugi's state was very much like what the anarchists wanted but denied was a state in their definition.

Uesugi was heavily indebted to the thought of the Russian anarchist Peter Kropotkin for this idea that the true character of man was not the struggle for existence but mutual cooperation. In *Mutual Aid: A Factor in Evolution*, Kropotkin made one of the most persuasive arguments against social Darwinism, maintaining that cooperation was an even more powerful factor in life than struggle and best ensured the survival of the species.

The emergence of anarchism in Western civilization signified for Uesugi a revolt against Western theories of the state that were based on the mechanistic organizational principle of society. From this principle, institutions and practices were designed to benefit parts of the whole at the expense of the whole, to allow the preponderance of private interests, and to permit individuals to endeavor for commercial profit and gain, devoting themselves to thinking of the community only for their own, individual advantage. By contrast, in the Japanese state of sōkan and renzoku, all people constituted one body in which no one in society had any advantage over another. It ensured that one sector of the whole would not benefit at the expense of all. The problem with Western state theories was that they made the profit of a certain class of people the only source of solidarity. Uesugi charged that even the modern nation-state was not a state in which the people were united as one, let alone a state in which they were continuously striving to create the state of ultimate morality.

Starting from the position that the state is made up of the sum total of its individuals, Western state theorists and political thinkers defined the state in a most mechanistic fashion: a fixed majority of people on a fixed landmass that was united and ruled over by a fixed sovereign power. Uesugi charged that this was just a formalistic definition and that, by such a definition, one could not understand the true nature of the state. This mechanistic view of state born out of the European Enlightenment did not say anything about the type of people in the state, the real relationship between the sovereign power and the people, or, in the case of Japan, the deep emotion and affectionate attachment Japanese felt toward their state. Uesugi was concerned that the Japanese were being educated in a mistaken understanding of the state because textbooks had been replete with mechanistic Western definitions that had defined the Japanese state for the past fifty years or so, since the introduction of Western learning in the Meiji period. Uesugi admitted that he, too, was guilty of using mechanistic Western theories of the state to define the Japanese state for over a decade at Tokyo Imperial University.

To deny that an authoritarian structural relationship was at the political core of the Japanese state, Uesugi devoted a chapter to clarifying the nature of politics. For him, politics was non-rule. He charged that no one should use the state to permit the rule of others. The fundamental source of national solidarity was essential being. The purpose of politics was to develop and perfect man's moral nature, man's essential being, and, unlike in the West, Japanese politics was not based on power relationships. Neither did the motivation of politics lie in the private benefit of individuals. Uesugi tried to channel the political energies of the masses into a non-Western political mode. It was not that he objected to the involvement of the masses in the affairs of the state. He certainly favored this. In fact, he claimed that it was the moral duty of the individual to actively serve the emperor, giving him advice on matters pertaining to the affairs of state. He charged that the "responsibility of serving the emperor by giving him advice on matters pertaining to the affairs of state does not rest solely on the ministers of state."[49] It was the responsibility of all subjects to assist the emperor. This idea of service to the emperor was the ideal behind the Constitution of the Empire of Japan. In other words, the constitution had broadened the way for the subjects to assist imperial rule.

Finally, following Hozumi, Uesugi posited that the Japanese state was an "ethnic nation-state (*minzoku kokka*),"[50] a concept that maintained that the state and the ethnic or völkisch group should be identical. In general, the völkisch state was also the only natural state. He defended this idea of the völkisch state on the grounds that people everywhere—in Eastern civilization and Western civilization and from ancient times to the present—tried to form a state based on ethnicity, even if there were truly no pure ethnic states. Thus, even if the term "ethnic nation-state" was of recent origin, it was actually not peculiar to the modern period. In general, the state takes ethnicity as the basis of its ideal. The nation-state should be an ethnic group where those related by ancestry and blood share a feeling and sentiment of their own identity. He also suggested that the members of the völkisch state must be consciously aware that they are of one ethnic group and have the desire to maintain that ethnic unity. Uesugi noted that among the various states in the world, the Japanese state was the most ethnically pure, and that the Japanese should unite on the conscious conviction that they are fellow countrymen, brothers and sisters united in the feeling of love and attachment. This was why their ancestors established the state (*kokka*); it was the reason why it should be maintained, and why it should be handed down to their descendants. Uesugi claimed that only in the völkisch state could one develop and perfect oneself and realize his essential being. Consequently, ethnic purity was also inextricably linked to his theory of ultimate morality. The Japanese state, consisting of ethnic Japanese, constituted one body under the rule of the emperor. Other criteria of the state—the size of the territory, land features such as mountains, customs, religion, industrial production—did not constitute a basis on which to establish the value of the state.

Western History through the Eyes of a Radical Shintō Ultranationalist

For Uesugi Shinkichi, the history of human civilization was a journey in nation-state building. The whole of human history was a process through which mankind had been making moral progress, which was a process of state building. In other words, he viewed history as a march toward a moral perfection that could be achieved only through a process of state building, because he could not imagine man's existence outside the state. Indeed, he saw man as a subject of history acting only through the state. Individuals, as we have seen in his theory of the metaphysics of being, were really parts of a greater "state being."

In this march toward moral perfection, the Japanese state was superior to all other states. It alone sought and had the inner capacity to attain the ultimate morality. It alone could achieve the total unity of the people, and Uesugi believed that this could be achieved only by the Japanese state because it alone was governed by the emperor, a "god incarnate" or "a god made manifest as man (*ara[hito]gami*)."[51] According to this doctrine, the emperor was the perfect being. In the emperor, there is no distinction between man's existential being and his essential being, man's existence and his essence. The emperor is the essential being, the ultimate norm, the ultimate morality. In man's essential being dwells the emperor, for man was made in the likeness of the emperor, for all beings were descendants of Amaterasu Ōmikami. As superior being, the emperor was also the goal of all created beings. The emperor was the final activity toward which all Japanese must work. In short, much like God is to man in Christian theology, the emperor was the glory of all creation. The state was called into existence by the will of Amaterasu Ōmikami, who was at the origin of the Japanese state and who was also the final end to which all activities of the Japanese state were directed. In many ways, Uesugi was very much like Hegel, for Hegel also glorified the state as "the march of God in the world," as a developing natural organism whose own worth transcended the separate interests of its members, who in fulfilling their duty to the state achieved moral purpose and freedom.

Derived from the doctrine of the emperor as god, only the emperor, as the embodiment of ultimate morality, could rule with absolute fairness and impartiality, totally disinterested in any personal profit or consideration. By contrast, the human Western king or emperor or elected head of state could not rule with this total impartiality and represent the will of the people entirely. He could only hope to express the will of the majority of the people. The Japanese state was able to do precisely what no Western state could claim: rule with a total impartiality that expressed the will of *all* the people.

Uesugi urged his countrymen to abandon all attempts to Westernize the Japanese state. In Uesugi's mind, those who sought to do so were not only totally misguided; they posed a threat to the very existence of the Japanese state. He sought to convince especially his already semi-secularized countrymen that the tradition of state building in the West had been a wrenching experience, and that it was the West, not the Japanese, that could not form a stable cohesive state. He argued that if one closely examined the history of state building in the West, one would find that the value placed on the state had always been weak and that to the present day the national cohesion of Western states continued to lag far behind that of the Japanese state. This lack of national cohesion was the source of the problems besetting Western state building.

Uesugi expanded on this view in part 2 of *A New Thesis on the State*, taking the reader on a journey through the history of Western thought, expounding on what he called the "anguish" of the state-building process in the West.[52] Uesugi attributed the problems of the Western state to the predominance of anti-statist thought in the intellectual tradition of the West—namely, that of Christianity and the Enlightenment. He charged that these religious and ideological constructions had placed a low value on the state and that, in consequence, the moral value of the state was not considered in the major Western ideologies and thought systems. He argued that the concept of the state itself did not emerge as a central sociocultural concept within the Western intellectual tradition, that it did not have cultural significance, and furthermore that the state was considered useful only as a means to achieve some other end that had nothing to do with the state itself. The state was usually portrayed as a means to enrich one group or sector of society at the expense of the rest of the society. Consequently, Western thought in general held a highly restrictive view of the state, considering it, for instance, as a system of legal norms. The philosophical concept of the state in the West was largely associated with specific institutions and bureaucratic structures and rarely went beyond them to include religious or cultural significance.

The source of the problem of most Western state theory was that it tended to emphasize a struggle between state and society. In other words, the central problem of Western state building was that the concept of state was separated from the concept of society. This meant that society, made up of the people who were interacting on the basis of shared beliefs, values, customs, and activities, was not dependent on the state. It was a type of thought that implied that society could exist without the state, while the state, of course, could not exist without society. Being associated with only material interests, effectively disassociating it from the moral idea, the Western state was condemned to continuous internal conflict and instability. In the worst scenario, it meant the destruction of the state altogether, as proposed by those who advocated anarchism.

Nevertheless, Uesugi saw the Greek tradition as a great bright spot in Western civilization. The Greeks were the first to recognize the state as the sphere of morality, as the sphere in which all virtue could be realized. According to Plato, man could realize his ethical ideal in the polis, which was the great pedagogue of man whose function was to bring men to morality and justice. Uesugi paid homage to the Greek concept of the state by admitting that he, too, was a student of Plato.

Moving on to survey the Roman tradition, he noted that the Romans at first valued the state highly, but with the rise of Christianity the value of the state in the minds of the people fell to its lowest depths. In Uesugi's opinion, Christianity was the first great anti-statist movement in the West. It made light of the state: it sought to save humanity, not the state. The Christian ideal was outside the state, instead seeking a community for the whole human race. Nevertheless, he did acknowledge that St. Augustine of Hippo (354–430) was a great philosopher, a man who saw a divine plan for human history, interpreting it not in economic or political terms but in moral terms. The collapse of the Roman Empire led to the rise of feudalism in the West, one thousand years of darkness in terms of state building. Uesugi argued that from the feudal period up to the rise of the modern nation-state, mainstream European state theory passed through several stages, each one corresponding to a fundamental change in economic activity. The first stage was the age of monarchism. In this age, the state was considered the private property of one person, the monarch, and the state existed for the ruler's private profit. But ultimately, a revolt occurred against the idea of the state existing for the profit of one person, and the feudal monarch was transformed into an absolute monarch. This revolt led to the idea of the Divine Right of Kings—the idea that the king's rule was based on the will of God. But what this really did, according to Uesugi, was merely make the profit of the king God's will. In areas that had a strong aristocracy, it gradually removed power from the monarch, but what that process involved was merely to extend the profit of the state to include a few more people instead of just the ruler.

In the feudal period, culture was in the hands of the Christian church rather than the feudal state. Therefore, little value was given to the state. However, it was also during this period that the seeds of the German conception of state were planted. Uesugi cited a very diverse group of intellectuals who were concerned with the moral quality of politics. One of them was Dante Alighieri (1265–1321). Dante, of course, was not just a poet but also a man deeply immersed in the politics of his age, writing his great political essay *On Monarchy*. Other intellectuals around this time who also gave importance to the state were the Florentine political theorist Niccolo Machiavelli (1469–1532), author of *The Prince*, and Sir Thomas More (1478–1535). Although Machiavelli effectively advocated an amoral state, one whose goal was to perfect the exercise of power, More's *Utopia* depicted an ideal commonwealth whose citizens were honored not for their wealth or ancestry but for their service to the state. Each of these thinkers in his own way made an important contribution to state building in the West. But from Uesugi's perspective, the major event that contributed to state building was the Protestant Reformation, which he interpreted as a revolt against Catholicism's "making light" of the state and ethnic identity in Western history.

Despite early contributors to state building in the West by such thinkers, state building suffered again as a result of the next wave of anti-statist philosophy: the Enlightenment. This marked the next great stage in European history. Uesugi interpreted the individualism in this era as a reaction against the medieval state. Nevertheless, central to Enlightenment thought was the idea that the state was the source of oppression and inequality. Therefore, Enlightenment thinkers tried to limit the power of the state, although some may have supported enlightened absolute states as the only means to effect substantive social change. They championed the concept of "natural law" that transcended the laws of the state, thereby separating man from the spirit of the state. In this sense, natural-law theory was a continuation of Christian values in secular form. The state was seen as useful only insofar as it could guarantee the freedom of individuals. But in eighteenth-century ideology, these individuals usually were the wealthy people, the bourgeoisie, who saw the state in terms of its usefulness for making profit. They wanted to be as free as possible from state control to pursue their own economic activities, a fundamental notion behind laissez-faire economic theory.

From the Enlightenment, however, came the idea of the nation-state. This constituted a giant step forward in Western state building. Absolutism collapsed in England with the so-called Glorious Revolution of 1688, but the French Revolution was the great event in the history of state building in the West. The basis of the modern nation-state was the involvement of the masses in politics when the people as a whole were politicized. According to Uesugi, however, the parliament or national assembly did not actually represent the people as a whole. These institutions were part of a process designed by the bourgeoisie to protect its privileges against all other classes.

Uesugi believed that one positive outcome of the Enlightenment and the French Revolution was that they generated a reaction that led to the

Romantic movement in the first half of the nineteenth century. The Romantic movement incited a feeling of affection for the state and ethnicity, and Uesugi noted Hegel's contribution to state building. However, despite Romanticism's emotional appeal, in the latter half of the nineteenth century the movement declined in its importance to state building. Materialism again established dominance, as Westerners began to think of the state in terms of profit. But late-nineteenth-century materialism took a different form. This time, no one class was to receive special benefit. The newly emerged but powerful socialist movement demanded common ownership of property, and the state was to be used for the profit of all the people. In trying to realize socialism through the state, the workers either had to take control of the government or, at least, participate in government with the bourgeoisie, the former resulting in communism and the latter in social democracy. Uesugi noted that the social democrats in the West called for universal suffrage to put labor at the center of government while in Japan they wanted socialism to create national unity.

In short, Uesugi's brief sketch of Western intellectual history in terms of the value of the state did contain some simple truths, and the message to his Japanese readers was clear: Western state theories were based on the fundamental notion of personal profit seeking, whether it be the profit of one, as in the case of monarchy; the profit of the few, as in the case of aristocracy; the profit of many, as in the case of liberal democracy; or the profit of all, as in the case of socialism. In all cases, he insisted, people sought to use the state as a means to enhance their own ends. This type of thinking was the result of considering the state a mechanistic material entity. The state was merely a means for other ultimate ends.

As Uesugi perceived it, the source of the problem was this conception of the separation of the state from the society. Looking at the history of Western state building, the worth of the state was weak because it did not extend to the social totality. In the Middle Ages, the Christian church, the basis of culture and society, was outside the state. With the rise of the liberal theories of the Enlightenment, the second great wave of anti-statist thought, society took priority over the state again. In theory, society was to be a self-regulating sphere. Liberal economic theory said that economic production should be carried on outside the sphere of the state, and when the state was given importance by intellectuals, it was seen in terms of power and oppression. As a result, the history of state building in the West was a history of "anguish." According to Uesugi, such a grim outlook on the state ultimately led to the rejection of the state itself: anarchism. The anarchist movement was a result of disappointment with the state; its solution was to destroy the state.

Uesugi nevertheless was fascinated by anarchism. While he saw it as the ultimate manifestation of "anguish" with state building in the West, he also saw it as a fundamental rethinking of the state. In other words, anarchism had a positive side: it got to the heart of the problem of state building in the West by rekindling a fundamental rethinking about the ideal state. In fact, Uesugi called anarchism one of the most important theories of the ideal state that had come out of Western thought. He believed that anarchism attacked the evils of the existing Western state, but it did not reject all human organization. Anarchists aimed to establish a stateless society in which harmony was maintained by voluntary agreements among individuals and groups. Society was to be run by means of networks of agreements among individuals and groups associating on the basis of freedom and equality.

Uesugi was particularly interested in the thought of the Russian anarchist Peter Kropotkin. What attracted Uesugi was Kropotkin's idea that man's original nature was good and that man progressed on the basis of mutual cooperation. Although the new society that anarchists hoped to create was something they claimed was completely different from existing Western states, their ideas of the ideal society were in fact very close to Uesugi's concept of sōkan and renzoku. The only difference, of course, was that Uesugi called such an ideal society a state while the anarchists did not.

Uesugi did, however, see a change in the history of state building in the West during his own lifetime. The historical significance of the Great War in terms of state building was that it led to a revolt against prewar materialism. The Great War frightened the world, but for good or for bad, the process of state building was greatly enhanced by it. During the war, nationalism reached its highest peak. The feeling of love of country burned in the hearts of people around the world. Extreme patriotism flourished, and nationalism became spiritual and romantic. The state developed and its powers expanded during the war because cooperation of all people in support of the war was the main preoccupation of governments attempting to conduct the largest, most costly war in human history. Uesugi maintained that if there had been no mobilization of the masses, this Great War could not have been carried out. But the horrors of war and the staggering loss of life also produced confusion in the hearts and minds of some people, which Uesugi believed sent some nations, such as Russia, on a mistaken historical course. Still more, the Great War made other people turn to internationalism, calling for an end to, or the regulation of, the nation-state by a supranational body.

It is worth noting here that Uesugi did not only criticize state building in the West. He also made disparaging comments about China, alleging that traditional Chinese thought likewise had separated the conception of society from that of the state. Noting again that although society can exist without the state, the state cannot exist without society, he claimed that China was almost all society and no state. Further, he pointed out that in traditional Chinese thought, society was always the main concern, while the state was of secondary importance. He did, however, give some praise to Confucius for seeking to make morality the central aim of the state. But he condemned Mencius's theory to justify revolution, saying that it stirred the hearts of the people against the state and that it was no different from Western revolutionary theories. Taoist thought despised the state, and Buddhism was fundamentally an anti-statist religion.

In contrast to the mainstream thought in the Western and Asian traditions, Uesugi continued to argue that the Japanese never seriously entertained the notion that Japanese society was separate from the Japanese state. State and society were inseparable. Indeed, in Japan, state, society, and ethnicity were identical. Politics, economics, religion, art, and learning were all in the sphere of the state. The Japanese state was one spiritual, organic, and moral union. Reflecting on the two thousand five hundred years of Japanese state history, Uesugi noted that it had passed though several periods. In ancient times, there was a direct relationship between the emperor and the people. With the passing of time, however, people emerged who obstructed this intimate relationship. They privatized the land and the people. In the Middle Ages, military aristocrats took power and turned their backs on the emperor, defying the emperor's way and privatizing land and control of people. All people suffered under the Shōguns, and they abandoned the founding ideal of the nation. The Meiji Restoration, however, represented a great event in the history of Japanese state building that restored the original relationship between the people and the emperor. But Uesugi insisted that these changes in the process of continual state building in Japan were merely reforms, not revolutions, so there were no major upheavals like those found in Western history. Thus, in theory the Japanese state has been ruled under the unbroken line of emperors descended from Amaterasu Ōmikami from the founding of the state to the present.

The promulgation of the Constitution of the Empire of Japan on February 11, 1889, was an important event in modern Japanese history. Uesugi regarded the constitution as a sacred text. He called it and the Imperial Rescript on Education the "two great canons" of the state.[53] These state documents were sacred to Uesugi not because of their inherent content, but solely because they were the words of the emperor. Uesugi regarded the constitution as the will of the emperor, conveniently forgetting that it had been drawn up in secret by Itō Hirobumi and his colleagues and his German adviser on constitutional law, Hermann Roessler. And for Uesugi, "The will of the emperor is absolute, and the standard of behavior of Japanese subjects depends solely on his will."[54]

In the essay "The Primary Intent in Establishing the Constitution" (1915), Uesugi stated that the constitution was established to mobilize all power in the nation to actively assist the sovereign emperor in pursuing the essence of the state.[55] But the essence of the state was the will of the emperor, which, of course, was identical to the pursuit of ultimate morality. Stressing the importance of Article 4 of the constitution, which states, "The Emperor is the head of the Empire, combining in Himself the rights of sovereignty, and exercises them, according to the provisions of the present Constitution," Uesugi declared that "the emperor is the sovereign of our Japanese empire."[56]

This simple statement had great meaning for Uesugi, who bluntly asked, "What is sovereignty?"[57] For him, sovereignty was more that just the location of ultimate power or authority in the state. The rule of the sovereign existed to fulfill the ethical purpose of the state. In other words, the state and the emperor had a mission to expand and perfect the good and the moral to the "total of human society (*ningen shakai zentai*)" throughout "the entire universe (*uchū zentai*)."[58] In other words, according to Uesugi's emperor ideology, the Japanese state had the right—indeed, the moral duty—to spread emperor ideology and imperial rule on a global scale. This was the goal of the "our imperial ancestors (*kōso kōsō*)."[59]

Uesugi believed that the function of the parliament was "to approve this great aim of the emperor."[60] Furthermore, he actively sought to use the politicized masses to support the emperor. Unlike Hozumi Yatsuka, who had an instinctive mistrust of the masses, Uesugi tried to incorporate them into his Shintō ultranationalist ideology. Terribly frustrating for Uesugi, however, was Minobe's constitutional theory that the state, rather than the emperor, was sovereign. He attacked Minobe and his emperor-as-organ theory of the state in the essay "Kokutai ni kansuru

Isetsu (A Different Theory of the Kokutai)," but, simply put, Uesugi thought Minobe's organ theory was heretical. From his perspective, the Constitution of the Empire of Japan was designed to ensure unlimited state power to be exercised by the emperor for unlimited expansionism on a global scale.

Totalitarian Ideology

In the late Meiji period, Hozumi had worked out an "orthodox" ideology of State Shintō in support of absolute monarchy. It was a state ideology in which the subject was a kind of political child personally subordinated to the paternal emperor. The family was the model for describing most political and social relationships, not only between the emperor and his subjects, but also between all superiors and subordinates throughout the whole society. In other words, personal dependent relationships constituted the ligaments that held the state together and made it work. It was a state in which the masses were not supposed to be involved in politics.

Despite Hozumi's efforts to keep the masses depoliticized, a decade or so later this task proved impossible. The traditional bonds of society were loosening, and the patriarchal construction of society was breaking down as people became politically active. Uesugi, who was aware of this, had constructed his theory of the state on the assumption that the masses had already become politicized and that no force could hold back this process. He could see that the people, through their actions in the streets, were willing and able to take matters into their own hands. For that reason, he formulated a state theory based on very different sorts of human relationships from that of patriarchy. His theory of sōkan and renzoku, man's relationship in a spatial-temporal matrix, linked people with one another in a horizontal social structure, not in a vertical patriarchal structure. People were linked by new bonds of mutual cooperation and affection, respect and consent. Uesugi was a revolutionary in this respect; in effect, he sought the reconstruction of the basic social relationships of society.

Nevertheless, Uesugi seemed to have had the same fundamental aim of Hozumi: the neutralization of the masses. He sought to do this by displacing politics with morality, the political state with a moral state. He sought to ensure that the masses were no longer political in the sense of representing different sorts of interests in society and different ideas of how the state ought to be managed. He sought to channel the politicized masses into one mold. Ultimately, the goal of Uesugi's *A New Thesis on the State* was to displace power politics with absolute morality.

As this analysis of Uesugi's state theory shows, an important transformation had taken place in the Shintō ultranationalist ideology between the Meiji period and the Taishō period. Uesugi's idea of the Japanese state as an undifferentiated mass of people interacting in a spatial-temporal matrix in pursuit of ultimate morality represented a fundamental transformation of State Shintō ideology. First, since all subjects were placed in a condition of equality under the emperor, Uesugi had displaced the traditional patriarchal bonds of society that had been central to Hozumi's theory of absolute monarchy. By breaking the individual's consciousness of traditional patriarchal bonds, Uesugi in effect sought to create a mass society encompassed by the emperor.

It is misleading to claim, as Maruyama Masao and others did, that the patriarchal family system was a central feature of Japanese "fascism" that distinguished it from German Nazism or Italian Fascism. The idea of the Japanese state as an extension of the primary family group had been official state ideology from the beginning of the Meiji period, and it was certainly integral to Hozumi's state theory, but this was not a period of fascist thought. On the contrary, the development of the intellectual structure of Shintō ultranationalist ideology from the Meiji period to the Taishō and Shōwa periods points to a *rejection of the family principle as a fundamental component of State Shintō ideology*. We find in the evolution of State Shintō ideology from the Meiji period to the Taishō and Shōwa periods a tendency to move beyond the idea of the Japanese state conceptualized as an extension of the family system. Uesugi's metaphysics totally displaced the family principle as a key component of State Shintō ideology. Uesugi clearly understood that the theoretical focus on the family system and family consciousness would actually work against the creation of "mass man" with total devotion to the emperor. When consciousness of the family, man's primary social group, is strengthened, identification of the self and one's own being with the emperor is necessarily weakened. Under Hozumi's patriarchal theory of the state, the emperor was not identical with the self; the emperor remained ultimately something external to the self, thus not achieving absolute control over all spheres of the individual's life. Under Uesugi's state theory, the emperor had become totally internalized. The separation between the emperor and the individual had been closed theoretically. Under Uesugi's state theory, conservative, reactionary, or counter-revolutionary

Shintō ultranationalist ideology had become radical Shintō ultranationalist ideology or totalitarian ideology and militant radical Shintō fundamentalism. The emperor invaded the essence of one's very being, becoming one's consciousness, one's self-identification. From total control over the individual, it sought to embrace everything and everyone in the state and beyond on the road to total domination on a global scale. This is the essence of totalitarianism as posited by Hannah Arendt.[61]

Uesugi's radical Shintō nationalist ideology had a major impact on the Shintō ultranationalist movement in the 1920s and the 1930s. I suggest that it was Uesugi, not Kita, who was a chief inspiration for members of the Imperial Way Faction of the military and other civilian rightists who attempted the coup d'état of February 26, 1936. One must remember that Uesugi's theory of state involved a dynamic process. He sought to organize the masses and set them in a perpetual state of motion in pursuit of the imperial way. In his metaphysics, it was man's moral duty to strive relentlessly to close the gap between existential being and essential being. Seeking actualization of one's essential being became, in effect, the search for total identity with the emperor, which morally justified— indeed, required—the destruction of all existing institutions of government that separated the emperor from the masses. In short, Uesugi's thought was the inspiration for one of the most extreme forms of radical Shintō ultranationalism in prewar Japan.

7

Kakehi Katsuhiko:

The Japanese Emperor State at the Center

of the Shintō Cosmology

Government is true religion. . . . Faith and patriotism are the two great thaumaturges of the world. Both are divine. . . . Once a man divorces himself from the divinity, he corrupts himself and everything he touches. His actions are misguided and end only in destruction. As this powerful binding force weakens in the state, so all conserving virtues weaken in proportion. . . . But once the idea of the divinity is the source of human action, this action is fruitful, creative, and invincible.
— JOSEPH DE MAISTRE, *Study on Sovereignty*, quoted in Jack Livery, *The Works of Joseph de Maistre*, 108–11

"The world," says Dr. Martin Luther, "is ruled by God through a few heroes and pre-eminent persons." The mightiest of these ruling heroes are the princes of intellect, men who without sanction of diplomacy or force of arms, without the constraining power of law and police, exercise a defining and transforming influence upon the thought and feeling of many generations. — HOUSTON STEWART CHAMBERLAIN, *Foundations of the Nineteenth Century*, 3

Constitutional Legal Scholar and Shintō Theologian

Uesugi Shinkichi's imagined political community of an undifferentiated mass of people interacting in a spatial-temporal matrix in pursuit of ultimate morality represented a major ideological rearticulation of Shintō ultranationalist ideology in the post-Meiji period. It was also, perhaps, the most radical form of radical Shintō ultranationalist thought in pre-war Japan. To reiterate, his thought justified terrorism both theoretically and morally, for it made it the individual's duty to eliminate, in the popular refrain of radical Shintō ultranationalists at the time, "wicked advisers, corrupt politicians, capitalists and weak-kneed bureaucrats" who separated the masses from the emperor. Such thinking, in my opinion, was the chief inspiration behind the terrorist actions by radical Shintō ultranationalists in the 1930s.

However, Uesugi's Shintō state theory and the movements it inspired were not the only school of radical Shintō ultranationalist thought to emerge in the first two decades of the twentieth century. Unlike the cases of Italian Fascism and German National Socialism, the prewar Japanese radical Shintō ultranationalist movement was highly politically fractured, and radical Shintō ultranationalists mobilized the masses not through single mass parties but by spreading their ideology through the existing institutions of government and the political parties and through ultranationalist associations and societies. These associations and societies began to proliferate after the end of the First World War. In his pioneering essay "The Ideology and Dynamics of Japanese Fascism," Maruyama Masao pointed out that "the birth of groups related to the Japanese fascist movement suddenly became very prolific from about 1919."[1] The reason for the fractured nature of the ultranationalist movement, I believe, has much to do with the emperor system and the nature of the Japanese social structure. The Japanese emperor was neither Il Duce nor Der Führer. Ironically, the particular individual who actually happens to occupy the position of emperor is largely irrelevant to the strength of the radical Shintō ultranationalist movement. The Japanese emperor was not revered or worshipped because of his personal charisma or his individual accomplishments. Proof of this can be seen by the fact that radical Shintō ultranationalist ideology began to spread throughout the country in the late 1910s and the early 1920s precisely at a time when the Taishō emperor himself became mentally unstable. This became obvious to all when the emperor, at the opening of parliament in 1915, did not read his carefully prepared speech but, instead, rolled it up and, holding it as if it were a telescope, peered intently at the startled and embarrassed members of parliament. Although he was mentally unfit to carry on even such ceremonial functions, this did not lead to the lack of devotion or commitment by the masses to the emperor in any fundamental way. Accordingly, we find rightist societies and associations formed around certain thinkers or leaders who took it upon themselves to promote radical Shintō ultranationalist ideology as they interpreted it.

Nevertheless, in very broad terms, there seem to have been two major strands of radical Shintō ultranationalist ideology. Uesugi's "revolutionary" or "militant" radical Shintō ultranationalism was one of those. However, it was suppressed in the late 1930s by what we might refer to as the "controlled" faction of radical Shintō ultranationalism.[2] The state theory of Kakehi Katsuhiko (1872–1961) probably best represented this strand of radical Shintō ultranationalist thought. The fundamental difference between the "revolutionary" or "militant" radical Shintō ultranationalists such as Uesugi and the "controlled" radical Shintō ultranationalists such as Kakehi had more to do with means than with fundamental or ultimate goals. The former, an extremely utopian ideology, tended to support and encourage terrorism or violent revolution to destroy existing structures and institutions of government that separated the emperor from the masses and to promote unlimited expansionism abroad. Kakehi, however, sought to unite the emperor with the masses through a spiritual revival and religious transformation, accepting at the same time the practical necessity of operating through the existing structures and institutions of government ultimately to obtain direct imperial rule, and then work to spread the emperor's rule throughout the world.

Although virtually unknown in Western scholarly literature on Japanese thought,[3] Kakehi was a towering intellectual figure among prewar radical Shintō ultranationalist state theorists and legal and religious scholars. His works were quoted often as an authority on constitutional matters in the great debates over state and sovereignty in the Taishō and Shōwa periods by both emperor-as-organ state theorists and supporters of the emperor-as-sovereign theory of the state.

Kakehi was born in Nagano Prefecture in 1872. In 1897, he graduated from Tokyo Imperial University's School of Law, where he majored in administrative law under Hozumi Yatsuka and Ichiki Kitokurō, who was then a professor of law and special councilor to the Home Ministry. His academic career began in 1900 when he was appointed to a position as assistant professor in the Faculty of Law at Tokyo Imperial University to teach administrative law, a field he would share with Minobe Tatsukichi. He would go on to have a distinguished career as a scholar. He was promoted to full professor in 1903, and in 1904 he received his doctor of law degree. A man with a broad academic focus, he taught a variety of subjects: principles of law, state law, politics, and constitutional law. In addition to his teaching duties at Tokyo Imperial University, he took on additional teaching responsibilities in the 1910s that included instructing foreign students from China in Japanese state law. He also began teaching in the Law Department of the Naval Academy in 1914. Through his teaching position in the Naval Academy, he had a direct link with the Japanese military.

In addition to a noted career as a legal scholar, Kakehi had a distinguished career as a scholar of the Shintō classics. He was often sought to teach the Shintō "scriptures" to the elite of society. For instance, in the early 1920s he gave lectures for a time on the *Kannagara no Michi* (The Way of the Gods as Such) to Prince Chichibu and to Empress Teimei, Hirohito's mother. Furthermore, he was selected by the government in 1944 to lecture on *The Way of the Gods as Such* to China's last emperor, Xuāntŏng (Pŭ Yi), who served as a figurehead leader of the Japanese-controlled state of Manchukuo. Kakehi was also employed at various times by the government as a consultant on State Shintō affairs. In this capacity, for example, he was a member of the government's Board of Inquiry on the State Shintō shrine system. After his retirement from Tokyo Imperial University, he taught concurrently at the Tokyo University of Commerce, Hōsei University, and Kokugakuin University.

Kakehi was a prolific writer. The publication and re-publication of his writings span almost a century. Among his well-known works are *Kō Shintō Taigi* (The Great Principles of Ancient Shintō; 1912); *Kokka no Kenkyū* (A Study of the State; 1913); *Kokka Gyōsei Hō* (State Administrative Law; 1920); *Kannagara no* Michi (The Way of the Gods as Such; 1926); *Kōkoku Kempō* (The Constitution of the Imperial State; 1935); *Dai Nihon Teikoku Kempō no Konpongi* (Fundamental Principles of the Constitution of the Empire of Great Japan; 1936); *Kōkoku Seishin Kōwa* (Lectures on the Spirit of the Imperial State; 1937); and *Kannagara no Daidō* (The Great Way of the Gods as Such; 1940). He was well versed in Western intellectual history and a recognized expert on traditional Japanese thought. As in the case of Uesugi Shinkichi, the state theory of Kakehi was also heavily influenced by German organic state theories. He acquired his knowledge of German state theory not only from his teacher Hozumi Yatsuka, but also from German mentors with whom he came into personal contact during his independent study in Europe from 1898 to 1903. At the University of Berlin, he became acquainted with Otto Gierke (1841–1921). He also studied philosophy under Wilhelm Dilthey (1833–1911). We are told that he was not only close to Dilthey himself but became intimate with other members of Dilthey's family.

Whatever his contacts were with German theorists, the most significant and lasting characteristic of Kakehi's state theory is that it is inextricably linked to Shintō theology. Kakehi was a Shintō fundamentalist, and he channeled his religious passions into his professional work as a constitutional-law scholar and state theorist. I think one can say that Kakehi was a theologian, a state theorist, and a constitutional-law scholar all wrapped up into one. Accordingly, one finds in his state thought the total integration of a Shintō worldview and the Japanese state.

My interpretation of Kakehi's state theory in this study comes primarily from a reading of *Kokka no Kenkyū* (A Study of the State), a work first published in 1913. This text, which is nearly five hundred pages long, is a collection of essays, articles, speeches, and other writings by Kakehi on the state in the early Taishō period, although a few of the articles date back to the last few years of the Meiji period. In other words, Kakehi emerged as a radical Shintō ultranationalist thinker in the early 1910s, just a decade or so after the publication of Hozumi Yatsuka's *National Education: Patriotism*. How can we account for this rapid shift from a conservative or counter-revolutionary form of Shintō ultranationalism such as that seen through Hozumi Yatsuka's thought and the radical Shintō ultranationalist thought just a decade later? The answer is that radical Shintō ultranationalism, or what Breuilly called radical-right nationalism (fascism), emerged politically out of the breakdown of a quasi-democratic, quasi-theocratic Meiji political system and, more important, out of the need to recruit and control the masses, who were rapidly becoming highly politicized. Breuilly stated, "Fascism comes into its own at times of intense popular involvement in politics and the breakdown of established political parties."[4] As this study has already argued, Hozumi's and Minobe's state theories emerged in response to the problems of politics under the Constitution of the Empire of Japan. However, by the middle of the first decade of the twentieth century, the problems and protests of the masses could no longer be ignored. As Andrew Gordon noted, a profound transformation of Japanese society had begun to occur around 1905. This transformation, according to Gordon, "was not limited to politicians, intellectuals, journalists, and the urban bourgeoisie. The process that generated imperial democracy touched the lives and drew upon the energies of common people throughout the nation."[5] Gordon's thesis is that the Taishō democracy period, coinciding with the emergence of the masses, began in 1905, six years before the Emperor Meiji died, and lasted until 1932: "The 1905 Hibiya riot inaugurated the 'era of popular violence.' "[6] He further stated: "The events of September 1905 were indeed the first time that the crowd acted as a political force."[7] Much the same argument can be used in terms of this study of prewar Japanese ideology. Ideologically, the Taishō period can be said to have started in 1905. In other words, radical-right nationalist (fascist) ideology appeared in Japan several years before World War One, which may have been earlier than in Europe.[8] Suzuki Sadami has noted that Kakehi felt that the spiritual foundations underpinning the Japanese nation began to crumble after the Japan–Russia War of 1904–1905.[9] In response to this, Kakehi wrote *The Great Principles of Ancient Shintō* in 1912, following the death of Emperor Meiji. Kakehi was concerned about what he had perceived as a weakening or an erosion of the bonds uniting the emperor and the Japanese people. In other words, as with Uesugi Shinkichi, Kakehi was conscious of the fact that a new era was about to begin and was deeply troubled with the uncertainty regarding Meiji formulations of the Japanese state and the future direction of the Japanese people. Kakehi urged the Japanese to return to the core religious belief of ancient Shintō. In connection with these concerns, it is instructive to note that Kakehi had been opposed to the position taken by the framers of the Constitution of the Empire of Japan and other Meiji leaders that State Shintō was not a religion, a topic to be discussed further.

Kakehi's radical Shintō ultranationalist ideology subsequently made inroads among the Japanese political and academic elite, as well as with the Imperial Court, throughout the 1920s. For example, as Suzuki noted, "Kakehi Katsuhiko, a close confidant of Empress Teimei, in November 1926 lectured to Crown Prince Hirohito, who had been serving as regent for the sickly and weakly Emperor [Taishō] since 1921. These lectures were published (1926) by the Bureau of Shrines, Ministry of the Interior, [in] the *Kannagara no Michi*, and, in the following month, [the contents of] the *Kannagara no Michi* were incorporated into the imperial edicts [issued on the occasion of] the Shōwa Emperor's coronation ceremony."[10] Hirohito, of course, would become emperor just one month later upon the death of his father, the Taishō emperor, on December 25. Suzuki went on to note that Kakehi's ideas spread in the 1920s among those connected with Shrine Shintō, who were enlivened by his political theology. Armed with Kakehi's State Shintō theology as a kind of universal religion, the Shintō Shrine movement was also energized and began to expand not only within the "Japanese area (*naichi*)," but outside the

Japanese area (*gaichi*), as well. Particularly noticeable was the building of Shintō shrines in Korea.

As further indication of Kakehi's influence on Japanese ultranationalists, ideologues such as Ōkawa Shūmei highly respected Kakehi and were very familiar with his writings. Suzuki also noted that Kakehi's ideas, such as the "great life of the ethnic-nation (*minzoku no daiseimei*)" and his *kami* spiritualism (*kamigakatta seishinshūgi*) served as the pillar of the ideology of a clique of army officers identified with the Imperial Way Faction. Suzuki noted that "the Imperial Way Movement was suppressed by the February 26, 1936 Incident, but the ideology of Kakehi Katsuhiko was then swallowed up by the Control Faction (*Tōseiha*)."[11]

The purpose of this chapter is to give a very brief introduction to the thought of Kakehi Katsuhiko and to situate him and his ideas in the great debate over state and sovereignty and within the context of the development of radical Shintō ultranationalist ideology and the radical Shintō religious movements within the established State Shintō religious tradition constructed by the Meiji state.

Rebirth of a Völkisch National Religion

In the first decade following the end of the First World War, one finds in Japan the rise of powerful radical Shintō religious movements emerging out of branches of Shintō religious conservatism, as we saw in the case of Uesugi Shinkichi and the followers of his radical Shintō ultranationalist ideology. These movements sought either to overthrow the existing order by terrorist means or to fundamentally transform it by non-terrorist means, all in the name of reviving a puritanical ideal religious community perceived to have existed in the ancient past. These ancient Shintō revival movements took on various forms and involved all sectors of the Japanese ruling elite, as well as broad sections of the masses. For example, Hiranuma Kiichiro and Prince Kan'in Kotohito were involved with the Shintō Rites Research Council, an organization formed to research ancient Shintō rites and study their application in modern government. Kakehi was very much the central theologian and state theorist in the rebirth of the völkisch Shintō national religion. However, it must be emphasized that the movement to reestablish a pure form of the Shintō religious community imagined in an idealized archaic past did not mean the rejection of modern institutions of government and state. It is similar to what Roger Griffin stated with regard to fascism: "When fascists appeal to healthy, uncontaminated elements of the national tradition (for example the Roman Empire, the Aryan past, chivalric culture) this can create the impression that they long to return literally to a legendary golden age, whereas such elements are being used with an essentially mythic force as the inspiration of the new order because of the 'eternal' truths they contain for the nascent national community."[12]

The best place to begin to understand Kakehi and his effort to reestablish a Shintō theocratic state uncorrupted or contaminated by decadent Western secular thought may be by examining his writings compiled in *A Study of the State*. The ideas he articulated in the essays in this volume would remain at the core of his later writings. Kakehi begins the first essay in *A Study of the State*, "The True Essence of the Imperial State," by noting that the Japanese state in many respects was not unlike other states.[13] That is to say, he rejected the argument by people who claimed that because the Japanese state had absolutely no equal in the world, one must not even try to discuss it in comparative context with other states. Kakehi thought from a global perspective, acknowledging that the peoples of other states had developed many admirable things and that the Japanese people had unabashedly borrowed much from foreign nations, absorbing cultural elements from other civilizations throughout Japanese history. Therefore, Japan could not be said to be superior to all other peoples in every way. Nevertheless, Kakehi believed that the Japanese state was inherently unequaled and superior to all other states of the world because the Japanese people had remained faithful to the original, true essence of the state, while the peoples of other states had presumably abandoned theirs at some point in their history.

What, asked Kakehi, was the "true essence of the Japanese state"? In short, he maintained that it was the unique unity of all the Japanese people, superiors and inferiors, living at different times and places throughout history under the rule of the divine emperor. He coined a word to describe this state of unity: *isshin dōtai*, which literally means "one heart, same body," but might be rendered into English as "being of one heart and the same body."[14] Kakehi asserted that the Japanese state was founded on the basis of this concept and that this organic unity of the Japanese people had been preserved throughout the ages since the establishment of the Japanese state. What made the preservation of the original Japanese state possible was the people's steadfast faith in the religion of their ancestral deities. In this context, Kakehi stressed that the state was founded neither on brute force, a case in which the strong had suppressed the weak, nor on the basis of a compact among equal peoples, thus rejecting both the autocratic idea that the essence of the state was force or power and the classical Western liberal notion that the state originated with a voluntary compact among men. Rather, he insisted that the Japanese state was founded on a basis much more profound and fundamental: the ideals of a national faith. This faith was, of course, Shintō, or the "Way of the Gods," in which the true essence of the Japanese state was the manifestation of "*Takama-ga-Hara* (the Plain of High Heaven)" in this world,[15] something that was made possible by the faithfulness of the Japanese people to the "*Kannagara-no-michi*," a complex term that refers to the relationship between the Japanese people, their ancestors, and their gods.[16]

For those unfamiliar with the doctrines of the Shintō religion, Kakehi's usage of theological concepts such as the "Plain of High Heaven" and "*Kannagara-no-michi*" presents a major problem, because he wrote on the assumption that his Japanese readers were already familiar with them. Therefore, some background information may be in order. First, the "Plain of High Heaven" refers to a place in the Shintō cosmology, and it is best explained by quoting from the famous Western scholar of the Shintō religion, Daniel Holtom:

> The oldest Shintō cosmology presents merely a particular form of the ordinary tripartite division of the visible universe into the upper world of the firmament where the gods and goddesses dwell and where they settle their affairs in tribal council under the authority of the great deities of the upper sky, the middle world of men on the surface of the earth, and the lower world of darkness where live evil and violent spirits ruled over by the great earth mother. The lower world is called *Yomo-tsu-Kuni* or *Yomi-no-Kuni*, with a probable meaning of "The Night Land." The domain of the living men is *Utsushi-yō*, "The Manifest World." The upper world of everlasting felicity is called *Takama-ga-Hara*, meaning "The Plain of the High Heaven."[17]

Thus, the Plain of High Heaven is a place in the heavens where the ancestral deities dwell. It was the supernatural divine world that existed alongside the natural world but existed in time before the creation of the natural world.

Kakehi assigned to the Japanese state the religious goal of realizing the essence of the Plain of High Heaven in this world. He also indicated that this could be accomplished by being faithful to the *Kannagara-no-michi*. According to Holtom, this term appeared in the eighth-century Shintō classic *Nihongi* in a passage on the reign of Emperor Kōtoku (a.d. 645–54).[18] He further noted that the passage in the *Nihongi* that uses the words *Kannagara-no-michi* can be translated as, "We have commanded Our son to rule according to the will of the *kami*."[19] Breaking this word further down into its components, Holtom says, the *nagara* of *Kannagara* means "as such" or "as it is,"[20] so "*Kannagara*" means "following the will of the gods without question." In a nutshell, Holtom suggested that "The Way of the *Kami* [Gods] as Such" should be taken to mean "following implicitly the will of the gods with no introduction of one's personal will whatsoever."[21] Holtom's analysis of the meaning of the phrase "*Kannagara-no-michi*" is the same as Kakehi's definition: the *Kannagara-no-michi* is nothing less than "to praise and realize the inherent state of 'being of one heart and the same body' while preserving from ancient times the proper relationship between superiors and inferiors."[22] In another passage, Kakehi gave a similar but slightly different explanation of "*Kannagara-no-michi*": "the realization of this intrinsic being of one heart and the same body of all people high and low unified by, and under, the superintendence of the single line of emperors established and unchanged since from the beginning [of creation]."[23] In short, this was the essence of the Japanese state. However, this explanation needs elaboration. First, Kakehi imagined the Japanese state as an organic unity, a unity of heart and body. He asserted this ideal consistently in passages such as, "The imperial state is a corporation (*dantai*), an intrinsic being of one heart, same body."[24] He gave serious attention to this theme in a lengthy address to the members of the Japanese Armed Service titled simply, "Isshin Dōtai (One Heart, Same Body)":[25]

> We abandon the self and offer our entire body and soul to the emperor. When you think that you are what you are, you are not a true Japanese. Because Western influences have been coming into Japan rapidly in recent years, there are some people who have been imbued with bad aspects of Western culture. Of course, such a thing is not supposed to happen in a sound military. But it cannot be said that there is absolutely no one like that among the many people [in the military]. A true Japanese is not like that [thinking of one's self interest]. One forgets one's own concerns and completely offers oneself to the emperor. . . . When we speak from our innermost feelings, we live without regard to ourselves. This is especially

true for soldiers. When you enlist in the military, you die and are reborn again to the armed forces under the command of the emperor himself. You give up your life, and do not think for a moment that you are what you are. This [way of thinking] applies not only to the armed forces, but also to ourselves [civilians] as well.[26]

To achieve this "one heart, same body," the individual must discard the self or, in stronger terms, annihilate the self. Any consideration of one's own personal needs was wrong, according to Kakehi. One must totally submerge the self into the collectivity of "one heart, same body." When he referred to the bad aspects of Western culture that had entered Japan in recent years, Kakehi was, of course, referring to the evils of Western secularism and individualism. Kakehi believed the focus on the value of the individual in Western thought was the greatest threat to the Japanese nation, and it is important to stress that he applied "one heart, one body" to all Japanese, not just military personnel.

What becomes of the self after individual consciousness is denied? In Kakehi's political theology, the individual enters into the mystical body of the emperor once one's own individuality is abandoned. He stated, "Subjects cast aside their individual selves and 'enter into the emperor (tennō no naka ni haite iru).' "[27] He went on to assert that all Japanese people living at the present time existed inside the emperor. All Japanese who have ever lived, from the origins of the state onward, also exist within the emperor. The emperor, then, is this intrinsic and sacred "being of one heart, same body" of all Japanese past and present (and to come). He is a "universal self (fuhenga)" or "universal person (fuhenjin)" but a person different from the total aggregate of each individual person. He is a particular person whose true nature is its intrinsic "being of one heart, same body."

Kakehi was careful to emphasize the voluntary nature of becoming a part of the emperor. To obey the will of the state (kokken), which, of course, was the emperor, was not to submit to an outside, coercive force:

To obey the will of the state is not to be forcefully bound by an external force like a slave or a piece of wood, but to obey the will of the state voluntarily based on one's own sincere desires and one's own conscience. . . . There is no contradiction in obeying the will of the state and following one's own conscience.[28]

"The will of the state is none other than the power of all the Tarōs and Jirōs," wrote Kakehi.[29] What he seems to have been saying is that in this collectivist type of thinking, one accomplishes one's own desire in submitting to the will of the state, which in this case is the will of the emperor. Ideally, there must be a total identity between the individual and the collectivity subsumed in the emperor.

One could easily argue that this obsession with the notion of total identity between each and every Japanese subject and the emperor is also a classic tenet of fascist ideology.[30] Eugen Weber's discussion of the relationship between the leader and the masses in *Varieties of Fascism* is directly relevant to Kakehi's theory of the emperor and the Japanese masses:

> When a people achieves true national self-consciousness, . . . the leader is no longer a master, a dictator who does what he wants and leads where he wills. He is the state of consciousness. He does not do what he wants. He does what he must. And he is led [by the interest] of the eternal nation which the people has sensed.
>
> Here is the basis of that cult of the leader as the emanation of his people, produced by his people as the materialization of its profound will and purpose. Such a leader is neither elected nor appointed. He affirms himself as the "truly democratic" chief of a group that freely accepts him. . . . Fascists and National Socialists stress this oneness between the statesman and his people, a people that gives itself to him, trusts him, and loves him. . . . The general will of the nation is now concentrated in one person in whom the people, his people, can glimpse their true historical selves, their true destiny, as a magic mirror in which they see themselves magnified and exalted.[31]

In another part of his speech to the armed forces, Kakehi said that "one does not possess oneself. This life is not one's own life. All are the Tarōs and Jirōs of the emperor. One did not create oneself. The Tarōs and Jirōs were created by the grace of the emperor."[32] In other words, one's own life from the beginning was never one's own; it came from the emperor. This heavy emphasis on the notion that the individual's existence was totally dependent on the grace of the emperor also served to undercut the family-state concept that Hozumi Yatsuka formulated. In Hozumi's state theory, loyalty to the emperor is an extension of filial piety. But Kakehi's state, like Uesugi's, is not based on an internal patriarchal family-state structure. In fact, Kakehi went to great lengths to deemphasize the individual's ties to the family. For example, he even argued that one was born, in the ultimate sense, not from one's parents but from the emperor:

Nowadays, if we say that we were born from our parents, everyone agrees. I do not think that there is anyone who does not understand that we were born from our parents. However, if we say that we were born from the emperor, foreigners would shake their heads and say they do not understand that we were born from the emperor. The reason that they do not understand this is because they are foreigners. We were indeed born from the emperor. It is a plain and true fact that our parents gave birth to us, but when we seek for the greatest, and the most fundamental cause of our birth, or our parents' birth, it derives from the emperor's grace. It would be awful to say that there was no emperor. But if one were to say hypothetically that the emperor did not exist, we would never have been born at all. No Japanese subject would have been born.[33]

That is to say, Kakehi argued that we owe our birth not to our parents but to the emperor, virtually severing the individual's dependence on the family principle. This is a very revealing point because, theoretically, there are no intermediary loyalties between the emperor and the individual in Kakehi's totalitarian ideology. Because Kakehi's state is not based on a patriarchal construction of society, it is fundamentally different from Hozumi Yatsuka's premodern family-state. However, it is also different from Uesugi Shinkichi's state, in which people were seen as cells or elements interacting in a horizontal spatial-temporal matrix within the mystical body of the emperor. Kakehi constructed the internal structure of the state in a hierarchical fashion. All people were supposed to interact with one another and work to realize the *Tama-ga-Hara* in this world from their "proper place" in the social hierarchy. Kakehi stressed this continuously throughout his writings. For example, in his same speech to the armed forces, he said:

Lower-ranking people must respect their superior officers if they feel obliged to the emperor. Even if you say that you will directly render devoted services to the emperor by abandoning your superior, it cannot be done. You have to do it through your superiors, who you should regard as a substitute for the emperor. Furthermore, this applies not only to soldiers, but also to [civilians].[34]

In other words, Kakehi said that one had to accept one's "proper place (*honrai no bun*)" in the social-political order. Each and every individual in the state imbued with the consciousness of "one heart, same body" had to inwardly accept the restraints of organizational life as a functional necessity. Kakehi did not condone insubordination in the military. Neither did he allow one to disobey one's superiors in civilian life. Suzuki Sadami also seems to concur on this point.

The Emperor as the Great Life of the Universe

In "An Evening's Conversation on the Essence of the State" (chapter 7 in *A Study of the State*), Kakehi, as the title implies, discussed the essence of the Japanese state. In his opening remarks, he said that a state is much more than just a group of people on a given piece of territory united under a political and legal system. The legal and political institutions were only the outward manifestations of the essence of the state, and it was of utmost importance for everyone to understand just what that essence was. The previous section on "one heart, same body" and the "Way of the Gods as Such" has provided Kakehi's essential philosophy of state, but this work gives us a few more details. In "An Evening's Conversation on the Essence of the State," Kakehi also said that the state was our "universal self (*fuhenga*)"; this "universal self" was the intrinsic "being of one heart, same spirit," as discussed earlier. More precisely, this "universal self" was at the same time the unique "great life (*daiseimei*)" existing in each individual, high or low, in time and space. Kakehi also used this term in his address to the military, saying that the "great life" was the "emperor and the masses (*Tennō oyobi okuchō*)" united as "one heart, same body."[35] The state, which he also referred to as the "universal great life (*fuhenteki daiseimei*),"[36] was composed of the emperor and the masses (*okuchō*) who had abandoned their individual selves to serve the emperor. The state was an entity that had a life of its own, something more than the sum total of the emperor and each individual member among the masses, yet not apart from them. It was a national community, a *Volksgemeinschaft*, that had a life that transcended the lives and interests of any particular emperor or any member of the state. In "An Evening's Conversation on the Essence of the State," Kakehi offered a set of proofs to illustrate that this great universal life or universal self actually existed.

First, Kakehi cited what he called "subjective" proof for the existence of the universal self.[37] This subjective proof was something like a mode of consciousness naturally contained within each individual. It was a consciousness of identity that essentially became an organizational force inasmuch as the state is constituted in part by the belief that people hold about it. For instance, Kakehi stated that the individual possesses various levels of consciousness and acts on them in his or her daily experiences.

There is a particular consciousness that limits the individual to his or her own physical body; a child, for example, is conscious of the self in contrast to the selves of his parents. The child is conscious of the fact that he or she has a body that is separate from the parents' bodies. This is one level of consciousness—a consciousness of the self in the narrowest sense. But the child naturally also has another level of consciousness: the consciousness of identity with his or her parent. This consciousness comes to the child naturally during daily life. Kakehi cites a concrete example of this: a child who senses that the parent is being treated cordially by an outsider naturally feels that this cordiality is also extended to himself or herself. When the child experiences this unity of his or her self with the selves of the parents, it illustrates a smaller universal self—the parent and the child becoming one self. In other words, in that particular mode of consciousness the child and the parent constitute one universal self.

Expanding this analogy to an even greater level of conscious identity, the individual self can be identical to the state. To illustrate this, Kakehi cited an incident in the Japan–Russia War of 1904–1905 when Port Arthur capitulated. During the euphoria over the victory of the Japanese forces, all Japanese felt as if they had personally won the battle. In this case, the individual identified with the state, and the individual became identical to the state and to the Japanese Volk as a collectivity. At that moment, the individual self merged totally with the universal self. Thus, in this way, the great universal life exists as "one spirit," something that spiritually unifies the beings that constitute the state.

Second, Kakehi cited what he called "objective proof" of the existence of this great universal being,[38] which he subdivided into three categories: "physiological," "spiritual," and "economic." It is sufficient to illustrate just one of them here: the "physiological" category. At the outset of his argument, Kakehi reminded readers to think about the life process: the individual is born from the union of two physical parents, who also had parents, and so on, going back to the origins of the national-ethnic group. That individual also grows and produces new life. In other words, the individual has the power to continue the ethnic group. In this sense, the individual has within his or her own self the capacity to continue his or her own life. The life that exists within the individual is at same time old and new. It is not something that is different in each of us, for each and every one of us has come from the same ancestor.

In short, the individual is a constituent component of the whole. Similarly, the state is a natural person, and within it are individual persons who have within them the life that has existed from the time of the origin of the state. This life, or universal being, is present in every individual being; it is something that was there from the time of our ancestors. We are the reality of life that existed before our parents were born. In other words, this universal life—meaning something like the essence of existence or the absolute existence in its perfect and unqualified state—existed in each individual and was permanent, something that has continued to exist since very ancient times, or from the origin of the state. Each individual is a product of (and literally a part of) his ancestors. What the individual is today is literally, physically, and spiritually a part of his ancestors.

Physically, the self was originally one with the body of the parent. But now it is separated. However, this separation is not a complete break. The body of the self is not totally separated from the rest of the environment—that is, the state—for the self is nourished from the environment and is part of the environment. The individual expands his or her own body, grows, takes in and assimilates food from outside the body. The food one eats enters the body and becomes absorbed into the bloodstream. The self as a body is linked with other bodies in this environmental system, much like a large ecological system. It is in such a sense that the universal self may be considered the "same body." In other words, Kakehi came close, it seems to me, to characterizing the state as a kind of great ecological-biological system of this great universal being.

Kakehi's theology of the emperor distinguished the Japanese emperor from all other monarchs. The essence of the emperor rests on the faith that he is not merely a mortal. Rather, he is a divine being transmuted into human form. He is a "god manifest as man," or a living incarnation of Amaterasu Ōmikami, a living *kami*. As a living deity, a being both deity and man at the same time, the emperor is somewhat analogous to a permanent Christ on earth, the "anointed one" who received an unction from Amaterasu Ōmikami that enables him to establish the reign of the gods in the Japanese state and in the world. The emperor, as *kami*, is the embodiment of *magokoro*, the spirit of total "impartiality and disinterestedness (*kōhei-mushi*)."[39] As totally impartial and disinterested, he is brought to universality, which means that the emperor's self-identity is equated with the great universal life. The essence of the emperor is that he is a personal manifestation of the great universal life. In this way, he is the sovereign universal self who determines itself and yet at the same time binds itself together with the whole state, the unifying spirit of "one heart, same body." Accordingly, without the emperor, the people would constitute an amorphous mass, a shapeless form lacking any organization or structure. Without the emperor, the Japanese ethnic state would cease to exist. As with the state, the emperor is eternal. He exists without change in the past, present, and future. The physical body of his manifestation may change, as it actually has more than one hundred and twenty times, but he is still the same emperor—namely, the deity Amaterasu Ōmikami manifest as man, the deity of total impartiality and disinterestedness. Thus, there has been only one emperor and the masses.

In a section of *A Study of the State* titled "The Emperor and the Amida Butsu," originally an address delivered in 1913 to a religious association in Tokyo, Kakehi equated the relationship between the emperor and the people to that between Amida Butsu and the devout followers of Amida Butsu.[40] Loyalty to the emperor was religious devotion. The subject was totally dependent on the emperor for his spiritual existence. Kakehi preached that the emperor was the source of the individual's life, his raison d'être, whether that be the common man on the street or the prime minister. It was by trust in the emperor that the individual was united in the great universal life. From this perspective, the emperor was the source of "affection and love (*jiai*)."[41] The fact that the individual existed and developed was due solely to the compassion and mercy of the emperor. Personal union with the emperor was the individual's ultimate objective; it was this objective that was at the heart of radical Shintō ultranationalist ideology. The individual was driven beyond the self to his essential being, to the emperor, to total impartiality and disinterestedness. This was the essence of the dynamic that motivated the individual and propelled the state to action.

Unlike Uesugi Shinkichi, Kakehi recognized the existence of hierarchical structural relationships within the state. But a close look at Kakehi's recognition of hierarchical organization in the state definitely did not constitute the same type of hierarchical structure as that in Hozumi Yatsuka's patriarchal state, which assumed an authoritarian relationship between the emperor and his subjects much like that of a father and his family. Rather, Kakehi's imagined political community was a non-authoritarian hierarchical organization of society. That is, one it was a hierarchical system that supposedly lacked any coercive element in the real sense. Kakehi, in fact, took great pains to show that hierarchical structures in the state did not constitute a power relationship. He explained that while the existence of the emperor was the source of the hierarchically structured state, the emperor was also the source of the unity of "one spirit, same body," which joined and united superior and inferior, or those above and those below, as one universal life. The emperor did not rule by brute force.

Kakehi stressed the identity of those above and those below. Those above had love and respect for those below in this hierarchical relationship. Likewise, those below had the same love and respect for those above. This was what tied those above with those below as "one spirit, same body." The virtue of love and respect that those above had for those below was called *jin* in the culture of the emperor state; the love and respect that those below had for those above was called *chū*. Although these words were of Chinese origin, it was a mistake to think that the substance of jin and chū of the emperor state was the same as that in the Chinese state. In the Japanese imperial state, the names of the virtues might be different, but in substance they were identical. Mutual warmth and respect existed because they were an expression of "one spirit, same body." Accordingly, to follow directives from those above was not to be restricted by an external force. To obey and follow the directives of those above was to advance one's own true heart or, as Uesugi would say, one's essential being. In other words, Kakehi denied any authoritarian nature of the state; in his theory of the state, one finds no emphasis on obedience as was characteristic of Hozumi's authoritarian absolutism and paternalism. That is, Hozumi's paternal obedience had given way to the emphasis on *consent* in the state thought of Kakehi. As did Uesugi, Kakehi assumed that his audience was the politicized masses. The masses would obey only what they consented to and, in doing so, were obeying themselves.

In a lecture to students at Tokyo Imperial University's School of Agriculture in 1913, titled "The Shintō Shrine and the Agricultural Village," Kakehi singled out the importance of the farmer and the value of the occupation of the farmer to the state.[42] He stressed that it was the farming communities that preserved the values and daily lifestyle that constituted the concept of "one spirit, same body," and it was the farming communities that served as the wellspring of values for the rest of the nation. Kakehi noted that in ancient times, the farmer was synonymous with the state. When one spoke of the farmer, one spoke for the nation as a whole, for all the people in the country were essentially farmers. He stressed that one could not have real faith in Shintō and not recognize the special role of the farmer and his work in the state, an idea that, of course, was an element of the ultranationalist agrarian movement.

He noted that in ancient times, one of the words for the state—that is, for Japan—was "Tōyōashihara (Land of the Abundant Rice)," which means not simply that there was an abundance of rice in the country but that the gods participated in the daily lives of the farmers to help them and ensure an abundant supply of food in the state. Kakehi also noted that the farmer was less likely to forget ancestor worship, the source of the Shintō religion, because he was attached to the land of his ancestors. The farmer thus functioned to preserve the religious base of the state at a grassroots level. The farmer's agricultural work was sacred work. The emperor's activities were also inextricably bound up with sacred rites related to agriculture. For example, at the beginning of the new year the emperor conducted the Shihōhai, the New Year's religious service at the Imperial Court, praying that there would be no natural disasters throughout the year and that there would be a good harvest of the five grains (wheat, rice, beans, and two kinds of millet—*awa* and *kibi*). The farmer and his agricultural work were important to the emperor state and at the core of Shintō. However, it would be reading too much into Kakehi to ascribe to him the opinion that industrialization and urbanization had destroyed the moral fabric of society. Nevertheless, agrarianism was a large part of Kakehi's thought.

In a greater comparative context, it is instructive to note that Japanese agrarianism in radical Shintō ultranationalist thought was not unique to Japanese right-wing ultranationalist movements. It was also present in German völkisch thought. Mosse noted that in the formation of the völkisch ideology, "The concept of the peasantry came to play a cardinal role."[43] Other parallels between Japanese radical Shintō ultranationalist thought and German völkisch thought deserve attention. For example, the organic conceptualization of the state of the Japanese minzoku and the German Volk is very close. Mosse writes:

But if the individual was tied to the Volk, which, in turn, as the repository of the "life force," found a unity with the "higher reality," how was this trinity actually expressed? Common to both the individual and the Volk was the romantic pantheistic concept of nature. For the romantics, nature was not cold and mechanical, but alive and spontaneous. It was indeed filled with a life force which corresponded to the emotions of man. The human soul could be in rapport with nature since it too was endowed with a soul. Every individual could therefore find an inner correspondence with nature, a correspondence which he shared with his Volk. In this way the individual linked himself with every other member of the Volk in a common feeling of belonging, in a shared emotional experience.[44]

The other segment of the population that Kakehi singled out for attention were the armed forces, which he thought occupied a special position among the emperor's subjects in the modern Japanese state. In the address "One Spirit, Same Body," discussed earlier, he quoted a passage from the *Gunjin Chokuyū* (Imperial Rescript to the Armed Forces):

> Soldiers and Sailors, We are your supreme commander-in-chief. Our relations with you will be the most intimate when We rely upon you as Our limbs and you look up to Us as your head. Whether We are able to guard the Empire, and so prove Ourself worthy of Heaven's blessings and repay the benevolence of Our Ancestors depends upon the faithful discharge of your duties as soldiers and sailors. If the majesty and power of Our Empire be impaired, do you share with Us the sorrow; if the glory of Our arms shine resplendent, we will share with you the honor. If you all do your duty, and being one with Us in spirit do your utmost for the protection of the State, Our people will long enjoy the blessings of peace, and the might and dignity of Our Empire will shine in the world.[45]

This passage states that the emperor is the supreme commander of the armed forces, but the most striking thing about it is that it emphasizes the direct and intimate ties between the emperor and the soldier and sailor. It was precisely this idea of a direct and intimate relationship with the emperor that was the core of Kakehi's message to the servicemen. While the military man was responsible for executing the will of the emperor, he also shared with the emperor the glory or sorrow in victory or defeat.

For Kakehi, the thoughts of the soldier or sailor were to be preoccupied with serving the emperor in a very direct way. It was the military man who exemplified purity of heart, who on entering the service shed all concern for his personal life and was prepared to put his life on the line in direct service to the emperor. A businessman who was preoccupied in his daily life with making a profit in his business could not serve the emperor in the same way as the serviceman. Nevertheless, Kakehi also insisted that selfless service to the emperor by those in military life was also to be the ideal for those in civilian life. Kakehi's teachings on this matter no doubt reinforced the sense of superiority that servicemen already felt toward civilians, a feeling that was based on the concept of being the emperor's personal force. It is worth noting that a strong connection existed between farmers and servicemen, because in the prewar days 80 percent of Japanese conscripts came from rural areas.

The special place for the military found in Kakehi's state theory would be pushed to new heights in the 1930s. Holtom quoted the following article from a 1938 issue of the journal *Teikoku Shimpō* about the Japanese military man:

> No matter how much of a wrongdoer, no matter how evil, a Japanese subject may have been, when once he has taken his stand on the field of battle, all his past sins are entirely atoned for and they become as nothing. The wars of Japan are carried on in the name of the Emperor and therefore they are holy wars. All the soldiers who participate in these holy wars are representative of the Emperor; they are his loyal subjects. To put the matter of what kind of person he may be, possesses the inherent capacity of becoming a loyal subject and of being empowered to put that loyalty into operation. The matchless superiority of the Japanese national life lies just here. . . .
>
> Those who, with the words "*Tennō Heika Banzai* [May the Emperor Live Forever]" on their lips, have consummated tragic death in battle, whether they are good or whether they are bad, are thereby sanctified.[46]

A couple of points from this passage deserve attention. First, even a person who may have committed unspeakable atrocities in his life would still be worthy of worship in the minds of radical Shintō ultranationalists. Yoshino Sakuzō had difficulty justifying such thinking and wrote about it in the article "The Ethical Significance of Worship at the Shrines."[47] Second, as Holtom noted, "All the wars of Japan are holy wars since they are under the supreme command of an emperor who can do nothing wrong."[48]

The Japanese State in a Shintō Cosmology

We have examined Kakehi's conception of the state as a great universal life. We now turn our attention to his vision of the Japanese state projected in a Shintō cosmology, a vision that later became official state ideology designed to replace liberal-democratic internationalism and challenge the Marxist vision of a communist world order. Kakehi's vision of a new world order, like the visions of most messianic political theorists, centered on his religious faith. At the core of his conception of this new world order was the Shintō cosmology. The Shintō version of the story of creation was not only a story of how the cosmos began and developed. It was a story of the creation of the Japanese state and its place in the world. Drawing on ideas from Western secular and religious thought, he reinterpreted the "biblical" Shintō story of origins to find in it the raison d'être for the Japanese state: the unification of the world under the emperor. Under the rule of the emperor, the world, as he put it, was to be "one great universal life (*ichidai fuhen seikatsu*)."[49]

Kakehi saw the world of his times as ruled by people and nations who thought in Darwinist terms—that is, as a struggle for existence. In a speech he gave in Ehime in 1915, Kakehi attacked this Darwinian worldview, saying, "A dog is a dog; a monkey is a monkey; the descendant of the *kami* is a *kami*. We here today are descendants of the *kami*. Our ancestors are not monkeys or pheasants. Our ancestors are the humans—that is, gods—of the Age of the Gods."[50] He thought the world was a constant struggle among entities called "universal selves" from which only the fittest emerged victorious. Not all universal selves, however, were states. There were collective entities endowed with personal qualities of will and intention that did not take the form of a state. Kakehi, in fact, identified various categories of universal selves (he actually made a diagram of these collective entities) and distinguished among their various properties, such as inner structure, membership, spiritual makeup, economic organization, and essential nature.[51] As examples of universal selves that did not constitute a state, he cited prefectures, counties, cities, and towns, as well as village communities. Such universal selves were self-governing bodies, but they were not sovereign states because they lacked a sovereign representative to determine their affairs and represent them in the sovereign state.

The state, however, was the most important universal self. It was the principal actor in history. It was the most natural in origin, structure, and development, and it belonged to a higher type among the categories of organic entities. Kakehi declared sovereignty to be a necessary and indispensable attribute of the state. The state was a universal self that was sovereign; there could be no state that was not a sovereign state. It was a sovereign universal life that could acknowledge its own personality through the sovereign representative and could pursue this recognition within and outside of society. As a sovereign entity, the state was free to determine its own internal form and its own laws and to pursue its own goals. Recognition, however, was another necessary feature of the state. The sovereign state was sovereign in that it was recognized as sovereign by like sovereign states or other universal selves.

Kakehi distinguished between what he called the "highest sovereign state (*saikō shuken koku*)" and other "autonomous corporations (*jishu dantai*)."[52] The former were the great and powerful states, states that were virtually independent from the practical restraints imposed on them by other states. These states were either self-sufficient or had the military power to secure the natural resources they needed. Sovereignty was theoretically unlimited in these states' external affairs with other sovereign states. Kakehi included in the category of highest sovereign states the great European powers as well as the Japanese state.

Finally, Kakehi cited another important sovereign universal self that did not, however, constitute a state in common political discourse because it lacked definite territorial boundaries essential to the sovereign state. Furthermore, it was different from the universal selves, which were living entities existing between the individual, on the one hand, and the cosmos, on the other hand, in that it did in a sense encompass the entire world and included the whole of mankind. This was the Roman Catholic church, with its sovereign pontiff, the sovereign representative of a universal civilization. Despite his deep faith in Shintō fundamentalism, Kakehi nevertheless cited the Roman Catholic church, with its global institutional organization, as a magnificent manifestation of man's impulse for a world order based on a divine sovereign. It is noteworthy that at one point in his career, during his study in Europe, Kakehi involved himself profoundly in Christianity and the study of Christian theology. This Christian influence is apparent in his writings on Shintō theology. He appropriated certain Christian concepts for his own use and used Christian theology as a means to develop his radical Shintō ultranationalist ideology.

Kakehi envisioned a new world order that was was based on a universal faith. It was a world order that had as its sovereign a divine universal sovereign. A world order involved a common unifying force, and that unifying force could be none other than a sovereign. But the only true sovereign was a sovereign derived from the gods, and it was impossible to imagine a new world order without a divine sovereign as the world sovereign. That sole sovereign was the Japanese emperor, the "god manifest as man," the only living being who was totally impartial and disinterested, the only being through which world justice could be dispensed. Only under the emperor could there be global political unity and lasting stability. And it was only the Japanese state that had retained the religious essence of the state since its origins. For Kakehi, the true state was by definition religious. The formation of the state was a religious act on the part of the gods, and the sovereign was the goddess Amaterasu Ōmikami. Accordingly, sovereignty—that is, the location of ultimate power in the state—could not derive from man. State and religion were identical. Only the Japanese state, which had retained the centrality of religion within the life of the modern state, could unite the world into a political-religious community.

The crux of the problem of order in Kakehi's contemporary world was that powerful, secularized Western states were struggling with one another to enhance their own interests. What brought this situation about was that Western civilization, now the dominating political force in the world, had turned its back on the divine sovereign. Western states had established states and governments founded on the mistaken notion that sovereignty came from men, not from the divine. Kakehi saw this as an ominous development because he believed that the ultimate source of political authority had to be found outside human society. The secularization of politics had made the Western states internally unstable; more important, this had led to the breakdown of global order. There was no sovereign moral force to unite mankind. And no truly moral force ultimately could be derived from man, since man was both partial and interested. Severed from the divine, sovereignty in the Western states came to be placed in a variety of secular localities: in the temporal monarch; in the parliament; jointly in the monarch and in the parliament; in the state; and in the people as a whole. With the severance of the concept of sovereignty from universal faith, a basis for world order no longer existed in Western thought. For Kakehi, world order as a concept was a meaningless abstraction, a concept devoid of any structure, without universal faith and a universal sovereign.

Such religious elements of Kakehi's state theory and polemical arguments against the secularization of state and society were surprisingly close to those of the Roman Catholic theorists of divine right such as Joseph de Maistre and Louis de Bonald who maintained that the root of the problems of state were to be found in the ecclesiastical revolution of the sixteenth century as well as in the liberal theories of popular sovereignty of the seventeenth century and the eighteenth century. Both de Maistre and de Bonald placed all political power in God, the only power from whom all political power could be legitimately derived, and stressed the need for a strong universal church under which the Roman pontiff was the supreme authority representing God's will. Kakehi no doubt would have agreed wholeheartedly with de Maistre's idea that "government is a true religion."[53] He attacked Western liberalism for its fundamental political doctrine of the separation of state and religion. He interpreted the revolt against monarchical rule as essentially a theory of secular individualism. The will of the independent individual was the starting point of the theory of all liberal political ideas and institutions. The contract theory of the origins of government and its doctrine of popular sovereignty was centered on the idea of the individual as an independent entity who was a law unto himself. Accordingly, he urged the Japanese government to abandon its official policy, which tried to work out a compromise between the idea of freedom of religion and the state sponsorship of Shintō shrines by claiming that state-sponsored Shintō was not a religion, a policy he argued was hypocritical and ultimately damaging to the state, for national unity depended on the conscious common bond of religion. He openly challenged the government to proclaim Shintō as the official state religion.[54] Claiming that religious sentiment was the strongest force in the human character, he argued that it was also a prerequisite for a peaceful world order.

However, while universal faith had been severed from the concept of the state among the Western states and left in the hands of the Roman Catholic church, it was precisely this concept of universal faith that was central to the Japanese state. The core concept of emperor ideology was that the spiritual world was not severed from the material world. The Japanese state was not established on the idea that sovereignty comes from man; it was not built on the idea of secular power. In the emperor state, the State Founding Law, the law of the formation of the Japanese state, made state and religion identical. Furthermore, the linkage of the Japanese state to universal faith made the essential nature of the state a realization of a divine purpose on earth. The power of the state was to be redirected to the realization of a divine state on earth, to actualize the one great universal life on earth. By identifying the Japanese state with a leadership role in a global order and assigning to it the task of spearheading this new world order, he had theoretically released the Japanese state from any limitations, either internally or externally, on its own power. Most important, the power of the state was not restricted by its own, self-defining purpose in the world.

Kakehi claimed that the idea of the emperor as a world sovereign was not something new. It was there at the origins of the universe and could be found in Shintō scripture. He discussed this in the speech "The Emperor and the Amida Butsu" to a Buddhist religious group at the Hongan Temple in Asakusa in April 1913.[55] He stated, "In ancient Shintō, the emperor was identical to the universe."[56] He also noted that in ancient times, the Japanese state, which then possessed a great universal faith, had expanded gradually from a fixed territorial base with the ideal in mind to establish in this world the divine state of Takama-ga-Hara. "In today's world, the Japanese state, still guided by the same universal faith as that of ancient times, must again accept this same challenge to create a new world order, to re-create in this world that one great universal life envisioned not by the Roman Catholic Church with the Catholic Pope, who is the Bishop of Rome, as representative of God's will, but the vision of one great universal life, that 'spirit of harmony' that emanates from the emperor, the divine ruler on earth." In short, expansionism of the Japanese state is internally derived from the definition of its own inner essence. It had little to do with external events, although external events were pointed out and interpreted in such a way as to illustrate what misfortunes would befall the world if Japan were to shrink from its responsibility as leader of a world order. The secularized, atheistic world had to be saved from utter chaos. However, the divine global order on earth was not to replace or merge with the supernatural world. This one great universal life was to be established alongside the supernatural divine world.

At the end of "An Evening's Conversation on the Essence of the State," Kakehi stated:

> The imperial state made as its core the land that has been immovable since ancient times and has gradually expanded it. At the same time, it has respected the universal great faith (*fuhenteki daishinkō*) and universal feelings. It has striven to realize the Plain of High Heaven centered on Japan. Great Japan is a divine land. It based itself on faith long before the Roman Catholic church [came into existence]. Under the rule of the emperor it takes as its principle the Japanese spirit and tries to realize this one great universal Life in this world. At the same time, she does not make light of this world centering on this immovable land, but befriends this world, and tries to make this world a divine land. Thus we are superior to the Roman Catholic church. These are the reasons we are a splendid state. Before other states came into existence, Japan was a state possessing the perfect land and exalting the ideal universal life. Having centered ourselves on this magnificent and deep faith, state power is not simple secular power. Everyone from the emperor down to the lowest person is a manifestation of the *kami*. The fact that everyone is trying to realize the *kami* nature in this world is the reason Japan is a divine land.[57]

To reiterate, according to Kakehi, Japan was at the center of a messianic faith that had to be spread throughout the world. For those who are interested in comparative radical religious movements and religious terrorism, it might be instructive to examine the parallels between radical Shintō ultranationalism and today's Salafist and Salafist jihadist movements in the Islamic world, which have called for a restoration of a world order based on the original teachings of the Quran.

The Fundamental Principles of the Constitution of the Empire of Great Japan

In *A Study of the State*, Kakehi wrote that the state law of the Japanese imperial state was the legal manifestation of the *Kannagara no Michi* (The Way of the Gods as Such) in ancient Shintō.[58] Accordingly, he did not consider the Constitution of the Empire of Great Japan to be the supreme law of the land. That is, he referred to a higher law that transcended the Meiji Constitution. This higher law was established at the time of the origin of Japanese state, and it was this law that had been in effect from the founding of the state to the present. He called this the "State Founding Law (*kenkokuhō*)."[59] This fundamental law of the state was the law on which the Constitution of the Empire of Great Japan was ultimately based. The State Founding Law established the kokutai for all time. It was the law that determined forever the structural distinction between the emperor and the people; it was a manifestation of ancient Shintō, the *Kannagara no Michi* in legal form. In other words, the State Founding Law was the unwritten law of the Way of the Gods. It was also the legal expression of "one heart, same body." In this way, Kakehi tried to eliminate the notion of secular law, the idea of the secular state and the secular foundations of government that emerged out of the historical struggle of the Meiji Restoration. What was really binding was this "biblical law." Some twenty years later, Kakehi would incorporate these fundamental ideas into *Essential Meaning of the Constitution of the Empire of Great Japan*, a revised, written version of his lecture notes for a course on the constitution that he made on behalf of the Ministry of Education in July 1935.[60]

Essential Meaning of the Constitution of the Empire of Great Japan is divided into four large chapters, titled, respectively, "Introduction," "The Imperial State," "The Emperor," and "The Imperial Family and Subjects." Each of the chapters is subdivided into a number of sections. The most striking feature about this work, however, is the great pain Kakehi took to subsume the constitution into his Shintō worldview. The first dozen pages consist of preamble-like passages in which he asserted that the

Meiji Constitution was designed to clarify the injunctions of the imperial ancestors and the founder of the imperial line, which is the *Kannagara no Michi*. Accordingly, Kakehi believed that the Constitution of the Empire of Great Japan should be based not on secular principles but divine law, perhaps much as Islamic fundamentalists believe that state law should be based on the *sharia*, or Islamic divine law, or possibly like religious Zionists who want to build a Jewish state in Israel in which Jews can live according to the laws of the Torah and Halakha. Kakehi maintained that the constitution must be correctly interpreted according to the Way of the Gods and that the Way of the Gods must be put into practice in daily life.

It was actually in the chapter "The Emperor" in which Kakehi began to discuss the specific articles of the Constitution of the Empire of Great Japan. Interestingly, following a short section of "general remarks" at the beginning of this chapter, he devoted the next seventy of the remaining seventy-three pages of the chapter to discussing only the first four articles of the constitution. For Kakehi, Articles 1–4 enunciated the kokutai, "The great law upon which the [Japanese] state was founded."[61] He devoted a mere three pages to the remaining articles (5–76). It was only in the last chapter, "The Imperial Family and [Japanese] Subjects," that Kakehi discussed to any extent the meaning of Articles 5–76. Noteworthy for the theme of this study was Kakehi's interpretation of the following articles of the Constitution of the Empire of Great Japan.

First, as might be totally expected, Kakehi denounced the emperor-as-organ theory of the state because placing sovereignty in the state was in contradiction to, or a denial of (*hitei*), the *Kannagara no Michi*.[62] In a section titled "Spirit of the Way of the Gods," he again clarified the meaning of the *Kannagara no Michi*, noting that *Kannagara* meant the *Kami sono mama*, or "the Gods as they are," "the Gods as such," or "the Gods in the original condition." The word "*kaminagara*" was first recorded in the reign of Emperor Kōtoku, as Holtom has noted. Accordingly, government according to the "spirit of the Gods (*Kami no seishin*)" meant that "government must be in accordance with the Gods in the original condition."[63]

Kakehi noted that the emperor-as-organ theory was also in error because it set up the state in opposition to the emperor as well as opposing elements within the state structure. For instance, he emphasized that imperial authority (*taiken*) could not be limited by, or be in opposition to, legislative powers (*rippōken*) or judicial powers (*shihōken*) or even by the rights of the subjects as stipulated in Chapter II of the Constitution of the Empire of Great Japan.[65] As evidence, he quoted Article 31, which states, "The provisions contained in the present Chapter shall not affect the exercise of the powers appertaining to the emperor, in times of war or in cases of a national emergency."[66] Kakehi also referred to Article 67 to bolster his argument that there could be no conflict in government over the annual budget. Article 67 stipulates, "Those already fixed expenditures based by the Constitution upon the powers appertaining to the Emperor, and such expenditures as may have arisen by the effect of law, or that appertain to the legal obligations of the Government, shall be neither rejected nor reduced by the Imperial Diet, without the concurrence of the Government."[67] According to Kakehi, any arguments or constitutional interpretations that allowed for the emergence of any oppositional forces within the imperial state meant that those who made such arguments or interpretations of the Constitution of the Empire of Great Japan were thinking along individualistic lines. Approaching the Constitution of the Empire of Great Japan from the viewpoint of individualism would lead to the Western notion of the independence of the legislative, executive, and judicial branches of government (*Seiyō no sanken bunritsu*).[68] Under Kakehi's state based on the *Kannagara no Michi*, the separation of powers of the threefold structure of government was a recipe for disaster rather than the basis for maintaining liberty or avoiding tyranny, as interpreted in liberal and democratic Western political thought.

In the final analysis, according to Kakehi, the purpose of the Japanese subjects within the state was to serve as assistants (*hoyokusha*) or aides in carrying out the imperial will. Ultimately, the imperial will was to establish the ideal imperial state in accordance with the *Kannagara no Michi* and expand the emperor and his power to "all the peoples of the world (*sekai no banmin*)."[69] This was the message he presented in a section of chapter 3 titled, "Article 4 of the Imperial Constitution." For Kakehi, in the statement in Article 4, "The Emperor is the head of the Empire, combining in Himself the rights of sovereignty, and exercises them, according to the provisions of the present Constitution,"[70] sovereignty did not simply refer to sovereignty over the Japanese state and the empire that it had up to that time acquired but imperial sovereignty over all the peoples of the world. As scriptural authority for global imperial rule, he quoted a passage from the reign of Emperor Kōtoku, which states, "Heaven covers us: Earth upbears us: the Imperial way is but one. . . . The Lord will eschew double methods of government, and the Vassal will avoid duplicity in his service of the sovereign."[71]

Another subject that is of interest to this study of the ideology of radical Shintō ultranationalism and its relationship to the state is the treatment of foreigners or non-Japanese. What role, if any, did non-Japanese have within the Japanese state or Japanese empire? This is an important question because by the time Kakehi was writing *Essential Meaning of the Constitution of the Empire of Great Japan,* Japan had already acquired for itself an empire containing a large number of non-Japanese people. The role of all Japanese in the Japanese empire—from the members of the imperial family to all subjects—was to serve as "assistants (*hoyokusha*)" in contributing to the "increasing prosperity of the emperor (*Tennōsama no iyasaku*)."[72] "Foreigners (*gaikokujin*)" and "stateless persons (*mukokusekijin*),"[73] however, should be treated differently. Although Kakehi commented that he had hoped foreigners would also revere and serve the emperor with sincerity, ultimately, in his mind, they were at best "guests (*hinkyaku*)" or, at worst, merely "objects (*kyakutai*)" who could not possibly consider the emperor their parent and worship the emperor as did Japanese.[74] He went on to assert that foreigners were fundamentally different from Japanese in the way that they viewed authority, too. Simply put, he adamantly believed that foreigners inevitably viewed themselves as "independent people (*dokuritsujin*),"[75] and that state authority in their minds was inevitably conceived in terms of a power relationship. Unlike Japanese, they were individuals (*kojin*) who thought of themselves as autonomous human beings (*dokuritsu no ningen*).[76] Foreigners would always be foreigners. After all, they were not descendants of the ancestral gods (*yaoyorozu no kami*).[77] This argument denied people of other races and ethnic groups participation in the Japanese State Shintō religion, saying that only Japanese could be the true people of the gods. In other words, a group of individuals who follow the religion of the emperor are not Japanese (*Nihonzoku*); Japanese are Japanese because of the "ethnic type (*zokushū*)" from which they are born.[78] Thus, because of biology or heredity, non-Japanese could not be spiritually Japanese.

Among Japanese within the Japanese empire, Kakehi categorized the population into three parts: the emperor (*Tennō sama*), members of the imperial family (*kōzoku sama*), and subjects (*shinmin*). Together they constituted the Japanese tribe (*Nihonzoku*).[79] In other words, "faith in the emperor was the faith of the Japanese Volk."[80] Likewise, the imperial state was a polity founded on the basis of "the unity of religion and state (*saisei itchi*),"[81] the "universal self" that envelops all activities.

Fired up by a religious fundamentalism in an imagined pure theocratic community, one might expect that Kakehi would find fault with Article 28 of the Constitution of the Empire of Japan, which reads, "Japanese subjects shall, within limits not prejudicial to peace and order, and not antagonistic to their duties as subjects, enjoy freedom of religious belief."[82] This was not necessarily the case, however. Somewhat astonishingly, he interpreted Article 28 as a proclamation of a line of reasoning in support of the *Kannagara no Michi* and the great law of the land going back to the founding of the Japanese state. In a different chain of reasoning, he asserted that this article, as it was expressed in the constitution, resembled similar articles in relation to freedom of religion and freedom of belief in Western constitutions, but it was fundamentally different in nature and significance. Freedom of religion in Western countries means that the state shall not, through the use of force, interfere in the freedom of the religious life of the individual and that the state shall not impinge on the spiritual sphere of the church. Kakehi interpreted this to mean that a compromise had been worked out in Western countries between the states, on the one hand, and the individual and church, on the other hand. Underlying this formula of compromise was the fundamental presumption that the individual obeys the laws of the state while at the same time acknowledging and maintaining the notion of an autonomous and independent individuality. In other words, the "people of the Church (*kyōkaijin*)" were presumed to have a moral and religious sphere of life above and beyond the authority of the state.[83] In the Japanese ethnic state, however, the individual and his moral life and moral consciousness were totally subsumed into the religious belief of the imperial theocratic state. From this vantage point, Kakehi interpreted Article 28 to mean that Japanese were free to uphold other faiths as long as they were not in conflict with beliefs and doctrines of the State Shintō *Kannagara no Michi*, into which all Japanese were born.

Kakehi also argued that the Chinese state, no different from Western states, was based on individualism: "In China, too, the state is a group of citizens."[84] He lashed out at the popes of the Roman Catholic church for not recognizing the freedom of religion in Roman Catholic states. He even referred to the dogmas of the "Tribes of Israel (*Isuraeru zoku*)."[85] For Kakehi, faith in the Way of the Gods of the imperial ancestors was absolute. Accordingly, there had to be restrictions on the following of dogmas of foreign religions. In short, he tried to convey the idea that Article 28 of the Constitution of the Empire of Japan in no way placed restrictions on the emperor and in no way diminished religious devotion to the emperor on behalf of Japanese subjects.

Kakehi's "Myth of the Twentieth Century"

How might one sum up Kakehi's ideology in the context of the general theme of this study and try to understand it in a broader comparative context? This study has demonstrated that an important transformation took place in the internal structure of the ideology of State Shintō from Hozumi Yatsuka's articulation of the traditional patriarchical family-state in the late Meiji period to Uesugi Shinkichi's metaphysical moral state and Kakehi's theocratic state in the post-Meiji period. By the 1910s, one could not say, as Hozumi had done in the 1890s, that the masses must meekly obey the state or that they should not be allowed to have some direct input in the affairs of state. Hozumi had tried to block the expansion of suffrage, arguing in effect that the masses politically were children and incapable of governing themselves. He insisted that the emperor was their paternal father and that it was the duty of all Japanese subjects to be passively obedient. In addition to arguing for imperial absolutism from the position of patriarchalism, he also cited the Shintō scriptures, claiming that Japan must be reigned over and governed by an unbroken line of emperors for ages eternal, and he expected the majority of the population to accept this doctrine unquestioningly.

But because of the politicization of the masses in the first and second decades of the twentieth century, Hozumi's argument in support of absolute monarchy was falling on deaf ears within a mere decade after he had articulated it. People were already beginning to gravitate toward Minobe Tatsukichi's emperor-as-organ-of-the-state theory as the chief ideology in support of parliamentary government. Accordingly, arguing in defense of extreme nationalism based on Shintōism, Uesugi and Kakehi had to recast the old doctrine of absolute monarchy in a new form. They could not go back to the simple authoritarian ideology of Hozumi.

Nagao Ryūichi, a leading scholar of the history of Japanese state thought and the history of Japanese constitutional law, also recognized that an important change had taken place in Shintō ultranationalist ideology between Hozumi Yatsuka and Uesugi Shinkichi and Kakehi Katsuhiko.[86] In *Nihon Kokka Shisō Shi Kenkyū* (A Study of the History of Japanese State Thought; 1982), Nagao stated,

Hozumi Yatsuka, in a sense, was an evolutionist under the influence of Katō Hiroyuki. His theory of the *kokutai* entirely focused on the issue of power. . . . His theory of government by direct imperial rule and the rejection of party cabinets lost its realistic foundation after Itō Hirobumi assumed the Presidency of the *Seiyūkai*. . . . What gave the final blows to the *kokutai* theory of Hozumi's constitutional science were the death of Emperor Meiji and the coronation of the sickly Emperor Taishō. With these events, the fictitious nature of justifying the activities of the clan clique in power under the name of the emperor was exposed to the public eye.[87]

Nagao argued that Hozumi's family-state theory lost all credibility after the death of Emperor Meiji. He went on to note that while Hozumi's theory of absolute monarchy faded away, Minobe's emperor-as-organ theory in support of parliamentary rule emerged to become the dominant theory of state.

But Nagao also went on to say that "it does not mean that the lifeblood of the kokutai theory was terminated even in this period" of gravitation toward democratic government.[88] He cited several reasons for this. First, a strong ideological justification for expansionism was needed. Because of its successes in the Qing Dynasty–Japan War of 1894–95 and the Japan–Russia War of 1904–5, Japan was beginning to flex its muscles and emerge as a great imperial power. In 1910, Japan annexed Korea, and in 1915, it issued the "Twenty-One Demands" to China. Second, Nagao noted that people concerned with international security in Japan, particularly military officials, began to see the need to prepare for a second world war after observing the realities of "total war" of the First World War. This preparation for a total conflict would require the "full mobilization of the national spirit."[89] He wrote, "The necessity of 'kokutai education' for the preparation of full mobilization of the national spirit in case of a future great war was repeatedly emphasized by some people, especially in the military."[90]

Nagao also noted that early in his career, Uesugi, like his mentor Hozumi, had come out against the expansion of the franchise. However, Uesugi, strongly influenced by what had happened in the Great War in Europe, began to advocate universal suffrage in the spring of 1917. He felt that extending the franchise to the masses was the only way to totally mobilize the Japanese population. In other words, Nagao observed that Uesugi had undergone a *tenkō*, a sort of ideological conversion. But this ideological conversion was not a conversion to democracy. Although

Nagao does not specifically state this, I believe that Uesugi at this point broke with Hozumi and converted to what would become his totalitarian ideology, as discussed in chapter 5. Nagao's remarks, however, do corroborate the basic thesis of this book that Uesugi's 1921 work was written in reaction to Hozumi's patriarchal authoritarian theory of state: "The significance of saying 'The state is ultimate morality' means the exclusion of Hozumi's theory of an authoritarian view of the state."[91] Nagao then cited a passage in A New Thesis on the State in which Uesugi says that, in following an ideology such as Hozumi's authoritarianism, the "Japanese people's respect, affection, aspirations and enthusiasm toward the Japanese nation could not help but become dry and prosaic."[92] As has been discussed, Uesugi's state theory eliminated all power relationships from the internal structure of the state. Indeed, Uesugi stated in A New Thesis on the State that the emperor had a "colorless and transparent mirror-like existence" that reflected everything.[93]

Nagao referred to Kakehi Katsuhiko as the other major state theorist of the Taishō and Shōwa periods who adapted the Meiji formulation of imperial absolutism to meet the needs of the modern state. While Uesugi was a kind of "metaphysician," he said, Kakehi was a "totally religious person."[94] He further wrote that Kakehi tried to revive and promote the ancient Shintō way pioneered by Motoori Norinaga and Hirata Atsutane. Therefore, Nagao saw a direct ideological linkage between the great classical National Learning theorists of the Tokugawa period and Shintō ultranationalists such as Kakehi of the twentieth century.

How can one better understand Kakehi's ideology in further comparative context? First, in terms of political form or political structures, Kakehi's ideology, as in the case of Uesugi Shinkichi's, was classically totalitarian. As Hannah Arendt said, totalitarianism seeks the "total domination of the total population of the earth."[95] According to Arendt, "Even a single individual can be absolutely and reliably dominated only under global totalitarian conditions."[96] Kakehi's concept of "one heart, same body" sought to extinguish the individual, as was the case for Uesugi's state. Conceptually, this identity of the emperor and the Japanese masses is close to the totalitarian identity of Der Führer and the German masses in Nazi thought as described by Arendt:

Totalitarianism is never content to rule by external means. . . . In this sense, it eliminates the distance between the rulers and the ruled and achieves a condition in which power and the will to power, as we understand them, play no role, or at least, a secondary role. In substance, the totalitarian leader is nothing more nor less than the functionary of the masses he leads; he is not a power-hungry individual imposing a tyrannical and arbitrary will upon his subjects. Being a mere functionary, he can be replaced at any time, and he depends just as much on the "will" of the masses he embodies as the masses depend on him. Without him they would lack external representation and remain an amorphous horde; without the masses the leader is a nonentity. Hitler, who was fully aware of this interdependence, expressed it once in a speech addressed to the SA [Sturmabteilung]: "All that you are, you are through me; all that I am, I am through you alone."[97]

Likewise, in the state thought of Uesugi and Kakehi, the emperor was not "imposing a tyrannical and arbitrary rule" on the Japanese population. But there was one significant difference between the Japanese emperor and Arendt's analysis of the German leader: the Japanese emperor was not just a "mere functionary" who "can be replaced at any time." The Japanese emperor was the *arahitogami*, or "divine being in human form" descended from the unbroken line of emperors from the Age of the Gods. Also, radical Shintō ultranationalists were never concerned with something like the German *Führer-prinzip* in which Der Führer, as Mosse stated, "would be a representative member of the Volk, and would be greater only by virtue of his charismatic leadership."[98] The Japanese emperor did not need to give electrifying speeches to the masses; he needed only to come into the presence of the masses and perhaps make a slight motion of his hand to acknowledge his awareness of them, and the masses would shout with all their hearts, "*Tennō heika Banzai!* (Long live His Imperial Majesty!)" As Herbert Bix noted, "His charisma resided in his whole imperial being."[99]

Kakehi's concept of one great universal life was a justification for global domination. Arendt draws a distinction between the traditional type of imperialism and the totalitarian goal: "Just as the totalitarian claim to world rule is only in appearance the same as imperialist expansionism, so the claim to total domination only seems familiar to the student of despotism. If the chief difference between totalitarian and imperialist expansion is that the former recognizes no difference between a home and a foreign country,"[100] Kakehi, too, sought to eliminate the difference between the Japanese state and foreign countries, although, as discussed earlier, he clearly set boundaries between the Japanese Volk and other peoples. For example, in *The Great Principles of Ancient Shintō*, he even stated that "Amaterasu Ōmikami is not only the ancestor of the Japanese,

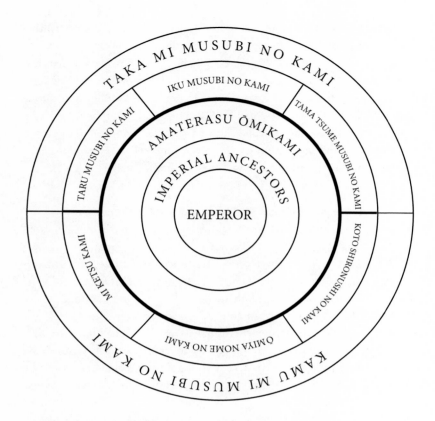

Kakehi Katsuhiko's Shintō cosmology.

but also the ancestor of all human beings."[101] He also said that "Japan is the center of the world,"[102] and he used ancient Shintō scriptures to justify the claim. Japan was the center of the world because the emperor was at the center of a Shintō cosmology.

Kakehi was fond of diagrams. In *The Great Principles of Ancient Shintō*, he provided an illustration of the Shintō cosmology. At the center of this universe was the emperor. Going outward in concentric circles from the emperor were the spirits of the imperial ancestors; Amaterasu Ōmikami; the six deities Koto Shiro Nushi no Kami, Tama Tsume Musubi no Kami, Iku Musubi no Kami, Taru Musubi no Kami, Omiya Nome no Kami, and Mi Ketsu Kami, who had been the center of worship by the Department of the Shintō Religion since the Heian period; and Taka mi Musubi no Kami and Kamu mi Musubi no Kami, who were the divine creators of the entire universe.

One can easily imagine the Japanese state at the center of this diagram because the state consisted of the emperor and everyone else as a constituent element of the emperor, or the people as in reality a part of the mystical body of the emperor, as in Kakehi's theory of "one heart, one body." We should also keep in mind that his ultimate goal of attaining a divine-like world of Takamaga Hara on earth was, of course, not a rational conception of a future society or a future world order but a vision, a dream, which was still another facet of Kakehi's totalitarian emperor ideology.

Compared with Japanese radical Shintō ultranationalism and German National Socialism, Italian Fascism appears to have been merely a strong form of traditional authoritarianism, for the Italian Fascists did not attempt to eliminate the individual; nor did they have a plan for world domination. The Italian Fascist theorist and Minister of Justice Alfredo Rocco (1875–1935) stated: "The relations between state and citizens are completely reversed by the Fascist doctrine. Instead of the liberal-democratic formula, 'society for the individual,' we have 'individuals for the society.' With this difference, however: that while the liberal doctrines eliminated society, Fascism does not submerge the individual in the social group. It subordinates him, but does not eliminate him."[103] The important point of this statement is that, while the individual is subordinated to the state, it is not eliminated. As we have seen, Japanese Shintō ultranationalists wanted to eliminate the individual entirely. In this respect, therefore, Japanese radical Shintō ultranationalism and German National Socialism appear closer to each other theoretically than either was to Italian Fascism.

Second, in terms of ideological substance, scholars of German National Socialist thought reading Kakehi's radical Shintō ultranationalist ideology will no doubt be reminded of Alfred Rosenberg and his major work *The Myth of the Twentieth Century: An Evaluation of the Spiritual–Intellectual Confrontations of Our Age* (1930). Rosenberg's work was also of interest to Japanese radical Shintō ultranationalists, who saw in it a major development in the rebirth of religious ethnic nationalism on the European side of the Eurasian continent in the 1930s. The radical Shintō ultranationalist Fujisawa Chikao, in fact, commented that "pure Nazism was really a manifestation of the Japanese spirit on German soil."[104] Although the primitive German völkisch religion had nearly been lost forever in the consciousness of Germans due to the centuries-long onslaught of Christianity and, in modern times, to the dominance of universal secular ideologies, Nazis such as Rosenberg sought to revive it and bring it to the center of state ideology. Rosenberg's worldview, or *Welt-*

anschauung, in broad, conceptual terms, was nearly identical to that of Kakehi and other radical Shintō ultranationalists who had labored to revive the ancient Shintō völkisch religion and propel it to the center of the Japanese state as a national ideology. In other words, Japanese radical Shintō ultranationalists viewed German Nazis and, to a lesser extent, Italian Fascists as junior ideological partners in a worldwide revolutionary movement against the existing world order created and controlled by states established on the basis of universalistic religions or their derivative secular ideologies. For example, Rosenberg, quoting Paul de Lagarde's *Deutsche Schriften* (German Writings; 1878) saw the fundamental world struggle in the same way: "World religion in the singular and national religions in the plural—these are the beginning points of two diametrically opposed camps. . . . Nations are the ideas of God! Catholicism, Protestantism, Jewry and Naturalism must be cleared from the field before beginning a new world outlook."[105] From the perspective of Shintō ultranationalists such as Hozumi, Uesugi, and Kakehi, as well as German National Socialists, universalistic religions were the relatively new pagan religions in man's history that had attempted (and nearly succeeded) to destroy man's original völkisch religions—the true religions. These universalistic religions in the East were Buddhism and Confucianism. In the German case, it was primarily Christianity. From a German völkisch perspective, the only exceptions were the Jews, who had their own völkisch national religion, which had invaded the German völkisch homeland and therefore had to be exterminated.

Of course, Japanese radical Shintō ultranationalists such as Kakehi and Uesugi and German Nazis such as Rosenberg were merely the latest in a long line of völkisch thinkers in both countries, but Japan's völkisch movement went back much further than Germany's and was much more entrenched in the Japanese consciousness. As George Mosse wrote, the origins of German völkisch religion can be traced back to the nineteenth century to Paul de Largarde and Julius Langbehn and continued at the beginning of the twentieth century in Houston Stewart Chamberlain's massive *Foundations of the Nineteenth Century*.[106] The most revered ancient writing on the German Volk was, of course, written by the Roman historian Tacitus, who lived in the first century. Tacitus's *Germania*, which in the minds of German völkisch nationalists, is supposed to have described accurately the culture of the tribes that were the ancestors of the modern Teutonic nations before they came into contact with the Romans. However, this German völkisch tradition pales in comparison with the Japanese völkisch movement, with its revival by people such as Kamo

Mabuchi, Motoori Norinaga, and Hirata Atsutane during the Tokugawa period in the eighteenth century and nineteenth century. The Germans had nothing in comparison to the *Nihon Shoki* and the *Kojiki*, the large sacred Shintō texts, which describes Japanese society prior to the introduction of the pagan Buddhist religion and Confucian thought from continental Asian civilizations and reveals the descent of the imperial line from the origins of the universe. From the viewpoint of radical Shintō ultranationalist thinkers, German National Socialists, who also yearned for the rebirth of a pure völkisch religious state, and even Italian Fascists, were considered varied manifestations of radical Shintō ultranationalism. From the Japanese perspective, Italian Fascism was the weakest link in the Axis alliance and had the least developed national religious consciousness, which can be attributed to the fact that the original Volk religion of the Italians had been virtually lost because Christianity was centered in Rome. It is also worth noting that the Greek völkisch religion was outlawed by the Roman Empire in the late fourth century. Today, perhaps only a handful of people still honor the Olympian Zeus. Japanese Shintō ultranationalists viewed this as a great tragedy.

In *The Myth of the Twentieth Century*, which was translated from the German (*Der Mythus des 20. Jahrhunderts*) into Japanese as *Nijū Seiki no Shinwa* in 1938, Rosenberg articulated the intellectual and spiritual foundation of the ideology of National Socialism. As the subtitle of his book, "An Evaluation of the Spiritual-Intellectual Confrontation of Our Age" suggests, the great struggle was inherently religious in nature. In book 1, "The Conflict of Values," Rosenberg wrote:

> Today one of those epochs is beginning in which world history must be written anew. . . . A youthful life-force—which also knows itself to be age-old—is impelled toward form; an ideology, a *Weltanschauung*, has been born and, strong of will, begins to contend with old forms, ancient sacred practices, and outward standards. . . . And this sign of our times is reflected in a turning away from absolute values, that is to say, in a retreat from values held to be beyond all organic experience, which the isolated ego once devised to create, by peaceful or violent means, a *universal* spiritual community. Once, such ultimate aim was the "Christianizing of the world" and its redemption through the Second Coming of Christ. Another goal was represented by the Humanist dream of "Mankind." . . . Christianity, with its vacuous creed of ecumenicalism and its ideal of humanitas, disregarded the current of red-blooded vitality which flows through the veins of all peoples of true worth and genuine culture.[107]

For Rosenberg, National Socialism's leading ideologist, the great confrontation of the twentieth century was between the "religion of the blood" and universal religions of mankind and their secular derivatives.[108] In this sense, Rosenberg's characterization of this great conflict of the twentieth century as the völkisch religion of the blood versus universalistic religions encompassing all of mankind was, broadly, identical to that articulated by Hozumi, Uesugi, and Kakehi. German Nationalists, however, who lacked the long-surviving Japanese völkisch Shintō religious tradition, had to create a "German Volk Church."[109]

Again, this is not to suggest that the internal conceptualizations of Japanese and German völkisch societies are identical. They were not. The most notable difference was with the concept of leadership. While the god-emperor was central to radical Shintō ultranationalism, monarchy had nothing at all to do with German Nationalism. Rosenberg stressed that "whoever wishes to be a nationalist today, must also be a socialist."[110] Furthermore, Hegelian thought, in which the "State" and the "State Official" became separated from the organic body of the Volk,[111] was rejected by Rosenberg. Accordingly, he wrote, "The State does not even have a purpose unless it acts to preserve the concept of the Volk."[112] Likewise, Rosenberg argued that in the German tradition, the king or the kaiser—the dynastic concept—was severed from the "Volk-totality,"[113] and in 1918 the dynastic ideas of state collapsed. Soon thereafter, "All conscious German Nationalist circles came to realize the days of kingship were over."[114] One might conclude that it was the successful welding together of the emperor and the Japanese masses in the first two decades of the twentieth century by people such as Uesugi and Kakehi that prevented the collapse of the emperor system in Japan. That is to say, Hozumi Yatsuka's ideal of a traditional patriarchal authoritarian state could not have survived in the twentieth century.

Interestingly, unlike Adolf Hitler, who referred often to Japan in *Mein Kampf* (1924) and became increasingly infatuated with Japan,[115] Rosenberg spoke very little in *The Myth of the Twentieth Century* about Japan and the Japanese. It was only at the end of his book that he specifically referred to Japan. According to Rosenberg, the völkisch traditions in East Asia had come under attack by Western imperialism in the nineteenth century. In this context, he noted, "It was not in the name of necessary protection that the white race broke into China but in the service of profit-seeking by Jewish traders. As a result the white race has dishonored itself. It has disintegrated an entire culture and precipitated a just rebellion against itself."[116] In response to this Western intrusion into East

Asia, Chinese and Japanese were leading movements in their countries aimed at racial renewal and the liberation of the region. The German renewal movement also sought war against the Jewish trader race that controlled all global capital markets. Similarly, it planned to dominate Japan, which "was still independent of high finance."[117] Rosenberg sympathized with Japan's predicament, saying that Japan was strengthening its forces in Manchuria out of an instinct for self-preservation.

I will now turn to the triumph of radical Shintō ultranationalism in the Shōwa period.

III

RADICAL SHINTŌ
ULTRANATIONALISM AND
ITS TRIUMPH IN THE EARLY
SHŌWA PERIOD

8

Terrorism in the Land of the Gods

In this book I explore this dark alliance between religion and violence. In examining recent acts of religious terrorism I try to understand the cultures of violence from which such acts emerge. . . .

Religion is crucial for these acts, since it gives moral justification for killing and provides images of cosmic war that allow activists to believe that they are waging spiritual scenarios. This does not mean that religion causes violence, nor does it mean that religious violence cannot, in some cases, be justified by other means. But it does mean that religion often provides the mores and symbols that make possible bloodshed—even catastrophic acts of terrorism.—MARK JUERGENSMEYER, "Preface," *Terror in the Mind of God*, 3rd. ed., xi

Japanese Militant Ultranationalist Movements

What is truly remarkable about the inter-prewar period of modern Japanese history was the sheer amount of politically, ideologically, and religiously motivated violence and acts of terrorism that plagued the nation. Three serving prime ministers (Hara Takashi [1856–1921], Hamaguchi Osachi [1870–1931], and Inukai Tsuyoshi [1855–1932]) and two former prime ministers (Saitō Makoto [1858–1936] and Takahashi Korekiyo [1854–1936]) were assassinated between 1921 and 1936. Within the same period, Prime Minister Okada Keisuke (1868–1952) had escaped an assassination attempt while he was prime minister, and Suzuki Kantarō (1867–1948), the man who would become Japan's last prime minister in the prewar period, narrowly survived an assassination attempt. (The would-be assassin's bullet remained inside Suzuki's body for the rest of his life.) Had the assassination attempt on Okada been successful, an astonishing six prime ministers or former prime ministers would have been murdered within a fifteen-year period and five of them within the final six years of that period. It is also noteworthy that two-time Prime Minister Wakatsuki Reijirō (1926–27 and 1931) had been slated for assassination by terrorists in the "October [1931] Incident." In addition to all this, we can add the number of related high-profile terrorist "incidents" that occurred between 1930 and 1936, resulting in the murder or attempted murder of leading intellectuals, political figures (including entire cabinets), top military officers, and prominent business leaders. Political violence and assassinations had become so commonplace that Hugh Byas, a foreign correspondent, political observer, and longtime resident of Japan at the time, wrote about it in a book, characterizing the pronounced feature of politics in the early 1930s in Japan as *Government by Assassination*.[1] Finally, one must also keep in mind that there was much violence on the political left wing, as well. Even Emperor Meiji was targeted for assassination by a group of radical socialists and anarchists, including Kōtoku Shūsui in the so-called High Treason Incident of 1910–11, and Regent Hirohito narrowly escaped being shot by the anarchist Namba Taisuke in the infamous Toranomon Incident in December 1923. And, of course, we should not forget that Minobe Tatsukichi had to deal with more than one attempt on his life.

How can one account for all this political violence and terrorism in a disciplined society that prided itself on harmony and consensus? This is not an easy question to answer, but one thing is quite certain: the wave of political violence did not suddenly appear in an ideological and political vacuum. There had to have been years, if not decades, of preparation within a particular political and ideological environment for this kind of terrorism to have taken place.

In his superb analysis of postwar Japanese politics, Gerald Curtis referred to the fact that one cannot predict precisely the changes to come in Japanese politics, writing, "We can understand the forces propelling political change, and stalling it as well, and discern the political opportunity structure within which Japanese political leaders will make the choices that will decide the future of Japanese politics."[2] A similar thing, I believe, can be said about the ideological forces propelling political change and violence, and we can discern the "ideological opportunity structure" within which Japanese make ideological choices and political choices. Curtis's assertion about incrementalism in the pace of political change in Japan also applies to the prewar period. Throughout his book, he stressed "how the interplay of change and continuity in Japanese political development created resistance at all levels of the political system to anything more than cautious incremental policy adjustments. There has not been public support for radical departures in Japanese government policy, whether the issue relates to the economy or foreign policy."[3]

Curtis also stated that "resistance to radical change is anchored deep in Japanese society and its political institutions. Those leaders who have tried to make a case for drastic change have been notably unsuccessful in persuading many people to agree with them."[4] I wholeheartedly agree with his analysis. Even after years of spectacular acts of terrorism, which served as a catalyst for changes in national political policy, rapid radical change in government proved impossible, and only in incremental stages did Japan go forward toward full-scale war in Asia and beyond.

E. Bruce Reynolds's insightful analysis of the peculiar characteristics of the prewar Japanese political system also shows that there was no simple institutional framework and political tradition within which sudden radical changes in government policy could emerge, given that the Constitution of the Empire of Japan was a sacred document (bestowed by the emperor, so modification of it was not a viable option) and that the Meiji oligarchs had created a constitution that masked the realities of a unusual separation of powers. Accordingly, he argued that this led many Japanese advocates of the "third way [fascists]" to the conclusion that it would be better "to co-opt, rather than to overturn, the existing [state] structure" and "achieve their goals within the existing political structure,"[5] certainly a position taken by the Control Faction within the military. Other radical ultranationalists, however, who felt it was futile to force radical change through the existing political system engaged in terrorist activities and unauthorized military actions to try to bring about a Shōwa Restoration and to mobilize the nation for war. Foreign observers of Japanese politics at the time found it almost impossible to comprehend the course of events in Japan by standards that they were accustomed to. For instance, Reynolds observed that "[Herbert] von Dirksen [German ambassador to Japan in 1933–38] pointed out that Japan's ultranationalists were able to launch overseas expansion in Manchuria in 1931 before gaining control of the government at home, while the Nazis had to gain power first before pursuing expansionism."[6] In other words, events in Japan seemed to unfold in ways quite unlike what one might expect to happen.

The purpose of this chapter is to try to understand radical Shintō ultranationalist terrorism between 1930 and 1936 in the context of the broader parameters of ideological and political developments already presented in this work. One of the conclusions I have drawn from this study is that the use of terrorism was absolutely essential to gradually nudge the Japanese state toward launching a global war. Whenever possible, I have tried to place Japanese ultranationalist terrorism within a broader comparative framework of global terrorism, incorporating ideas on this topic by noted scholars such as Walter Laqueur, Mark Juergensmeyer, Ariel Merari, Walter Reich, and Bruce Hoffman, as well as a Japanese author on right-wing terrorism who writes under the pseudonym Tendō Tadashi.

Laqueur wrote, "History shows that terrorism is not a static phenomenon; what is true for a terrorist group in one country at a certain time is not necessarily true with regard to terrorism in another period on another condition. Hence the great difficulties associated with any attempt to generalize about terrorism. Specific political, social and cultural conditions predicate the way in which we will form an understanding of any given situation."[7] Laqueur went on to say, "What is true with regard to, say, the Irish patriots of the nineteenth century or the anarchists and the Russian terrorists of the early twentieth century does not necessarily carry through to the Islamic terrorist of today."[8] He further stated that "one example should suffice: The old terrorism was selective in the main, directed against leading figures of the 'establishment.' The Al Qaeda-type terrorism, on the other hand, is indiscriminate; the aim is to annihilate a more generalized enemy, not carry out 'propaganda by deed,' as the anarchists put it."[9] Japanese terrorism in the prewar period was also rooted in its specific political, social, cultural, and ideological conditions. But what is striking in the Japanese case is the sheer amount of terrorist violence *across* the ideological spectrum, from the extreme left to the far right. Furthermore, the prewar Japanese ultranationalist terrorist phenomenon differed from the pattern of terrorism carried out by Japanese anarchists and other leftists groups. Still more striking is the complexity and shifting nature of terrorism on the extreme radical right. Although a shared common ideology united ultranationalist terrorists, a kaleidoscope of patterns and trends characterize terrorism. Ultranationalist terrorism under the rule of the authoritarian Meiji oligarchs, for instance, evolved into something distinctively different in the increasingly secular and more democratic Taishō period, which in turn evolved still more dramatically in the early Shōwa period.

"Terrorism is violence—or, equally important, the threat of violence— used and directed in pursuit of, or in service of, a political aim."[10] If one defines terrorism in this way, terrorist groups in Japan emerged within the early years of the formation of the modern Japanese state. For instance, Ōkubo Toshimichi, one of the great leaders of the Meiji Restoration revolution, was assassinated in May 1878 in Kioizaka, Tokyo, by Shimada Ichirō, who had conspired with a group of discontent former samurai to kill him. Ōkubo argued against war with Korea in 1873 and had been considered a traitor to Satsuma when he opposed Saigō Takamori in the Satsuma Rebellion of 1877.

In 1881, the ultranationalist, terrorist organization Genyōsha (Dark Ocean Society), founded by Hiraoka Kotarō (1851–1906), emerged. The assassination attempt on October 18, 1889, by Kurushima Tsuneki on Foreign Minister Ōkuma Shigenobu over a treaty revision is one early example of a terrorist activity planned and carried out by the organization.[11] Another example of the organization's domestic terrorist activities came during the general election of 1892, when "the society exerted itself to terrorize anti-government candidates in the Fukuoka area."[12] The Dark Ocean Society and the Kokuryūkai (Black Dragon Society), founded in 1901, were among Japan's earliest ultranationalist terrorist groups. Both organizations during the Meiji period, however, are probably best remembered for their influence in pushing the Japanese nation toward military expansionism on the Asian continent, especially in Korea and Manchuria. With the assistance of Dark Ocean Society members such as Fuji Katsuaki and Kajikara Hikaru, Japanese operatives under orders from Miura Gorō, the Japanese ambassador to Korea, assassinated Empress Myongsong (also known as Queen Min) in the Korean royal palace on October 8, 1895. Miura's key man in the plot was Adachi Kenzō, who would later become home minister in the Wakatsuki cabinet of 1931.

The wave of rampant radical Shintō ultranationalist terrorism that would plague the Japanese nation in the first decade of the Shōwa period and fundamentally change the nature of Japanese politics, however, had its roots in the increasingly secularized, liberal, and democratic period of the 1920s. It can said to have begun with the assassination of Yasuda Zenjirō, the Japanese entrepreneur who founded the Yasuda financial and industrial combine, one of Japan's great prewar conglomerates that would dominate the economy in the prewar period, by Asahi Heigo on September 28, 1921. The assassination of Prime Minister Hara Takashi in November 1921 by the eighteen-year-old Japan railway switchman Nakaoka Konichi occurred less than two months later. The context of Hara's assassination remains somewhat unclear. Nakaoka's motives for stabbing the prime minister to death were apparently not pursued to the fullest during his court trial, which is astonishing, considering the gravity of the crime. However, it is believed that he had close ties to ultra-nationalist organizations. In other words, it is assumed that the assassination of Hara involved more than one individual. At any rate, these two cases of terrorism were the beginnings of a trajectory that would engulf the Japanese nation by the end of the decade in the early Shōwa period.

The next significant terrorist act by Japanese radical ultranationalists took place not in Japan, but in Manchuria. This was the assassination of the warlord Zhang Zuolin in June 1928 by army officers of the Kwantung Army led by Colonel Kōmoto Daisaku and his commanding officer Muraoka Chōtarō. Other military officers involved in Zhang's assassination included Captain Tomiya Kaneo, the man who operated the switch to detonate the explosion on the railway line, and Lieutanant Kirihara Sadatoshi, a military engineer from the Japanese army in Korea who took care of the technical aspects of the bombing operation. Japanese army terrorists planned Zhang's assassination with precision. They had planted the bomb on the railway line near a junction in which the train was moving en route to Shenyang (Mukden) from Beijing. The terrorists waited in a nearby shed for the eighth car from the front of the train, in which they learned from military intelligence sources Zhang was aboard, to pass over the spot where the bomb had been placed, then detonated the explosives. They were successful in carrying out the attack. Zhang died in a Shenyang hospital several hours later. Seventeen others close to Zhang were also killed in the blast. Apparently, it was Dohihara Kenji, head of military intelligence in Manchuria (one of the twenty-five found guilty by the International Military Tribunal for the Far East and sentenced to death), who had masterminded Zhang's assassination.

Zhang's assassination was, of course, a setback for Prime Minister Tanaka, who had orchestrated a plan to manipulate Zhang in order to control Manchuria. The junior-officer terrorists, dissatisfied with Tanaka's foreign policy with regard to Manchuria, were trying to push Japan toward war, however. An extensive network of officers was bent on resorting to terrorism to push the Japanese state into war. Not only that: accomplices and sympathizers went all the way to the top of the military establishment, including Tanaka's own minister of war. The irony is that Tanaka, who had departed from previous administrations in the 1920s by taking an aggressive policy toward China, would fall victim to radical elements within the military. Richard Storry noted, "Kawamoto's [Kōmoto's] Manchurian plot in 1928 can be called the first notable indication of terrorist activity on the part of the younger officers of the modern Japanese army."[13] The assassination of Zhang did not lead to war, but Tanaka was unable to bring the terrorists to justice. Nevertheless, this incident clearly illustrates the weakness of the Japanese government and that radical ultranationalist elements in the military were spiraling out of control. No one was held accountable, although Kōmoto resigned his post as senior staff officer in the Kwangtung Army. (Lieutenant-Colonel Ishihara Kanji, the man who planned the Manchurian Incident, replaced him.)

A wave of assassination attempts by ultranationalists within Japan was soon to follow. It began with the murder of Yamamoto Senji (1889–1929), a left-wing leader and politician, in March 1929 by Kuroda Okuji, a member of the Shintō ultranationalist Shichi Sei Gi Dan (Seven Lives Righteousness Association).[14] In November 1930, Prime Minister Hamaguchi Osachi was attacked at Tokyo Station by Sagoya Tomeo, a member of the radical Shintō ultranationalist Aikoku Sha (Patriotic Society),[15] who was enraged at the prime minister for, among other things, having infringed on the emperor's prerogative of supreme command of the military, as they saw it, by signing the London Naval Treaty. Hamaguchi died the following year, in November 1931. The next four prime ministers who would hold office from 1931 to 1936 would be targeted for assassination by radical Shintō ultranationalist groups. It took radical Shintō ultranationalists more that half a decade of selectively targeted assassinations to destabilize the government to the point where major change of course in the nation's domestic and foreign policies became inevitable.

The formation of the secret society Sakura Kai (Cherry Blossom Society) within the army in September 1930 by mid-ranking army officers on the active-duty list led by Hashimoto Kingorō and Chō Isamu was another important development in the history of radical Shintō ultranationalist terrorism.[16] The purpose of the organization was to carry out a program of national reform—a euphemism for the elimination of political-party government, although there was much disagreement over how this should be done, and the promotion of Japanese military expansionism on the Asian continent. This, of course, is the radical Shintō ultranationalist agenda, which advocated personal government by the emperor and the abolition of parliamentary government in addition to unlimited expansionism to establish imperial rule in Asia, and then the world. As is well known, members of the Cherry Blossom Society, in coordination with members of civilian ultranationalists, planned the so-called March (1931) Incident to overthrow the government headed by interim Prime Minister Shidehara Kijurō, who was substituting for the incapacitated Hamaguchi Osachi. The plan never materialized, because General Ugaki, who was to have taken over as head of a military government according to the planned coup d'état, changed his mind at the last minute and refused to go along with it. Impatient with their inability to overturn the civilian leadership in Japan, military officers in the Kwangtung Army in Manchuria started the military takeover of Manchuria, creating the so-called Manchurian Incident on September 18, 1931, the start of the Japanese military's takeover of Manchuria, which arguably started the Second World War. This incident took place during the administration of Wakatsuki Reijirō, who had been in office just four months.

Shortly after the Manchurian Incident came the October (1931) Incident, an attempted coup d'état planned to bring about a "Shōwa Restoration," a euphemism for political action ostensibly designed to restore power to the emperor and expand imperial power in Manchuria. The plan, which included senior military officers, involved the assassination of almost the entire Wakatsuki cabinet (April–December 1931). The terrorists were enraged by Prime Minister Wakatsuki's "non-expansion policy (fukakudai hōshin),"[17] which was an attempt by Wakatsuki and his administration to contain military hostilities in Manchuria and restrain the Kwantung Army from further action. That is to say, acts of terrorism within Japan were inextricably linked to expansionism overseas, although not necessarily coordinated. The evolving ultranationalist movement was far from unified, but sympathizers were inspired by the terrorist actions of like-minded individuals. Ironically, the plot was foiled by Lieutenant-General Araki Sadao. But the instigators of this Kinki Kakumei (Revolution of the Imperial Flag), Hashimoto Kingorō and Chō Isamu, were never punished. Neither was Ōkawa Shūmei, who was involved in both the March (1931) Incident and the October (1931) Incident. The Wakatsuki cabinet, however, would soon be brought down under pressure from Home Minister Adachi Kenzō for "a national unity cabinet."[18]

Radical Shintō ultranationalists struck again in February 1932 by assassinating Inoue Junnosuke, finance minister in Inukai Tsuyoshi's cabinet. Inoue was shot by Onuma Shō,[19] a member of the Ketsumeidan (Blood Pledge Corps) radical Shintō ultranationalist organization. The Blood Pledge Corps had planned to assassinate a number of political and business leaders, who they thought were responsible for agrarian suffering and a weak national government in Tokyo. Just one month later, in

March 1932, Hishinuma Gorō, a member of the Blood Pledge Corps, succeeded in assassinating Dan Takuma, chairman of the board of directors (*rijichō*) of the Mitsui Gōmei (Mitsui Holding Company),[20] which controlled the Mitsui conglomerate. Hisanuma shot Takuma in front of the Mitsui Bank in Nihonbashi, Tokyo.

The next major terrorist attack by radical Shintō ultranationalists came to be known as the May 15 (1932) Incident. This was a plot by several dozen naval and army officers and civilian ultranationalists to overthrow the government of Prime Minister Inukai Tsuyoshi, destroy the system of parliamentary government, and establish direct imperial rule, which many of the conspirators hoped would then lead to war on the Asian continent. Inukai was shot to death in this incident. Compared with the military terrorists who had planned the assassination of Zhang Zuolin, the level of sophistication of the May 15 insurrection was much lower.

In July 1933, during the administration of Saitō Makoto, who was appointed prime minister after the assassination of Inukai, still another major coup d'état was planned by army and naval officers and members of the Dai Nihon Seisan Tō (Great Japan Production Party) and the Aikoku Kinrō Tō (Patriotic Labor Party),[21] which was formed in 1931 by former students of Uesugi Shinkichi, who, as this study has argued, was the preeminent theorist for radical Shintō ultranationalist terrorism. Leaders of the Shimpeitai Incident, also known as the July 11 (1933) Incident, included such people as Amano Tatsuo and Maeda Torao. Amano was admitted to the Tokyo Imperial University Law School in 1913 and became a disciple of Uesugi,[22] later actively spreading his radical teachings for the overthrow of parliamentary government and the restoration of imperial rule. Amano was deeply troubled by the fact that the Blood Pledge Corps assassinations and the May 15 (1932) Incident did not lead to any fundamental changes in the political and economic systems. He had made it his lifelong purpose to bring about a Shōwa Restoration. Amano and the other Shimpeitai (Divine Soldiers) conspirators had planned to kill Prime Minister Saitō and the other members of his cabinet, Makino Nobuaki, Lord Keeper of the Imperial Seal, and attack the offices of the Minseitō, Seiyūkai, and the Social Mass Party. Forty-nine persons were arrested in this coup conspiracy. This is another indication of how radical ultranationalist organizations inspired by Uesugi and other ultranationalist theorists of the 1920s had by the 1930s morphed into small terrorist cells and affiliated groups.

Prime Minister Saitō Makoto had been given the task of forming a "united, national" government by Saionji, but it certainly did not lead to a united government. Just the opposite. Radical Shintō ultranationalist terrorists rejected all forms of compromise, and it merely led to an increasing radicalization of the military and Japanese society in general. Although Japan withdrew from the League of Nations in March 1933 and advanced farther into China under Saitō's administration, radicals such as Amano were far from satisfied. In short, the idea of a national unity government and a more moderate foreign policy was not working because radical Shintō ultranationalists were edging Japan closer toward revolution and expansionism.

By 1935, radical Shintō ultranationalist terrorists were targeting for assassination rival radical Shintō ultranationalist military officers who belonged to other factions. An example of such an incident came in August 1935, during the administration of Okada Keisuke (1934–36), when Lieutenant-Colonel Aizawa Saburō murdered Major-General Nagata Tetsuzan, then the director of the Bureau of Military Affairs in the War Office.

The culmination of the wave of terrorism that began in 1930 came with the so-called February 26 (1936) Incident. This incident was really a repeat of the May 15 (1932) Incident, but on a grander scale. This insurrection was carried out by 1,400 soldiers of the First Division of the army, which was then stationed in Tokyo. It was led by Captain Nonaka Shirō, a company commander in the Third Infantry Regiment of the First Division. The troops surrounded and occupied the Japanese parliament building, the residence of the prime minister, the Ministry of War building, the Metropolitan Police Headquarters, and the Sanno Hotel. Death squads were also sent out to find and murder a number of high-ranking or former high-ranking government officials, such as Admiral Suzuki Kantarō, Grand Chamberlain; Admiral Saitō Makoto, Lord Keeper of the Imperial Seal; General Watanabe Jotarō, Inspector-General of Military Education; and Makino Nobuaki, former Lord Keeper of the Imperial Seal and a longtime adviser to the emperor. A number of the targeted officials were brutally murdered. According to Byas, who observed the insurrection from the windows of his home just outside the area in Tokyo occupied by the insurrectionists, wrote that Prime Minister Okada Keisuke had hidden in a closet of a maid's room while the terrorists, who were unable to identify him, mistakenly murdered his brother-in-law. "Two days later, dressed as a mourner, he followed his own coffin, in which his brother-in-law's body lay, out of the residence under the noses of the mutineers."[23] Takahashi Korekiyo, finance minister at the time and a former prime minister, was "shot with an automatic weapon and brutally hacked to death with a sword."[24] Admiral Saitō was with his wife when his life was taken. "She was wounded in the arm as a stream of bullets was pumped into the old admiral."[25]

Radical Shintō Ultranationalist Terrorism

The wave of rampant ultranationalist terrorism in the early Shōwa period can be traced to both the legacy of the tension within the Japanese ruling elite over foreign policy, particularly with regard to Korea and Manchuria, in the early Meiji period, and, more important, to the major ideological cleavages splitting Japanese society over the issues of state and sovereignty that had begun in the late Meiji period. As Japan slid into a de facto secular parliamentary government in the 1920s, the seeds of radical terrorism were sown. If one examines Japanese ultranationalist terrorism from the Meiji period to the early Shōwa period, one can see several important trends.

First, Japan's early terrorists were civilian ultranationalists, and their targets were civilians. This should not be particularly surprising, since Yamagata's Imperial Rescript to the Soldiers and Sailors (1882) specifically forbade Japanese soldiers and sailors from becoming involved in politics.[26] Yamagata's injunctions were largely obeyed by military personnel in the Meiji period, but military discipline began to slacken in the Taishō period. By the late 1920s, it had become virtually impossible for military authorities to prevent army and navy officers from meddling in politics. Also, as has been discussed, civilians first articulated the theological imperative for religious terrorism. One should keep in mind that military officers got their radical ideological and political ideas from Japan's top civilian state theorists and from legal scholars at Tokyo Imperial University and other leading universities. The influence of Uesugi Shinkichi's ideas on the military is particularly noteworthy. Uesugi's teachings "were required at the military schools,"[27] and "it was with Uesugi and Hiranuma that the senior military barons made common cause in the ultranationalist movement of the 1920s."[28]

"Colonel Kawamoto's [Kōmoto's] plot [to assassinate Manchurian warlord Zhang Zuolin] in 1928 can be called the first notable indication of terrorist activity on the part of the younger officers of the modern Japanese military."[29] From the beginning of the Shōwa period, civilians and military officers actively cooperated to carry out terrorist activities, primarily against civilian politicians, bureaucrats, and financial leaders.

Finally, the ultranationalist terrorist movement evolved to the point that terrorists' activities were planned and led primarily by military officers against other military officers, as well as against civilians. The best-known case of this was the assassination of Major-General Nagata Tet-suzan of the Control Faction by Lieutenant-Colonel Aizawa Saburō of the Imperial Way Faction in August 1935. However, a more intriguing case in the context of the overall theme of this study was the assassination of General Watanabe Jotarō in the February 26, 1936, insurrection.[30] Why was General Watanabe specifically targeted for assassination? Tak-ahashi Masae offered an important perspective on this question. In October 1935, General Watanabe, who had become the superintendent-general of military education (*kyōiku sōkan*) following the forced resignation of General Mazaki Jinsaburō in July,[31] lectured to officers of the Third Division in Nagoya on the emperor-as-organ theory of the state. According to Takahashi, Watanabe had explained to the assembled officers that he had first been exposed to the controversy over the emperor-as-organ theory when he served as an assistant to Army General (*gensui*) Yamagata Aritomo in the 1910s.[32] At that time, he told his audience, Yamagata had gathered together a group of constitutional-law scholars for opinions on the issue, on the advice of Uesugi Shinkichi. Watanabe then related how he had come to the conclusion that the emperor-as-organ theory was not necessarily wrong, citing the words in Emperor Meiji's *Imperial Precepts to the Soldiers and Sailors* that the emperor was the "head (*tōshu*)" of the Japanese state,[33] which, of course, implied that the Japanese state was an organic body composed of organs, with the emperor as its head or main organ. He then urged the officers not to make a great fuss about the current controversy over the emperor-as-organ theory of the state. He apparently did not sincerely believe that the emperor was literally the state, as Shintō religious doctrine proclaimed.

Needless to say, in the highly emotionally charged political, religious, and ideological atmosphere in 1935 revolving around the emperor-as-organ theory of the state, Watanabe's instructions to the soldiers of the Third Division were not well received. His lecture did nothing but enrage a large number of the junior officers in attendance. But that was not the only problem. Since Watanabe was officially speaking as the highest military authority on spiritual training, his remarks soon appeared in print, which, of course, meant that they were read throughout the army. Watanabe was subsequently flooded with letters of protest. At the same time, rumors were circulating that Watanabe had ousted Mazaki from his position as superintendent-general of military education, and, more important, it had been only a few months since General Kikuchi Takeo had denounced Minobe Tatsukichi's emperor-as-organ theory in the House of Peers and the Home Ministry had banned several of Minobe's writings. From that time forward, a group of officers was determined to assassinate General Watanabe. By the mid-1930s, it had become extremely dangerous for anyone openly and publicly to advocate that the emperor was an organ of the state. One was essentially putting one's life on the line by doing so. In connection with this, it must be emphasized that the emperor-as-organ theory had been festering like a sore in the ranks of the Japanese military's officer corps for more than two decades, as the Watanabe incident revealed. After the Manchurian Incident in 1931, the cabinet, controlled by civilian political parties, found itself unable to control the independent actions of the army. The May 15 (1932) Incident, in which Inukai was assassinated, may have marked the end of party-controlled cabinets, but it did not lead to the dissolution of the political parties, which tried to rebound. However, the attacks on the political parties and constitutional government intensified, and their legitimacy was further undercut by the attack on the emperor-as-organ theory of the state, which was the ideological basis of constitutional government. The denunciation of the emperor-as-organ theory made it virtually impossible for party-based politics to revive.

A shift occurred from acts of terrorism to achieve primarily limited, secular political goals in the Meiji period to acts of terrorism for purely or predominantly religious goals in the Shōwa period. But how does one clearly distinguish between acts of terrorism for political and secular reasons from acts of terrorism for purely religious purposes and goals? This is unquestionably a difficult issue, as a number of writers on terrorism have discovered. Bruce Hoffman grappled with this problem in *Inside Terrorism*.[34] He argued, for example, that "anti-colonial, nationalist movements such as the Jewish terrorist organizations active in pre-independence Israel and the Muslim-dominated FLN in Algeria . . . , the overwhelmingly Catholic [Irish Republican Army]; their Protestant counterparts, arrayed in various loyalist paramilitary groups like the Ulster Freedom Fighters, the Ulster Volunteer Force and the Red Hand Commandos; and the predominantly Muslim [Palestine Liberation Organization]" all have a strong religious component,[35] but "in all these groups it is the political, not the religious aspect of their motivation that is dominant."[36] In contrast, Hoffman asserted that terrorist incidents and organizations in which the religious motive is overriding can be classified as religious terrorism. The young Jewish extremist Yigal Amir, who assassinated Israeli Prime Minister Yitzhak Rabin, was a case of religious terrorism. Amir had told the police, "I acted alone and on orders from God."[37] Hoffman asserted that "Amir's words could just as easily come from the mouths of the Islamic Hamas terrorists responsible for the wave of bombings of civilian buses and public gathering-places that have convulsed Israel; the Muslim Algerian terrorists who have terrorized France with a campaign of indiscriminate bombings; the Japanese followers of Shōko Asahara in the Aum Shinrikyo sect who perpetrated the March 1995 nerve gas attack on the Tokyo subway in hopes of hastening a new millennium; or the American Christian Patriots who the following month . . . bombed the Alfred P. Murrah Federal Office Building in Oklahoma City."[38] These were cases of religious terrorism because they were "motivated either in whole or in part by a religious imperative, where violence is regarded by its practitioners as a divine duty or sacramental act [that] embraces markedly different means of legitimization and justification than that committed by secular terrorists."[39]

Likewise, the assassination of General Watanabe was motivated in whole or in part by religious imperatives. In the eyes of the Japanese terrorists in this case, the emperor was a "divine emperor (*kami naru tennō*, or *arahitogami*),"[40] and it was the divine emperor for whom they were willing to die and to kill. To refer to the divine emperor as a mere bureaucratic organ of the state was a sacrilege, an attack on the core Shintō doctrine, and such a desecration or profanation of the sacred emperor was punishable by death. These terrorists were radical Shintō fundamentalists—or what this study calls radical Shintō ultranationalists. For radical Shintō ultranationalist terrorists, as with other religious terrorists, "Violence is first and foremost a sacramental act or divine duty executed in direct response to some theological demand or imperative."[41] Radical Shintō religious doctrine may sound unimportant or irrelevant to a Westerner or to a Chinese, but to place this in a more contemporary and familiar perspective, it was much like the case of the British Indian author Salman Rushdie, whose *The Satanic Verses* provoked the Muslim community. Rushdie subsequently received death threats and a *fatwa* by Ayatollah Ruhollah Khomeini. A similar example of religious terrorism was the murder of the Dutch filmmaker and newspaper columnist Theo van Gogh,[42] who was a critic of Islamic fundamentalism, by Mohammed Bouyri, a Dutch-born member of a radical Muslim network.

As mentioned in the discussions of the state theories and theologies of Uesugi Shinkichi and Kakehi Katsuhiko, a fundamental purpose of life for a radical Shintō ultranationalist was to bring about a "Shōwa Restoration (*Shōwa Ishin*)" and to spread the divine emperor's rule throughout the world.[43] In his *Government by Assassination*, Byas insightfully focused on the story of the men and the ideas for which they were ready to kill and be killed. For instance, during the trial of the assassins in the May 15, 1932, insurrection, Sub-Lieutenant Itō Kamahiro, when asked by the judge to explain the philosophy of "constructive destruction," stated that the group that had killed Prime Minister Inukai was an "organization without organization. . . . My life's desire will be fulfilled if a state is established on the principle that the Emperor and his subjects are one."[44] During the cross-examination by the judge, Itō said, "We demand direct imperial rule by the Emperor. Our center today is the imported egotistical notion of popular rights. It is wrong. Manhood suffrage and the grant[ing] of social and political rights to the people are a gigantic mistake."[45] Itō's remarks clearly illustrate that secular democracy was the ideological enemy of the ideal theocratic religious state that he and his group were trying to bring about.

Another army officer who participated in the terrorist plot said at the same trial: "The Imperial Way should be spread through the world, the Asiatic nations being first consolidated into a unit and thereafter the rest of the world."[46] In other words, imperial rule was to be established in all nations or civilizations in stages or phases, beginning with the conquest of Asia. Again, it is instructive to keep in mind radical Islam and its confrontation with the secular Western world today. Similarly, Ayatollah Khomeini declared in March 1980, just a year after the establishment of the Islamic Republic of Iran, "We must strive to export our Revolution throughout the world."[47] Similarly, Sayed Abu al-Maududi, one of the leading radical Islamic theorists of the twentieth century, stated, "The objective of the Islamic jihad is to eliminate the rule of a non-Islamic system and establish in its stead an Islamic system of state rule. Islam does not intend to confine this revolution to a single State or a few countries; the aim of Islam is to bring about a universal revolution."[48] What we have in enunciations by both radical Shintō ultranationalists and radical Islamic fundamentalists are proclamations for what Mark Juergensmeyer calls a "cosmic war," a divine struggle between good and evil to be carried out on a global scale.[49]

The stabbing to death of Major-General Nagata Tetsuzan on August 12, 1935, by Lieutenant-Colonel Aizawa Saburō is another striking example of radical Shintō ultranationalist terrorism. During the military trial, Aizawa explained: "The Emperor is the incarnation of the great god who made the universe. The Emperor is absolute; he has been so in the past, he is so now, and will be so in the future."[50] Byas noted, "In those phrases Aizawa declares that he acknowledges the Emperor's power alone. The statesmen who exercise power are intruders between the sovereign and his people, and he does not recognize any responsibility for obeying their orders."[51] Aizawa also explained the concept of the Shōwa Restoration to the court:

> The Emperor is the incarnation of the god who reigns over the universe. The aim of life is to develop according to His Majesty's wishes, which, however, have not yet been fully understood by all the world. The world is deadlocked because of communism, capitalism, anarchism, and the like. As Japanese we should make it our object to bring about happiness to the world in accordance with His Majesty's wishes. As long as the fiery zeal of the Japanese for the Imperial cause is felt in Manchuria and other places, all will be well, but let it die and it will be gone forever. Democracy is all wrong. Our whole concern is to clarify the Imperial rule as established by the Emperor Meiji. Today is marked by arrogation of Imperial power. The Premier has propounded the institutional [Minobe's organ] theory of the Emperor.[52]

This is a clear indication that the assassination of Major-General Nagata was a case of "religious terrorism, by pious people dedicated to a moral vision of the world."[53]

This global struggle between good and evil was definitely evident in the minds of the leaders of the February 26, 1936, insurrection, as well. It is instructive to quote in its entirety the manifesto issued by officers of the insurrection:

> The essence of the Japanese nation consists in the fact that the Emperor reigns from times immemorial down to the remotest future in order that the national glory be propagated over the world so that all men under the sun may enjoy their lives to the fullest extent. This fundamental fact has been from the earliest days down to the present time the glory of Japan. Now is the time to bring about an expansion of the power and prestige of Japan.
>
> In recent years many persons have made their chief purpose in life the amassment of wealth regardless of the general welfare and prosperity of the people, with the result that the majesty of the Empire has been impaired. The people of Japan have suffered in consequence. Many troublesome issues now confronting our country are due to this situation.
>
> The Elder Statesmen, the financial magnates, the government officials,

and the political parties are responsible. The London naval agreements and the unhappy events which have occurred in the Japanese army in recent years prove this statement. That Prime Minister Hamaguchi was assassinated, that a Blood Brotherhood arose, that the May Fifteenth incident occurred, and that Aizawa killed Nagata last summer are not without reason.

Those incidents, however, have failed to remind men of their responsibility. The recent strained relations between Japan and the other powers are due to our statesmen's failure to take appropriate measures. Japan now confronts a crisis. Therefore, it is our duty to take proper steps to safeguard our fatherland by killing those responsible. On the eve of our departure to Manchuria we have risen in revolt to attain our aims by direct action. We think it is our duty as subjects of His Majesty the Emperor.

May Heaven bless and help us in our endeavor to save our fatherland from the worst.[54]

But how could these radical Shintō ultranationalist terrorists really believe that the emperor would sanction their use of terrorism? How did they know what was in the mind of their emperor? In other words, how could they legitimize their actions in speaking for the emperor? One must adequately address these questions, because I believe they hold the key to understanding the essence of radical Shintō ultranationalism as a radical, mass-based revolutionary religion of völkisch nationalism. This goes back not to Hozumi Yatsuka's conservative or reactionary Shintō fundamentalism of the Meiji period but, rather, to Uesugi Shinkichi's and Kakehi Katsuhiko's formulations of radical Shintō ultranationalist thought of the Taishō period. In Hozumi's reactionary Shintō ultranationalism, the individual was an object to be acted on. He or she simply was instructed to obey orders from above. But in radical Shintō ultranationalist ideology / theology, the individual was not a passive object but the subject or agent who acted on the world and changes the world to suit his or her goals. That is, the Shintō faith demanded that they carry out the insurrection.

After the September 11, 2001, attacks on the World Trade Center, Juergensmeyer recalled, Osama bin Laden said in a videotape released to Al Jazeera television that it was "by His will the twin towers of the World Trade Center had collapsed."[55] The "His" in the statement, of course, meant Allah's will. Juergensmeyer also cited the case of a young man who beamed into a video camera the day before he was to blow himself up and become a martyr in a Hamas suicide operation that he was "doing this for Allah."[56] Regarding these two cases, Juergensmeyer commented:

In both cases they were demonstrating one of the remarkable facts about those who have committed acts of terrorism in the contemporary world: they would do virtually anything if they thought it had been sanctioned by divine mandate or conceived in the mind of God. The power of this idea has been enormous. It has surpassed all ordinary claims of political authority and elevated religious ideologies to supernatural heights.[57]

Indeed, the power of this idea has been enormous. The same can be said about the radical Shintō ultranationalist terrorists. They committed acts of terrorism because they believed that they were "carrying out the will of the Emperor" and "doing it for the Emperor." But, again, how did they become convinced that they were doing what the emperor had wanted them to do? To my knowledge, radical Shintō ultranationalists had never claimed that they were in direct communication with the emperor. They did not claim that the emperor-deity had spoken directly to them. However, there are two other methods of interpreting God's will in most religions: through interpretations of scripture and by theological formulations. Uesugi's new theory of the state was in effect a theological formulation of State Shintō. Kakehi relied much more heavily on scriptural interpretations. The radical Shintō ultranationalist terrorists were justifying terrorism on the basis of the type of theology best articulated by Uesugi. Their own, "essential being" was the emperor, and they resorted to violent measures to empower the emperor as well as themselves by destroying moderate secular nationalist thought, which had functioned to sideline religion from political public life. In short, Uesugi's thought was the spiritual force behind radical Shintō ultranationalist terrorism. Without doubt, these are clear examples of how Uesugi's complex metaphysical ideology had resonated with the common Japanese soldier—as representative of the Japanese masses—and the profound emotional impact of this ideology translated into a vehicle for terrorism. "Ideology relates people's problems to society as a whole: that is why it can serve the emotional and political functions it does," wrote John Breuilly. The manifesto by Captain Nonaka and his colleagues about the February 26, 1936, insurrection illustrate with unmistakable clarity they had related the people's problems to society as a whole and sought salvation in the emperor.

This shift from political terrorism in the Meiji period to religious terrorism in the Taishō and Shōwa periods was also pointed out by Tendō Tadashi, who states that, from the emergence of the Blood Pledge Corps we find a type of terrorism that is no longer carried out by single individuals but is "systematically planned terrorism by groups" and a terrorism characterized by a "religiosity that transcended a certain kind of politics (*aru shū no seiji o koeta shūkyōsei*)."[58] Tendō also pointed out that the ideal Japanese religious state was conceptualized by the radical right wing—that is, radical Shintō ultranationalists—as being conterminous with the world, and certainly in the case of Kakehi's theocratic state, in accordance with the "law of the universe (*uchū no hōsoku*)."[59] David Rapoport refers to terrorist activities justified in theological terms as "sacred terror."[60]

This is not to suggest that each and every individual involved in terrorist activities in the 1930s was inspired solely by the purely religious beliefs of radical Shintō ultranationalism. There were exceptions. A good case in point is Ishihara Kanji. As Mark Peattie has shown, Ishihara was heavily influenced by Buddhism.[61] Ishihara had attempted to work out his own, unique philosophy of, and justification for, war. According to Peattie's account, Ishihara seems to have amalgamated core Shintō ideas with Buddhist concepts. It was an awkward combination of inherently contradictory beliefs, as many critics have stated. Ishihara seems to have been confused about radical Shintō ultranationalist goals. Before his conversion to Nichiren Buddhism, Ishihara was influenced by Kakehi Katsuhiko's ancient Shintōism, as Seike Motoyoshi, a writer on Shōwa nationalism, has pointed out.[62] Others also have had difficulty understanding Ishihara. For example, Lieutenant-Colonel Kanda Masatane, a member of the staff of the Japanese Korean Army at the time of the Manchurian Incident who had gone to Port Arthur a number of times to confer with Ishihara before September 18, 1931, remarked that "Ishihara was a genius, but [he was one who] left everything half-finished (*shirikire-tonbo*)."[63]

No matter how much Ishihara Kanji may have believed personally in Buddhism, he could not have used Nichiren Buddhism or Buddhist arguments to change the course of Japanese politics or justify military expansionism. That is, he could not very well have tried to approach his colleagues in the military and argue for Japanese expansionism on the basis of Buddhist doctrine. Buddhists had to accommodate themselves to the prevalent Shintō ultranationalist ideology and bend their religious principles to support it. Similarly, a Japanese Christian or a Japanese Muslim, for example, could not have argued for the creation of an Islamic state or a Christian world order. Ishihara had to work within the ideological opportunity structure of radical Shintō ultranationalist ideology. The Japanese masses could understand Japan's mission in terms of spreading the emperor's powers on a global scale or sacrificing their life for the emperor. That is to say, radical Shintō ultranationalism had become the prevailing ideology of the Japanese nation. In *The Crisis of Islam*, Bernard Lewis wrote, "Most Muslims are not fundamentalists, and most fundamentalists are not terrorists, but most present-day terrorists are Muslims and proudly identify themselves as such."[64] Much the same can be said about the prewar Japanese within the context of the prewar Japanese empire. Most Japanese were not radical Shintō fundamentalists,[65] and most radical Shintō fundamentalists were not terrorists, but most terrorists in the 1930s were radical Shintō ultranationalists, and they were extremely proud of themselves when they carried out these terrorist activities.

Also, I would not deny that there were certain individuals controlling the Japanese state who might have used radical Shintō ultranationalist doctrines as a means to mobilize the people for expansionist policies that were based on perceived strategic imperatives. Further, one should assume that not all the elites who used radical Shintō ultranationalist rhetoric were true believers. Nevertheless, it was within this framework of radical Shintō ultranationalist ideology that actions were justified.

Third, many of Japan's earliest ultranationalist leaders and terrorists held strong pan-Asian ideas in the sense that they were sympathetic to and supportive of Asian nationalist movements that sought to overthrow traditional regimes in their own lands and free themselves from Western domination. For instance, Tōyama Mitsuru saw the Western colonial powers as the great threat to Asia, as well as to Japan, and actively supported Asian nationalists such as Kim Okkyun (1851–94), a leader of the Korean reform movement; Sun Yat-sen, the father of the modern Chinese revolution; various activists in the Indian independence movement against the British, such as Rash Behari Bose; and a number of Philippine and Vietnamese independence leaders.[66] The pan-Asianism is significant because this aspect of Tōyama's ultranationalist ideology is in stark contrast to that of later radical Shintō ultranationalists, who proclaimed the superiority of the Japanese Volk over all the other peoples of Asia, attempted to force Koreans and Taiwanese to abandon their own languages for Japanese, and pushed the Shintō religion on them, building Shintō shrines in their conquered territories. The Japanese totally alienated other Asians in trying to persuade them to worship Japan's ethnic community's (*Volksgemeinschaft*) Shintō gods.[67]

Japanese ultranationalists shifted their policy from actively supporting Asian liberation movements to cruelly suppressing them. The turning point perhaps came with ultranationalists such as Uchida Ryōhei, who founded the Black Dragon Society in 1901 and published the monthly managine *Kokuryū* (Black Dragon). Uchida apparently began to push for military expansionism on the Asian continent with his "Manchuria and Mongolia independence thesis (*Mammo dokuritsu ron*)" after he came to the conclusion that China was hopeless in being able to form a nation-state after the disaster of Sun Yat-sen's republican revolution.[68] He charged that the Chinese people had "no political ability (*seiji nōryoku nashi*)" to form a cohesive modern nation-state.[69] Accordingly, he became convinced that Japan had no choice other than to take it upon itself and defend Asia against the Western powers. This was an idea that would be adopted by many Japanese ultranationalists. Suzuki Sadami pointed out that, for some time, the Japanese government had a double strategy of suppressing other peoples under its control such as the Taiwanese and the Koreans while supporting independence for peoples under Western colonial rule.[70] It should also be noted that Ishihara Kanji's ideas fell out of favor with radical Shintō ultranationalists between the time he instigated the Manchurian Incident in 1931 and the February 26, 1936, insurrection, which he urged be suppressed. According to Tendō Tadashi, Ishihara became gravely concerned about the powerful anti-Japanese sentiment in Manchuria and was appalled by the racial and ethnic prejudices displayed by the Japanese troops in Manchuria.[71] In relation to Ishihara's belief in ethnic harmony, Kevin Doak noted that "drawing on the idea of Kyōto Imperial University Professor Sakuda Sōichi that the ideals of ethnic national harmony and integration within the political state were compatible goals, Ishihara founded the Kenkoku University (National Foundation University) in Manchuria in May 1938, placing Sakuda effectively in charge of the University. At that university, ethnic harmony was not only an idea, but enacted through admissions policies that yielded a remarkable ethnic balance among the students enrolled."[72] I believe that Ishihara's ideas diverged from those of the Shintō ultranationalists.

Fourth, we find that the Shintō ultranationalist terrorist movement had become more unified in its vision for the future Japanese state. For example, in the May 15, 1932, insurrection, the so-called agrarianists (*nōhonshugisha*) played a central role. Agrarianists such as Tachibana Kōsaburō and Gondō Seikyō had envisioned a highly decentralized state composed of autonomous agrarian communities somehow linked with the emperor at the apex of the nation. This, of course, differed greatly from the radical Shintō ultranationalists, who at this stage, at least, had imagined a political community consisting of the emperor on top of a highly centralized and industrialized state. Maruyama Masao noted in "The Ideology and Dynamics of Japanese Fascism" that one of the distinctive features of the Japanese ultranationalist movement was the idea of agrarianism.[73] He further stated: "The right wing may be divided into two sections: those who advocated an intensive development of industry and who wished to increase state control for this end, and those who flatly rejected the idea and thought in terms of agrarianism centered on the villages."[74] However, the radical Shintō ultranationalist agrarianist terrorists quickly faded from the scene and played no central role in the February 26, 1936, insurrection. Hosaka Masayasu also noted that a major change had taken place within the radical Shintō ultranationalist terrorist movement between the May 15 (1932) Incident and the February 26 (1936) Incident: "The influence of agrarianism-type thought," he wrote, was "all but missing" from among the officers who had carried out the February 26 Incident.[75] In the rapidly changing goals of radical Shintō ultranationalist terrorism in the 1930s, the agrarianism movement was no longer a major factor.

Finally, radical Shintō ultranationalist terrorist acts increased in number and frequency and involved larger numbers of individuals as time went by, especially from the Taishō to the Early Shōwa period. A clear lesson to be drawn from the radical Shintō ultranationalist terrorists was that giving in to their demands did not serve to alleviate the problem.

In addition to these trends, the Japanese radical Shintō ultranationalist terrorist movement has characteristics that distinguish it from terrorist movements elsewhere. First, the assassinations and terrorist attacks by radical Shintō ultranationalists were selective: they were not indiscriminate killings of innocent people, such as in the case of the September 11, 2001, attacks on the World Trade Center in New York and on the Pentagon building in Washington, D.C., by radical Islamic members of al-Qaeda. Nor were they similar to the indiscriminate, al-Qaeda-type terrorism in East Asia, as seen in the the bombing of Korean Airlines Flight 858 on November 28, 1987, in which the 115 passengers aboard were killed by the North Korean terrorist operatives Kim Seung Il and Kim Hyun Hee.[76] This is not to suggest that innocent people were not killed by Japanese radical Shintō ultranationalists. If people happened to be in the wrong place at the wrong time or in some way tried to interfere with the assassinations of targeted individuals, radical Shintō ultranationalist terrorists had no qualms about killing them.

The discriminate terrorism carried out by radical Shintō ultranationalists made them immensely popular in the minds of the Japanese masses, who were becoming increasingly radicalized. Martha Crenshaw has noted that a possible cost of terrorism is the loss of popular support.[77] This was definitely not a problem in the case of prewar Japanese radical Shintō ultranationalists. Their assassinations were widely popular with the Japanese public. For instance, the reaction to the murder of Prime Minister Inukai by the common man on the street, according to Byas, was something like, "The Japanese people will not be angry about the Prime Minister's murder. . . . Many of us think the politicians needed a lesson."[78] Radical Shintō ultranationalist terrorism was succeeding in creating the grounds for revolutionary changes that were to come by undermining what was conceived as corrupt government authority and by demoralizing its leadership.

Second, many Japanese scholars who study ultranationalist thought point out that radical Shintō ultranationalist terrorists displayed a tendency to take personal responsibility for their actions either by committing suicide or by giving themselves up to authorities. There are many examples of this type of behavior. For instance, on October 18, 1889, Kurushima Tsuneki, a member of the Dark Ocean Society, hurled a bomb at Foreign Minister Ōkuma Shigenobu's horse-drawn carriage as it was approaching the front gate of the Foreign Ministry building compound. Ōkuma was wounded and eventually lost one of his legs. The bomb was supplied by Tōyama Mitsuru, a founding member of the Dark Ocean Society. Kurushima then committed suicide by slitting his throat. The point, of course, is that Kurushima, according to Shintō ultranationalist reasoning, killed himself to show his sincerity and the selflessness of his act to the world. This arguably was a highly religious form of purification (junka) characteristic of Shintō ultranationalist terrorists' behavior, whether conservative or radical.[79] It was a kind of suicidal terrorism that transcended the mere political act of the assassination itself. Tendō Tadashi has also noted that ultranationalist terrorists had strong religious convictions and believed that they were carrying out the "will of the gods (kami no ishi)."[80] Assassinations in this context were not to be construed as shameful or disgraceful acts. On the contrary: it was the most pious thing to do. Through assassination, Kurushima believed he was selflessly removing a poison from society.

Another example of radical Shintō ultranationalist terrorists taking responsibility for their actions by committing suicide or turning themselves over to law-enforcement authorities, which, of course, most likely meant that they would face the death penalty, was in the May 15 (1932)

Incident. In *Government by Assassination*, Byas recorded that, at five o'clock on Sunday evening on May 15, "nine naval and military officers of ages between twenty-four and twenty-eight alighted from two taxicabs at the side entrance of the Yasukuni Shrine in Tokyo."[81] He continued, "They worshipped at the shrine, doffing caps, clasping hands, and bowing towards the unseen mirror of the Sun Goddess in homage to the souls of the dead soldiers whose names are inscribed in the books and whose spirits dwell there."[82] They then departed and headed for the Prime Minister's official residence, where they would take part in the plot to murder Inukai. The fact that they went to Yasukuni Shrine, a Shintō shrine where Japan's war dead are worshipped, is significant. This is just one more indication that religion did play a role in this act of terrorism. As Byas pointed out, for these military officers there was "no holier place in Tokyo" than Yasukuni Shrine.[83] The murder in which they were about to participate was an act that was morally sanctioned by the gods. Keep in mind that from a religious perspective, walking into a Shintō shrine to pray is the functional equivalent of a Christian going into a church to worship or a Muslim going into a mosque to pray. At any rate, after completing their terrorist mission, Byas recounted, "The first cab-load drove on to the headquarters of the military police, commonly called the gendarmerie, and gave themselves up."[84] The second cab load, in their final act, "drove to the Bank of Japan, hurled a grenade at the door, and went back to the gendarmerie [military policy] building, where they surrendered."[85] As it turned out, however, the terrorists who participated in the assassination of Prime Minister Inukai did not receive the death penalty. They were each sentenced to fifteen years in prison. Others involved received smaller terms. But no one served out his sentence fully. By the time of the February 26, 1936, insurrection, all had been freed.

The same thing cannot be said of all those who carried out the February 26, 1936, insurrection, however. The radical Shintō ultranationalist terrorist leaders involved were given a chance to commit suicide, but they chose not to, except for Captain Andō Teruzo, who shot himself inside the Sanno Hotel. The other leaders were summarily executed. Nevertheless, one could argue that there was a high expectation that the radical Shintō ultranationalist insurgents would voluntarily commit suicide for their actions. This was an established practice, as illustrated by the fact that the generals who crushed the revolt tried to give the "rebels a chance to commit hara-kiri."[86] Again, this can be understood only in the overall context of Japanese radical Shintō ultranationalist thought.

Nevertheless, many of the rank-and-file soldiers who were involved in the insurrection did surrender rather than be branded traitors to the emperor. "The soldiers had been trained to obey the orders of their officers as if they were the orders of the Emperor."[87] Major Okubo drafted the following message, which was announced by radio and dropped from planes, to the non-commissioned officers:

Hitherto you have obeyed your officers believing their commands to be just. His Majesty the Son of Heaven (*Hieka Tennō*) now orders you to return to your barracks. If you fail to obey you will be traitors. If you return you will be pardoned. Your fathers and brothers and all the people are praying you to return. Come back to your barracks.

"They surrendered their arms and were packed into trucks and rushed to their barracks."[88] At any rate, even with the February 26, 1936, insurrection, it was not a case of rebellious troops trying desperately to evade responsibility or fighting to the bitter end.

A factor that is thought to have contributed to the readiness of radical Shintō ultranationalists to take their own lives is that the "responsibility to the gods (*kami e no sekinin*)" in the minds of Japanese right-wing terrorists was connected to the traditional Shintō "outlook on death (*shiseikan*)."[89] Tendō believed that for a Japanese person, death did not bring the same kind of finality that it might for an individual in Western society. The psychologist Ariel Merari differentiates between *ready* to die and *seeking* to die and has argued that, in most of the cases of suicidal terrorism, the terrorists consciously wanted to live.[90] In the many cases of radical Shintō ultranationalista, the terrorists wanted to die, however, because death was seen as the ultimate way to merge spiritually with the emperor, which leads to a third feature of radical Shintō ultranationalism: a very powerful anarchistic element in the thought and behavior of the radical Shintō ultranationalist movement, as seen clearly in the ideology of Uesugi Shinkichi and Kakehi Katsuhiko. This was also pointed out by Tendō, who noted the existence of the idea to "eradicate the wickedness around the Emperor."[91] Radical Shintō ultranationalist terrorists believed that rooting out evil in society by eliminating corrupt officials and the special interests of the wealthy, and thus removing all barriers between the emperor and the people, would lead to salvation— not individual salvation but a kind of social redemption of the völkisch nation as a whole in which each individual was conceived to be only a constituent element of the emperor.

The smashing of the February 26, 1936, insurrection by Emperor Hirohito in cooperation with the Control Faction of the military was by no means a victory of moderate military forces against radical militants and terrorists. Failing to understand this critically important issue leads to a total misunderstanding of the vast difference between the moderate nationalists and pragmatic leadership of the Meiji period and the fanatical leaders of the Shōwa period who were driving Japan into a war with the world. There are at least three reasons for this. First, although the Control Faction of the army had crushed its rival Imperial Way Faction, which had revolted against the civil authority (the constituted constitutional government), the purge of the Imperial Way Faction within the military was not as thorough as one might think. Although Richard Storry pointed out that "the position of the Tōsei-ha [Control Faction] seemed virtually unassailable" in terms of controlling the overall agenda for state policy, like mushrooms, members of the Imperial Way Faction sprang back up throughout the army, society, and government. Moreover, radical Imperial Way Faction officers who had been disciplined after the February 26, 1936, insurrection were later recalled to active duty.

Hashimoto Kingorō (1890–1957), a leader of the Cherry Blossom Society and a terrorist "who had linked his gospel of Japanese domination of the world with his own searing hatred of the white man,"[93] for example, was later put in charge of the shore batteries ordered to clear the Yangtze River of enemy shipping while Japanese military forces were trying to capture the city of Nanjing (which led to the infamous "Rape of Nanjing"). He was responsible for firing on the USS *Panay* of the U.S. Asiatic Fleet in December 1937. "His object was to provoke the United States into a declaration of war, which would eliminate civilian influence from the Japanese government and complete the Shōwa Restoration."[94] After the *Panay* was sunk by air attacks, American sailors were machine gunned as they tried to reach the shoreline.

Chō Isamu, a co-founder of the Cherry Blossom Society, is another good example of a radical Shintō ultranationalist terrorist who subsequently held important positions in the army. Chō was a member of the inner circle of advisers of Matsui Iwane, commander of the Central China Area Army, and was allegedly responsible for terrorism and mass murder during the Rape of Nanjing.[95] In the final months of World War Two, Chō, chief of staff of the Thirty-Second Army in Okinawa, committed suicide at the end of the battle for Okinawa.

Araki Sadao, a leader of the Imperial Way Faction who had served as war minister in the Inukai and Saitō cabinets, was placed on the inactive list following the February 26 (1936) Incident. He subsequently served as education minister (1938–39) in the Konoe cabinet and thus had considerable influence in promoting the radical Shintō ultranationalist agenda. Araki was tried as a Class A war criminal after the war and sentenced to life imprisonment.

Yamashita Tomoyuki, who had clashed with Tōjō Hideki, commanded the Fourth Infantry Division in northern China in 1938–40. In 1941, he was put in command of the Twenty-Fifth Army and launched the invasion of Malaya, which concluded with the fall of Singapore in February 1942 and the capture of 130,000 British, Indian, and Australian troops. Many readers may have seen the famous picture of Yamashita pounding his fist on a table, demanding that General Percival surrender. These are just a few examples of Imperial Way Faction members who were active and influential after the February 26 (1936) Incident.

Second, the military officers of the Control Faction were certainly no friends of liberal democracy; nor did their victory over their rivals represent the triumph of a traditionally conservative, authoritarian type of leadership such as that in the Meiji period, as some scholars have suggested. Neither is it quite accurate to say that the radical Shintō ultranationalist movement had evolved by the 1930s into just two radical sectarian factions in the eyes of the rapidly dwindling moderate, Western-oriented Japanese who still continued to struggle to support party politics and parliamentary government. This also obscures the complex nature of the radical Shintō ultranationalist movement, which was highly fragmented, and terrorism was not the only method of pursuing radical goals. The two factions originally emerged within the army over the issue of whether to attack next the Soviet Union or China. Those identified with the Control Faction were just as ruthless as, but perhaps more cunning and calculating than, the Imperial Way Faction followers. As E. Bruce Reynolds pointed out, "An effort to co-opt, rather than to overturn, the existing structure made the 'third way' [fascists] advocates in Japan appear more conservative that their counterparts in Italy or Germany, but their ultimate intentions were hardly less radical."[96]

Long before the wave of radical Shintō ultranationalist terrorism and terrorist movements in the early 1930s, radical Shintō ultranationalists had paved the way for the eradication of parliamentary government by destroying its ideological basis of support. This three-decade struggle between the adherents of the emperor-as-sovereign theory of the state, on the one hand, and the proponents of the emperor-as-organ theory of the state, on the other hand, would culminate in the mid-1930s with the "movement to clarify Japan's national structure (*Kokutai Meicho Undō*)." The triumph of this movement came with the suppression of Minobe's emperor-as-organ theory of the state. Three of Minobe's books were banned: *Essentials of Constitutional Law, A Course on the Constitution of Japan Article by Article,* and *Fundamental Doctrines of the Japanese Constitution.* Others who expounded the emperor-as-organ theory were purged from positions of power, too. In contrast to the failed attempted "bloody coups d'etat" by radical Shintō ultranationalist terrorists, this came to be known as the successful "bloodless coup d'etat (*muketsu kudeta*)."[97] In other words, the movement to clarify the kokutai was very much a part of the radical Shintō ultranationalist movement to purge anyone who was trying to block the nation from going in a radical direction.

Internally, as Storry wrote, the Control Faction opted for "co-operation with capitalists and with the Diet, so long as it was amenable to army wishes."[98] The Control Faction also took practical measures to alleviate some of the worst economic problems, which was a source of much social discontent, to ensure that the terrorist-driven insurgency would lose its base of support and not resurface again in the future. The more disciplined or "controlled" radical Shintō ultranationalist faction, which included Tōjō Hideki, ultimately would prove to be the more dangerous of the two groups. Internal peace was somewhat restored within Japan but at the price of a reckless pattern of unlimited expansionism of imperial power overseas.

Third, the defeat of the February 26, 1936, insurrectionists did not serve to curb radicalism, regardless of the involvement in these two factions of the army. The radical trajectory continued with even greater momentum. For instance, the China Incident, which took place in July 1937, triggered Japan's major thrust into China and full-blown war in East Asia. Those who argued for expansion into China, such as Colonel Muto Akira, section chief of the Army General Staff Headquarters,[99] and General Tanaka Shinichi, chief of the Military Affairs Department in the War Ministry, were not Meiji-type, authoritarian military officers like Yamagata Aritomo. They won out over Prime Minister Konoe and Ishihara Kanji, who urged caution and containment of the incident.

A number of incidents also occurred along the border with the Soviet Union, culminating in the so-called Nomonhan Incident in 1939. It was the Imperial Way Faction that urged attacking the Soviet Union. This reckless adventure into Soviet-controlled areas while Japanese forces were fighting in China led to defeat by the forces of Red Army General Georgy Zhukov—Japan's greatest military defeat of the modern era. After an armistice was signed, Japanese Commander Umezu Yoshijirō was forced to take measures to ensure that Japanese troops would be situated far from disputed territory to prevent another incident from occurring. Umezu, a member of the Control Faction, along with Koiso Kuniaki and Tōjō Hideki, were radical Shintō ultranationalists. In the final days of the Second World War, Umezu, chief of staff of the Army; Toyoda Soemu, chief of staff of the Navy; and Anami Korechika, minister of war, opposed surrender in August 1945. They wanted to fight on and force the Allies to sustain heavy casualties in a ground invasion of Japan. They were extremists by any measure.

In addition, radical Shintō ultranationalist ideology permeated the entire officer corps, which numbered in the tens of thousands. In reality, only a very small fraction of military officers had any type of affiliation with either the Imperial Way Faction or the Control Faction.

The July 15 (1940) Incident, during the administration of Prime Minister Yonai Mitsumasa (January–July 1940), was the last plot by radical Shintō ultranationalist terrorists to effect a Shōwa Restoration. The plot was uncovered eight years after the initial attempt to bring about an imperial restoration (in the May 15 [1932] Incident). But what did it take to stamp out radical Shintō ultranationalist terrorism? War against the rest of the world. As Storry pointed out, "The price of peace at home was, of course, armed expansion abroad."[100]

Two well-known scholars have argued that Japan was in a very different category from Nazi Germany and Fascist Italy. In the article "A New Look at the Problem of Japanese Fascism," George Wilson argued against Maruyama's theory that a particularly Japanese form of fascism came about by transforming the existing Meiji state into "emperor-system" or "military-bureaucratic" fascism and suppressing liberalism and socialism.[101] He maintained that too many differences existed between Japan and the European cases for the fascist model to be useful in understanding Japan. He further asserted that there was no fundamental difference between the character of the regime of the Meiji state, which "came to power in order to guarantee national independence and security and to foster modernization so that national security could not be threatened,"[102] and the regimes in power in the 1930s and the early 1940s. Borrowing terminology and a thesis advanced by Robert C. Tucker, who argued that a nationalist regime "is apt to become totalitarian only when it undergoes 'metamorphosis' to a communist or fascism form," Wilson claimed that there was no "movement-regime"—that is, a transformation from the Meiji national movement to a fascist state.[103] The modernization process set in motion by the Meiji regime did bring about social problems, which caused fascist-like nativist forces to emerge, culminating in the February 26 (1936) Incident. But this "fascism from below" movement was crushed by the conservative government to maintain the Meiji state. In short, he argued that there was no "metamorphosis" from the nationalist Meiji state to a fascist state—a state that had the "utopian goal of totally transforming society."[104] The prewar Japanese state advanced to a variation of a developmental authoritarian state, but it was not fascist. Wilson ended his essay by saying, "If we wish to find fault with the conservative leaders of early Shōwa Japan, we might do so not because they were 'fascists' but, paradoxically, because of the inflexibility of their very commitment to the institutional framework and national security conceptions that grew out of the Meiji system."[105]

This study, however, has documented that there was indeed a metamorphosis from the nationalist Meiji state to a fascist state, a state that had the "utopian goal of totally transforming society," as seen in the state theories of Uesugi Shinkichi and Kakehi Katsuhiko, even though the Meiji institutional framework was still in place. Further, Wilson's assertion that there was no fundamental difference between the character of the regime of the Meiji state, which "came to power in order to guarantee national independence and security and to foster modernization so that national security could not be threatened" and the Japanese state in the early Shōwa period is puzzling. Radical Shintō ultranationalists sought global rule, as has been discussed. This utopian objective was different from nationalist goals of Meiji leaders such as Yamagata, who was thinking rationally of Japan's independence and national security in terms of "line of sovereignty" and "line of advantage."[106] In reference to the foreign policy Japanese leaders pursued in the 1930s, Kenneth Pyle, who is aware of this fundamental difference in the mentality of the Meiji leadership and the Shōwa leadership, remarked that the "Meiji leaders would have been appalled at the incautious way in which policy commitments were made that exceeded the nation's capabilities."[107]

When one considers Shōwa political military leaders such as Anami Korechika, Umezu Yoshijirō, and Toyoda Soemu, members of the Supreme Council for the Direction of the War who were unwilling to surrender even after the atomic bombs were dropped and the Soviet Union entered the war, or Ōnishi Takijirō, vice chief of the Naval General Staff who, on August 14, 1945, argued that "Japan should be ready to sacrifice twenty million lives in a Kamikaze attack to win the war,"[108] one is tempted to ask Wilson whether he considers them "conservative" and committed to "national security" in the same way that Itō Hirobumi and Yamagata Aritomo had been in the Meiji period. For those radical Shintō ultranationalists, the choice was either global rule or utter destruction. In comparison, it is instructive to recall that Itō and Yamagata made rational decisions based on strategic interests and decided to withdraw and return the Liaodong Peninsula to the Qing Dynasty when Russia, Germany, and France intervened in the so-called Triple Intervention following the Qing Dynasty–Japan War of 1894–95. Again, on the other hand, it is worth quoting what Konoe allegedly remarked to his secretary in the closing months of the Pacific War about the type of people in charge of the Japanese state: "The army will increasingly brandish the notion of fighting to the death. But Kido['s] . . . mind is completely set on [Chief of the General Staff] Anami. Considering our kokutai, unless the emperor assents to it, we can do nothing. When I think of the madmen leading the present situation, I can't help but feel weary of life."[109] In other words, toward the end of the war, radical Shintō ultranationalists were branding rival radical Shintōists "madmen."

It is also worth noting that the Control Faction members were "branded as 'true fascists' by their rivals [in the Imperial Way Faction]."[110] And anyone who was somehow able to break away or step back from this whirlpool of Shintō fanaticism became a target for assassination. One should not forget that Konoe himself had once been marked for death by a radical Shintō ultranationalist group called the Squad of Heavenly Punishment.[111] The group had intended to kill Konoe on September 18, 1941, the tenth anniversary of the Manchurian Incident. At any rate, Konoe seems to have come to his senses and realized that fanatics were willing to sacrifice the entire Japanese population. Yonai Mitsumasa apparently did, too. Realizing that national suicide and the destruction of the imperial system was a real possibility, he remarked to Admiral Takagi Sōkichi on August 12, 1945, that the "atomic bombs and the Soviet entry into the war are, in a sense, gifts from the gods."[112] Hirohito's close adviser Kido Kōichi made a similar statement, saying that the atomic bombs and the Soviet entry into the war were "useful elements for making things go smoothly."[113] Finally, Hiranuma Kiichirō, who at the end of the war insisted that "even if the entire nation is sacrificed to the war, we must preserve both the kokutai and the security of the imperial house,"[114] had once survived an assassination attempt. Nishiyama Naoshi, a Shintō priest and a member of the radical Shintō ultranationalistic group Kinnō Makoto Musubi Kai,[115] shot him, wounding him in the neck and jaw, in August 1941. The group had wanted immediate war with the United States and was upset about any attempt by the Konoe government to meet with U.S. President Franklin D. Roosevelt. In short, these were the type of people pushing Japan towards disaster. Japan of the 1930s and 1940s was not Japan of the Meiji era.

Peter Duus and Daniel Okimoto also argued that comparing prewar Japan to German Nazism and Italian Fascism is misguided. In "Fascism and the History of Pre-War Japan: The Failure of a Concept" (1979),[116] they seem irritated by the fact that anyone might want to pursue this kind of historical analysis, stating in their opening paragraph, "Old paradigms never die; they just fade away, though often not soon enough."[117] They went on to write that "neither Maruyama, nor anyone else until recently, has pressed on to the obvious conclusion: the Japanese case is so dissimilar that it is meaningless to speak of Japan in the 1930s as a 'fascist' political system."[118] In their analysis of the inappropriateness of the fascist label to describe Japan of the 1930s, Duus and Okimoto cite a problem of ideology. While they acknowledged that fascist ideology appeared in the 1930s and cite an article by Kamishima Jirō,[119] who "traces the origins of 1930s ideology to the structure of village social relations, which shaped the values and behavior of the bulk of the Japanese population before World War II,"[120] they also noted that "the problem with this line of analysis is that it does not explain why structural factors and the collectivist ethic produced a fascist ideology only in the 1930s and not before. Why, for example, did it have little or no effect on the intellectual elite in the 1920s, when left-wing ideology carried the day?"[121] Duus and Okimoto raised a very important question. They theorized that the emergence of fascist thinking must be viewed in the broader context of events that took place between the 1910s and the 1930s:

> While the collectivist ethic may have provided some of the important unspoken assumptions of fascist thinking in the 1930s, its emergence has to be seen within the broader context of the socioeconomic developments from 1910 through the 1930s. It was during this period that the process of economic development and industrialization began to have a major impact on all segments of Japanese society. By the end of World War I, 19 percent of the labor force had moved into manufacturing and construction, and if the service industries are included, 43.4 percent of the labor force had been concentrated in the modern sector; 28 percent of the

[gross national product] was produced by the manufacturing industries; including the services, the modern sector had already accounted for 62 percent of the [gross national product]. Perhaps more important than these quantitative changes was the emergence of corporate capitalism, and of a small but militant labor movement. These vociferous social forces were not easily contained by appeals to the family state ideology devised in the 1890s or by the operation of the collectivist ethic more diffusely embedded in Japanese political culture. This development required a new political theory—and if possible a new political practice—that would meld these forces into the same consensual framework adumbrated by these earlier modes of sociopolitical thought.[122]

This analysis is excellent. Duus and Okimoto intuitively understood that there had to be another political theory besides the Meiji family-state ideology constructed by Meiji ideologues such as Hozumi Yatsuka and the "structure of village social relations" analysis of Kamishima. They were absolutely correct in saying that the potentially explosive forces emerging among the Japanese urban masses could not be contained by the family-state ideology of the Meiji period. But the problem in Duus's and Okimoto's analysis is that they did not know where to find the answer to what they referred to in one of the article's subheadings: "The Problem of Ideology."[123] They commented, "The subtle interplay between the emphasis on the collective and the need to respond to the masses is one that requires further exploration in studies of intellectual developments."[124] This study of the transformation of the intellectual structure of Shintō ultranationalist thought from the Meiji period to the Taishō and Shōwa periods should fit into their analysis perfectly, because it provides the missing ideological link between the Meiji period and the 1930s for which they had been looking. As I have argued, the ideological break between Hozumi's family-state ideology and Uesugi's and Kakehi's ideological reformulation of radical Shintō ultranationalism in the Taishō period was truly revolutionary. Using Wilson's analysis, there was an ideological metamorphosis at the heart of State Shintō ideology in the 1920s, as Duus and Okimoto theorized there should be.

The triumph of the ideology of radical Shintō ultranationalism in the wake of the February 26, 1936, insurrection, however, had to be spelled out in a statement of official government ideology. This was forthcoming. It would, of course, be *Kokutai no Hongi* (Fundamentals of Our National Polity), the subject of the next chapter.

9

Orthodoxation of a Holy War

One of the biggest changes in politics in my lifetime is that the delusional is no longer marginal. It has come in from the fringe, to sit in the seat of power in the Oval Office and in Congress. For the first time in our history, ideology and theology hold a monopoly of power in Washington.—BILL MOYERS, quoted in Kevin Phillips, *American Theocracy*, 218

Ionian philosophers departed fundamentally from the Oriental worldview by rejecting vitalistic principles. Despite local diversities in Middle Eastern intellectual traditions, all agreed that the processes of nature depended on the acts and wills of superhuman living beings. The universe was interpreted in the image of man: things were believed to happen because some god or spirit, susceptible to impulses like those which men experience, made them happen that way. But the Ionian philosophers neglected the gods and conceived of the universe as lawful and therefore intelligible. They did not deny the existence of spirits or souls, but thought that souls, like other things were subject to natural laws.

Civilizations built around a doctrinally developed religion demanded orthodoxy; and orthodoxy meant not only the acceptance of a single cultural model, but the rejection of all others as dangerously heretical or leading to heresy.—WILLIAM H. MCNEILL, *The Rise of the West*, 232–33

The Japanese Disenlightenment

"For over four hundred years, the nation states of the West—Britain, France, Spain, Austria, Prussia, Germany, the United States, and others—

constituted a multipolar international system within Western civilization and interacted, competed, and fought wars with each other. At the same time, Western nations also expanded, conquered, colonized, or decisively influenced every other civilization."[1] "This unprecedented expansion of Europe was made possible by three great revolutions—scientific, industrial, and political—which gave Europe irresistible dynamism and power."[2]

Japan, of course, was one of those nations decisively influenced by Western countries. Since the arrival of the Americans in the mid-nineteenth century, the Japanese embraced the scientific and industrial revolutions pioneered by the Europeans with an eagerness, speed, and success that amazed the world, dramatically demonstrating their new-found industrial power to the world by astonishingly defeating two of the world's largest empires within a ten-year period: the heavily populated Qing Dynasty in 1895 and the vast Russian Empire in 1905. But the Japanese reaction to the Western political revolution was mixed. Elements of nationalism, liberalism, and even socialism were hastily grafted onto the native emperor-centered Shintō religion in awkward and conflicting ways in the Meiji period, subsequently producing a major cleavage in the body politic. The ideological struggle for the hearts and minds of the Japanese people that emerged in the Meiji period raged on through the Taishō period and finally came to a violent showdown in the early Shōwa period, generating a wave of political and religious assassinations that terrorized the nation. Once in control of the critical organs of the Japanese state, radical Shintō ultranationalists embarked on a massive campaign to purge the nation of basic features and values of the European Enlightenment: faith in reason and rational thought, intellectual freedom and curiosity, and the secularization of society. With this flight from science and reason, the Japanese can be said to have had experienced a type of "disenlightenment" in the early half of the twentieth century. Following the establishment of a state orthodoxy, radical Shintō ultranationalists declared all-out war on the eighteenth-century European Enlightenment, and European and American influence and presence in East Asia and the world, sparking a chain of events that would lead to the Second World War, which Niall Ferguson referred to as "the greatest man-made catastrophe of all time."[3] Japan, of course, was the first non-Western nation to make a bid for global power in modern times.

Radical Shintō ultranationalist ideology was finally established as the orthodox ideology of the Japanese nation in 1937. The principles of this ideology were articulated in the document *Kokutai no Hongi* (Fundamentals of Our National Polity), issued by the Japanese government.[4] *Fundamentals of Our National Polity* can be best understood as a kind of state religious document addressed to all Japanese subjects that was designed to guide them in matters of religious faith and government. It was a direct outcome of the "movement to clarify the *kokutai* (*Kokutai Meichō Undō*)*.*" I do not want to suggest that it solved all ideological issues, however. Nor do I wish to convey the idea that all the political theories discussed earlier came to a dead end in this text. That would reduce the value of the depth and range of analysis of political thought in the preceding chapters. But it did settle once and for all a fundamental cleavage in Japanese society that had existed since the Meiji period between the powerful and influential state theorists and constitutional-law scholars such as Minobe Tatsukichi, who argued that the emperor was an organ of the state, and their Shintō ultranationalist opponents, who asserted that the emperor was the state. It was, of course, within this overarching debate that Shintō nationalism was radicalized. *Fundamentals of Our National Polity* was distributed to the masses and studied throughout the late 1930s and the early 1940s. Commentaries on it were produced by many of its authors, as well as by the Japanese intellectual elite and teachers throughout the nation, in the years following its publication to teach the masses. In short, this was one of the most important government documents in the prewar and wartime period of modern Japanese history.

Fundamentals of Our National Polity

The doctrine that the Japanese state had been ruled over and governed by an unbroken line of emperors from the Age of the Gods, which had been embedded so deeply in the Shintō tradition, was at the center of radical Shintō ultranationalist orthodoxy: "The unbroken line of Emperors, receiving the Oracle of the Founder of the Nation, reign eternally over the Japanese empire. This is the eternal and immutable national entity [*kokutai*].*"*[5] Accordingly, Minobe's emperor-as-organ theory was declared a heresy. *Fundamentals of Our National Polity* states, "The emperor is the holder in essence of supreme power; so that the theory which holds the view that sovereignty lies in essence in the State and that the Emperor is but its organ has no foundation except for the fact that it is a result of blindly following the theorists of Western States."[6] The authors of the text adamantly maintained that the emperor rules directly.

In other words, it was not a case, as in the British type of government, that "the sovereign reigns, but does not rule."[7] Neither was it joint government by sovereign and subjects. The emperor's rule was absolute rule. Connected with this, *Fundamentals of Our National Polity* stressed that the emperor was the commander-in-chief and that the sole purpose of the armed forces was to carry out the will of the emperor. Thus, each Japanese soldier was supposed to carry out the duties assigned to him as if he were carrying out the will of the emperor.

The fundamental ideological cleavage in Japanese society that had begun over the Constitution of the Empire of Japan in the late Meiji period, evolved into radical, mass-based ultranationalist movements in the Taishō period, and finally terrorized the nation for more than half a decade in the early Shōwa period, almost plunging Japan into civil war, was finally resolved. The publication and subsequent enforcement of the ideological orthodoxy spelled out in *Fundamentals of Our National Polity* constituted a "bloodless revolution" in that it brought down secular, democratically oriented government. In other words, it was designed to achieve what radical Shintō ultranationalist terrorists could not achieve directly through violence.

Fundamentals of Our National Polity also proclaimed that the Constitution of the Empire of Japan was really no more than an imperial edict. Its authors stressed that the concept of the constitution in the Japanese context was fundamentally different from that in in foreign countries, where constitutions, in one way or another, were designed to limit the powers of the monarch:

> The substance of this constitution [the Constitution of the Empire of Japan] granted by the Throne is not a thing that has been turned into a norm in order to stabilize forever, as in foreign countries, the authoritative factors to the time of the enactment of a Constitution. Nor is it the fruit of a systematization of abstract ideas or practical requirements of such things as democracy, government by the law, constitutionalism, communism or dictatorship.[8]

This interpretation of the Constitution of the Empire of Japan meant the demise of the nascent form of constitutionalism and parliamentary government that had been developing in Japan since the promulgation of the constitution in 1889. The constitution was merely claimed to be a continuation of the "Great Law" of government bequeathed by the imperial ancestors,[9] which was what Kakehi Katsuhiko had theorized.

Fundamentals of Our National Polity did more, however, than just attack the German-derived emperor as organ of the state theory to clarify the meaning of the Constitution of the Empire of Japan. Its authors went to great lengths to attack the source of all modern, Western, secular political thought: the European Enlightenment. They began that attack on an optimistic note, stating: "Japan faces a very bright future."[10] Their reasons for such optimism can be summarized as follows: (1) the Japanese people had freed themselves from the fetters of feudalism; (2) Japan had followed a very energetic policy of development overseas; (3) Japan's industries were strong; (4) Japan's way of life had grown richer; and (5) progress has been made in the area of cultural development. In short, they acknowledged that Japanese civilization had been greatly enhanced by the introduction of European and American civilization; they also noted that, in earlier times, the Japanese had been successful in adopting many things from continental Asian culture while at the same time assimilating this Asian culture into Japan's unique national entity, or kokutai. Nevertheless, *Fundamentals of Our National Polity* issued a stern warning to the Japanese people: in recent times there has been "immeasurable disquiet within and without, many difficulties in the path of advance, and much turmoil in the house of prosperity."[11] Its authors claimed that the real problem, in essence, was the lack of thoroughly digested, imported foreign ideologies. They asserted that the "ideological and social evils of present-day Japan" had resulted from the fact that "since the days of Meiji so many aspects of European and American culture, systems, and learning, [had] been imported, and that, too rapidly."[12] These ideologies stemmed from the European Enlightenment. "The views of the world and of life that form the basis of these ideologies are a rationalism and a positivism, lacking in historical views, which on the one hand lay the highest value on, and assert the liberty and equality of, individuals, and on the other hand lay value on a world by nature abstract, transcending nations and races."[13]

It is clear from the opening statements in *Fundamentals of Our National Polity* that Japanese radical Shintō ultranationalists traced the origins of Japan's internal problems to the ideas of the European Enlightenment, which had been filtering down into the population. The most important of those ideas were personal liberty and the equality of individuals. In short, they attributed the evils that then existed in Japan to the fact that the Japanese people had become, consciously or unconsciously, somewhat individualistic. From the concept of the value of the individual came such disruptive things as the freedom and rights movements and the establishment of the institutions of parliamentary government.

The authors of *Fundamentals of Our National Polity* stated that this "Age of Europeanization" had brought injury to the Japanese spirit, and that it had caused confusion in the minds of the people.[14] They claimed that individualism manifested itself in many ways and was the underlying basis for the ideologies of democracy, socialism, anarchism, and even communism. "Paradoxical and extreme conceptions, such as socialism, anarchism, and communism, are all based in the final analysis on individualism, which is at the root of modern Occidental ideologies, and are no more than varied forms of their expressions."[15] It is interesting to note that the authors felt that the Europeans also were having doubts about the value of individualism and that they saw in Europe the rise of fascism, Nazism, and totalitarianism as desirable trends in European politics. Since Japanese people in varying degrees had already been infected by the European ideologies based on individualism, radical Shintō ultranationalists were convinced that they had to be thoroughly reeducated on the basis of the fundamental Shintō ultranationalist ideology. In brief, they declared a holy war on rational discourse and the essence of modern Western society itself, much as radical Islamic fundamentalists in the Middle East regard Western-style thought as a direct threat to their vision of a pure Islamic state. With this aim in mind, *Fundamentals of Our National Polity* was published and disseminated to the Japanese masses.

"Dying to the Self and Returning to the One"

The authors of *Fundamentals of Our National Polity*, true believers in the divine origins of the Japanese islands and convinced that the Japanese emperors were the flesh-and-blood descendants of Amaterasu Ōmikami, demanded that the Japanese people, who in their minds were the deities' chosen people, be guided strictly by Shintō biblical principles to root out from the Japanese psyche any notion of Western individualism. Accordingly, the document recounts the Shintō religious origins of the Japanese nation and the divine ancestry of the emperor, drawing directly and extensively from the holy scriptures *Kojiki* and *Nihonshoki*. The reason for this, of course, was to ground Japanese subjects in solid Shintō religious principles and firmly implant in their minds a Shintō worldview; to instill in the Japanese people the ideas that their land was sacred because it was created by the purposeful act of the deities and that the emperor was indeed a flesh-and-blood descendant of Amaterasu Ōmikami. This was, in effect, the government-proclaimed orthodoxy on Shintō biblical creationism. This discussion was, of course, designed to preempt any rational examination of Shintō creationism as a belief system. As G. E. R. Lloyd stated, "Holy scripture may invite ruminative reflection, meditation, learned commentary, yet be anything open to skeptical, critical evaluation."[16]

Fundamentals of Our National Polity also discusses "The Way of the Subjects." Its authors pointed to a fundamental distinction between the relationship of the ruler and subjects/citizens in foreign lands and the unique relationship between the emperor and Japanese subjects. They charged that in foreign lands, even when subjects/citizens—who are thought of as separate individuals independent of each other and the ruler—support the ruler, no deep bonding force exists between them. But Japan was different, because an inseparable unity existed between the emperor and the Japanese people:

> Loyalty means to reverence the Emperor as [our] pivot and to follow him implicitly. By implicit obedience is meant casting ourselves aside and serving the Emperor intently. To walk this Way of loyalty is the sole Way in which we subjects may "live," and the fountainhead of all energy. Hence, offering our lives for the sake of the Emperor does not mean so-called self-sacrifice, but the casting aside of our little selves to live under his august grace and the enhancing of the genuine life of the people of a State.[17]

Offering one's life for the sake of the emperor was not to be construed as a sacrifice of the self, they maintained. On the contrary, one would gain something, which, the authors of *Fundamentals of Our National Polity* said, is something that cannot be fully grasped by those whose ideas are premised on the notion of European individualism and rational thought. "Our relationship between sovereign and subject is by no means a shallow, lateral relationship such as the correlation between ruler and citizen, but is a relationship springing from a basis transcending this correlation, and is that of 'Dying to the Self and Returning to [the] One (*botsuga kiitsu*),' in which this basis is not lost."[18] This notion of "Dying to the Self and Returning to the One," however, was not new. As should already be clear, it was very much the type of theology present in the writings of Uesugi Shinkich and Kakehi Katsuhiko.

Fundamentals of Our National Polity also contains a brief subsection on "filial piety." At first glance, this might appear to be a throwback to Hozumi Yatsuka's patriarchical völkisch state. It states, "The relationship between parent and child is a natural one, and therein springs the affection between parent and child. Parent and child are a continuation of one chain of life; and since parents are the source of the children, there spontaneously arises toward the children a tender feeling to foster them. Since children are expansions of parents, there springs a sense of respect, love for, and indebtedness toward, parents."[19] But a closer examination shows that this was not the case. Filial piety towards one's parents had no intrinsic value in itself. It was only a means to an end, and that end was totally subsuming the individual into the emperor. For example, *Fundamentals of Our National Polity* noted, "In our country there is no filial piety apart from loyalty, and filial piety has loyalty for its basis."[20] It also emphasized this point, saying, "When filial piety is elevated to loyalty, then for the first time it becomes filial piety."[21] It takes care to note that filial piety in Japan is not the same as filial piety in other countries: "In China, too, importance is laid on filial duty, and they say that it is the source of a hundred deeds. In India, too, gratitude to parents is taught. But their filial piety is not of the kind related to or based on the nation. Filial piety is a characteristic of Oriental morals; and it is in its convergence with loyalty that we find a characteristic of our national morals, and this is a factor without parallel in the world."[22] What the authors did here with regard to the Confucian-derived concept of filial piety was to gut it of any genuine value, much in the same way they gutted any real notion of constitutionalism from the Constitution of the Empire of Japan. Equally important, the notion of filial piety in *Fundamentals of Our National Polity* does not constitute a traditional, conservative, family-based authoritarianism, as in Hozumi's völkisch state in the Meiji period. On the contrary, it illustrates radical Shintō ultranationalism's anti-hierarchical faith centered on a personal relationship with the emperor.

A chapter of *Fundamentals of Our National Polity* titled "Harmony and Sincerity" asserts that only in Japan can there be real harmony among the people.[23] According to the authors, in the Western world, where each individual tries to assert his own individuality, one finds nothing but contradictions and confrontations in society. In Western societies, where the individual reigns supreme, "It may be possible to have cooperation, compromise, sacrifice, etc., so as to regulate and mitigate this contradiction and the setting of one against the other; but after all there exists no true harmony."[24] In other words, the authors argued that Western states were inherently fragmented. Likewise, there was no real possibility of achieving total harmony within the Western state because of the individual-centered contract theory of the origins of government. In contrast, the source of harmony within the Japanese state derives from the unique origins of the Japanese state. It originated from the "creation (*musubi*)" act of the deities Izanami and Izanagi; accordingly, it is based on the spirit of *musubi* (organic development), an inherent oneness of sovereign and subjects and between subjects alike. They acknowledged that problems do arise in Japanese society, but this was not due to an inherent fragmentation of society but the behavior of some people acting contrary to the spirit of musubi, which brings about harmony.

The fact that harmony was a major topic in *Fundamentals of Our National Polity* is important. Certainly a central aim of the authors was to unite the nation under a controlled orthodoxy of radical Shintō ultra-nationalism after decades of political crisis, violence, and terrorism that had been ripping Japanese society apart. In short, there had been everything but harmony in Japanese society, so the articulation and enforcement of a national religious orthodoxy was designed to ensure political, social, and cultural stability in the Japanese nation.

It is interesting to note further that the authors cited fundamental distinctions in the relationship between God and man in the Christian religious tradition, on the one hand, and the relationship between the gods and the Japanese people in the Shintō tradition, on the other hand. For example, they referred to the fact that according to the Holy Scripture in Christianity that God expelled and severely punished man; therefore, the authors concluded, man possesses an inherent fear of God. But no such thing ever happened to the Japanese people in their intimate relationship with their divine ancestors, they claimed. The authors argued that this harmonious spirit of musubi extended throughout the society, starting with the family. In the workplace, people must follow the way of harmony. Harmony was the thing that cemented relationships— vertical as well as horizontal. Each person in society was to strive to do one's best at one's task or in one's occupation. For instance,

> Those serving in Government offices as well as those working in firms must follow this Way of Harmony. In each community there are those who take the upper places while there are those who work below them. Through each one fulfilling his position is the harmony of a community obtained. To fulfill one's part means to do one's appointed task with the utmost faithfulness each in his own sphere; and by this means do those above receive help from inferiors, and inferiors are loved by superiors; and in working together harmoniously is beautiful concord manifested and creative work carried out.[25]

This was essentially the same thing that Kakehi Katsuhiko had argued, although Kakehi was not among the authors of *Fundamentals of Our National Polity*.

The second book of *Fundamentals of Our National Polity*, titled "The Manifestation of Our National Polity in History," contains six chapters. In chapter 1, "The Spirit That Runs through History," the authors claimed that there was a particular Japanese spirit (*seishin*) that was at the core of Japanese society and that this spirit had nurtured Japanese society from ancient times to the present, despite the changes and the transitions of the times. They also asserted that this spirit had become strengthened and clearer rather than diluted through the ages. However, in foreign countries the "life cords of the nation have been cut off through revolutions and downfalls, so that the spirit of the founding of the nation is disrupted and dies off, giving birth to another national history."[26] Therefore, when seeking to find the spirit of their nation, they have looked to general rules based on "abstract reason."[27] The authors argued that as a consequence of being cut off from the original inner life of the nation, the historical views of Westerners tend to transcend the nation, an argument that is essentially the same as that in Uesugi Shinkichi's analysis of the history of the state in Western European thought. But to understand the history of the Japanese nation, one must understand "the great spirit of the founding of the Empire and the unbroken line of Imperial rule."[28] They argued that this spirit had been maintained and nourished throughout the ages, and proof of this was that in Japanese history there had been reformations, but not revolutions. The distinction they made between reform and revolution is important and must be grasped in order to understand radical Shintō ultranationalist thinking. To say that there has been a revolution is to say that the national polity (the kokutai) has changed in history. This is unacceptable because that would destroy the idea of the rule of Japan by the unbroken line of rulers descended from the deity Amaterasu Ōmikami. There have been major reforms—that is, the restructuring of the "form of government"—but not an overthrow of the "form of state," which is, of course, the national polity.

The chapter then gave readers a sketch of Japanese history that began with the founding of the Japanese state by the deities and the expansion of the imperial state through the efforts of Emperor Jimmu. It then mentioned that Emperor Sujin (97–30 BC) enshrined Amaterasu Ōmikami in a village called Kasanui in Yamato and that Emperor Suinin (29 BC–AD 70) built the Grand Shrine of Ise, acts that indicated the emperors' reverence of the spirits of the ancestral deities. Next mentioned were the Taika Reforms carried out by Emperor Kōtoku (AD 645–54) and by Prince Naka no Ōe. It noted that the reforms were carried out to correct the abuses of the clan system, especially the Sōga Clan. The emperor adapted Chinese institutions of government to strengthen imperial rule. The Taika Reforms were made because the powerful clans had gradually usurped the powers of the imperial court until they controlled the people and the lands. In essence, the Taika Reforms were designed to give back to the emperor all the people and the lands belonging to the clans, as well as the administrative powers of government. This was the first great example of returning to the spirit of ancient times, which means direct rule by the emperor, the "god made manifest as man (*arahitogami*)." It is important to note that, although the reformers used ideas from Chinese philosophy and Chinese institutions of government, those ideas were selectively adapted. Elements of Chinese thought that were incompatible with the concept of the unbroken line of imperial rule were rejected.

The next era in Japanese history began with the establishment of the Kamakura military government by Minamoto Yoritomo (AD 1147–99). Yoritomo had seized control of the land and the reins of government and set up a rival government in Kamakura. The authors of *Fundamentals of Our National Polity* regarded these acts as "administrative abnormalities that run counter to our national structure."[29] Indeed, the whole history of feudalism from the twelfth century to the end of the nineteenth century was considered an aberration from imperial rule. The document cited this long era of military rule as the reason for Emperor Meiji's Rescript to the Armed Forces, which, in regard to the rule by the Shōguns, stated that "it is indeed contrary to our national structure and indeed in violation of the laws set by Our Imperial Ancestors, and a thing to be truly ashamed of."[30] *Fundamentals of Our National Polity* praised the attempts by Emperor Go-Daigo to restore imperial rule in the so-called Kemmu Restoration (AD 1334–35). Probably the most hated person in the feudal period was Ashikaga Takauji (AD 1305–58). Takauji's actions, which totally disregarded the spirit of the national polity, were regarded as "high treason."[31]

The Tokugawa regime received positive treatment because its leaders were regarded as having felt or shown honor and respect to the imperial court. The Tokugawa regime also promoted learning that gave rise to the various schools of thought that eventually contributed to the rise of the prestige of the Imperial Family and laid the necessary intellectual foundations among the Japanese people for the restoration of imperial rule with the Meiji Restoration. In short, the essential point that the authors of *Fundamentals of Our National Polity* tried to convey about the feudal period of Japanese history was that, despite rule by the feudal military leaders, the ancient spirit of imperial rule endured to the extent that it was never overthrown; finally, that spirit was revived and strengthened during the Tokugawa period to the point that the Meiji Restoration of 1868 could succeed:

> Thus we have seen that the unfolding of our history consists, in the case of the Emperor, in taking over and appropriating the injunctions bequeathed by the Imperial Ancestors and, in the case of his subjects, in "dying to the self" in order to fulfill their duties and in loyally guarding and maintaining the prosperity of the Imperial Throne. Hence, this great spirit of union between high and low is a thing that has already been clearly shown in the founding of the Empire; and it is this great spirit that runs throughout history.[32]

This "dying to the self" is a selfless devotion to the emperor. Under this philosophy, one becomes totally devoid of any self-interest, eager to obey and carry out the will of the emperor.

The third chapter of *Fundamentals of Our National Polity*, "The Inherent Character of the Nation," discussed the special character of the Japanese nation. The Japanese were said to have a "clean and cloudless heart."[33] In "dying to one's ego and one's ends," one finds one's purpose in life in the fundamentals of the ancient spirit.[34] The text emphasized that this "dying to the self" should not be construed as a form of denial of oneself but as a means of enhancing one's true great self, a type of thinking seen in the state theories of Kakehi and Uesugi. In organic theories of state, the concept of the individual is not an individual as understood within the Western liberal-democratic philosophical tradition. The individual is fundamentally an element of the collective whole. The spirit of "dying to the self and returning to the One" meant "death to oneself with one's mind centered on the Imperial Household and for the sake of the Throne."[35] This spirit was at the core of the Japanese nation and it is because of the strength of this spirit throughout Japanese history that the national polity had been maintained. The authors of *Fundamentals of Our National Polity* claimed that this spirit was embedded in the Japanese language, the manners and customs of the people, and Shintō ceremonial rites. The deities enshrined in the Shintō shrines were the imperial ancestors, ancestors of the clans descended from the heavenly deities, and those who had served and defended the imperial court.

On the basis of this spirit, foreign ideologies and systems of thought had been imported, assimilated, and sublimated, contributing to the enhancement of the imperial way. Chapter 4, "Ceremonial Rites and Morality," noted that Buddhism, originally from India, was imported into Japan to strengthen imperial rule. Chapter 5, "National Culture," reiterated this theme, stating in its opening paragraph: "Our culture is a manifestation of the great spirit that has come down to us since the founding of the Empire. In order to enrich and develop this, foreign culture has been assimilated and sublimated." The text then went on to state something of fundamental importance: in the Ming Dynasty Chinese text *Gozatsuso*, it was written that, "if there should be anyone going over to Japan carrying with him the works of Mencius, his boat would be overturned and those aboard drowned."[36] The point is that anyone who attempted to bring into Japan a philosophy that was contrary to the spirit of the national polity would be destroyed. Mencius's political philosophy emphasized the importance of the people in the state. He taught that rulers should rule for the benefit of the people, and that should a monarch fail to do so, his subjects had the right to rebel because in that case the monarch forfeited his right to rule. This political philosophy, which advocated the right of revolution, was obviously a threat to the kokutai and therefore unacceptable. In other words, foreign ideologies had to be sanitized and stripped of all concepts of universality before being allowed to enter and flourish in Japan.

Japan's Holy War

Mark Juergensmeyer, one of America's foremost scholars of religious nationalism and religious terrorism, wrote that many religious activists who have turned to terror and war have been driven by "an image of a cosmic war."[37] A cosmic war is a divine war:

> I call such images "cosmic" because they are larger than life. They evoke great battles of the legendary past, and they relate to metaphysical conflicts between good and evil. Notions of cosmic war are intimately personal but can also be translated to the social plane. Ultimately, though, they transcend human experience. What makes religious violence par-

ticularly savage and relentless is that its perpetrators have placed such religious images of divine struggle—cosmic war—in the service of worldly political battles. For this reason, acts of religious terror serve not only as tactics in a political strategy but also as evocations of a much larger spiritual confrontation.[38]

Radical Shintō ultranationalists were fighting what Juergensmeyer referred to as a cosmic war. Japan's cosmic war was a holy war of good against evil.

In the opening paragraph in the concluding section of *Fundamentals of Our National Polity*, the authors asked the following question: How should the Japanese nation deal with the various problems of the day? As has already been discussed, the "problems" referred to in *Fundamentals of Our National Polity* were the various ideological and social evils of Japan at that time. The underlying cause of the ideological and social evils was modern Western civilization, which stemmed from the European Enlightenment. The authors argued that the Japanese people had not been able to digest Western culture fully. In other words, they had not been able to introduce it, assimilate it, and then sublimate it to the fundamental principles of the kokutai as they had done with ideas and ideologies that had come into Japan from Indian and Chinese civilizations in the ancient period. On the contrary, the rapid influx of European and American civilization had confused them, causing them to lose their own cultural bearings.

What should the Japanese nation now do? The answer was this: "Our first duty is the task of creating a new Japanese culture by assimilating and sublimating foreign cultures which are at the source of the various problems in keeping with the fundamental principles of our kokutai."[39] To assimilate and sublimate Western culture, Japanese had to have a solid understanding of the principles on which Western culture was based. Accordingly, the next several pages of *Fundamentals of Our National Polity* presented in capsule form the fundamentals of Western culture and provided examples of the methodology the Japanese used to assimilate and sublimate Chinese culture. The authors' view of the spirit of Western civilization was stated as follows: Western ideologies originated from Greek ideologies. The core concepts of Greek ideologies were rationalism, objectivism, and idealism. Toward the end of classical Greek civilization, individualistic tendencies gradually appeared. The Romans subsequently adopted and developed these Greek concepts into laws, statecraft, and other facets of their civilization. They also adopted Christianity, which was a universal faith that transcended the state. The modern European nations had arisen with the aim of achieving a "Kingdom of Heaven on earth" by reviving Greek ideologies and by seeking the liberation of the individual in opposition to the religious and despotic oppressions of the Middle Ages. Hence, they reasoned that the core spirit of modern Western civilization was individualism and universalism.

The authors of Fundamentals of Our National Polity claimed that the Western nations were based on faulty principles. They warned that this "individualistic explanation of human beings abstract[ed] only one aspect of an individuality and overlooks the characteristics of a nation (kokuminsei) and historicity (rekishisei)."[40] Accordingly, Westerners have lost sight of the real nature of human existence. This was the problem of liberalism and the ideological derivatives of it. The authors reiterated the fact that Western thinkers had finally awakened to the problems of individualism and had devised various new ideologies, such as fascism, Nazism, and totalitarianism, to overcome them. But they noted that the future for the Western world was basically hopeless, for the new ideologies would "furnish no true way out or solution."[41] On the other hand, the prognosis for Japan was good. The reason given for this optimism was that the Japanese had been guided by the true spirit, and this spirit was alive and well. Furthermore, Japan had had an impressive record of importing, assimilating, and sublimating foreign cultures in the past and, in the process, strengthening its own spirit while enhancing its own civilization.

Japanese must be clearly aware of the fact that although European culture, especially natural science, had greatly contributed to the national prosperity of the nation, "their individualistic qualities brought about various difficulties in all the phases of the lives of our people, causing their thoughts to fluctuate."[42] Having already introduced various Western ideologies and practices, the authors argued that the Japanese now had to begin "with the clearest insight to adapt their merits and cast aside their demerits."[43] The document noted that many Japanese had accepted Western doctrines at face value, without even realizing that they contradicted the national structure. It also noted that Western learning had created a gap between the Japanese educated class, which had come under the influence of Western ideologies, and the Japanese masses.

Communism and the emperor as organ of the state theory were cited as concrete examples of ideologies imported from the West that had disrupted the Japanese. However, the authors optimistically noted that communism "appears to have fallen into decay"[44] and the emperor as organ theory had "exploded."[45] Nevertheless, they warned that the problems had by no means been solved, for while the case of communism and the emperor as organ of the state theory were clearly in violation of the national polity, other dangerous Western ideologies were much more difficult for Japanese to grasp. This presented a greater danger to the Japanese state because many Japanese might unwittingly be trying to incorporate abstract Western theories that disguises underlying individualistic values. The authors cautioned that those ideologies had to be discerned and weeded out. As an example of this, they warned about being duped by the notion of internationalism:

> Such things as an international community comprising the entire world and universal theories common to the entire world were given importance rather than concrete nations and their characteristic qualities; so that in the end there even arose the mistaken idea that international law constituted a higher norm than national laws, that it stood higher in value, and that national laws were, if anything, subordinate to it.[46]

The conclusion of *Fundamentals of Our National Polity* ended with a section subheaded "Our Mission (*Warera no Shimei*)," which stated, "Our present mission as a nation is to build up a new Japanese culture by adopting and sublimating Western cultures with our *kokutai* as the basis."[47] It also noted that Japan was at a historic juncture and seemed to suggest that the massive cultural borrowings from Western civilization might already be coming to a close. Moreover, it stated that it was now time for Japan to contribute to world culture:

> Our contributions to the world lie only in giving full play more than ever to our Way which is of the Japanese people. The people must more than ever create and develop a new Japan by virtue of their immutable National Polity which is the basis of the State and by virtue of the Way of the Empire which stands firm throughout the ages at Home and abroad, and thereby more than ever guard and maintain the prosperity of the Imperial Throne which is coeval with heaven and earth. This, indeed, is our mission.[48]

This was the cosmic or divine struggle that Juergensmeyer talked about. Japan's war against the Western world was to be an all-or-nothing struggle.

From a liberal-democratic viewpoint, totalitarianism is the ultimate evil form of government, for the individual is totally annihilated. But from the perspective of radical Shintō ultranationalism, totalitarianism and totalitarian ideology were praiseworthy. In fact, the authors of *Fundamentals of Our National Polity* boasted of the totalitarian traits in Japanese culture—for instance, in passages such as, "Bushido may be cited as showing an outstanding characteristic of our national morality. In the world of warriors one sees inherited the totalitarian structure and spirit of the ancient clans peculiar to our nation."[49] In another passage discussing how the Japanese were able to sublimate Buddhism to the Japanese spirit, they wrote, "Their doctrines were likewise adapted and sublimated through our clans and family spirit and our self-effacing and totalitarian spirit."[50] Furthermore, as mentioned earlier, they openly lauded the fact that some European nations were beginning to turn their backs on the ideas of the liberty and the equality of individuals by embracing fascism, Nazism, and totalitarianism.[51]

According to *Fundamentals of Our National Polity*, the positive purpose of the Japanese nation was to promote harmony (*wa*) in the world. But at what price was this harmony to be achieved? Ultimately, Japanese radical Shintō ultranationalists reasoned that individualism was the main source of disharmony in the world of the twentieth century. Accordingly, it had to be eradicated from within and from without. This was a dual call for the eradication of any lingering notions of individualism among Japanese within the Japan nation and for unlimited expansionism abroad to destroy the liberal international world order created by the Anglo-Saxon people. This was a gigantic task: trying to destroy ideas in the minds of people throughout the world is not an easy thing to do. Nevertheless, it had to be attempted if world harmony was to be achieved. Internally, the state propaganda machine stepped up the pace of indoctrination in the thought of "Dying to the self and returning to the One," the basis of Japan's national morality and national culture. It was on the basis of this spirit, of course, that foreign ideologies had been successfully assimilated and sublimated in Japan in the past. It was now crucial that Western ideologies based on individualism be assimilated and sublimated. But how was this actually done?

As a rule, all inklings of universalism and individualism had to be rooted out. Take, for example, the Constitution of the Empire of Japan. First, the fact that the authors of *Fundamentals of Our National Polity* distinguished between constitutions of foreign countries and the Japanese constitution must be made clear. They noted that in the Western tradition, constitutions were designed to place restraints on the ruler. The underlying philosophical principle was that rulers or political leaders should be held accountable, and that nobody was above the law. This is a form of universalism and therefore could not be accepted. The emperor was absolute. Therefore, the authors claimed, the Constitution of the Empire of Japan was not a constitution in the Western sense. They announced that it was nothing more than an imperial edict. There could be no limitations on the powers of the emperor; there could be no notion of the separation of powers. The constitution said that subjects had rights and duties. But they could not be rights and duties for the subject in the usual sense in that the subject had inherent rights that had to be protected. The subject could not have inherent rights, either, to protect him or her from the ruler or from intrusions from other members of the society. The subject was supposed to be dead to the self and one with the emperor. This is what is meant by the Constitution of the Empire of Japan being sublimated. The net result of this process of sublimation was that, while Japan was to have the formal trappings of constitutional government, that government became something quite different in content. In this way, the sublimation of democracy meant that it was no longer democracy. Recall that Kita Ikki was also concerned that socialism was being gutted because his fellow socialists were compromising its fundamental principles to satisfy the orthodox State Shintōists.

Under pressure from radical Shintō ultranationalists, even the principles of reason and logic were stripped of their universalism. The authors of *Fundamentals of Our National Polity* noted that "Shōtoku Taishi adopted the teachings of Confucius, Buddha, and Lao-tzu to further the Imperial Way, and built up a Code of Laws in Seventeen Chapters, and also produced the *Sangyogissho*."[52] But even in these cases, they claimed, in expounding "reason"—namely, the "logic of things"—it was by no means an abstract, universal law to which they were referring. Universal values of logic were unacceptable. As discussed earlier, Minobe was rebuked by Kikuchi Kakeo for emphasizing that his textbooks focused on "the influence of actual circumstances and vigorously expound[ed] logic and reason." As this example suggests, irrationalism was a fundamental characteristic of radical Shintō ultranationalist ideology. The importation, assimilation, and sublimation of foreign thought was really a process of ideological sanitization, which resulted in the very destruction of individualism.

In terms of foreign policy, Japanese expansionism meant the expansion of totalitarian rule on a global scale. As the authors of *Fundamentals of Our National Polity* argued, the struggle between Japan and the outside world had always been a struggle between universal values and the totalitarian values of Japan's unique national polity. If one follows the logic of radical Shintō ultranationalist thought, the emperor system could never be safe until "the permanent domination of each single individual in each and every sphere of life" was achieved.[53] The cosmic or holy war that radical Shintō ultranationalists were waging was what Juergensmeyer called an "all-or-nothing struggle against an enemy whom one assumed to be determined to destroy. No compromise is deemed possible. The very existence of the opponent is a threat, and until the enemy is either crushed or contained, one's own existence cannot be secure. What is striking about the martial attitude is the certainty of one's position and the willingness to defend it, or impose it on others, to the end."[54]

Commentaries on *Kokutai no Hongi*

In his introduction to John Gauntlett's translation of *Kokutai no Hongi* (translated as *Cardinal Principles of the National Entity of Japan*), Robert Hall noted that the original draft of *Kokutai no Hongi* was written by Hisamatsu Senichi, a scholar of Japanese classics at Tokyo Imperial University. However, he further noted that Hisamatsu's original manuscript was rewritten twice and that it underwent further, extensive revisions by Itō Enkichi, chief of the Ministry of Education's Bureau of Educational Reform (Thought Control). The first revisions of the original manuscript were done by a committee of academics, which included Yoshida Kumaji, a member of the Research Section of the Kokumin Seishin Bunka Kenkyūjo (National Spirit Cultural Research Institute); Kihara Masami of the National Spirit Cultural Research Institute; Watsuji Tetsurō, a professor in the Ethics Department of Tokyo Imperial University; Inoue Takamarō of the National Spirit Cultural Research Institute; Sakuda Sōichi, a professor at Kyōto Imperial University; Kuroita Katsumi, a professor emeritus of Tokyo Imperial University; Otsuka Takematsu, an official compiler of materials for the history of the Reformation; Hisamatsu Senichi, a professor at Tokyo Imperial University; Yamada Yoshio, a professor at Tōhoku Imperial University; Iijima Tadao, a professor at the Peers' School; Fujikake Shizuya, a professor at Tokyo Imperial University; Miyaji Naokazu, the official in charge of historical research; Kōno Seizō, president of Kokugakuin University; and Ui Hakuju, a professor at Tokyo Imperial University.[55] Another board of specialists was created by the Ministry of Education to conduct research and assist in the compilation of *Fundamentals of Our National Polity*. Members of that board included Yamamoto Katsuichi, Ōgushi Toyō,

Shida Nobuyuki, Ogawa Gisho, Kondo Toshiharu, Yokoyama Shumpei, Shimizu Gisho, Fujioka Tsuguhei, Sano Yasutaro, and Fujimoto Manji. According to John Brownlee, the National Spirit Cultural Research Institute was established in 1932 by the Ministry of Education to promote the Shintō ultranationalist ideology.[56]

All of these scholars contributed something to the drafting of *Fundamentals of Our National Polity* except, possibly, Kuroita Katsumi. He "fell ill six months after his appointment to the committee, and he attended none of the general meetings."[57] Moreover, many of the scholars were recruited to write commentaries on *Fundamentals of Our National Polity* in the years following its publication. The commentaries were written between 1937 and 1940 and published in the series *Kokutai no Hongi Kaisetsu Sōsho*, compiled by the Educational Affairs Bureau of the Ministry of Education. Several of the commentaries elaborated on the mission of Japan's holy war and are, therefore, worth mentioning.

In December 1937, Iijima Tadao (1874–1954), who at the time was professor emeritus of literature at the Peers' School, wrote an article titled "Nihon no Jugaku (Japanese Confucianism)," which dealt with the ideology of Confucianism in Japanese history and with the historical and ideological relationship between Confucianism and the Japanese kokutai. He started the article by noting that Confucianism had been introduced into Japan from the Korean peninsula by the scholar Wani during the sixteenth year of the reign of Emperor Ōjin (circa AD 285). He further noted that Confucianism had been in Japan for 1,653 years. Iijima then traced the history of Confucianism throughout each period of Japanese history up to 1937. The key point of his article was that Confucianism was accepted in Japan only after Confucian doctrines that inherently contradicted, or came into conflict with, the Japanese kokutai had been removed. In other words, it was only after Confucianism had undergone a process of sublimation (*junka*),[58] or a kind of sanitization, that it was accepted. Chinese Confucian notions of individualism and "ideas of revolution (*kakumei shisō*)" had to be eliminated. Confucian values such as harmony (*wa*), sincerity (*sei*), and loyalty and filial piety (*chūkō*) were acceptable as long as they could be rendered in harmony with the kokutai. What Iijima was arguing in effect was that Confucianism had to be stripped of any sense of universal values before it could be accepted as an ideology in Japan. The result was that it left Japanese Confucianism without any real content independent of radical Shintō ultranationalist ideology.

Kōno Seizō (1882–1963), another scholar on the Compilation Committee, wrote a fascinating and important commentary on *Fundamentals of Our National Polity*. It is worth noting here that Daniel Holtom, a renowned scholar of Shintō who wrote in English in the prewar period, commented that Kōno, as a scholar, ranked "among the foremost of the students of Shintō history."[59] In March 1938, Kōno wrote the lengthy essay "Our *Kokutai* and Shintō."[60] As this title suggests, he discussed the relationship between the kokutai and the Shintō religion. Kōno divided his essay into eight subtopics. In the first section, he talked about the awakening of the Japanese spirit; in the second, he discussed Shintō's essence and special characteristics; in subsequent sections, he focused on the belief in Kamunagara; sincerity and the Japanese ethnic group; the *jinja* as a manifestation of Shintō; and the unity of Shintō and the Japanese state. In his final two subsections, Kōno summarized developments in Shintō doctrine and discussed the kokutai and its relationship to national life.

In the opening sentence of the essay, Kōno stated, "The *kokutai* is [our] national characteristic."[61] He then elaborated on the meaning of the national characteristic of the Japanese state, saying that it was the manifested form of Japan's distinctive national essence. Central to Japan's national essence was its "state organization (*kokka shoshiki*),"[62] the idea that Japan would be reigned over and governed by a line of emperors unbroken for ages eternal. Japan's national essence further encompassed the belief in the destiny of the Imperial Throne "originating and existing with heaven and earth (*tenjō mukyū*),"[63] which was the essential life of the nation and the motivation for national action. This was the belief and spirit of the Japanese people and the Japanese Volk. Accordingly, the essence of the kokutai was directly connected to Shintō, the Way of the Gods. Kōno emphasized that this belief in the imperial destiny of the Imperial Throne coeval with heaven and earth, the essence of the Japanese state, continued to live in the hearts of the emperors and had been the belief and sentiment of the Japanese people who had served the successive generations of emperors. In Kōno's opinion, this belief had been at the core of Japanese "ethnicity (*minzokusei*)" since ancient times.[64] In other words, he argued that the foundations of the Japanese state were religious. Shintō was the traditional belief of the Japanese ethnic group. It was this traditional belief of the Japanese people that shaped the Japanese spirit throughout the ages and the ideal that continued to drive the passions of the Japanese people in the present. Holtom quoted Kōno, the man responsible for the training of Shintō priests in Japan, saying many of the same things in an article in 1940:

This august message of the Imperial Ancestors has been looked upon by later generations as an expression of the Divine Will co-existent with heaven and earth. It is also considered as the fundamental faith of the nation and the motivating force of all activities. Furthermore, it is the source and foundation of Article I of the Japanese Constitution which reads, "The Empire of Japan shall be reigned over and governed by a line of Emperors unbroken for ages eternal."[65]

Kōno noted that the consciousness of this ethnic spirit (*minzoku seishin*) among the Japanese people had advanced even more since the Meiji Restoration. As examples, he stated that people constantly referred to the Japanese spirit (*yamato damashii*) during the Qing Dynasty–Japan War of 1894–95 and to Bushidō, the spirit of the samurai, during the Japan–Russia War of 1904–1905.[66] With the establishment of the modern nation-state, the "ethnic spirit" that had existed throughout Japanese history had become the "national spirit (*kokumin seishin*)" or the "Japanese spirit (*Nihon seishin*)." Kōno further stated that Shintō, the imperial way (*kōdō*), the national spirit, and Japanese ethnicity were all expressions of the same traditional belief. It had been the "guiding spirit (*shidō seishin*)" that had governed national life throughout Japanese history.[67] Since the Meiji Restoration, the policy of the new Japanese state had been the "unity of Shintō and the state (*saisei itchi*),"[68] which in turn was also the "great principle of *kamunagara* (*kamunagara no daidō*)."[69]

He lamented the fact that the Japanese people seemed to have temporarily become confused after the Great War, during the economic depression and because of the corrupting influences of democratic thought in Japan. However, he noted that the Japanese spirit revived toward the end of the Taishō period, and the Japanese people successfully confronted the disaster of the Great Kantō earthquake and subdued the radical communist movements. By the end of the Taishō period, the Japanese people had again awakened to the national spirit; a popular saying of the time was, "Return to the spirit of nation-building (*kenkoku no seishin ni kaere*)."[70] Kōno stated that the Japanese spirit was further aroused by the Manchurian Incident in 1931 and again by the China Incident in 1937.

In short, Kōno argued that Shintō religious ethno-nationalism—or what this study calls radical Shintō ultranationalism—was at the center of a great Japanese belief system and that it was the spirit driving the Japanese state toward its inherent mission of global rule. He reiterated this throughout the essay, and there is no reason to doubt his sincerity. Holtom noted:

Indeed, the doctrine that her state structure is the strongest and most excellent of all the world must have as its corollary the idea that non-Japanese peoples can benefit only by being brought under its sway. It would be a misreading of the facts if we should be content to account for the vigor and steadfastness with which this conviction of mission is asserted, merely as a search for compensation in the presence of frustration and insecurity, or as a pious verbiage that cloaks desperate economic need, on the one hand, and bitterly inconsistent severity toward conquered people, on the other.[71]

Holtom devoted several pages to talking about the importance of the Shintō "doctrine of benevolent destiny" or the "benevolent destiny dogma" in motivating the Japanese. This is the same thing—"the destiny of the imperial throne co-existent with heaven and earth (*tenjō mukyū no koun*)"—that Kōno focused on in his commentary on *Fundamentals of Our National Polity*.

By the 1930s, it had become dangerous for any Japanese in Japan to challenge this state doctrine. Holtom wrote:

We have examined in some of its major aspects a situation that introduces us to the pattern according to which the Japanese mind is molded from the cradle to the grave and to forms of nationalistic dogma that are so successfully imbued through constant reiteration in the schools, in the newspapers, in magazines, in books, over the radio, in all the manifold agencies of propaganda of an all-powerful state, and which are so inextricably merged with the sanctions of religion that rejection of the stereotype becomes an indignity offered to deity and criticism a form of treason. The rare professor who dares to turn the light of scientific historical research into the amazing mixture of mythology, rationalization, and historical fact that makes up the texture of the Japanese state structure and its official interpretation finds his writings confiscated, himself apprehended by the police and prosecuted in the courts of law, and his family subjected to social censure. There was a time when the mythological elements in the traditional picture of the sun-goddess *Amaterasu Ōmikami* or the impossible idealization of history that places the first accession to the throne at 660 b.c. could be brought up for open discussion. To raise the questions now would involve serious consequences. Japanese scholarship is in the hands of a modern inquisition.[72]

Holtom's statement reconfirms the contention of this study that Japan of the late 1930s was not the same as Japan of the Meiji period or even of the

Taishō period. Although fundamental state structures may have been the same, the Japanese state had changed dramatically in terms of thought and leadership. Internally, a rigid ideological and religious conformity had gripped the nation as never before. Externally, the radical Shintō ultranationalists who controlled the Japanese state believed in Japan's destiny of unlimited expansionism to further the ideal of "the whole world under one roof (*hakkō Ichiu*)." Kōno equated this "destiny of the imperial throne co-existent with heaven and earth" with the concept of "the whole world under one roof."

When Japan, Germany, and Italy formed the Axis in September 1940, Emperor Hirohito issued an imperial edict. It stated that the purpose of the alliance was "to enhance justice on earth and make of the world one household . . . , bequeathed by Our Imperial Ancestors, which We lay to heart day and night."[73] There should be no question in anyone's mind that Japan after the 1930s was controlled ideologically by what the philosopher and longshoreman Eric Hoffer has referred to as the "true believer,"[74] a man of "fanatical faith who is ready to sacrifice his life for a holy cause."[75]

Ōgushi Toyō, a member of the second board of specialists established to assist in the compilation of *Fundamentals of Our National Polity*, also wrote a commentary on *Fundamentals of Our National Structure*. The aim of Ōgushi's essay, "The Imperial Constitution and the Subjects' Assistance," was to explain that the Constitution of the Empire of Japan was the framework within which Japanese subjects assisted the emperor in his task of direct imperial rule.[76] Ōgushi went to great lengths to illustrate that the imperial constitution was not based on the premise of a contract between ruler and the people or on some notion of power sharing, as one found in Western constitutions. He stressed that the Constitution of the Empire of Japan did not come about as the result of a confrontation between the emperor and his people, as had been the case of the Magna Carta in thirteenth-century England.[77] The constitution was a gift from the emperor to his people (*kintei kempō*).[78] He further emphasized that the relationship between the emperor and the people was an indivisible unity. The form of government was "direct imperial rule (*tennō goshinsei*),"[79] and the task of the people was to assist in the emperor's rule. The existing executive, legislative, and judicial branches of the Japanese government did not represent a separation of political powers, as in foreign systems of state. It merely represented a "separation of assistance functions (*hoyoku kikan no bunritsu*)" of direct imperial rule.[80]

Toward the end of his essay, Ōgushi attacked the emperor as organ of the state theory, according to which "the subject of sovereignty was the state and the emperor was merely an organ of the state."[81] He noted that the word "organ (*kikan*)" was part of the larger "organism (*yūkitai*),"[82] and argued that the emperor as organ theory was ultimately premised on individualistic Western legal thought, which implied a disconnection between the state and the individual. This, of course, was in direct conflict with the Japanese kokutai. By this time, Minobe's emperor as organ theory had already been banned.

The final section of Ōgushi's essay, subtitled "Direct Imperial Rule and the Subjects' Assistance," echoed arguments made by Uesugi Shinkichi and Kakehi Katsuhiko decades earlier.[83] Ōgushi went to great lengths to argue that direct imperial rule (*tennō goshinsei*) by the emperor differed fundamentally from "an absolute [a despotic] monarchy (*sensei kunshū-sei*)" found in foreign countries.[84] He emphasized that what was meant by imperial rule (*tōchi*) was not the control or domination (*shihai*) of the land (*tochi*) and the people (*jinmin*), as with foreign absolute or despotic monarchs. On the contrary, the subjects absorbed themselves into the life of the emperor, becoming one with him, and assisted him in working for the unity and development of the Japanese state. Rule by the emperor was not "rule by force (*kyōsei shihai*)."[85] In the last two pages of his essay, Ōgushi, quoting Article 5 of the Constitution of the Empire of Japan, which stated, "The emperor exercises the legislative power with consent of the Imperial Diet," asserted that the "supreme power of legislation (*rippō no taiken*)" resided in the emperor and noted that it was the function of the parliament to assist the emperor in the passing of legislation:[86] "It goes without saying that legislative (lawmaking) power resides in the emperor; legislative power does not reside in the Diet."[87] This argument, too, as has already been discussed, went back to the debate over state and sovereignty between Hozumi Yatsuka and Minobe Tatsukichi in the late Meiji period. But by the time Ōgushi wrote his essay, in the late 1930s, the issue had already been resolved. He brought it up again as part of the massive propaganda campaign of the radical Shintō ultranationalists that Holtom mentioned.

Ōgushi ended his essay by quoting from the Imperial Rescript on Education: "Always respect the Constitution of the Empire of Japan and observe the laws; should emergency arise, offer yourselves courageously to the State; and thus guard and maintain the prosperity of Our Imperial Throne coeval with heaven and earth."[88] The official English translation of the Japanese "*tenjō mukyū no kōun*" is "the prosperity of Our Imperial

Throne coeval with heaven and earth." But in the context of the late 1930s and the early 1940s, these lines from the Imperial Rescript took on even greater meaning: they meant that Japanese subjects were to work to assist the emperor in making this "destiny" of the imperial throne conterminous with heaven and earth a reality through the power of the emperor's military.

Another commentary on *Fundamentals of Our National Polity* was written in 1939 by Hisamatsu Senichi (1894–1976), who, as noted earlier, was the primary author of the original draft of *Fundamentals of Our National Structure*. In his commentary "Our Climate, Nationality and Literature," Hisamatsu discussed the relationship between climate and Japanese literature and the linkage of Japanese "nationality (*kokuminsei*)" and Japanese literature. He argued that a distinctive characteristic of Japanese literature was that it represented and revealed an aspect of Japanese nationality. He pointed out, for example, that Japanese tended to express content rich in meaning by using as few words as possible. Also, countless Japanese words had multiple meanings. Further, in the history of Japanese literature, one tended to find a very strong antitheoretical or anti-logical bent—a "theory hell (*rikutsu jigoku*)"—as well as word clusters or a propensity to combine and unite concepts that were not found in the languages of other peoples.[89]

An example of a distinctive feature of Japanese nationality was a special reverence for deities, or, as Hisamatsu put it, a "spirit of reverence [toward gods] (*keishin no seishin*)."[90] Although he admitted that reverence toward gods was not limited to the Japanese, he maintained that nowhere except in Japan could one find the identity of the concepts of "reverence toward the deities (*keishin no seishin*)" and "loyalty and patriotism (*chūkun aikoku*)."[91] The identity of these concepts was comprehensible only in the Japanese cultural context because only in Japan was the supreme deity a national deity who had founded the Japanese state. This deity, of course, was Amaterasu Ōmikami, and the special spirit of reverence stemmed from absolute belief in Amaterasu Ōmikami, whose descendants ruled the Japanese state as emperors and were manifestations of Amaterasu Ōmikami. To be loyal to the emperor was automatically to worship Amaterasu Ōmikami, which was also to possess the spirit of love of country. That is to say, Hisamasa argued that only in the Japanese context could one find a complete identity of *kami* (god), *kimi* (ruler), and *kokka* (state).

The center of Japanese nationality lay not only in respect for the deities and loyalty and patriotism. Respect for the family was also important for maintaining Japanese national identity. The spirit of respect for the family consisted of filial piety that a child has towards his or parents, as well as the parents' love for their offspring. At the same time, the attitude of respect for the family was based on the spirit of loyalty to the emperor and love of country. Hisamatsu insisted that the primary value of the family lay in the fact that the family was like an arena in which to train the individual in the spirit of loyalty to the emperor and love of country. The descendants of the divine deities who founded the Japanese state were the emperors and the Imperial Family. Likewise, Japanese subjects were descendants of the gods. Thus, the Imperial Family was the head family of the nation, making the Japanese state "one large family state (*ichidai kazoku kokka*)."[92] In this family state, the emperor treated his subjects as if they were his children, and subjects as family members were loyal to the Imperial Family as the head family. The concept of filial piety (*kō*) could not be separated from the concept of loyalty to the emperor (*chū*). Further, Hisamatsu reasoned that without loyalty there could be no filial piety. And if loyalty and filial piety were not an identity, true filial piety could not exist. This, of course, sounds like a throwback to the family-state ideal articulated in the late Meiji period by Hozumi Yatsuka. However, I think it is safe to conclude that, for Hisamatsu, the family idea had only utilitarian value. He did not value filial piety or the institution of the family as an end in itself. Rather, he saw the importance of the family principle as a vehicle to inculcate the values of loyalty and love of country (which were the same thing in his mind). And certainly, anyone with knowledge of Chinese thought would quickly realize that Hisamatsu's notion of "respect for the family" had little or nothing to do with Confucianism or Confucian family values.

In the last few pages of this essay, Hisamatsu discussed the meaning and significance of the concept *botsuga kiitsu* in the text of *Fundamentals of Our National Polity*. This, in my opinion, is one of the most important concepts in radical Shintō ultranationalist thought and therefore deserves careful attention. The words "*botsuga kiitsu*" appear in the original Japanese text of *Fundamentals of Our National Polity* on page 36, in a section subtitled "Chūkun Aikoku (Loyalty and Patriotism)." In his translation of the Japanese text, John Gauntlett translated the concept as "self-effacement and a return to [the] one."[93] In a footnote, however, he explained that "self-effacement and return to [the] one" is represented by four characters—"sink–self–return–one"—and can be paraphrased as "casting oneself away and returning to the one great Way."[94] In *Sources of Japanese Tradition*, these words are translated as "dying to the self and returning to [the] one."[95] Hisamatsu, who wrote these words in the original manuscript, explained that the spirit of *botsuga* or *mushi* meant to abandon one's selfish or individualistic attitude, to absorb oneself into the larger state, and to live as "one element (*ichi bunshi*)" of the state. In other words, according to Hisamatsu, the individual was supposed to dissolve the self within the state. That was the way the subject was to "live" in loyalty and patriotism to the state, which was identical to the emperor. In effect, Hisamatsu was saying that one must live as "one element" in the mystical body of the emperor. According to him, this was the spirit of the poem in the Manyōshū:

> By the sea our corpses shall steep in the water.
> On the hills our corpses shall rot in the grass.
> We will die by the side of our sovereign,
> we will never look back.[96]

These ideas can be found in the state thought of Uesugi Shinkichi and Kakehi Katsuhiko, whose theories have already been discussed. Hisamatsu further said that the spirit of "dying to the self and returning to the one" was the special characteristic of the Japanese people. It was this spirit that existed from the origins of the Japanese state, and it transformed the foreign ideologies of Confucianism and Buddhism in Japanese history to bring them into accordance with the kokutai. It was also the spirit behind the idea of "the whole world under one roof."

In March 1939, Yamada Yoshio (1873–1958) wrote "The Spirit of the Founding of the Nation," an elaboration of book 1, chapter 1 of *Fundamentals of Our National Polity*.[97] He began his essay by reminding readers that the title of the first chapter of *Fundamentals of Our National Polity* was "Founding of the Nation (*chōkoku*)."[98] He then provided a brief explanation of the origins and the meaning of the two-character word *chōkoku*, reminding readers that the meaning of the word could be found in the first line of Emperor Meiji's Imperial Rescript on Education, which stated: "Our Imperial Ancestors had founded Our Nation on a basis broad and everlasting (*kuni o hajimuru koto koen ni*)."[99] He noted that the *kun* reading of the character *chō* was *hajimu* (to found) and that the word *chōkoku* was first used in Chinese classical literature but was later used in Japanese classical literature, such as in the *Nihon Shoki*, in the chapter on Emperor Sujin. He pointed out that *chōkoku* (*kuni o hajimu*) did not merely mean the founding of the nation, citing various examples from the *Nihon Shoki* and the *Kojiki* in which *chōkoku* was linked to more than just the concept of creation and founding of the Japanese state. The Japanese state was founded by the gods and for a purpose: the growth and prosperity of the nation and the realization of imperial rule conterminous with heaven and earth.

Yamada quoted the first line of the first chapter of book 1, which states:

> The unbroken line of Emperors, receiving the Oracle of the Founder of the Nation, reign eternally over the Japanese empire. This is our eternal and immutable national entity. Thus, founded on this great principle, all the people, united as one great family nation in heart and obeying the Imperial Will, enhance indeed the beautiful virtues of loyalty and filial piety. This is the glory of our national entity. This national entity is the eternal and unchanging basis of our nation and shines resplendent throughout our history. Moreover, its solidarity is proportionate to the growth of the nation and is, together with heaven and earth, without end. We must to begin with, know with what active brilliance this fountainhead shines within the reality of the founding of our nation.[100]

The kokutai, or "form of state," of Japan was established with the origins of the Japanese state and the origins of the universe. Yamada then noted that this truth of the kokutai was "embodied in the text of the law (*hōbunka*)" in Article 1 of the Constitution of the Empire of Japan, thus defining the purpose of the modern Japanese state.[101] *Fundamentals of Our National Polity* further stated Japan's national purpose by quoting directly from the *Nihon Shoki*:

> His August Izanagi no Mikoto and Her August Izanami no Mikoto consulted together and said: "We have already brought forth Oh-yashima no Kuni (Land-of-Great-Eight-Islands) as well as mountains, rivers, grasses and trees. Wherefore should we not bring forth one that shall be sovereign throughout the whole world?" They then together brought to birth the Sun Goddess. She is called Ohirume no Muchi (Great-noon-female-of-possessor). In one place she is called Ohmikami. In another place she is called Amaterasu Ohhirume no Mikoto (Heaven-illumine-great-noon-female-of-augustness). The luster of this child was resplendent and shone throughout the six quarters.[102]

Gauntlett noted in a footnote that the "six quarters" in this referred to "East, West, South, North, Above, and Below, hence the world and the universe."[103] Accordingly, *Fundamentals of Our National Polity* provided the Japanese masses with a doctrinal faith that had a purpose and vision of a future and a specific role for them to play in undertaking a great change. The emperor was given this great task, and it was the duty of the Japanese subjects to assist the emperor in carrying it out. It is interesting to note that Yamada, while carefully emphasizing the immutable distinction between sovereign and subject and the "great duty (*taigi meibun*)" of the subject to defend and protect this distinction,[104] carefully sought to bridge the gap between the emperor and the Japanese masses. He stressed that the distinction between the imperial family and Japanese subjects was not based on the principle of blood lineage. Rather, it was more or less based on a distinction of names. He noted that the emperor's subjects had surnames (*seishi*) or family names (*ie no na*),[105] but that, from ancient times, the Imperial Family did not have a surname. Yamada explained that surnames originated in ancient times when someone from among the Imperial Family descended to the status of a subject. Other than making this distinction, he said that the Japanese subjects, too, were gods. In fact, he said that possessing the spirit of the founding of the nation, the subject of his essay, was based on the individual's mental and emotional awareness of the fact that the nation was a divine nation and that every Japanese thus had divine parents, and, by extension, that each and every individual had a divine character (*shinkaku*).[106] He asserted that the land of Japan as well as its people and the ruler were all the offspring of the deities. The Japanese state was thought to be one great blood-related family. The fact that the nation was born from the gods also meant that the people were endowed with a special "life spirit (*seimei seishin*)" from the gods and that this life spirit, properly nourished, was the source and inspiration for action.[107] He was convinced the Japanese nation had never been invaded and taken over by foreigners because of the concerted efforts of the Japanese people to prevent their divine nation from being contaminated by foreign barbarians (*gaii*).[108]

In short, what Yamada, the true believer, was attempting to accomplish through this deification of the common person was to infuse the Japanese masses with a desire for radical change at home and abroad and with the desire to pursue the holy cause of an emperor conterminous with heaven and earth. Eric Hoffer pointed out that the desire for radical or revolutionary change or action could not be brought about by those who were totally "awed by their surroundings,"[109] regardless how miserable their condition. What he meant was that people who are completely awed by their surroundings fear change. "They face the world as they would an all-powerful jury," he noted.[110] On the contrary,

The men who rush into undertakings of vast change usually feel they are in possession of some irresistible power. The generation that made the French Revolution had an extravagant conception of the omnipotence of man's reason and the boundless range of his intelligence. Never, says de Tocqueville, had humanity been prouder of itself nor had it ever so much faith in its own omnipotence. And joined with this exaggerated self-confidence was a universal thirst for change which came unbidden to every mind. Lenin and the Bolsheviks who plunged recklessly into the chaos of the creation of a new world had blind faith in the omnipotence of Marxist doctrine.[111]

Much of this can be said of the Japanese of the 1930s and early 1940s. Constantly bombarded with radical Shintō ultranationalist thought, the common Japanese was no doubt coming to feel invincible. By teaching the masses that they possessed a divine character (*shinkaku*), Yamada was empowering them and driving them to action. Again, the only difference between them and the Imperial Family, Yamada told them, was that they had surnames while the Imperial Family did not. That is to say, he was consciously trying to create a mass movement.

Furthermore, Yamada's preaching of the faith of the blood identity between the emperor and his subjects worked to prepare the masses for the ultimate struggle and self-sacrifice. Again, Hoffer's insight into the nature of mass movements is relevant:

To ripen a person for self-sacrifice he must be stripped of his individual identity and distinctiveness. He must cease to be George, Hans, Ivan, or Tadao—a human atom with an existence bounded by birth and death. The most drastic way to achieve this end is by the complete assimilation of the individual into a collective body. The fully assimilated individual does not see himself and others as human beings. When asked who he is, his automatic response is that he is a German, a Russian, a Japanese, a Christian, a Moslem, a member of as certain tribe or family. He has no purpose, worth and destiny apart from his collective body; and as long as that body lives he cannot really die.[112]

Yamada, as we have seen, was not the only one who preached this. It was taught by Uesugi Shinkichi and Kakehi Katsuhiko in the Taishō period, as well as by all later radical Shintō ultranationalist theorists. The total assimilation of the individual into a collective body is the goal of all totalitarian movements, of which radical Shintō ultranationalism was one variety. However, none arguably had better success in instilling the masses with this totalitarian mentality than Japanese radical Shintō ultranationalists.

Japanese radical Shintō ultranationalists had always imaged a primitive Golden Age of history when a primitive totalitarian identity existed between the emperor and his people. Again, Hoffer saw this characteristic as common to all totalitarian thinkers and totalitarian mass movements:

> The effacement of individual separateness must be thorough. In every act, however trivial, the individual must by some ritual associate himself with the congregation, the tribe, the party, etcetera. His joys and sorrows, his pride and confidence must spring from the fortunes and capacities of the group rather than from his individual prospects and abilities. Above all, he must never feel alone. Though stranded on a desert island, he must still feel that he is under the eyes of the group. To be cast out from the group should be equivalent to being cut off from life.
>
> This is undoubtedly a primitive state of being, and its most perfect examples are found among primitive tribes. Mass movements strive to approximate this primitive perfection, and we are not imagining things when the anti-individualist bias of contemporary mass movements strikes us as a throwback to the primitive.[113]

As with all radical Shintō ultranationalists, Yamada lamented the breakdown of the ideal primitive state of being in subsequent Japanese history. For example, he noted that the ancient Japanese way of government, when a unity of religion and government (*saisei itchi*) existed, began to break down during the reign of Emperor Sujin. Until that time, there had been a total unity of religious rites and government (*saishi to seiji*).[114] However, during Sujin's reign, he wrote, a separation occurred between the Shintō shrine (*jingū*) and the imperial palace (*kōkyo*). Officials (*kanjin*) who worshipped the deities and officials who administered the affairs of state were no longer the same.[115] Occupations then became divided among the clan (*shizoku*) groups.

In connection with his discussion of the ideal of the blood-based unity of the Japanese state, Yamada made what I believe were some stunning comments about foreigners in Japanese history. He stated: "It goes without saying that there is a blood relationship between the imperial family and subjects. However, it is not that there is no foreign blood mixed in among the Japanese people."[116] He then noted that it was recorded in the *Shinsenshojiroku*, a multi-volume work completed in 815, that approximately one-fourth of the Japanese population were the descendants of foreigners. He further claimed that the ratio had not changed. He concluded that in the 1930s, roughly one-fourth of the Japanese population was originally of foreign extraction. Nevertheless, this did not seem to be a problem for Yamada. He stressed that those people who were of foreign origin quickly assimilated into the dominant Japanese population in a physical and spiritual sense. In fact, he claimed that this assimilation of foreigners was so complete that very few Japanese were even aware that there were so many non-ethnic Japanese among the population. The assimilation of people of foreign blood lineage had in no way destroyed the blood-based principle on which the solidarity and unity of the Japanese state were based.

Finally, in the last section of his commentary, Yamada discussed the deity Ame no mi-naka-nushi no kami in connection to the concept of "coeval with heaven and earth (*tenjō mukyū*)." His discussion was an elaboration on a subsection of part 1, chapter 1, of *Fundamentals of Our National Polity*, titled "The Throne's Being Coeval with Heaven and Earth." Yamada's use of complex metaphysical terms and concepts in this discussion makes this section difficult to comprehend, so it might be useful to begin by quoting *Fundamentals of Our National Polity* on the meaning of the Imperial Throne's being "coeval with heaven and earth":

> By being coeval with heaven and earth is meant to be endless together with heaven and earth. It seems that one has not yet quite fathomed the full import of endlessness if one thinks of it as being successions of time. Ordinarily, words such as "eternity" or "endlessness" convey simply the ideas of perpetuity in succession of time; but the so-called expression "coeval with heaven and earth" has a far deeper significance. That is to say, it expresses eternity and at the same time signifies the present. In the august Will and great august undertakings of the Emperor, who is deity incarnate, is seen the great Will of the Imperial Ancestors, and in this Will lives the endless future of our nation. That our Imperial Throne is coeval with heaven and earth means indeed that the past and the future are united in one in the "now," that our nation possesses everlasting life, and that it flourishes endlessly. Our history is an evolution of the eternal "now," and at the root of our history there always runs a stream of eternal "now."[117]

Yamada asserted that Ame no mi-naka-nushi no kami (Heaven-of-august-center-master-god) itself was this coevalness with heaven and earth. He began his inquiry with a question: What is the meaning of "center (*naka*)" of Ame no mi-naka-nushi no kami? He said that if you see *naka* from the viewpoint of a plane surface, it merely indicates a middle point on a diagram. However, he noted that since reality was not a plane surface, *naka* indicated the center of a three-dimensional or solid body. This *naka* was like an absolute entity that was in the center of space and in the center of time. But *naka* embodied the universe, too. It had spirit and life, and spirit and life did not lie motionless in the middle of space. While *naka* was without beginning and without end, it was not static. It was at the center of space and time, but it was a center that developed eternally in time. In short, Ame no mi-naka-nushi no kami was conterminous with heaven and earth.

Yamada also noted that this idea of conterminous or "coeval with heaven and earth" was linked to the idea of *nakaima* (center-present). The "present (*ima*)" of the "center-present (*nakaima*)" included the past and the future, as well as this eternity in the center. In other words, the concept of *nakaima* meant that everything in the past and the future was united in the present. When one combined these metaphysical concepts with the imperial throne, the "eternal now" meant that the imperial throne was conterminous with heaven and earth and that all the events that occurred in the past existed at this very moment. It is as if to say that the existence of the imperial throne cut across a time axis through space. At the same time, the imperial throne conterminous with heaven and earth was constantly expanding and flourishing. Maruyama Masao referred to Yamada's thought in "Theory and Psychology of Ultra-Nationalism":

> The contemporaneousness of the myth of the national foundation has been expounded by Professor Yamada Takao [sic; Yoshio]: "If we cut across the time axis, the events that occurred 2,600 years ago constitute the central layer. . . . The happenings in Emperor Jimmu's reign are therefore no ancient tales but facts that exist at this very moment."
>
> Here we find a truly skillful expression of ultra-nationalist logic according to which the extension of the axis of ordinates (time factor) represents at the same time an enlargement of the circle itself (space factor).
>
> The fact of being "coeval with heaven and earth" guaranteed the indefinite expansion of the range in which the ultimate value was valid, and conversely the expansion of the "martial virtues of the Empire" reinforced the absolute nature of the central value.[118]

It is the duty of the emperor, and of the subjects who assist the emperor, to ensure that the emperor's virtue develops and spreads eternally.

These are just a few examples of some of the ideas of those who were involved in the compilation of *Fundamentals of Our National Polity* and who subsequently wrote commentaries on it for the Ministry of Education. It is obvious that these writings contain a lot of redundancy. But I have used the seemingly needless repetition in this study for a purpose: to show the massive impact of the ideology of radical Shintō ultranationalism on the Japanese nation. As shown earlier, this ideology was fostered by the intellectual elite at Japan's most prestigious imperial universities, as well as by the leaders of Japan's Shintō universities.

In this context, it is also instructive to reflect on what one does not find in the writings of Japanese ultranationalists in the late 1930s and the early 1940s. For instance, where are the ideas of Kita Ikki, who argued for an emperor as organ of the state theory; who argued that the emperor was a "people's emperor"; and who argued that the kokutai, Japan's "form of state," had undergone a fundamental transformation with the Meiji Ishin? Why were these ideals not taken up and elaborated on? The answer is quite simple: Kita's ideology had nothing to do with Shintō nationalism.

It is now more than sixty years since German and Japanese ultranationalism were defeated. Is it not time for the taboo on the discussion of radical Shintō ultranationalism to be lifted so scholars can scrutinize this ideology with the same objectivity and intensity and with the same critical perspective and passion that Western scholars have applied to the cases of German National Socialism and Italian Fascism? Let us not abandon the old ideal of searching for the truth.

Conclusion

In reading the history of nations, we find that, like individuals, they have their whims and their peculiarities; their seasons of excitement and recklessness, when they care not what they do. . . . We see one nation suddenly seized with a fierce desire of military glory; another as suddenly becoming crazed upon a religious scruple; and neither of them recovering its senses until it has shed rivers of blood and sowed a harvest of groans and tears, to be reaped by its posterity.
— CHARLES MACKAY, *Memoirs of Extraordinary Popular Delusions and the Madness of Crowds*, xix

The success of the Islamic revolutionary ideology is the novel and teleologically distinct mark of the Islamic Revolution in Iran. . . . In a sense it has considerable ideological advantages over Nazism and communism, both of which clashed with religion. Rather than creating a new substitute for religion, as did the Communists and the Nazis, the Islamic militants have fortified an already vigorous religion with the ideological armor necessary for battle in the arena of mass politics. In doing so, they have made their distinct contributions to world history.— SAID AMIR ARJOMAND, *The Turban for the Crown*, 210

In *War without Mercy*, John Dower exposed the racism in America toward the Japanese people as a whole during the Pacific War. Japanese were considered "subhuman and repulsive" by many Americans. In daily conversation, Americans tended to refer to their wartime enemies, Germany and Japan, as "Hitler and the Japs" or "the Nazis and the Japs." Dower pointed out that the implication of perceiving the enemy as "Nazis" and "Japs" was enormous, for "this left the space for the recognition of the 'good German,' but scant comparable place for 'good' Japanese."[1] Racism was certainly a major factor in the inability or the unwillingness of many Americans to distinguish between "good Japanese" and "bad Japanese," but another, important but overlooked factor may have significantly exacerbated the problem: the failure to identify our real enemy in Japan. What was the Japanese ideological equivalent of German Nazis or Italian Fascists? The average American on the street during World War Two simply did not know, but this was certainly not due to Americans' personal faults or prejudices. It was not clear even to the director Frank Capra. In his wartime propaganda film *Prelude to War*, the first in the series of seven *Why We Fight* films, Capra presented a picture of the development of the dictatorships in Germany, Italy, and Japan. When the time came to identify America's ideological enemies, Capra told viewers that the enemy in Germany was National Socialism, or simply "Nazism," and in Italy it was "Fascism." When he came to the case of Japan, he said, "They [the Japanese] have lots of names for them [the extremist nationalists]." Simply put, Capra and the U.S. War Department could not identify a specific ideological enemy in Japan. But one should not fault him, either, because even after more than six decades since the end of the Second World War, the average American still does not know. The blame must lie with the failure of American scholars to deal adequately with one of the most fundamental issues in modern Japanese history, as well as in the history of World War Two: the failure to identify the enemy. Clearly, we must recognize that this is a conceptual void that must be filled.

If we do not wish to continue to make villains of all Japanese when we speak about the Second World War and Japan's role in waging that war, we must make an effort to identify this ideological enemy. One can give easy reasons for this failure to identify the ideology of extreme nationalism in prewar Japan. For example, unlike in the cases of Germany and Italy, no one, easily identifiable radical nationalist group took power in Japan. This presents a major problem, but it is not the whole problem. Who were the Japanese theorists of the radical right? What did they write? This study was first undertaken at least in part to attempt to fill this ideological void. I hope it has succeeded in laying the ideological foundations for further studies of the interaction of ideology and political groups or individual actors in prewar Japan.

In this study of the main developments and trends within State Shintō ideology from 1890 to 1937, I have argued that the ideological equivalent of Nazism and Fascism in Japan was radical Shintō ultranationalism. I have also argued that radical Shintō ultranationalism was a totalitarian ideology and a massed-based radical religion of völkisch nationalism, much like Nazism in Germany. It grew out of an extreme form of religious fundamentalism that had begun to emerge at the center of political and ideological discourse in Japan at the beginning of the twentieth century. The story of the rise and fall of radical Shintō ultranationalism is not just about ideological contestation in the past century. It may also offer a lesson about the extent of the immense challenges we face at the beginning of this new century between extremist political religions, particularly radical Islamic fundamentalism, and other radical religious movements that now confront Western-style secular nationalism.

It may be instructive to begin by noting the striking similarities between the rise of radical Shintō ultranationalism in Japan and the rise of radical Islamic fundamentalism in the Muslim world, a subject that deserves further examination and analysis. First, both radical movements seem to have grown out of powerful religious traditions that had deep roots of seeking ideological or religious purity to explain and overcome outside challenges to orthodoxy, most recently in response to globalized secularization and materialism. For example, in *The Crisis of Islam*, Bernard Lewis noted that the rise of Wahhabism in the eighteenth century could be traced back to the retreat of Islam and the corresponding advance of Christianity.[2] Wahhabism's founder, Muhammad ibn Abd al-Wahhab (1703–92), was a theologian who in 1744 "launched a campaign of purification and renewal" whose "declared aim was to return to the pure and authentic Islam of the Founder, removing and where necessary destroying all the later accretions and distortions."[3] Often considered the first modern Islamic fundamentalist, al-Wahhab made the central point of his reform movement the notion that anything added to Islam after the tenth century was false and should be eliminated. Wahhabists in the nineteenth century and the twentieth century continued this search for religious purity, rejecting Islamic reform movements that tried to bring Islamic law closer to Western standards in regard to such things as civil liberties and participatory democracy. Wahhabism was extremely successful in the sense that it subsequently became the "official, state-enforced doctrine of one of the most influential governments [Saudi Arabia] in all Islam—the custodian of the two holiest places of Islam."[4] And Yossef Bodansky noted that Osama bin Laden was strongly influenced by the Saudi Islamists, who "claimed that the agony of the Lebanese [during the outbreak of civil war there in the 1970s] was a punishment from God for their sins and destructive influence on young Muslims."[5] The assassination of Saudi Arabia's King Faisal in 1975 by his thoroughly Westernized nephew Prince Faisal ibn Musaid was taken by Islamic fundamentalists as a "warning against the sinful and perilous influence of the West." It "created a grassroots backlash [against the West] and sent many of these youth, including bin Laden, back into the fold of Islam."[6] Similarly, in the case of Iran, the Ayatollah Ruhollah Khomeini, following the Islamic Revolution in 1979, began to purge the country of Western influences. According to Bodansky, he

> issued an order ensuring the Islamization of the higher-education system. Student committees, composed of hard-core Islamist activists, complied by evicting leftists, both students and faculty, from the campuses and then supervised the Islamic "correctness" of both the material taught in classes and the research conducted by the surviving faculty. Finally the government closed the universities between 1980 and 1983 to complete a proper Islamic approach, that is, the elimination of all departments and courses the mullahs considered un-Islamic as well as the banishment and at times arrest and execution of all the related faculty.[7]

These are just a few examples of the Islamic search for religious purity and revolt against the secularized Western world.

In a very similar way, the aim of the pure Shintō fundamentalist revival movement of the late Tokugawa period was to fight a religious and ideological battle against all things foreign, particularly Chinese. The attack on Chinese and other Asian ideologies, religions, and systems of thought by Shintō fundamentalists such as Kamo Mabuchi and Motoori Norinaga in the eighteenth century did not cease, however, with the end of the Tokugawa regime and feudalism. The pure Shintō fundamentalist movements of the late nineteenth century and early twentieth century led by Hozumi Yatsuka, Uesugi Shinkichi, and Kakehi Katsuhiko represented a revival of the Kokugaku (National Learning) Movement of the Tokugawa period in a new form. They were religious purists who sought to purge the Japanese state of foreign ideologies. The Shintō ultra-nationalists' assault on Asian thought, as well as on the new ideological threat from the Western world, continued until the end of the Second World War.

A prime example of this search for religious purification and anti-foreignism can be found in the thought of the radical Shintō ultra-nationalist Yamada Yoshio (1875–1958), who was just briefly introduced in the previous chapter. Yamada was a well-respected scholar of Japanese language and literature who hailed from Toyama Prefecture in central Japan. Very much a self-made man, having achieved success and recognition by his own efforts, he earned a teaching certificate mostly through independent study. Upon obtaining his teaching credentials, he secured a job as a schoolteacher and taught at a number of elementary and middle schools. He eventually worked his way up to teach in higher education and finally became a professor at Tōhoku Imperial University in 1927. However, the pinnacle of his professional academic career came with his appointment as president of Kōgakkan University in 1940, one of the two large Shintō theological universities responsible for the training of Shintō priests. Kōgakkan had been established in 1882 under the name Jingū Kokugakuin near the Ise Shrine as part of a government effort to establish an institution of higher learning with the mission to develop a coherent Shintō doctrine following the so-called pantheon dispute of the 1870s.[8] The school was later moved to Uji Yamada, where it was reestablished as a Shintō training institute of the Ministry of Home Affairs. As a government-funded State Shintō religious institution, Kōgakkan would be forced to close down by General Douglas MacArthur's occupation authorities in 1945, but it reopened in 1952 at its original location as a private university. As mentioned in the previous chapter, Yamada also moved into the political limelight at the height of his academic career when he became a member of the House of Peers in 1944.

During the American occupation of Japan, MacArthur carried out purges that aimed to "eliminate for all time the authority and influence of those who [had] deceived and misled the people of Japan into embarking on world conquest." Purge Directive SCAP AG 091.1 (January 4, 1946) GS, "Removal and Exclusion of Undesirable Personnel from Public Office," guided the removal from public office of all persons who had been "active exponents of militaristic nationalism and aggression."[9] Yamada was among the people forbidden by the directive to hold public or educational office. It is noteworthy that although Yamada was one of the members of the official compilation committee that rewrote the original manuscript of *Fundamentals of Our National Polity*, he apparently was purged not on that basis but because of his numerous other ultranationalist activities and writings. In other words, Yamada is an excellent example of a radical Shintō ultranationalist who came to dominate the prewar Shintō religious establishment.

Taken as a whole, Yamada's writings during the wartime period reveal a fixed mental attitude that predetermined the responses to, and interpretations of, any given set of situations. A classic example of this was that he continued to spout the rhetoric of Japan's purity and divine nature and its invulnerability to defeat and failure while stubbornly clinging on to the erroneous notion that the Chinese people somehow lacked a genuine sense of national cohesiveness and nationalism many years after the tenacity with which the Chinese resistance to Japan's occupation had been clearly and courageously displayed to the world. One example of this can be seen in his essay " Shinkoku Nihon no Shimei to Kokumin no Kakugo (Divine Japan's Mission and the Nation's Resolve)," which appeared in the September 1943 issue of *Chūō Kōron*.

Yamada began the essay by telling readers that Japan's unique kokutai could be understood in all its magnificence and glory only by adopting a purely Japanese perspective on Japanese history. He charged that Japanese history, for the most part, had not been written from a purely Japanese consciousness, as was in the case of earlier works in Japanese history, such as the Great History of Japan and the Chronicle of Gods and Sovereigns. He lamented that he could find very few books on Japanese history that were written from the perspective of Japan's miraculous kokutai. Yamada provided concrete examples of what he meant by saying that Japanese history was not being presented from a consciousness of Japan's kokutai. For example, he attacked Japanese historians for structuring Japanese history from what he considered essentially a Chinese-inspired perspective of history: the rise and fall of dynasties. Employing the Chinese historical method in analyzing Japanese history, Japanese historians had formulated the period in Japanese history in which the Fujiwara regency was powerful as the Fujiwara Period; the period of the regency of the Kamakura government was likewise called the Kamakura Period. The years in power by the Ashikaga and Tokugawa feudal clans were called the Ashikaga Period and the Tokugawa Period, respectively. Yamada asserted that viewing Japanese history as the rise and fall of these powerful families and governments was to use a historical interpretation very close to that used by Chinese historians to analyze their own history. Thus, this type of periodization of Japanese history by Japanese historians amounted to nothing less than a Sinofication of Japanese history—a Sinofication that subverted the spirit of Japan's true history based on the kokutai, which was a history of the unbroken line of emperors from the age of the gods:

> Conventional historians in our country . . . undoubtedly adopted this form of periodization as if to compare these periods in Japanese history with the rise and fall of dynasties in the history of China. Many modern scholars have mistaken this view of the repeated rise and fall of regimes in China and the Western world as the essence of history. They have based their theories on the fundamentally erroneous view of history which ignores the sacred essence of our country. The reason Rai San Yō (1780– 1832) wrote a kind of national history called "The Unofficial History of Japan" centered on the rise and fall of regencies generation after generation was because he fell into the trap [of writing from such a viewpoint] that any scholar of Chinese history might do. However, since this is an "unofficial history," there is no need to pursue this matter further, but it does go to show that this method of compiling history is, for the most part, easily copied by scholars who have learned Chinese history.[10]

Yamada also charged that the factual information Japanese were required to learn in schools also did not focus on Japan's unique kokutai. As a simple illustration of this, he noted that if one were to ask a Japanese subject who had completed at least compulsory education the name of the third Tokugawa Shōgun, one would expect to hear a correct answer. Similarly, an educated Japanese subject could readily answer that the eleventh Shōgun was Ienari. But if one were to ask any Japanese who was the third emperor from Emperor Jimmu, could he or she answer correctly? Or if one were to ask who was the eighth emperor or the eleventh emperor, could he or she reply correctly? Most likely not, Yamada lamented. Yamada charged that the problem lay in education based on the memorization of facts and terminology without providing the slightest clue as to what the facts meant or how they came to have historical significance from the Shintō perspective. Citing another example, a Japanese young person was likely to know the name Seiitaishōgun, Yamada said, but was very unlikely to know the name of the particular emperor who appointed the warriors Seiitaishōgun and the rationale for it.

In short, what all these examples added up to in Yamada's mind was that the Japanese people were learning Japanese history from a certain type of historiography that originated in China, that they were learning facts not centrally relevant to Japan's kokutai, and that they were memorizing facts without learning the ideas behind them.

Needless to say, this seeking of ideological and religious purity can be dangerous to an individual, a nation, and even an entire civilization, for ideological blinders distort reality, and that can lead to destruction. For example, Yamada claimed contemptuously that the history of China was not a history of a nation (*kuni*) that was born, matured, and continues to live and develop in the present. Rather, it was the history of a geographical region (*chiiki*) called China that had seen the rise and fall of some fifty-odd states in chronological order. These Chinese states had no common relationship or common connecting thread or logical link.[11] The history of each Chinese dynasty was no more than a history of a "victorious state (*shōkoku*)," which he defined as a state that had destroyed the imperial household of the previous dynasty and replaced it with its own rulers. Accordingly, the history of the Yuan Dynasty period was written by the Ming Dynasty; the history of the Ming Dynasty was written by the Qing Dynasty. If one read the history of China by Chinese scholars, according to Yamada, one could easily see that the people who wrote the history were neither tied by blood (*ketsueki*) nor were they sympathetic to the peoples concerned.[12] That is to say, such histories were written from the standpoint of conquerors who had revised the history of the previous dynastic period to cover their own crimes and present themselves in a favorable light among their contemporaries. Consequently, Chinese history lacked a continuous genuine national spirit. Crudely speaking, he said, it was the same as if a burglar or a thief had broken into somebody's house, killed the master of the house, occupied the house, and then had written a history of the house and the generations of its occupants from the viewpoint of a criminal. Anyone would be appalled by such events. Nevertheless, this was the kind of history that had been written in China by the Chinese for thousands of years.

For Yamada, the Chinese state represented a clear and obvious example of a typical non-ethnically based state. It therefore lacked a homogeneous historical culture. An alien group ruled over the Chinese masses. Accordingly, when one referred to "China," it meant merely a geographical or a territorial entity. He seems to have implied that China was a cluster of different races or ethnic groups in that no identifiable blood ties linked everyone to the nation:

It can be said that the history of our country is like one person's life history from its birth to the present if one compares it to a human being. The history of other countries is different. Take, for example, the case of China. From the age of the Three Sovereigns and the Five Emperors to the present it is merely a compilation of records of the rise and fall of various states. Accordingly, if one speaks of the history of China in general, it is not a history in which the country called China continued to survive, but it only refers to the histories of more than 50 individual, disconnected, states compiled chronologically as they rose and fell in a region called China. Furthermore, the history of each state is a history of a so-called victorious state. What is a victorious state? It is a state which destroyed the loyal family of a previous dynasty, and declared it the winning state over the state they overthrew and conquered. . . . As to the history of China, the people who write it are tied neither by blood nor emotional bonds; neither do they have common interest. It is written from the same standpoint of a disinterested third party. While that may have its good points, one writes what is good and rewrites what is not good. However, there is no way for ideals to be handed down and carried on, and absolutely no way for a coherent spirit to flow through its history. . . . To think that there is a coherent spirit . . . is to think that there is a spiritual connection between an assailant and a victim when the burglar breaks into a house and kills the master of the house and then settles down there. . . . This kind of history, even if it continues for 3,000 or 5,000 years, cannot be thought of as the history [of one nation].

For Yamada, this was not the case just for the history of China. It was the same for all countries in the Orient and the Occident.[13]

This idea that China was really not a nation was common among nearly all Japanese radical Shintō ultranationalist thinkers and was one argument they used to justify taking over territory in China. Herbert Bix also brought out this point and implied that Emperor Hirohito and Prime Minister Hirota (1936–37) also held such a view. "Also like the emperor," Bix wrote, "Hirota shared an assumption that many Japanese officers considered self-evident: China was neither a nation nor a people but merely a territorial designation, and Japan was entitled to rearrange that territory and take whatever parts it wished."[14] In another passage in which Yamada linked China and the West, he said, "Both the Chinese people and the Western peoples are similarly individualistic."[15] This is not to say that he felt the Chinese were similar to the Western peoples in all respects, but from the radical Shintō ultranationalist point of view, the

Chinese were considered to be closer to Western peoples in a fundamental way than they were to the Japanese. Yamada also insisted that while the Japanese people had a nation-centered ideology, the Chinese, like the Westerners, had an individual-centered ideology.

This perception of China was commonplace among Japanese radical Shintō ultranationalists, as has been shown in the thought of Hozumi Yatsuka, which completely demolished the erroneous notion that all Asians have common underlying cultural traits. Western historiography tends to emphasize a link between Shintō ultranationalist thought and pan-Asianism in the sense of having "Asian" values, and the Second World War in Asia is sometimes characterized as a war between Asia and the Western world. But the logic of the ideology of Shintō ultranationalism in Japan clearly denies this. State Shintō and Shintō ultranationalism were inherently anti-Asian. They were also anti-Buddhist and anti-Confucian, the two leading systems of continental Asian thought derived from India and China.

Bombarding the Japanese masses with outdated perceptions of China and the Chinese people, Yamada and other radical Shintō ultranationalists kept the Japanese people from acquiring any realistic understanding of the realities of China in the 1930s and 1940s. They simply reinforced the prevalent attitude among the Japanese that, since the Chinese people had no true sense of nationhood, they should be easily conquered. But nothing could have been further from the truth. Chinese nationalist consciousness grew more intense as Japan continued to wage war. The historian Ienaga Saburō blamed Japan's disaster in the Second World War on its contemptuous attitude toward the Chinese. Ienaga began his analysis of Japan's defeat in the Second World War in Asia, which he referred to as the "fifteen-year war," with a chapter titled "Misconceptions about China and Korea."[16] For Ienaga, the Second World War in Asia was all about Japan's attempt to conquer China. He emphasized that Japan's long-held misconception that the Chinese had no sense of nationhood blinded the Japanese leadership into thinking that China could be subdued with little effort. This was Japan's "colossal blunder" in the war, he stated.[17] He lamented the fact that "a domestic political force capable of preventing aggression against China just did not exist" in Japan.[18] But why? Ienaga's answer to this was that contempt toward the Chinese had been so ingrained in the minds of the Japanese, at least since Japan's victory in the Qing Dynasty–Japan War of 1894–95. But he did not mean to say that all intelligent Japanese were unaware of the rise of Chinese mass nationalism in the first decades of the twentieth century. As an example, he quoted Yanaihara Tadao, a Tokyo Imperial University scholar and specialist on Japanese colonial policy, warning the Japanese of danger in China in a lecture in November 1936:

> Assertions that the Chinese have no sense of nationhood and so forth are outdated. The Chinese of today are not the Chinese of old. I have heard that there are Chinese who say, "If China goes to war with Japan, we will probably lose at first. But there are 400 million of us, so we can afford to lose 300 million and still have 100 million left. With three Chinese soldiers to every one Japanese, we must resist and defend our nation's sovereignty.[19]

Again, in February 1937, just a few months before the China Incident, or the outbreak of Japan's full-fledged invasion of China, Yanaihara stated the following in an article in *Chūō Kōron*:

> The key to our relations with China lies in understanding that China is a national state on its way to unification and reconstruction. Only a policy based on a perception of China which affirms and asserts that national unity will help China, help Japan, and contribute to the peace of Asia. Implementation by force or arbitrary policies contrary to this rational view will bring a disaster that will haunt us for generations, will inflict suffering on China, and will destroy the peace of Asia.[20]

This turned out to be a very prophetic statement.

What is remarkable is that Yamada and other radical Shintō ultranationalists were still preaching the same fallacies about the lack of nationalism in the Chinese collective consciousness six years after Japan's full invasion of China and after Japan had clearly become bogged down in its war with China and was fighting a world war, as well. By 1941, "nearly 300,000 Japanese soldiers had died in China, and over a million were deployed across the country, occupying most of its major cities, all of its ports, and most of the rail lines connecting them. Millions of Chinese had perished, and still no end was in sight."[21] Clearly, with such a high death toll, the Chinese were in no mood to surrender. What Yanaihara had heard from nationalistic Chinese in 1937 was turning out to be quite accurate. And the "rational views" regarding China that Yanaihara mentioned were apparently still not being heard in Japan. The rational views of secular thinkers had long been silenced by the Japanese state in the hands of radical Shintō ultranationalists who promoted the rise and spread of militant Shintō fundamentalism. The thoughts of most Japanese had been formed by the writings of the true believers such as Yamada, who were motivated and driven by theology. Since they genuinely believed that Japan had never been defeated in war in its 2,600 year history, to even entertain the idea that Japan could possibly be defeated in war was considered blasphemy toward the collective Japanese national entity, the kokutai. After all, was not Japan destined to lead the world prophesied under "Eight Corners of the World under One Roof"?

For Yamada, Japan was the nation of the gods: "When we say that our Japan is a divine country, it is of course based on the fact that the two gods Izanagi and Izanami created this country."[22] That is to say, Yamada was a committed creationist, a true believer in the Japanese Shintō story of creation. He further reasoned that since the imperial ancestors were gods and the Japanese people were descendants of those gods, all of the Japanese people, too, as children of the gods, must also be gods. Therefore, "Being a divine country is not just a metaphor, or a figure of speech, but a fact and a reality in our country."[23]

Being a divine nation and a divine people also dictated that there must be a divine mission for the country:

The fact that our country is a divine country created by the gods also directly indicates the mission of the Empire. . . . This country was not born by chance, but was born in order to fulfill the purposes prescribed by *Amaterasu Ōmikami*. It may be that she is a sacred country in order to realize this mission. Looking back on our real history, we find that Japan has gradually become prosperous since the Age of the Gods, and it has never yet been invaded or suppressed as other foreign countries have. Upon deep reflection, this seems to be due to sacred and profound facts that are unfathomable to us.[24]

But what was that mission? Yamada was clear on that issue, too:

What should be the work of the divine nation of Japan? What should its mission be? As every Japanese person nowadays knows, it was clearly indicated in the Imperial Proclamation of Emperor Jimmu "Eight strings make a house (*Hakkō o motte ie to nasu*)." What is a house? We can understand this when we look at our individual life. Even if we go out, engage in various activities, encounter difficulties, and feel uneasy, once we go home, we can enjoy our own living there. Thus, a house is a base where people feel at ease and carry on their lives. The "eight strings (*hakkō*)" in the phrase "eight strings make a house" means "in all directions (*shihohappō*)." I believe that "eight strings make a house" signifies Emperor Jimmu's desire to let everyone and everything have peace of mind and enjoy living. . . . It is conceivable that the thought of "the whole world makes a house" is the purpose of the Greater East Asian War at the present time. However, we can clearly see that this desire of Emperor Jimmu did not start only with Emperor Jimmu when we read the Imperial Proclamation of Emperor Jimmu. This is the desire of *Amaterasu Ōmikami.*[25]

As indicated in this statement, the idea of "eight strings make a house" was taken from a passage in the chapter on Emperor Jimmu in the *Nihon Shoki,* which reads, "Thereafter the capital may be extended so as to embrace all the six cardinal points, and the eight cords may be converted so as to form a roof."[26] In prewar Japanese literature, this phrase became popularly known as *hakkō ichiu,* or "the whole world under one roof," and was used to justify carrying out the Greater East Asian War as the necessary first step in the establishment of a new world order by the Japanese nation.

Yamada made another comment on the ultimate purpose of the Greater East Asian War, which is worth quoting at length:

What we have to seriously consider about the current Greater East Asian War is that our enemies England and America are also making a desperate effort in this war. At this time, even if there is the slightest inattention on our part, the enemy may seize the opportunity, and this could possibly lead to disaster. Therefore, our hundred million people must unite and become one in heart and show not one bit of carelessness. But by that alone we cannot achieve the purpose of this sacred war. . . . [S]ince the war naturally came about as a result of the destruction of the League of Nations, it must be said that the focus of the war should now be on whether or not England and America are still allowed to maintain a world order. When the war broke out, England and America were still in control of the world. We the Japanese people may end up by facing the same fate as our fellow countrymen encountered in Guadalcanal. We Japanese should first realize this point. . . . Our immediate mission is to . . . realize the Imperial ideal of "the whole world under one roof." For this purpose, we must engage in fixing, solidifying, and stabilizing other countries in the world who are wandering aimlessly. This is the original mission of the divine country of Japan. This Greater East Asian War was started to force England and America to relinquish their position of world leadership, and ultimately to establish a new order to secure a just and lasting peace.[27]

Thus, from what we have found in the writings of Yamada Yoshio, Japanese expansionism was internally derived from its sense of mission to establish a new world order. Accordingly, anything short of achieving that objective would be tantamount to defeat.

Second, both radical Islam and radical Shintō ultranationalism are similar in the sense that they were not unified movements and they took on several religious forms that were organized into many splinter organizations, some of which had worked out a theological justification for terrorism, which in turn moved from being on the periphery of the mainstream to the point where it coalescenced into a mass-based movement. Lewis noted that "there are several forms of Islamic extremism current at the present time."[28] He then cited the "subversive radicalism of Al-Qaida and other groups that resemble it all over the Muslim world; the preemptive fundamentalism of the Saudi establishment; and the institutionalized revolution of the ruling Iranian hierarchy."[29] Likewise, as we have seen, there were several forms of Shintō ultranationalism. Hozumi Yatsuka's Meiji Shintō ultranationalism was an ultraconservative form of Shintō ultranationalism that sought to push back the clock, at least in a political sense, and re-create a Shintō theocracy. The most militant of the radical Shintō ultranationalist movements, which encouraged terrorism, can be loosely associated with the thought of Uesugi Shinkichi. This is by no means to imply that all terrorist groups or individual terrorists in the 1920s and 1930s who saw themselves as executioners carrying out the will of the emperor can be traced to a cohesive network that Uesugi had built. It does, however, suggest that autonomously operating radical Shintō ultranationalist groups and individuals shared his religious ideology. Uesugi provided the ideological leadership and the theological justification for terrorism. In prewar Japan, radical Shintō ultranationalist groups frequently disbanded and reemerged under new names. We find that the radical Shintō ultranationalist groups with no apparent connections to each other nevertheless advanced the same extremist agendas.

The ultimate purpose of the individual in Uesugi's radical Shintō ultranationalist ideology was to die for the emperor, the act through which one's own being would merge into the mystical body of the emperor, thus closing the gap between one's existential being and one's essential being. This meant in actual practice seeking death by eliminating individuals who refused to follow what they considered the true will of the emperor or by destroying corrupt institutions that stood in the way between the emperor and the masses. Accordingly, such terrorist activities were directed primarily not against foreigners but against Japanese in positions of power and influence who were considered apostate. As has been discussed, the Japanese state was gripped by a religious fundamentalism so powerful and pervasive that even the radical Shintō ultranationalist terrorists were praised by the masses for their purity and devotion and purely innocent victims were thought to have deserved death at the hands of the true believers. By contrast, the ultimate purpose of Kakehi's radical Shintō ultranationalism was to die for the emperor by carrying out the emperor's task of destroying the Western-controlled secular world order—beginning with the "liberation" of China from the clutches of Western ideology and Western civilization—and creating a Japanese emperor-centered world order in its place. This was very much the ideology of the Control Faction in the military and was more directed toward outsiders by waging war and dying on the battlefield to create the emperor-centered world order.

Third, there is an inherent linkage of politics and religion in both Shintō and Islamic traditions, and radical Shintō ultranationalists and radical Islamic militants such as Al Qaida both want or wanted a "holy war" against the rest of the world. Lewis wrote that Osama bin Laden's "declaration of war against the United States marks the resumption of the struggle for religious dominance of the world that began in the seventh century."[30] He further warned us of the current worldwide dangers of radical Islam:

> If the leadership of Al-Qaida can persuade the world of Islam to accept their views and their leadership, then a long and bitter struggle lies ahead, and not only for America. Europe, more particularly Western Europe, is now home to a large and rapidly growing Muslim community, and many Europeans are beginning to see its presence as a problem, for some even a threat. Sooner or later, Al-Qaida and related groups will clash with other neighbors of Islam—Russia, China, India—who may prove less squeamish than the Americans in using their power against Muslims and their sanctities.[31]

That is to say, radical Islam is waging a war against the rest of the world.

In the prewar period, Japan, together with its German and Italian allies, waged war against the rest of the world. How to win this war was an important topic of discussion in Japan in the early 1940s. For instance, in November 1943, on the eve of the second anniversary of the start of the Pacific War, a symposium was held in Tokyo to discuss the theme "The Greater East Asian War and National Politics." This was just one of a number of symposiums organized during the Pacific War years. A wide range of issues on war goals and the means necessary to achieve these goals were discussed at the symposium, which appeared in print in the December 1943 issue of the widely read and highly respected intellectual journal *Chūō Kōron*. The participants in this particular round-table discussion, conducted on November 6, 1943, were Hanami Tatsuji, editor-in-chief of the *Yamato Newspaper*; Mitsuda Iwao, a political and social critic; Nakano Tomio, a professor at Waseda University; and Tsuguno Kunitoshi of the General Affairs Department of the Imperial Rule Assistance Political Association.[32]

The moderator of the symposium opened the session by asking the panelists to restate the meaning of the Greater East Asian War and, in light of the current situation, to reflect on some of the problems facing Japan in China and elsewhere in East Asia. Hanami began by saying that the Greater East Asian War was a war that was being fought to create a "new world order."[33] He also stated that this was something that everyone in Japan should know. But he also said that many people still had to have a clearer understanding of the role that Japan was to play in the East Asian community and the new world order. On this point, he emphasized that Japan would play a pivotal role in this new world order because that order itself ultimately had to be based on the imperial way (*Kōdō*),[34] the spirit of the Japanese state since its founding in ancient times. He firmly believed that the imperial way was the original way of mankind and of the world and that humanity had no choice other than to return to this great way if global order and peace were to be maintained.

Nakano Tomio also placed much emphasis on the point that Japan's kokutai spirit was the only viable basis for a world order. He agreed with Hanami's remarks and added to them by pointing out that the spirit of Japan's kokutai was fundamentally opposed to constitutional forms of government. He further noted that Western theories of liberalism, democracy, and Marxism were not comprehensive worldviews. They were no more than partial views of the human condition. If one wished to take as a worldview a perspective that encompassed the entire universe, including all aspects of human life, then the political theories and political principles devised by the Western world thus far would not qualify. On the contrary, Nakano asserted: "It is Japan's world view that is a real worldview."[35] In other words, the Western world never really produced a true worldview; and it was the worldview founded on Japan's kokutai that was the only true worldview on which to establish a new world order. Nakano's reference to liberalism and Marxism implied that neither the American-inspired Wilsonian ideal of a world order based on liberal-democratic internationalism nor the Soviet-led Marxist vision of a world order was a worldview that could guarantee world peace and order.

The participants in the symposium sought to drive home the point that the Greater East Asian War was not merely a "defensive war (*jiei no sen*)" to free the peoples in East Asia from Western imperialism by expelling the Europeans and the Americans, only to let each individual country in Asia go its own way.[36] Hanami stressed this point in his opening remarks. He said that it had to be embedded in the people's minds that the political aim of the Greater East Asian War was the consolidation of East Asia using the imperial way as the foundation of unity. This was to be a major stepping stone to the establishment of the Japan-centered world order. Hanami also added that it was a "holy war."[37] Mitsuda Iwao also viewed the war in East Asia as the first step in the establishment of a new world order. In fact, he referred to the war as a "war for world reform (*sekai ishin sen*)."[38]

Having restated the fundamental goal of the Greater East Asian War to be the consolidation of East Asia as the first step toward a new world order, the participants then began to identify problems and discuss ways in which these problems might be solved if Japan were to be successful in establishing this new world order. As for unity in East Asia, the principal stumbling block was China. China, of course, is the largest country in East Asia in terms of both population and size. The Japanese could not possibly succeed in their initial goal of the Greater East Asian War without winning over the Chinese. As Hanami saw it, the crux of the "China problem (*Shina no mondai*) was that the Chinese still had their own vision for the construction of a modern state that was ultimately in conflict with Japan's vision of a new East Asian order under the emperor."[39] The Chinese ideals for the establishment of a new China were ultimately based on the ideals of the so-called *San Min Chui* (Three People's Principles)—nationalism, democracy, and land nationalization—articulated at the turn of the century by the father of the Chinese revolution, Sun Yat-sen. The first principle of Chinese nationalism was originally aimed against rule by the Manchu people as well against imperialist incursions by the Western powers and Japan. The Chinese wanted to be ruled by the Chinese people. The second of the Three People's Principles was that China was eventually to evolve into a democracy. This, too, was in opposition to the Japanese imperial way. With these visions of the state, Japan and China were bound to come into conflict.

Hanami did not frontally attack the Three People's Principles and insist that the Chinese abandon them. That would have been political suicide for furthering Japanese–Chinese relations. Instead, he called for a "correct interpretation of the Three People's Principles based on the imperial way."[40] That is, Hanami in effect suggested as a solution to the China problem that the Chinese be allowed to retain the ideals of the Three People's Principles but interpret them in such a way as to gut them of all real content. Recalling the discussion of *Fundamentals of Our National Polity* in chapter 9 about the sublimation of foreign ideologies, this was an inverse application of the same principle. The Japanese radical Shintō ultranationalists suggested that the only viable solution at the time was to bring about the complete sublimation of the ideals of the modern Chinese state into the Japanese kokutai.

The last topic brought up for discussion was the "Greater East Asian War as a War for World Reform (*sekai ishin sen to shite Dai Tōa Senso*)."[41] Mitsuda reiterated that the war ultimately was being fought to establish a new world order. The hegemonic kingly ways of European civilization and Chinese civilization in the past, as well as the present republican and democratic ways of America, could never serve as a solid basis of a world order for all people. The only viable way to achieve a lasting world order was the imperial way. It is instructive to note here that nobody suggested trying to find a way to unite the peoples of East Asia under a common spiritual heritage such as Buddhism, a universal religion that had spread throughout the major countries of the region. But the reason for this should be clear: that would have negated their justification for waging this war.

Finally, there is a striking similarity between the Iranian Revolution of 1979 and the radical Shintō revolutionary movement in Japan of the 1920s and 1930s. In *The Turban for the Crown*, Said Amir Arjomand wrote that the Islamic Revolution in Iran "ha[d] considerable ideological advantage over Nazism and communism, both of which clashed with religion. Rather than creating a new substitute for religion, as did the communists and the Nazis, the Islamic militants have fortified an already vigorous religion with the ideological armor necessary for battle in the arena of mass politics. In doing so, they have made their distinct contributions to world history."[42] Arjomand's comparison of the Islamic Revolution in Iran to Nazism and communism is interesting. He argued that modern revolutions do require political religions but asked rhetorically: Is there any necessary incompatibility between religion and political religions? His argument was that the Islamic revolutionaries had an advantage over the Nazis and communists in their revolutions against Western secular liberalism and atheistic communism because they were able to build on a thriving traditional religion and radicalize it to meet the battle for the hearts and minds of the people in an era of mass politics. The Nazis and communists faced the difficult task of creating new substitutes for religion. My interpretation of Nazism differs from Arjomand's in that I would argue that the Nazis did not try to create an entirely new religion from scratch but attempted to revive the long-dead völkisch religion of the pre-Christian German tribes. Nevertheless, I have shown that Japanese radical Shintō ultranationalists, like the Iranian Islamic revolutionaries, radicalized a vigorous religion and turned it into a revolutionary mass-based religion of extreme nationalism.

According to Arjomand, it was in the secularization policy of Reza Shah (who was inspired by Turkey's Ataturk) in the 1930s that the Islamic Revolution had its roots. Reza Shah's anti-Islamic policies included the prohibition of the "teaching of the Koran and religious instruction in the schools" and the ordering of police to "remove the women's veil."[43] His secularization policy continued under the new reform program of his son Mohammad Reza Shah. This sparked the Islamic antigovernment protests of the 1960s. In 1962, Ayatollah Ruhollah Khomeini emerged as one of the leading figures of the Islamic revolutionary movement. As we have seen, it was in the 1920s that Uesugi Shinkichi was actively involved in the radical Shintō ultranationalist movement against the secularization of Japanese society and the slide into parliamentary government.

The shah's policy of enfranchising women "was vigorously denounced [by the clerics] as a ploy to destroy family life and spread prostitution."[44] Khomeini began his bid to overthrow the Pahlavi regime around 1970. As in the case of Japanese population, not all of the population of Iran was secularizing. The rising middle class was part of the Islamic revival. At the same time, an Islamic fundamentalist ideology was emerging. According to Arjomand, "As an individual, Khomeini had the making of a revolutionary transformation of tradition."[45] His militant followers began referring to him as an imam. "Never since the majority of Iranians had become Shi'ite in the sixteenth century had they called any living person Imam," Arjomand noted.[46] Khomeini would later go on to destroy Western influence and set up a theocracy in Iran. It is also noteworthy that both revolutionary movements had millenarian elements: the radical Shintō ultranationalists wanted direct rule by Amaterasu Ōmikami, while the Islamic revolutionaries wanted government by a priesthood claiming divine authority.

In conclusion, I would suggest that the religious revolt against the secularized Western world started not with the Iranian Revolution based on the mass-based radicalization of the Islamic religion, but with the radical Shintō ultranationalist movement and its war against the Western world. At any rate, in this era of popularity of global studies, more comparative studies across civilizations and cultures are certainly needed.

The Failure of Radical Shintō Ultranationalism as a Universal Ideology

The ultimate goal of radical Shintō ultranationalism in the Second World War was to establish a new world order based on Japanese imperial rule to replace the Wilsonian-inspired world order of democratic international-ism, institutionalized through the League of Nations after the First World War. This goal was enunciated by virtually every radical Shintō ultra-nationalist thinker, politician, and military man in the 1930s and the 1940s. This study has introduced some of the principal theoreticians of radical Shintō ultranationalism who articulated this global vision, but there were many more. For instance, Daniel Holtom, who wrote on Shintō ultranationalism in the midst of the Pacific War in the 1940s, quoted Admiral Yonai Mitsumasa speaking as the newly appointed prime minister in January 1940: "The principle of the whole world under one roof embodies the spirit which the Empire was founded by Jimmu Tennō. My understanding is that this is the spirit of making the boundless virtues of the Emperor prevail throughout the whole world."[47] Holtom also cited Konoe Fumimaro, who in July 1940 replaced Yonai as prime minister, proclaiming: "The basic aim of Japan's national policy lies in the firm establishment of world peace in accordance with the lofty spirit of *Hakko Ichi-u*, in which the country was founded."[48] Holtom also noted a very interesting piece of information in a footnote:

> In the spring of 1940 a monument to the spirit of "the whole world under one roof" was erected in the city of Miyazaki, Kyushu, at a cost of some six hundred thousand yen. It stands on Hakko Hill in the form of a great tower of ferroconcrete, overlooking the Hyuga Straits and rising to a height of more than a hundred feet. In outline it suggests the shape of a

Shintō *gōhei*, the zigzag purification device in common use at the shrines. On each of the four sides of the pillar is a representation of a human figure, symbolizing the four primary agencies wherewith Japan attains the realization of her mission in the world—commerce and industry, fishing, agriculture, and war.[49]

General Araki Sadao, who was serving as minister of education in 1938, wrote in an article titled "State and Education" in the journal *Contemporary Japan* in December 1938:

> The Japanese conception of political origin lies in the very law of nature in conformity with Divine Will. According to our belief, Japan was founded by the Sun Goddess, *Amaterasu-Ōmikami*, who is revered by the entire nation for her all-pervading virtues, and from whom our Imperial House is descended. We, therefore, are proud to look upon our Emperor as the fountain-head of our national life. In this respect our Empire rests upon the foundation of blood relationship which far transcends mere morality, and our Ruler is viewed in the light of a super-moral being. . . .
>
> The *Tenno*, by which name our Sovereign is known, embodies in Himself the spirit of the deities of the primordial universe, as well as the guiding spirit of government, manifested by His divine ancestress, *Amaterasu-Ōmikami*. His august virtues thus pervade both time and space, and He reigns over His people with love and benevolence.[50]

One could go on and on citing such statements by Japanese leaders. Indeed, it would be no exaggeration to say that radical Shintō ultranationalist thought and the idea of global imperial rule deeply permeated the minds of the Japanese people as a whole as well as those of its its leaders. John Dower noted:

> Only a handful of academics emerged from the war with their reputations enhanced for not having been swept along by the tides of ultranationalism. . . . There was no counterpart to the principled resistance that a small but heroic number of intellectuals, leftists, church people, and military officers had mounted against National Socialism in Germany in the same period. There was very little indeed in which intellectuals could take pride where their behavior prior to August 15, 1945 was concerned.[51]

It must be noted that another explosion of radical Shintō ultranationalist writings occurred in the early 1940s, but covering this requires another study. For example, Satō Tsūji, a scholar of German literature and philosophy who in 1943 became a member of the Ministry of Education's

National Spirit Cultural Research Institute and later was president of Kōgakkan University, published his monumental *Kōdō no Tetsugaku* [The Philosophy of the Imperial Way] in 1942. Still another important work by a radical Shintō ultranationalist intellectual in the 1940s is Nakashiba Suezumi's *Kōdō Sekai Kan* (World View of the Imperial Way; 1942).

This vision of a new world order ruled over and governed by the Japanese emperor-deity was prophesied in scripture. Indeed, it was the radical Shintō ultranationalists' purpose in life to contribute to the fulfillment of this prophesy. It was their belief that only the emperor could rule the world with total impartiality and benevolence. And, as we have seen in the state theories of Uesugi Shinkichi and Kakehi Katsuhiko, for the Japanese people themselves, radical Shintō ultranationalist ideology envisioned an egalitarian society in which every individual was equal in the eyes of the emperor. The utopian objective for the individual in his or her relationship with the emperor was to lose the ego—that thinking, feeling, and acting self that is conscious of the self and aware of the distinction of the self from the selves of others—and merge the self totally into the mystical body of the emperor.

However, the problem of how to export this ideology to the non-Japanese people of the conquered lands became a more critical issue as the war progressed. Thinkers critical of Shintō ultranationalism such as Kita Ikki had raised this issue in the first decade of the twentieth century, during the early stages of Japanese expansionism. Radical Shintō ultranationalists, as well as other ideologues, were aware that one cannot create a world order based on sheer military power. This issue of how to rule over an empire composed of other ethnic peoples and races was also an issue of which Holtom was keenly aware. He wrote:

> The rise of modern Japan to ascendancy in Far Eastern affairs has been accompanied by an impressive geographical expansion. This territorial growth—achieved mainly by the force of arms—has been safeguarded by the extension of elaborate political and military administration, and this in turn has been accompanied by economic and cultural penetrations that are only beginning to reveal their vast possibilities for the reordering of the new areas of control. . . . In manufacturing, agriculture, mining, engineering, business, education, and religion, Japan is projecting something like a migration onto the mainland, which, if carried through even to partial conclusion, will leave very little as it was either for continental eastern Asia or for Japan. And even though the actual movements of

population may not be relatively large, the completeness of the controls which the Japanese genius for paternalistic organization is in process of establishing over conquered peoples threatens a momentous change to the story of mankind. . . . The part which the national religion has played in this great movement is not inconsiderable. The tenacity with which the Japanese government has pressed the Shinto issue in Korea and elsewhere points to its significance as the guarantee of the establishment of inner authority over subjected peoples.[52]

The goal, of course, was somehow to induce non-Japanese to embrace radical Shintō ultranationalist ideology. But this proved to be no easy task. The crux of the problem was that radical Shintō ultranationalism was in essence an ethnic or Volk-based ideology that lacked a universal message with which all peoples of the world could enthusiastically iden-tify. (This, of course, is where the similarities between radical Islam and radical Shintō ultranationalism end.) Further, the Japanese themselves, imbued with this ideology for decades, were unprepared mentally and psychologically for the task of converting the non-Japanese masses to radical Shintō ultranationalism. Holtom noted that Horie Hideo, an authority on Shintō, tried to deal with this vexing problem in an article titled "The Shintō Shrine Problem Overseas," in the 1939 issue of *Shūkyō Nenkan (Yearbook of Religion)*. In a summary of Horie's article, Holtom wrote:

> The major problem, argues Horie, is that of adjustment of the exclusively nationalistic aspects of State Shintō to the universalism that ought to inhere in constructive international intercourse. The existence of the former elements is first recognized and strongly emphasized. The author calls attention to the consciousness of unique racial integrity that under-lies the thinking of the Japanese people. He begins with the doctrine of the one-tribe origin of the nation. The true members of the Japanese race regard themselves [as offspring] of the gods. They believe that their state was brought into being by the *kami* and that the people are the descen-dants of these ancestral deities. They hold that, in spite of the infusion of the blood of other peoples in times past, the genuine Yamato stock pre-dominates and that for the most part the breed is pure. Communal solidarity is guaranteed and preserved by this fact of direct divine descent and by the bonds of spiritual communion with the gods.[53]

What Horie said about the essence of State Shintō is exactly what the radical Shintō ultranationalists had been articulating for decades. However, after Horie admitted that ethnicity was at the core of State Shintō, according to Holtom, he went on to say:

> The nationalistic character found in the shrines does not inevitably veto a universal character. In cases where members of our Japanese race [*sic*; ethnic nation]—so rich in the sentiment of reverence—are living together in a land with foreigners of like tendencies the practice of worshipping together at the shrines is not merely a matter to which there is no objection, rather it should be welcomed. Shinto, the Great Way of the Gods, is not a thing which the state or the people of the nation should regard selfishly. Shinto is broad. It includes humanitarianism and righteousness. The spirit of Shinto, which is the fundamental directive principle of our national life, must be utilized for the purpose of elevating the races of neighboring territories where the national relationships are complicated. Indeed, by means of this spirit of Shinto foreign peoples must also be evangelized. The self-interested internationalism, which has come into existence apart from the give and take of ordinary intercourse and which up to now fought with the weapons of craft and deception, must be brought to its senses by the saving presence of the pure and holy spirit of Shinto.[54]

There is no reason to doubt Horie's sincerity in wanting to lift up the neighboring Asian peoples by encouraging them to worship the Japanese gods in the shrines. But one should hardly be surprised to discover that such a message would fall on deaf ears. If Horie was addressing Asian peoples in Japanese conquered territories, this was the equivalent to a man throwing a few scraps of bones to hungry dogs running down the street. In terms of ideology, Japanese radical Shintō ultranationalists might as well have been from another planet; their State Shintō ideology was totally alien to Asian peoples. Besides, other Asians for the most part were already acting and operating within the ideological orbit of the Western world, whether republican or communist, which the Japanese utterly failed to understand. Even Douglas MacArthur alluded to this when he remarked, "Tucked away there in the North Pacific, the Japanese had little or no realization of how the rest of the world lived. They had evolved a feudalistic system of totalitarianism which had produced results which were almost like reading the pages of mythology."[55]

Holtom also had expressed strong reservations about this and noted that trying to spread State Shintō ideology was hampered by three factors: (1) the government-inspired doctrine that the essence of sincerity consisted of conformity to rule; (2) the conception of the national expansion process as involving the full assimilation of conquered peoples; and (3) the inseparable connection between Shintō and political administration. In regard to the first point, when asked what value Shintō had to offer applicable to all mankind, radical Shintō ultranationalists claimed that "sincerity" was the universal value of State Shintō that was the equivalent to Christian love and to Buddhist compassion. But this virtue of "sincerity"—the equivalent saying "one heart, one virtue"— meant becoming one with the emperor. When asked what this might mean to a Manchurian subject under Japanese rule, a non-Japanese resident candidly replied, "It means a heart of fear and a virtue of absolute obedience."[56] As anyone even remotely familiar with the history of modern Chinese history knows, nationalism had been spreading rapidly among the Chinese masses since the May 4, 1919, Movement, and the Chinese people were certainly in no mood to identify with a foreign emperor whose troops were occupying their land and when their people were being massacred in the name of that emperor. The original policy of "assimilation" in Korea and Taiwan, for all practical purposes, meant "cultural genocide"—the cultural extermination or destruction of an entire people or ethnic group. These Asians in essence were expected to become fictive Japanese. Needless to say, this was no way to establish an "inner authority over the subjected peoples." Finally, Holtom acknowledged that radical Shintō ultranationalism was a religion of national expansionism. Its ideal of egalitarianism of all people under the emperor did not apply to non-Japanese peoples. Therefore, the ideal could not be realistically exported and accepted beyond the Japanese völkisch or ethnic group.

To circumvent this ideological dilemma and come up with some kind of viable blueprint or set of ideological guidelines for Japanese officials involved in the practical planning and administration of Japan's conquered areas, radical Shintō ultranationalists finally resorted to a partial resurrecting of the Meiji conceptualization of a hierarchical order of rule articulated by theorists such as Hozumi Yatsuka. They also incorporated new ideas from abroad, especially German Nazism. This authoritarian model of "conservative Shintō ultranationalism" was resurrected and rearticulated to apply to Japanese rule of non-Japanese peoples. Insofar as it served as an ideological basis of a world order, this development within radical Shintō ultranationalist ideology was a sure indication of the theoretical breakdown of the ideology when it came to justifying global rule. It simply did not contain egalitarian universal values. But the potential long-range outcome of a failure to articulate adequately an ideological justification for ruling over a vast empire would also result in certain disaster. For that reason, Japanese radical Shintō ultranationalists had to come up with alternative solutions to the dilemma. An excellent example of this can be seen in the 1943 document *An Investigation of Global Policy with the Yamato Race [sic; Ethnic Nation] as Nucleus* that Dower discussed in his powerful work *War without Mercy*.[57] More than anything, this document seems to indicate that Japan's global ideological policy was in shambles and that its fanatical militant Shintō ultranationalist leaders were desperate to try anything.

As shown in Dower's analysis of *An Investigation of Global Policy*, which was compiled by forty researchers working for the Population and Race (Ethnic Nation) Section of the Research Bureau of the Ministry of Health and Welfare, the Japanese were even seriously contemplating drastic measures such as a long-range plan to relocate on a massive scale Koreans and Taiwanese:

> Concerning the Koreans and Formosans, the report was exceedingly harsh. They were described as being especially suitable to carry out the heavy physical work of a protracted war. Given their high birth rates, resistance of Japanization, and strategic locations, special care had to be taken to prevent them from becoming "parasites" within the empire. Once the war was over, Koreans living within Japan proper should be sent home; those living near the Soviet border should be replaced by Japanese settlers; and, in general, Koreans should be encouraged to emigrate to harsh and thinly populated places such as New Guinea.[58]

It is instructive to keep in mind that the Taiwanese and Koreans were the first people to fall under Japanese rule. By the 1940s, the Koreans had been under direct Japanese rule for more than three decades and the Taiwanese more than four decades. Obviously, the Japanese policy of cultural genocide was not working, and the Japanese were by that time clearly fed up with having the Taiwanese and the Koreans living in the core area of the new world order they were trying to create. It seems that they had no real, "proper place" within that order. Advocating the physical removal of the Koreans was only one or two steps away from a final solution such as the one the Nazis developed for the Jews. This Japanese proposal to encourage the Koreans to emigrate to New Guinea recalls the Nazi proposal to have the European Jews emigrate to Madagascar.

But the radical Shintō ultranationalists were not having problems with just the Taiwanese and the Koreans. Contact with the peoples of Asia that was too close was also considered dangerous for the long-range survival of the empire and, eventually, global rule. Dower noted: "Concerning overseas Japanese, admonitions against racial [ethnic] intermarriage were a standard part of policy documents, and the 1943 report spelled out the rationale for this: intermarriage would destroy the 'national spirit' of the Yamato Race [ethnic nation]."[59] Not only would it destroy the national spirit of the Yamato ethnic nation; it would, in the long run, destroy the ethnic nation itself. This is what the radical Shintō ultranationalists feared most, and this mind-set goes back to what Hozumi Yatsuka was talking about in the late nineteenth century. With this attitude toward other races and ethnic groups, the only way to secure the stability of the empire and the conquered lands theoretically was to export Japanese overseas in numbers large enough to dominate them. The detailed plan for the "blood of the Yamato race [ethnic nation]" to be "planted in the soil" of the various countries is just one of the fascinating aspects of this incredible document.[60] Everything according to radical Shintō ultranationalism was centered on Japan, and theoretically there was no room for anything else. They even went so far as to redraw the maps of the world. Since Japan was the first land created by the gods Izanagi and Izanami, Japan was considered the center of the world. Accordingly, one finds Komaki Tsuneki's proposal to place Japan at the center of a world map, going so far as to rename the continents and designate all the oceans of the world the "Great Sea of Japan."[61]

From our analysis of the ideology of radical Shintō ultanationalism, one should not be surprised by the fact that Japan had no reliable Asian ally in the Second World War. Radical Shintō ultranationalism was not the type of ideology that could give meaning for people outside the Japanese ethnic group. Only a universal ideology can unite peoples of different national origins and give them a shared sense of identity and a purpose to work together to make a better world for all. This study should make it very clear that the Japanese could never have won the ideological battle, for only the globalization of a universal religion or universal ideology ultimately could have succeeded. The United States, for example, attempts to promote democracy and human rights globally by supporting democratic elements in countries around the world. Democracy can also be induced from the outside by military forces as in the case of Germany and Japan after the Second World War, but it is not necessary. Various strategies can be utilized for that purpose. The critical point is that democratic institutions and values of human rights can be exported. Likewise, the other major ideology of the twentieth century, communism (and its various ideological derivatives), can also be exported. The communist nations had supported indigenous communist movements in countries around the world. This is not to suggest that exporting universal values is easy. One of the great lessons of the twentieth century and now the twenty-first century is that democracy is not easily exportable, as Americans are now finding out in Iraq and other areas of the Middle East. It is extremely difficult even under the best circumstances, and in places where relative success stories are found, such as Taiwan and the Republic of Korea, it has taken decades of careful nurturing and massive assistance from the United States. Radical Shintō ultranationalism could not be spread by such means. In other words, the globalization of an ethnic religion could not possibly have succeeded.

Shintō ideology and theology utterly failed to break out of the narrow confines of ethnicity within which it had been imprisoned since ancient times. It had not advanced beyond the late Tokugawa period, when Hirata Atsutane had first articulated his cosmology. In *Tama no Mihashira* (Pillar of the Soul), Hirata claimed that Japan and the Japanese were superior to all other lands and peoples because in the Shintō story of genesis Japan was born as the result of the union of the gods Izanagi and Izanami and its people were the descendants of the gods, while foreign peoples and foreign countries were formed out of the foam of the sea. The Shintō story contained no monogenetic theory of the origins of man, and no serious attempt was ever made to evolve Shintō into a genuinely universal religion.

Japanese Shintō ultranationalists were victims of their own delusions of grandeur and power. All of them were highly religious people—Shintō fundamentalists[62]—and as such they believed in the core doctrines of Shintō ultranationalism: the divine descent and divinity of the living emperor; the divine origins of the Japanese ethnic group as against the divine origins or natural evolutionary origins of man; and the divine source of political authority stemming from the ancestral deity Amaterasu Ōmikami. These doctrines were common to all Shintō ultranationalists as much as the crucifixion or resurrection of Jesus Christ is to Christians. Accordingly, for all these radical Shintō ultranationalist theorists, sovereignty resided in the emperor, and no human law was capable of restraining the sovereign emperor. Nevertheless, within this common framework, major differences did exist among Shintō ultranationalists in their articulations of emperor ideology. Hozumi Yatsuka started with the principle of the family, and on the basis of the family he built the structure of the state. Uesugi Shinkichi, on the contrary, virtually ignored the family and took the state, which to him was composed of individuals who were all equal in the mystical body of the emperor interacting in a spatial-temporal matrix, as his starting point. For Kakehi, the state was really religion. He focused on the divine nature of the emperor and the mystical relationship between the emperor and the masses. Shintō ultranationalism, in short, contained a multiplicity of distinct articulations.

Hozumi's conservative Shintō ultranationalism inherited the task of defending the authoritarian political order in the late Meiji period against liberalism and democratic institutions by demonstrating its ability to defend the sovereignty of the emperor and thereby the interests of the elite ruling oligarchy. Based on the traditional patriarchal construction of state and society, Hozumi's formulation of emperor ideology allowed for no participation of the masses in politics. Hozumi had linked the emperor system to the state much in the same way Europeans had connected the monarchy to the state in the sixteenth century and seventeenth century. But such a theory of state was effective as an ideology only in a premodern society. Consequently, by the second decade of the twentieth century it came to represent a reactionary force and was in danger of losing its appeal to the people, who were, using the words of Hegel, rapidly becoming "a law unto themselves." By then, no longer could it be correct to say that the state consisted of the emperor and his subjects, if by "subjects" one meant nonpolitical, scattered, and unorganized individuals.

Ideological challenges coming from liberalism and socialism articulated in the form of German state-sovereignty theories in the Meiji period and *minponshugi* in the Taishō period were, for the most part, responses to Hozumi Yatsuka's formulation of emperor ideology. If it were not to become ossified and corroded and thereby lose its ideological hegemony, Shintō ultranationalism had to be rearticulated. Correctly perceiving the inherent weakness of Hozumi's formulation of emperor ideology, Uesugi Shinkichi and Kakehi Katsuhiko reformulated it to accommodate the new political and social realities brought on by the politicization of the masses. It had to be redefined and its relevance reproduced without losing the validity of its central tenets.

To construct an ideology welding absolute monarchy to the politicized masses was a formidable task, indeed, that could be accomplished only by means of a fiction. Uesugi's emperor ideology had sought to convince the masses that what they desired was really what the emperor desired. He had to convince them that their wishes were identical to those of the emperor—that indeed, they were really a part of the emperor rather than independent beings who had consciousness of their own individuality. Kakehi's emperor ideology sought to create this identity between the emperor and the masses by indoctrinating the latter through devotion, prayer, adoration, and sacrifice to the emperor. In both Uesugi's metaphysics and Kakehi's mystical religious doctrines, this identity between the emperor and the masses was theoretically worked out. The findings of the study suggest that it was in this way that radical Shintō ultranationalist ideology, Japan's "myth of the twentieth century," succeeded in organizing and mobilizing the masses and in remaining the dominant ideology throughout the first half of the twentieth century. This transformation of emperor ideology from a traditional form of absolutism to a modern, mass-based egalitarian state structure under the emperor represented one of the most important political developments in modern Japanese history—more important than the turn from constitutional monarchy to absolute monarchy—for it required the transformation of the consciousness of men on a massive scale. The dynamics involved in the process of the mass transformation of the consciousness of the Japanese people from a traditional form of absolutism to a consciousness of totally identifying one's own being with the emperor is best illustrated by the story "A Sailor's Mother" that elementary-school children were required to recite throughout the Taishō and Shōwa periods:[63]

It was the time of the War of 1894–1895. One day on our ship the Takachiho, a sailor was weeping as he read a letter written in a women's handwriting. A passing lieutenant saw him and, thinking his behavior unmanly, said, "Hey, what have we here? Has life become so valuable? Are you afraid to die? Are you lonely for your wife and children? Don't you think it's an honor to become a soldier and go to war—What kind of attitude is that?"

"Sir, don't think that of me . . ."

[The officer reads the letter:]

"You said you did not fight in the battle of Feng-tao, and you did not accomplish much in the August 10th attack at Weihaiwei either. I am very disappointed in you. Why did you go into battle? Wasn't it to sacrifice your life to repay the emperor? The people in the village are good to me and offer help all the time, saying kindly: 'It must be hard for you having your only son off fighting for the country. Please don't hesitate to tell us if there is anything we can do.' Whenever I see their faces, I am reminded of your cowardice and I feel as if my heart will break. So every day I go to the shrine of Hachiman and pray that you will distinguish yourself in battle. Of course I am human, too, and cannot at all bring myself to hate my own child. Please try to understand my feelings as I write this letter. . . ."

[The officer apologized.]

"I'm sorry. I can only admire your mother's spirit."

The sailor, who had been listening with lowered head, saluted and, smiling, left.[64]

Irokawa Daikichi noted that "A Sailor's Mother" illustrated "the close relation between filial piety and loyalty on the part of the ordinary people and the common soldier."[65] Quite frankly, I am at a loss to explain what Irokawa meant by this statement. If the story was supposed to illustrate filial piety, it was a filial piety so twisted and mangled that it is unrecognizable. It is inconceivable that this story has anything to do with illustrating the close association between loyalty to the emperor and filial piety. Just the opposite: the story signified, if anything, the demise of the value of filial piety in Japanese society. Filial piety—and, definitely, filial piety in the Confucian ideal—required that a son should protect his own life to care for his parents. In the traditional patriarchal construction of state and society, loyalty to the king or the emperor was construed as an *extension* of filial piety. In other words, devotion one has to one's parents is extended to the emperor. Loyalty to the emperor is thus promoted alongside filial piety.

In the story, morality is used to destroy any emotional attachment that a person may have even to one's own family or spouse or children. It was designed to destroy the sphere of the individual's inner life of freedom from radical Shintō ultranationalist ideology. It recognized no limits on its penetration into the thoughts and daily life of the individual. The moral of the story is to induce total devotion to the emperor. To die for the emperor, the individual must obliterate any real affection between the individual and his loved ones. In the story, the lieutenant mistakenly chides the young sailor for weeping for what at first he imagines as his longing for his wife and children. "Are you afraid to die?" asked the lieutenant. The implication here, of course, is that any feeling that the sailor may have had for his wife and children would weaken his resolve to die for the emperor. The lieutenant is delighted when he reads the letter and finds out that the sailor's mother has scolded her son for not seeking death in battle for the emperor. In the mother's thinking, too, the son is not supposed to be concerned about her or the family. She feels that her "heart will break" if her son does not die in battle.

From the viewpoint of radical Shintō ultranationalist ideology, the mother and the lieutenant were the exemplary personalities. They were the ones responsible for sending millions of Japanese to their deaths in the name of the emperor. But to do this, the most fundamental of human emotions had to be destroyed. Even the slightest of feelings or emotions for loved ones indicated weakness and less than total commitment and devotion to the emperor. "A Sailor's Mother" portends the type of thinking that was to dominate the Japanese state in the 1930s and the 1940s. Anyone who had been in the way of this form of religious ultranationalism was driven from power and influence in Japanese society. What happened to Minobe Tastukichi and his organ theory of the state is a good example of this.

Of course, it is possible that not everyone in Japan in the 1930s and the 1940s came to believe in the divinity of the emperor, despite the decades of mass indoctrination of radical Shintō ultranationalist ideology. Perhaps groups and individuals resisted to the bitter end, as Ienaga Saburo tried to show in the chapter "Dissent and Resistance: Change from Within" of his book *The Pacific War, 1931–1945*. But one thing is unquestionable: the massive impact of this radical form of Shintō nationalism on the life of the Japanese people in the first half of the twentieth century.

Notes

Introduction

1   Holtom, *The National Faith of Japan*, 3–4.
2   In his well-crafted essay "The Fascist Era," Joseph Sottile surveyed the long-running, contentious scholarly debate on how to define and categorize fascism and the ongoing debate among American and Western scholars regarding the ideological placement of Japan within the Axis alliance. He notes, "Faced with a complex Cold War paradigm and the difficult problems of war guilt, . . . Western scholars have embraced Japan as different to avoid attaching to it the ugly word 'fascism'": Sottile, "The Fascist Era," 12.
3   Mosse, *The Crisis of German Ideology*, 1.
4   Ibid.
5   Huntington, *The Clash of Civilizations and the Remaking of World Order*.
6   Bodansky, *Bin Laden*, x.
7   Huntington, *The Clash of Civilizations and the Remaking of World Order*, 209.
8   Ibid., 217–218.
9   Juergensmeyer, *The New Cold War?*
10 Ibid., 1–2.
11 These are the words of Benamin R. Barber: see the introduction in Barber, *Jihad versus McWorld*.
12 Maruyama, "The Ideology and Dynamics of Japanese Fascism," 36.
13 Ibid.
14 Ibid., 37.
15 Ishida, *Meiji Seiji Shisō Shi Kenkyū*.
16 Irokawa, "The Emperor System as a Spiritual Structure," 245–311.
17 Ibid., 282.
18 *Hagakure* in *Nihon Shisō Taikei*, vol. 26, (Tokyo: Iwanami Shoten, 1974), 220. I studied formally with Professor Sagara as a graduate research student in the Department of Ethics of Tokyo University between 1975 and 1978. I also studied with him in an unofficial capacity until 1981, when I enrolled as a graduate research student in the Department of

Cultural Anthropology of Tokyo University and received instruction from Obayashi Tarō. While having dinner together, Sagara told me that *Hagakure* was his favorite book and that if I really understood *Hagakure*, I would understand the essence of Japan and the Japanese people.

19   Byas, *Government by Assassination*, 45.

20   Ibid., 46.

21   Ibid., 47.

22   Ibid., 42

23   Bix, *Hirohito and the Making of Modern Japan*.

24   Dower, *Embracing Defeat*, 283.

25   "State Shintō" refers to the linkage of the Shintō religion with the modern Japanese state. Helen Hardacre states that "the term *State Shinto* has been employed in two main ways in previous studies. Shinto scholars apply it only after the establishment of a Shrine Office (Jinja kyoku) within the Home Ministry in 1900, restricting its use to administrative measures regulating Shinto shrines and priests. For these scholars, State Shinto came to an end in 1945. Historians and historians of religions have tended to use the term in a broader way, thinking of State Shinto as a systematic phenomenon that encompassed government support of and regulation of shrines, the emperor's sacerdotal roles, state creation and sponsorship of Shinto rites, construction of Shinto Shrines in Japan and in overseas colonies, education for schoolchildren in Shinto mythology plus their compulsory participation in Shinto rituals, and persecution of other religious groups on the grounds of their exhibiting disrespect for some aspect of authorized mythology": Hardacre, *Shinto and the State, 1868–1988*, 5–6. She also remarks that historians of the latter category "are likely to speak of a resurgence of State Shinto in the Postwar era": ibid., 6. The meaning of State Shintō employed in this study comes closer to the latter definition, but I am not in any way concerned with, nor have I ever spoken of, the resurgence of State Shintō in the postwar period. Actually, I have come to the opposite conclusion.

Hardacre also noted that "State Shinto begins with the Restoration" and that "the years 1868 to roughly 1880 were characterized by state experimentation with Shinto": ibid, 22, 27. For the constitutional-law scholars who are the focus of this study, we might say that Shintō and the state became permanently linked and fixed in a new state order with the promulgation of the Constitution of the Empire of Japan in 1889. The Shintō myth was incorporated into the Constitution in Article 1, which states, "The Empire of Japan shall be reigned over and governed by a line of Emperors unbroken for ages eternal."

26   I am aware of the differences between the Iranian Revolution of 1979 and the emergence of radical Shintō ultranationalism in early-

twentieth-century Japan, including the scholarly debate over whether the Iranian Revolution was indeed a true revolution in the classical sense. Obviously, the Iranian Revolution of 1979 was not carried out in the name of attempting to restore an emperor to power—just the opposite: it overthrew the monarchy of the shah and established an Islamic republic. Khomeini had made it crystal clear that no political authority rested with the monarchy. Nevertheless, both revolutions, I would argue, were directed against Western secularization of thought and society and the secular world order established by the West.

27 Gluck, *Japan's Modern Myths*, 279.

28 Uesugi, *Kokka Shinron*.

29 Breuilly, *Nationalism and the State*, 54.

30 Hardacre, *Shinto and the State, 1868–1988*.

31 Holtom, *The National Faith of Japan*, 138.

32 Holtom, *Modern Japan and National Shintoism*, 60. It should be noted here that Hardacre stated that Holtom tended to accept the "wartime rhetoric" of Shinto as an "engine of war" and that "Holtom connected Shinto with nationalism, imperialism, and militarism, explaining that Shinto, originally a cult lacking political significance, had been "perverted by militarists": Hardacre, *Shinto and the State, 1868–1988*, 6, 135. I feel compelled to respond.

First, Holtom never accepted the "wartime rhetoric" of Shintō as the engine of war. Where did this wartime rhetoric come from? He was merely pointing out what the state documents and the leading intellectuals of Japan were saying and writing at the time and trying to warn the world of the role State Shintō played in fueling and justifying Japan's war in East Asia. And it is absolutely necessary for us to get away from using the term "militarists." State Shintō was not "perverted by militarists," if by "militarist" one means someone who espouses the glorification of the military profession or the predominance of armed forces in the administration or policy of the state. One should not try to blame everything on such a vague concept as "militarists"—that is, an amorphous group of individuals with no names. Although analysis of the political events of the 1920s and 1930s shows with unmistakable clarity that there was a definite shift in the balance of power from civilian to military authorities, Holtom referred to a large number of civilian thinkers and intellectual leaders—civilian scholars in the universities, including Kokugakuin University; bureaucrats in government; and politicians in society who enthusiastically promoted Shintō totalitarian ideology. One must also not forget that people in the military also have ideological convictions.

33 Antoni, *Shintō und die Konzeption des japanischen Nationalwesens (kokutai)*, 278–83.

34 Breuilly, *Nationalism and the State.*
35 Ibid., 1.
36 Ibid.
37 Ibid., 2.
38 Ibid., 9.
39 Ibid., 230–53.
40 Ibid., 230.
41 Ibid.
42 Ibid.
43 Ibid., 247.
44 For a brief discussion of the historical origins of *Kokugaku* ideology in Japanese history, see Antoni, "Karagokoro," 49–72.
45 Breuilly, *Nationalism and the State,* 247–48.
46 Ibid., 252.
47 Ibid., 272.
48 Juergensmeyer, *The New Cold War?* 6.
49 Ibid., 46.
50 Ibid., 41.
51 Juergensmeyer, *The New Cold War?* 195.
52 Ibid., 197.
53 Breuilly, *Nationalism and the State,* 288.
54 Ibid., 290.
55 Ibid.
56 Ibid., 290–91.
57 Ibid., 300.
58 Cohen, *Communism, Fascism and Democracy,* 262.
59 Mosse, *The Crisis of German Ideology,* 312–13.
60 Ibid., 313.
61 Breuilly, *Nationalism and the State,* 291.
62 Laqueur, *Fascism,* 6.
63 Holtom, *The National Faith of Japan,* 4.
64 Ibid., 5.
65 Ibid., 305.
66 Hall, *Cartels of the Mind,* 150.
67 Ibid.
68 Juergensmeyer, *The New Cold War?* 146.
69 Mosse, *The Crisis of German Ideology,* 8.
70 Among those who have argued in the affirmative are Scalapino, *Democracy and the Party Movement in Prewar Japan;* Storry, *The Double Patriots;* Maruyama, "The Ideology and Dynamics of Japanese Fascism"; Gordon, *Labor and Imperial Democracy in Prewar Japan* ; Bix, "Rethinking 'Emperor-System Fascism'"; McCormack, "Nineteen-

Thirties Japan." More recently, Sottile ("The Fascist Era") and E. Bruce Reynolds ("Peculiar Characteristics") have articulated powerful arguments for the case of Japanese fascism. Sottile's and Reynolds's essays appear in Reynolds, *Japan in the Fascist Era*, a work highly endorsed by Chalmers Johnson. Among those who have argued that the concept of "Japanese fascism" is mistaken are Wilson, "A New Look at the Problem of Japanese Fascism"; Kasza, "Fascism from Below?"; and Duus and Okimoto "Fascism and the History of Pre-War Japan."

71 Payne, *A History of Fascism, 1914–1945*, 329–30.
72 Weber, *Varieties of Fascism*, 9.
73 Laqueur, *Fascism*, 13.

1 Constitutional Monarchy

1   Tsunoda et al., *Sources of Japanese Tradition*, 137.
2   Ibid., 137–39.
3   Pittau, *Political Thought in Early Meiji Japan, 1868–1889*, 46.
4   Ibid., 49.
5   Ibid., 106.
6   Ibid., 59.
7   Ibid.
8   Ibid.
9   Harootunian, *Things Seen and Unseen*, 404.
10 Ibid., 378.
11 Ibid., chap. 8.
12 Pittau, *Political Thought in Early Meiji Japan, 1868–1889*, 88.
13 Brest, "The Misconceived Quest for the Original Understanding," 227.
14 Pittau, *Political Thought in Early Meiji Japan, 1868–1889*, 201. Pittau notes in regard to the outcome of the pre-constitutional debate over state that "A new theory of the state emerged from the framing of the Meiji Constitution: it was based essentially on an uneasy marriage of absolutist ideas with modern constitutional principles bound together by mythical traditions. . . . As long as the diet and the parties existed there could be no pure absolutism or pure bureaucratic transcendentalism. The Meiji political system both in theory and practice was a mixture of authoritarianism and constitutionalism, a hybrid 'absolute constitutional monarchy.' "
15 Scalapino, *Democracy and the Party Movement in Prewar Japan*, 150.
16 Itō, *Commentaries on the Constitution of the Empire of Japan*, 9.
17 Hane, *Modern Japan*, 129.
18 Quoted in Fairbank et al., *East Asia*, 554.

19   Wolferen, *The Enigma of Japanese Power*, 295–96.

20   This is from a passage of Kosaka's article "The Showa Era (1926–1989)," in Gluck and Graubard, *Showa*, 39.

21   Siemes, *Hermann Roesler and the Making of the Meiji State*, 43.

22   Pittau, *Political Thought in Early Meiji Japan, 1868–1889*, 150.

23   Ibid.

24   Itō, *Commentaries on the Constitution of the Empire of Japan*, 7.

25   Siemes, *Hermann Roesler and the Making of the Meiji State*, 45.

26   Pyle, *The Making of Modern Japan*, 162.

27   Keene, *Emperor of Japan*, 469.

28   Ibid., 539.

29   Keene, *Emperor of Japan*, 539.

30   Ibid., 539–40.

31   Ibid., 541–42.

32   Ibid., 541.

33   McGovern, *From Luther to Hitler*, 61–62.

34   Fairbank et al., *East Asia*, 531.

35   In his chapter "Constitutional Democracy: GHQ Writes a New National Charter" in *Embracing Defeat*, Dower noted that the *Guide to Japan* prepared for the U.S. occupation forces around the time of surrender stated the following in regard to the Meiji Constitution: "The new Japanese Constitution, with Prussian tyranny as its father, and British representative government as its mother, and attended at its birth by Sat-Cho [Satsuma and Choshu] midwives was a hermaphroditic creature," 346.

2   Hozumi Yatsuka

1   Minear, *Japanese Tradition and Western Law*, 22.

2   Ibid., 22.

3   Ibid., 22–23.

4   Ibid., 23.

5   Ibid., 24.

6   Nagao, *Hozumi Yatsuka Shū*, 291.

7   Minear, *Japanese Tradition and Western Law*, 29.

8   See ibid. for more detailed biographical information.

9   Hozumi, *Kokumin Kyōiku*, 1.

10   Ibid., 12.

11   Ibid., 16.

12   Ibid., 5.

13   Ibid., 16.

14 Ibid. Hozumi also used the word *kokka minzoku* in *Kempō Teiyō*, which is a direct translation of the German term *Staatsnation*.

15 Mosse, *The Crisis of German Ideology*, 32.

16 Ibid., 33.

17 Ibid., 44.

18 Nagao, *Hozumi Yatsuka Shū*, 365–66.

19 Ibid., 366.

20 Ibid.

21 Ibid.

22 Ibid.

23 Ibid., 398.

24 Ibid.

25 Doak, *A History of Nationalism in Modern Japan*, 225. In his chapter on ethnic nationalism, Doak noted that, in contrast to Japanese Christians who generally welcomed Koreans into the Japanese state, Shintō nationalists saw "Japan's annexation of Korea as proof of Japan's superior ethnic identity and the necessity of keeping Koreans in a separate and inferior social position": Ibid., 26.

26 Harootunian, "Review Article: *Hirohito Redux*," 619.

27 Laslett, *Patriarcha and Other Political Works of Sir Robert Filmer*, 11.

28 Figgis, *The Theory of the Divine Right of Kings*, 5. This work, published in 1896, was extremely popular among Japanese scholars of political theory in the twentieth century.

29 Hozumi, *Kokumin Kyōiku*, 5.

30 Ibid., 26. The last part of this passage about state law and state religion is a key point of Hozumi's state theory. This is taken up later, but suffice it to note here that law and morality are identical in Hozumi's theory, and it is the separation of them, he argued, that contributed to the downfall of the ethnic state in history.

31 Ibid., 4.

32 Hozumi, *Kempō Teiyō*, 1.

33 Ibid., 30.

34 Ibid. .

35 Ibid., 49.

36 Ibid.

37 See Minear's reference to *Hozumi Yatsuka Hakase Rombun Shū* (Collection of essays of Dr. Hozumi Yatsuka) in Minear, *Japanese Tradition and Western Law*, 57.

38 Hozumi, *Kempō Teiyō*, 3.

39 Hozumi, *Kokumin Kyōiku*, 3–4. I have used Minear's translation here with minor changes: see Minear, *Japanese Tradition and Western Law*, 73.

40 Hozumi, *Kokumin Kyōiku*, 16.

41 Ibid., 117.

42 Ibid., 16.

43 Tanaka, *Japan's Orient*, 132.

44 Ibid., 132.

45 Hozumi, *Kokumin Kyōiku*, 16–27.

46 Ibid., 29.

47 Ibid., 30.

48 Ibid., 30.

49 Irokawa, "The Emperor System as a Spiritual Structure," 282.

50 Hozumi, *Kokumin Kyōiku*, 89.

51 Ibid., 90.

52 Ibid.

53 Ibid., 5.

54 Ibid., 76.

55 Ibid., 23.

56 Ibid.

57 Minear, *Japanese Tradition and Western Law*, 77.

58 Doak, *A History of Nationalism in Modern Japan*, 223.

59 Hozumi, *Kokumin Kyōiku*, 44.

60 Ibid., 39.

61 Doak, *A History of Nationalism in Modern Japan*, 225–26.

62 Hozumi, *Kokumin Kyōiku*, 17.

63 Ibid., 18.

64 Ibid., 3–4.

65 Minear, *Japanese Tradition and Western Law*, 68.

66 Hozumi, *Kempō Teiyō*, 239.

67 Ibid., 230.

68 Ibid., 293–94.

69 Ibid., 294.

70 Ibid.

71 Ibid., 310.

72 These comments regarding Hozumi's state thought were made to me in an e-mail message from Roger Griffin on July 31, 2007.

73 Ida, *Uesugi Shinkichi*, 7.

3   Minobe Tatsukichi

1 Ienaga, *Minobe Tatsukichi no Shisōshi teki Kenkyū*, 3. Ienaga noted that Ichiki had published his book *Nihon Hōrei Yosan Ron* in 1892 while he was still studying overseas in Germany even before he had become a professor at the University of Tōkyō.

2 For a short discussion of Sueoka's constitutional thought, see Sueoka, *Nihon Kindai Kempō Shisō Shi Kenkyū*, 136–39.

3 Sueoka, *Minobe Tatsukichi no Shisōshi teki Kenkyū*, 3.

4 Ibid.

5 For more biographical information on Minobe, see Miller, *Minobe Tatsukichi*, 22–42.

6 See Hegel, *Philosophy of Right*.

7 See Emerson's classic *State and Sovereignty in Modern Germany*, 12.

8 Ibid., 13.

9 Ibid., 14.

10 Nagao, "Hans Kelsen in Prewar Japan," 3.

11 Miller, *Minobe Tatsukichi*, 12.

12 Nagao, *Nihon Kempō Shisō Shi*, chap. 4 ("Minobe Tatsukichi no Ho Tetsugaku [The legal philosophy of Minobe Tatsukichi])" 142–94.

13 Ibid., 144–45.

14 Ibid., 147.

15 Miller, *Minobe Tatsukichi*, 9.

16 Ibid., 9.

17 Ibid., 42.

18 Ibid., 56.

19 Ibid.

20 Ibid.

21 Ibid., 58.

22 Ibid., 58–59.

23 Ibid.

24 Ibid., 60.

25 Ibid., 63.

26 Ibid.

27 Ibid., 63–64.

28 Ibid., 64.

29 Kelly, "Revisiting the Rights of Man," 30.

30 Miller, *Minobe Tatsukichi*, 73.

31 Ibid., 129.

32 Itō, *Commentaries on the Constitution of the Empire of Japan*. A reprint edition of this work was published in 1979 by University Publications of America; the quote appears on p. 102. It should be pointed out that Itō was only nominally the author of *Commentaries on the Constitution of the Empire of Japan*. The real author (Itō's ghostwriter) was Inoue Kowashi, who also received advice from a number of scholars.

33 Miller, *Minobe Tatsukichi*, 79

34 Ibid.

35 Ibid.

36 Ibid.

37 Ibid.

38 Ibid., 81.

39 Constitution of the Empire of Japan, preamble.

40 Ibid., chap. I, art. IV.

41 Ibid., art. III.

42 Miller, *Minobe Tatsukichi*, 89.

43 Constitution of the Empire of Japan, chap. IV, art. LV.

44 Miller, *Minobe Tatsukichi*, 95.

45 Ibid., 297. Miller noted that for thirteen years Ichiki had been "active both as a university professor and a high-ranking officer in the home ministry secretariat, a paragon of the then current professor-bureaucrat in his continual coming and going between lecture hall and ministry. He subsequently became a member of the house of peers, chief of the cabinet legislative bureau, minister of education and home minister (in the Okuma Cabinet of 1914), member of the privy council, imperial household minister (1933), and president of the privy council (1934)."

46 Ibid., 200.

47 The most authoritative account of this incident in the Japanese language is in Miyazawa, *Tennō Kikan Setsu Jiken*, which was republished in 1998.

48 Miller, *Minobe Tatsukichi*, 200.

49 Ibid., 200.

50 Ibid., 207.

51 Ibid., 210.

52 It should be noted that the idea of the emperor-as-sovereign theory of the state as the "orthodox" interpretation of the Constitution of the Empire of Japan was not Miller's original creation. He apparently accepted this explanation based on a number of Japanese writings he consulted on the matter.

53 Ienaga, *Nihon Kindai Kempō Shisō Shi Kenkyū*.

54 Ibid., 129–56.

55 Ibid., 129.

56 Ibid.

57 For example, in the chapter "The High Tide of Prewar Liberalism" in the very important and popularly used sourcebook *Sources of Japanese Tradition*, it is noted that educators, particularly university professors such as Yoshino Sakuzō and Minobe Tatsukichi, "provided the intellectual foundations for Japanese liberalism and their writings showed how the democratic ideal could be adapted to the Japanese scene. They also implanted liberal ideas in the minds of students who passed through their lecture halls, frequently taking the initiative in organizing student groups dedicated to the spread and implementation of these ideas": Tsunoda et al., *Sources of Japanese Tradition*, 882. That is to say, demo-

cratic "ideals" were never accepted, which was precisely an important contributing factor in the weakness of this "liberal" school of constitutional thought in prewar Japan.

58 Miller, *Minobe Tatsukichi*, 52.

59 Ibid., 200–201. I think there are some problems with this statement. First, it is somewhat misleading to say that Kakehi's participation in this debate was marginal. Second, it was Uesugi Shinkichi who was known chiefly for his writing on the moral basis of the Japanese state. This will be covered in chapter 6 of this study, but suffice it to say here that the opening line in Uesugi, *Kokka Shinron*, is: "The state is ultimate morality."

60 Nagao, "Hans Kelsen in Prewar Japan," 10. This was a paper professor Nagao presented at an international conference on Han Kelsen in St. Louis, Missouri, in March 2006.

61 Ibid., 10.

62 Ibid., 11.

63 Miyazawa, *Tennō Kikan Setsu Jiken*.

64 Ibid., 551.

65 Ibid.

66 Ibid., 552.

67 Ibid.

68 Ibid.

69 Ibid.

70 Nagao, "Hans Kelsen in Prewar Japan," 4.

71 Miyazawa, *Tennō Kikan Setsu Jiken*, 554.

72 Ibid.

73 Ibid., 555.

74 Ibid.

75 Ibid.

76 Ibid., 556.

77 Ibid., 560.

78 Ibid.

79 Anderson, *Imagined Communities*, 15.

80 Ibid., 16.

81 Ibid.

82 Ibid.

83 Ibid., 15.

84 Ibid., 78

85 Ibid., 25.

86 Ibid., 27.

87 Ibid., 23.

88 Ibid.

89 Ibid., 24.

90 Ibid., 80.

91 Ibid., 20.

92 Ibid., 78.

93 Anderson explains this ibid., chap. 6 ("Official Nationalism and Imperialism").

94 Ibid., 83.

95 Ibid., 82–83.

96 Ibid., 90.

97 Ibid., 91.

98 Ibid.

99 Ibid., 92.

100 It is worth pointing out that there are real, fundamental theoretical problems with Minobe's general theory of the state, especially when we link it to his interpretation of the constitution. For instance, one could argue on very solid grounds that, by removing the emperor from any direct responsibility in government and arguing that ministers of state were responsible to the parliament, Minobe in effect had made the parliament the sole direct ruling organ of the state. Thus, Japan could no longer be considered as having a constitutional monarchy in which the people exercised a degree of power *jointly* with the emperor. Moreover, it is also worth keeping in mind that, while almost all nineteenth-century state theorists in Germany were captivated by Hegel's state sovereignty, a few were not. Romeo M. Maurenbrecker and Heinrich Zopfl were among those few who denied the validity of Hegel's conception of the state as a sovereign person. Zopfl took the standpoint that this was theoretically untenable. On this point, it is worth quoting Emerson's statement on Zopfl at length:

> Zopfl made a more radical attack upon the theory [of the state as a sovereign person], accepting Maurenbrecker's historical conclusions, but denying that the prince, as the concrete reality of the will of the State, could be conceived as the mandatory or representative of the power of any other abstract "personality." The State, he argued could have personality only through, in, and with its ruler. Contrary to the then current view he asserted that the sovereignty of the State appeared only when it had been embodied in a personal sovereign. Until the personality of the State received concrete embodiment, Zopfl held it to be an abstract concept, incapable of willing or acting, and without meaning (Emerson, *State and Sovereignty in Modern Germany*, 32).

Ultimately, sovereignty had to reside in real human people because only real people can make decisions and be responsible for those decisions. That is to say, Hegel's state sovereignty theory could not easily resolve the vexing problem of where sovereignty, as the location of ultimate power *within* the state, should reside.

101 Tsunoda et al., *Sources of Japanese Tradition*, 241.

102 Kelly, "Revisiting the Rights of Man," introduction.

103 Ibid.,15.

104 Miller, *Minobe Tatsukichi*, 85.

105 Ibid., 95.

106 Ibid.

107 Bix, *Hirohito and the Making of Modern Japan*, 288.

108 Ibid., 291.

109 Ibid.

110 *Constitution of the Kingdom of Prussia*, translated and introduction by James Harvey Robinson, in the supplement to the *Annals of the American Academy of Political and Social Science* (September 1894).

111 *The Constitution of Italy*, translated and introduction by S. M. Lindsay and Leo S. Rowe, in supplement to the *Annuals of the American Academy of Political and Social Science* (November 1894).

4 Kita Ikki

1 In most textbooks on modern Japanese history, Kita Ikki is cited as the chief theoretician of ultranationalism in the prewar period. For example, Andrew Gordon notes that "older ultranationalists such as Uchida Ryōhei (1874–1937) had supported Japanese imperialism in Asia since the 1880s, and they continued to demand expansionism on the mainland to bolster the glory of imperial rule. But probably the most influential intellectual to promote such as vision was Kita Ikki": Gordon, *A Modern History of Japan*, 179. Gordon then goes on to cite Kita's *An Outline Plan for the Reorganization of Japan*.

2 Kita, *Kokutairon*, 5.

3 By the time Kita wrote this work, Japanese socialists had been around for nearly two decades. They appeared in Japan in the late 1880s and formed a socialist party for the first time in 1901, which was called the Social Democratic Party: see Wilson, *Radical Nationalist in Japan*, 12. See also Hoston, *The State, Identity, and the National Question in China and Japan*, esp. chap. 3.

4 Kita, *Kita Ikki Chosakushu*, 210.

5 Ibid., 209.

6 Ibid., 210. Hence, the use of the words "pure socialism" in the title of his work.

7 Ibid., 210.

8 Ibid.

9   Ibid., 211.

10   Ibid., 246.

11   Ibid., 211.

12   Ibid., 228. This term seems to have been widely used by prewar Japanese state theorists of all political persuasions. But the State Shintōists or theorists of the official state kokutai ideology held the idea that the state was a gigantic mystical body of the emperor where the individual within the state was a constituent element of the organic whole.

13   Ibid., 244.

14   Ibid., 244–45.

15   Ibid.

16   Ibid.

17   Ibid., 353.

18   Ibid., 341–71. Nagao Ryūichi writes that *"Ishin"* came from a passage in the Chinese classic *Da Xué* (Great Learning): "Zhou sui jiu bang qi ming wei xin." He translated this into Japanese as "Shū wa kyūchō naredomo sono mei (inochi) Orata mari." In English, this reads: "Chou is an ancient state, but its mandate, this is new." The character "I" of *"Ishin"* stands for the pronoun "this." Therefore, *"Ishin"* here means the reconstruction of the state under a new mandate. A direct translation of *"Ishin kakumei"* would be the awkward "reform revolution": see Nagao, *Nihon Kokka Shisō Shi Kenkyū*, 10.

19   Ibid., 267–91.

20   Ibid., 253.

21   Ibid.

22   Ibid.

23   Constitution of the Empire of Japan.

24   Kita, *Kita Ikki Chosakuchu*, 295.

25   Ibid., 295.

26   Ibid., 254. It is interesting to note that in *Kokutairon oyobi Junsei Shakaishugi* (*On the Kokutai and Pure Socialism*), Kita used the English word "Bible," which was written in *katakana*.

27   Kita, *Kita Ikki Chosakuchu*, 221.

28   Ibid., 298.

29   Ibid., 306. *"Bushi"* is the Japanese word for the military aristocracy that governed Japan from the twelfth century to the middle of the nineteenth century. English texts usually use the word "samurai," but that word does not include all members of the military aristocracy in all of Japan's feudal periods.

30   Ibid.

31   See Minear, *Japanese Tradition and Western Law*, 57.

32   Kita, *Kita Ikki Chosakushu*, 224.

33 Ibid., 224.

34 See Hozumi, *Kokumin Kyōiku*, 5. Hozumi defined the state as an ethnic group protected by a sovereign power. He further broke this down and said that the ethnic group consisted of "blood relatives of the same womb," and the "same womb" referred to the originator of the line of descent of the unbroken line of emperors, Amaterasu Ōmikami. The sovereign power was the emperor, who was "Amaterasu Ōmikami existing in the present": ibid., 12, 16.

35 Hozumi, *Kempō Teiyō*, 1. This was, in fact, this work's opening statement.

36 Kita, *Kita Ikki Chosakushu*, 214–15.

37 Ibid., 264.

38 Ibid., 263–65.

39 Ibid., 264.

40 See chapter on Empress Jingū in Aston, *Nihongi*.

41 Kita referred to the passage in the *Nihongi* that states: "Achi no Omi, ancestor of the Atahe of the Aya of Yamato, and his son Tsuga no Omi immigrated to Japan, bringing with them a company of their people of seventeen districts." A footnote at "Aya" explains: "Aya is the traditional Japanese rendering of Han, the name of the Chinese dynasty."

42 Kita, *Kita Ikki Chosakuchu*, 265.

43 See Gluck, *Japan's Modern Myths*, 103. Also see Teruhisa, *Educational Thought and Ideology in Modern Japan*, chap. 3 ("Education and Human Cultivation in the Emperor State").

44 According to Kōsaka Masaaki, Hozumi Yatsuka and Inoue Tetsujirō were the central figures in spreading the orthodox nationalist ideology in the first two decades of the twentieth century. Kōsaka writes: "Thus both Hozumi Yatsuka and Inoue Tetsujirō, as influential members charged with the revision of the national moral education textbooks in the period from 1908–1911, were active in the establishment and dissemination of familial-state nationalist thought." See Kōsaka, *Japanese Thought in the Meiji Era*, 377.

45 Kita, *Kita Ikki Chosakuchu*, 269.

46 Ibid., 269.

47 The Polish astronomer Nicolaus Copernicus (1473–1543) first theorized that the earth and other planets revolved around the sun. This, of course, was a challenge to the Ptolemaic planetary theory. Galileo received copies of Copernicus's works and went to Rome in 1615 to argue for the acceptance of the theory. But this angered Pope Paul V, who held Copernicus's theory to be contrary to the teachings of the Bible. Galileo was subsequently admonished and ordered to abandon Copernicus's theory and ordered never to teach it again. In 1616, Co-

pernicus's work was banned by Pope Paul V. However, Galileo wrote his *Dialogue Concerning the Two Chief World Systems* in 1632, which again challenged accepted doctrines about physics, as well as about astronomy, for which the Inquisition sentenced him to life imprisonment, and all his works were forbidden to be printed.

48 Kita, *Kita Ikki Chosakuchu*, 370–71.

49 For a discussion of this, see Ida, *Kindai Nihon no Shisō Kōzō*, 169–97. Also, Nagao Ryūichi suggested to me that "*henkyokuteki shakaishugi*" might be rendered into English as "excessive dominance of society over individuals" or "one-sided emphasis of society over individuals."

5 Mass Nationalism

1 Nagao Ryūichi, "Hans Kelsen in Japan," paper presented at the Hans Kelsen conference in St. Louis, Missouri, in March 2006.

2 Kuno, "The Meiji State, Minponshugi, and Ultranationalism."

3 Ibid., 61.

4 Ibid., 66.

5 Ibid., 63.

6 Ibid.

7 Ibid., 64.

8 Weber, *Economy and Society*, 2:1382.

9 Ibid., 2:1385.

10 Ibid., 2:1392.

11 See Bix, *Hirohito and the Making of Modern Japan*.

12 Kuno, "The Meiji State, Minponshugi, and Ultranationalism," 65.

13 Maruyama, "The Ideology and Dynamics of Japanese Fascism," 25–83.

14 Ibid., 63.

15 Ibid., 59.

16 Harootunian, "Introduction," 12.

17 Ibid., 17.

18 Ibid., 9–10.

19 Najita, "Some Reflections on Idealism in the Political Thought of Yoshino Sakuzō," 43.

20 Ibid.

21 See Silberman, "The Political Theory and Program of Yoshino Sakuzō," 316.

22 See Scheiner, "Socialism, Liberalism, and Marxism," 677.

23 Ibid., 677.

24 Uesugi, *Kokutai, Kempō oyobi Kensei*, 187–97.

25 Mitani Taiichiro, "Shisōka to shite no Yoshino Sakuzō" in *Nihon no Meicho*, Volume 48 (Tōkyō: Chūōkōronsha, 1972), 22.

26 Yoshino Sakuzō, "Minshūteki Jii Undō no Ronzu" in *Nihon no Meicho,* Volume 48, 73–74.

27 Ibid.

28 Ibid., 78–79.

29 Yoshino, "On the Meaning of Constitutional Government and the Methods by Which It Can Be Perfected," 228.

30 Silberman, "The Political Theory and Program of Yoshino Sakuzō," 316.

31 Ibid.

32 Najita, "Some Reflections on Idealism in the Political Thought of Yoshino Sakuzō," 31.

33 Yoshino, "On the Meaning of Constitutional Government and the Methods by Which It Can Be Perfected," 218.

34 Scheiner, "Socialism, Liberalism, and Marxism," 683.

35 Ibid., 685.

36 Kuno, "The Meiji State, Minponshugi, and Ultranationalism," 73.

37 Kita, *Nihon Kaizō Hōan Taikō.*

38 Ibid., 1–16.

39 Ibid., 15.

40 Ibid., 1.

41 Tsunoda et al., *Sources of Japanese Tradition,* 267.

42 Kurosaki, *Renketsu,* 65.

43 Ibid., 66.

44 Ibid., 68.

45 Christopher W. A. Szpilman, "Kita Ikki and the Politics of Coercion," *Modern Asian Studies* 36, no. 2 (2002), 475.

46 Ibid., 488.

47 See Wilson, *Radical Nationalist in Japan,* 133. I might note here that I had a fascinating conversation with Nagao Ryūichi on March 11, 2006, during a visit we made together to the Jamestown Settlement in Virginia. While we were relaxing after lunch and discussing the state theories of Minobe Tatsukichi, Miyazaki Toshiyoshi, Hozumi Yatsuka, and Kita Ikki in comparative context, he admitted that Kita was being used as a scapegoat for the real radical Shinto ultranationalists who inspired the terrorism in the 1930s.

48 Kuno, "The Meiji State, Minponshugi, and Ultranationalism," 72.

49 Katō, "Taisho Democracy as the Pre-Stage for Japanese Militarism," 217–18.

50 These are Aristotle A. Kallis's words, used to introduce an excerpt from Griffin, *The Nature of Fascism.*

51 Ibid., 211.

52 Katō, "Taisho Democracy as the Pre-Stage for Japanese Militarism," 229.

53 Ibid., 239.

54 Ibid., 226.

55 Ortega y Gasset, *The Revolt of the Masses*, 22–23.

56 Griffin, *The Nature of Fascism*, 154.

6 Uesugi Shinkichi

1 In "Extinction du Pauperism; Oeuvre de Napolean III," quoted in Kulstein, *Napoleon III and the Working Class*, 5.

2 Pyle, *The Making of Modern Japan*, 160.

3 Gordon, *Labor and Imperial Democracy in Prewar Japan*, 1. Gordon states: "In the first two decades of the twentieth century, crowds of city-dwellers took to the streets of Tōkyō and launched the most vigorous urban protests yet seen in Japan. At least nine times from the Hibiya riot of 1905 to the rice riots of 1918, angry Tōkyōites attacked police-men, police stations, and national government offices, smashed street-car windows and beat the drivers, marched on the Diet, and stormed the offices of major newspapers. They destroyed public and private property, launching both symbolic and substantive attacks on the in-stitutions of the established order of imperial Japan."

4 Okamoto, "The Emperor and the Crowd."

5 Pittau, *Political Thought in Early Meiji Japan, 1868–1889*, 201.

6 This in Gordon's term: see Gordon, *Labor and Imperial Democracy in Prewar Japan*, 9.

7 Hegel, *The Philosophy of History*, 104.

8 Ibid.

9 Ibid. 120.

10 Ida quoting Miyamoto Moritarō in *Uesugi Shinkichi*, 59.

11 Ibid., 203.

12 Ibid., 207.

13 Ibid., 207, 211.

14 Miller, *Minobe Tatsukichi*, 301–2.

15 Ibid., 202.

16 Satō, *Nichibei Kaisen no Shinjitsu*, 264.

17 Ibid.

18 Ibid., 267.

19 Ida, *Uesugi Shinkichi*, 289.

20 Morris, *Nationalism and the Right Wing in Japan*, 371.

21 Ibid., 371.

22 Storry, *Double Patriots*, 320–21.

23 For more information on the internal structure of these two early ultranationalist societies, see Byas, *Government by Assassination*, chap. 14 ("Leaders and Gangs"). For example, Byas noted that in the first

meeting of the Black Dragon Society (Kokuryūkai), only fourteen people were present. The organization's purpose was to make propaganda for war with the Russian empire and to advocate extending Japan's sovereignty to the Amur River, the boundary between Siberia and Manchuria. He further noted that when a meeting of the Black Dragon Society was held in 1906, five years later, only a dozen people attended. "Nothing remained of the membership but a handful of the faithful who could not fit into any orthodox party or movement": ibid., 197. By contrast, mass ultranationalist societies such as the Dai Nippon Seisantō (Great Japan Production Party), organized in 1931 by Uchida; the Jimmukai; Kokuhonsha; and Kokusuikai all had memberships of more than a hundred thousand of people. In other words, mass ultranationalist societies emerged in the post-Meiji period.

24 Ida, *Uesugi Shinkichi*, 292.

25 Ibid.

26 Ibid.

27 There is still very little available about Uesugi Shinkichi by Japanese scholars and by Western scholars writing in the English language. To my knowledge, Ida Terutoshi was the first Japanese scholar to write a full-length book on Uesugi in the postwar period. Dealing with Uesugi's radical ideas is still taboo among Japanese scholars. However, I am certain that no Japanese scholar with in-depth knowledge of Uesugi and his writings would characterize him as a conservative.

28 For the meaning of this group, see ibid., 296–97.

29 Morris, *Nationalism and the Right Wing in Japan*, 274.

30 Ida, *Uesugi Shinkichi*, 297.

31 Ibid., 299.

32 Ibid., 298.

33 Maruyama, "The Ideology and Dynamics of Japanese Fascism," 349–50.

34 Storry, *The Double Patriots*, 36.

35 Morris, *Nationalism and the Right Wing in Japan*, 441. For a full list of the violent activities in which Akao was involved from the 1920s to the 1980s, see Ino *Hyōden*.

36 Schmitt, *The Crisis of Parliamentary Democracy*, 22.

37 Ida, *Uesugi Shinkichi*, 289.

38 Ibid., 289.

39 Uesugi, *Kokka Shinron*.

40 Ibid., 5–6.

41 Ibid., 7.

42 Ibid., 8.

43 Ibid., 5–8.

44 Ibid., 93.

45   Ibid., 93–94.

46   Ibid., 60.

47   Ibid., 62–65.

48   Ibid., 73–75.

49   Ibid., 84.

50   Ibid., 40.

51   See ibid., chap. 12 ("Tennō").

52   Ibid., 129.

53   Uesugi, *Kokutai, Kempō oyobi Kensei*, 2.

54   Ibid., 8.

55   Ibid., 257–91.

56   Ibid., 257.

57   Ibid.

58   Ibid., 258.

59   Ibid., 276.

60   Ibid. 280.

61   See Arendt, *The Origins of Totalitarianism*, part 3 ("Totalitarianism").

7   Kakehi Katsuhiko

1   Maruyama, "The Ideology and Dynamics of Japanese Fascism," 27.

2   The differences between Uesugi's ultranationalist ideology was, as we shall find out in this chapter, in broad terms, much like that we find between the Imperial Way Faction and the Control Faction in the military bureaucracy.

3   In correspondence with Suzuki Sadami, director of the International Center for Japanese Studies in Kyoto, I asked him why there has been no major scholarly work on Kakehi in postwar Japan. He said that Kakehi Katsuhiko has been taboo even among Japanese researchers.

4   Breuilly, *Nationalism and the State*, 290.

5   Gordon, *Labor and Imperial Democracy in Prewar Japan*, 3.

6   Ibid., 33.

7   Ibid.

8   There is a dispute about when fascism emerged in Europe. Zeev Sternhell argues that it emerged before World War One in France: see Sternhell, *Neither Right nor Left*.

9   Suzuki, *Nihon no Bunka Nashonarizumu*, 179.

10   Ibid., 182.

11   Ibid., 209.

12   Griffin, *The Nature of Fascism*, 49.

13   Kakehi, *Kokka no Kenkyū*, 1.

14   Ibid., 3.

15 Ibid., 4.
16 Ibid.
17 Holtom, *The National Faith of Japan*, 21.
18 Ibid., 14–15.
19 Ibid., 14.
20 Ibid.
21 Ibid., 15.
22 Kakehi, *Kokka no Kenkyū*, 4.
23 Ibid.
24 Ibid., 5.
25 Ibid., 27–79.
26 Ibid., 36–37.
27 Ibid., 52.
28 Ibid., 10–11.
29 Ibid., 11.
30 I am using "fascism" here in the generic sense to refer to both Italian Fascism and German National Socialism.
31 Weber, *Varieties of Fascism*, 35.
32 Kakehi, *Kokka no Kenkyū*, 41.
33 Ibid., 41–42.
34 Ibid., 77–78.
35 Ibid., 55.
36 Ibid.
37 Ibid., 216.
38 Ibid., 217.
39 Ibid., 12.
40 Ibid., 316–43.
41 Ibid., 326.
42 Ibid., 149–209.
43 Mosse, *The Crisis of German Ideology*, 24.
44 Ibid., 15.
45 Kakehi, *Kokka no Kenkyū*, 29–30.
46 Holtom, *Modern Japan and Shintō Nationalism*, 55.
47 This article, titled *Jinja Sūhai to Dōtoku teki Igi*, appeared in the December 1920 issue of *Chūō Kōron*.
48 Ibid., 54.
49 Kakehi, *Kokka no Kenkyū*, 249.
50 Ehime Kyōiku Kyōkai Onsen Bukai, *Kō Shintō* (Ehime: Fukuda Printing, 1916), 18.
51 Kakehi, *Kokka no Kenkyū*, 232–36.
52 Ibid.
53 Joseph de Maistre, *Study on Sovereignty*, 108.
54 See Nagao, *Nihon Kokka Shisō Shi Kenkyū*, 40.

55 Kakehi, *Kokka no Kenkyū*, 316.

56 Ibid., 331. It is worth noting that Kakehi gave speeches to Christian groups in Japan as well as to Buddhist groups.

57 Ibid., 248–49.

58 Ibid., 13.

59 Ibid., 12.

60 Kakehi, *Dai Nihon Teikoku Kempō no Konpongi*. Another translation of the title of this book might be "Fundamental Principles of the Constitution of the Empire of Great Japan." I have used the word "Great" here for emphasis. Normally the word "Great" is not translated into English, but it is actually there in the Japanese.

61 Ibid., 251.

62 Ibid., 254.

63 Ibid., 29

65 Ibid., 255.

66 Constitution of the Empire of Great Japan, chap. 2 ("Rights and Duties of Subjects"). It might be noted here that in most translations of the Meiji Constitution the Japanese word *Dai* (Great) is usually left out of the translation.

67 Ibid., chap. 6 ("Finance"), art. 67.

68 Kakehi, *Dai Nihon Teikoku Kempō no Konpongi*, 256.

69 Ibid., 270.

70 Constitution of the Empire of Japan, chap. I, art. IV.

71 Kakehi, *Dai Nihon Teikoku Kempō no Konpongi*, 270. The translation from the *Nihongi* here is from Aston, *Nihongi*, 197–98.

72 Kakehi, *Dai Nihon Teikoku Kempō no Konpongi*, 281.

73 Ibid., 277.

74 Ibid.

75 Ibid.

76 Ibid., 293.

77 Ibid., 281.

78 Ibid., 292.

79 Ibid., 291.

80 Ibid., 292.

81 Ibid., 294.

82 Constitution of the Empire of Japan, art. 28.

83 Kakehi, *Dai Nihon Teikoku Kempō no Konpongi*, 293.

84 Ibid., 295.

85 Ibid. I assume he was referring to the Twelve Tribes of Israel.

86 Nagao Ryūichi was a leading scholar of Japanese state theory and constitutional law at the University of Tokyo.

87 Nagao, *Nihon Kokka Shisō Shi Kenkyū*, 33–34.

88 Ibid., 34.

89 Ibid.

90 Ibid.

91 Ibid., 36.

92 Ibid.

93 Ibid.

94 Ibid., 37.

95 Arendt, *The Origins of Totalitarianism*, 392.

96 Ibid.

97 Ibid., 325.

98 Mosse, *The Crisis of German Ideology*, 285.

99 *Hirohito and Making of Modern Japan*, 441.

100 Arendt, *The Origins of Totalitarianism*, 422.

101 Kakehi, *Kō Shintō Taigi*, 44.

102 Ibid., 63.

103 Rocco, *The Political Doctrine of Fascism*.

104 See Reynolds, "Pecular Characteristics," 175.

105 Rosenberg, *The Myth of the Twentieth Century*, 296.

106 Mosse, *The Crisis of German Ideology*, 31. Mosse noted that "Chamberlain himself was a great admirer of Hitler. In a dramatic scene, Hitler visited the paralyzed and dying apostle of Germanism and kissed his hands. But Chamberlain died in 1927 and did not see the triumph of his prophecies."

107 Rosenberg, *The Myth of the Twentieth Century*, 3–4.

108 Ibid., 5.

109 Ibid., 393.

110 Ibid., 350.

111 Ibid., 342.

112 Ibid., 343.

113 Ibid., 351.

114 Ibid.

115 See Skya, "Fascist Encounters."

116 Rosenberg, *The Myth of the Twentieth Century*, 430.

117 Ibid., 432.

8   Terrorism

1   Byas, *Government by Assassination*. I might also note that Gerald Curtis wrote, "There have been times in Japan's modern political history marked by harmony and social peace, and periods where instability and conflict predominated. One of the standard Western-language works about Japanese politics in the 1930s was titled *Government by Assassination*. Although Japanese place a high value on consensus building, the

'spirit of harmony' (wa no seishin), and the avoidance of overt conflict, modern Japanese history is replete with intrigue, violence, and radical change": Curtis, *The Logic of Japanese Politics*, 11.

2 Curtis, *The Logic of Japanese Politics*, x.

3 Ibid., 19.

4 Ibid.

5 Reynolds, "Peculiar Characteristics," 161, 165.

6 Ibid., 158.

7 Laqueur, *Voices of Terror*, 1–2.

8 Ibid., 2.

9 Ibid.

10 Hoffman, *Inside Terrorism*, 15.

11 Tendō, *Uyoku Undō*, 26.

12 Storry, *The Double Patriots*, 11. Storry noted that "the leaders of the Genyōsha were assured by the Matsukata cabinet that the administration would pursue a strong foreign policy, and greatly increase the budget for the armed forces," and that "this unofficial agreement between the Home Ministry [of the Matsukata cabinet] and the Genyōsha is of interest; for it was the first notable example of the close, unavowed co-operation, over a limited period and for a special purpose, between the Home Ministry and the most powerful nationalist organizations."

13 Ibid., 44.

14 Tendō, *Uyoku Undō*, 90.

15 Ibid.

16 The literal translation of *Sakura Kai* is Society of the Cherry, but it is usually translated into English as the Cherry Blossom Society to denote reference to the life of the cherry blossom among Japanese ultranationalists.

17 Tendō, *Uyoku Undō*, 155. There are many books in Japanese that discuss this event.

18 Ienaga, *The Pacific War, 1931–1945*, 64.

19 Tendō, *Uyoku Undō*, 90.

20 Ibid.

21 Ibid., 91.

22 *2–26 Jiken to Shōwa Ishin*, 60.

23 Byas, *Government by Assassination*, 121.

24 Ibid.

25 Ibid.

26 Yamagata Aritomo's *Imperial Precepts to Soldiers and Sailors* (1882) instructed all members of the military to "neither be led astray by current opinions nor meddle in politics": quoted in Tsunoda et al., *Sources of Japanese Tradition*, 199. I find it puzzling that this document is not

included in the 2000 edition of this very important book of primary documents in modern Japanese history.

27   Miller, *Minobe Tatsukichi*, 211.

28   Ibid.

29   Storry, *The Double Patriots*, 44.

30   I think that the February 26, 1936, Incident should more appropriately be referred to in literature on this subject as the February 26, 1936, Insurrection, because this was an insurrection—an act of open revolt against civil authority or constituted government.

31   Takahashi, *Ni-Nijūroku Jiken*, 153.

32   Ibid., 153–58.

33   Ibid., 154. Watanabe had stated, "Tōshu to wa yūkitai taru ichi kikan de aru. Tennō o kikan to aogitatematsuru to omoeba nan no futsugō mo nai de wa nai ka."

34   Hoffman, *Inside Terrorism*.

35   Ibid., 87.

36   Ibid.

37   Ibid.

38   Ibid., 87–88.

39   Ibid., 88.

40   Takahashi, *Ni-Nijūroku Jiken*, 155.

41   Hoffman, *Inside Terrorism*, 94.

42   See Bawer, *While Europe Slept*.

43   Takahashi, *Ni-Nijūroku Jiken*, 163–67.

44   Byas, *Government by Assassination*, 46.

45   Ibid., 47.

46   Ibid.

47   Hoffman, *Inside Terrorism*, 95.

48   This is quoted from a lecture given in Lahore, April 13, 1939, by Syed Abul ala Maududi: in Laqueur, *Voices of Terror*, 398.

49   Juergensmeyer, *Terror in the Mind of God*. "Cosmic War" is the title of chapter 8 of this book.

50   Byas, *Government by Assassination*, 101.

51   Ibid.

52   Ibid., 113.

53   Juergensmeyer, *Terror in the Mind of God*, 7. These are the words of Juergensmeyer in a discussion how violence is motivated by religion in chapter 1 ("Terror and God").

54   Byas, *Government by Assassination*, 123–24.

55   Juergensmeyer, *Terror in the Mind of God*, 219.

56   Ibid.

57   Ibid.

58   Tendō, *Uyoku Undō*, 103.

59 Ibid., 104.

60 Rapoport, "Sacred Terror," 103. Rapoport considered the assassination of Egyptian President Anwar Sadat a case of religious terrorism, since the group Al-Jihad, led by Abd Al-Salam Faraj, said it had killed Sadat because it wanted Egypt to be governed by Islam's sacred law.

61 Peattie, *Ishiwara Kanji and Japan's Confrontation with the West.*

62 Seika, *Senzen: Shōwa no Nashonarizumu no Sho Mondai*, 48.

63 Ibid.

64 Lewis, *The Crisis of Islam*, 137.

65 I think that the terms "radical Shintō fundamentalism" and "radical Shintō ultranationalism" can be used interchangeably as long as it is understood that radical Shintō fundamentalism is the revolutionary, mass-based radical religion of nationalism that was articulated by theorists such as Uesugi Shinkichi and Kakehi Katsuhiko.

66 For this information on the activities of Tōyama in support of Asian nationalists, see Tendō, *Uyoku Undō*, 28.

67 These are the words Griffin used to describe the nature of the modern German nation-state in *The Nature of Fascism*, 85.

68 Tendō, *Uyoku Undō*, 32–32.

69 Ibid., 32.

70 Suzuki, *Nihon no Bunka Nashonarizumu*, 157.

71 Tendō, *Uyoku Undō*, 53.

72 Doak, *A History of Nationalism in Modern Japan*, 241.

73 Maruyama, "The Ideology and Dynamics of Japanese Fascism," 25–83.

74 Ibid., 38.

75 *Bessatsu Rekishi Dokuhon Senki Shireezu 35: 2–26 Jiken to Shōwa Ishin* (Tōkyō: Shin Jinbutsu Orai Sha, 1997); Hosoka Masayasu, "Seinen Shōko ga Yuso shita Kokka Zo," 14.

76 See Kim, *The Tears of My Soul.*

77 Crenshaw, "The Logic of Terrorism."

78 Byas, *Government by Assassination*, 34.

79 Tendō, *Uyoku Undō*, 88.

80 Ibid.

81 Byas, *Government by Assassination*, 22–23.

82 Ibid., 23.

83 Ibid.

84 Ibid., 26.

85 Ibid.

86 Ibid., 126.

87 Ibid., 124.

88 Ibid., 125.

89 Tendō, *Uyoku Undō*, 89.

90 Merari, "The Readiness to Kill and Die."

91 Tendō, *Uyoku Undō*, 107.

92 Storry, *The Double Patriots*, 191.

93 Lory, *Japan's Military Masters*, 196.

94 Ibid., 197.

95 Honda Katsuichi quoted a section from Tokugawa Yoshichika's book *The Last Lord* (Tokyo, 1973): "Several days after I finished my inquiries and returned to Japan, the Japanese military carried out a huge slaughter in Nanjing. When I say 'slaughter,' I'm not talking about cutting down ten people or even a hundred people. These days, I'm sometimes asked whether the Nanjing Massacre was a fabrication, but I heard at the time that tens of thousands of Chinese civilians had been killed or injured. Fujita Isamu told me that the ringleader of the massacre was Lieutenant Colonel Chō Isamu, a member of Commander Matsui Iwane's inner circle. I was also well acquainted with him": Honda, *The Nanjing Massacre*, 169.

96 Reynolds, "Peculiar Characteristics," 161.

97 Takahashi, *Ni-Nijūroku Jiken*, 155.

98 Storry, *The Double Patriots*, 140.

99 Hayashi and Cook, *Kogun*, 230. Muto was executed as a "Class A" war criminal on December 23, 1948. He was held responsible for the Nanjing Massacre and atrocities in Indonesia.

100 Storry, *The Double Patriots*, 193.

101 Wilson, "A New Look at the Problem of Japanese Fascism."

102 Ibid., 409.

103 Tucker, "Towards a Comparative Politics of Movement-Regimes"; Wilson, "A New Look at the Problem of Japanese Fascism," 409.

104 Wilson, "A New Look at the Problem of Japanese Fascism," 409.

105 Ibid., 412.

106 Pyle, *The Making of Modern Japan*, 135.

107 Ibid., 191.

108 Hane, *Modern Japan*, 338.

109 Bix, *Hirohito and the Making of Modern Japan*, 492.

110 Reynolds, "Peculiar Characteristics," 170.

111 Butow, *Tōjō and the Coming of the War*, 252.

112 Bix, *Hirohito and the Making of Modern Japan*, 509.

113 Ibid., 510.

114 Ibid., 513.

115 Butow, *Tōjō and the Coming of the War*, 251.

116 Duus and Okimoto, "Fascism and the History of Pre-War Japan."

117 Ibid., 65.

118 Ibid., 66.

119 Kamishima, "Mental Structure of the Emperor System."

120 Duus and Okimoto, "Fascism and the History of Pre-War Japan," 68.

121 Ibid.
122 Ibid., 69.
123 Ibid., 68
124 Ibid., 70.

9   Orthodoxation of a Holy War

1 Huntington, *The Clash of Civilizations and the Remaking of World Order*, 21.
2 Stavrianos, *The World since 1500*, 185.
3 Ferguson, *The War of the World*, xxxiv.
4 In the well-used sourcebook *Sources of Japanese Tradition* (Tsunoda et al.), *Fundamentals of Our National Polity* is interpreted as a "conservative affirmation" of conservative State Shintō control over the radical ultranationalist movement. I strongly disagree. There are many problems with the way nationalist thought is introduced in that volume. First, passages from Kita Ikki were introduced in *Sources of Japanese Tradition* as *the* prime source of radical nationalism. As indicated in this study, Kita's thought was not at the heart of the radical Shintō ultranationalist movement. Second, most of the authors of *Fundamentals of Our National Polity* were radical Shintō ultranationalists, as in the case of Yamada Yoshio and Kōno Seizō.
5 Hall, *Kokutai no Hongi*, 59.
6 Ibid., 165.
7 Ibid.
8 Ibid., 161–62.
9 Ibid., 163.
10 Ibid., 51.
11 Ibid.
12 Ibid., 52.
13 Ibid.
14 Ibid., 53.
15 Ibid., 54.
16 Lloyd, *The Ambitions of Curiosity*, 5.
17 Hall, *Kokutai no Hongi*, 80.
18 Ibid., 81–82. I have changed Gauntlett's translation here slightly. I prefer translating the character words *botsuga kiitsu* as "dying to the self and returning to [the] One," as done in Tsunoda et al., *Sources of Japanese Tradition*, 281, rather than as "self-effacement and a return to [the] one," as Gauntlett translated them. What is implied here is more than just self-effacement. It means the annihilation of the self and

returning to the mystical body of the emperor, who is in turn really Amaterasu Ōmikami living in the present.

19 *Kokutai no Hongi*, 88–89.

20 Ibid., 90.

21 Ibid., 91.

22 Ibid.

23 Gauntlett's English translation of the title of this chapter is "Harmony and Truth," the word "truth" being a translation of the Japanese word "*makoto*." I prefer to translate "*makoto*" as "sincerity."

24 *Kokutai no Hongi*, 93.

25 Ibid., 97–98.

26 Ibid., 105.

27 Ibid.

28 Ibid.

29 Ibid., 113.

30 Ibid.

31 Ibid., 115.

32 Ibid., 123.

33 Ibid., 132.

34 Ibid.

35 Ibid., 135.

36 Ibid., 150.

37 Juergensmeyer, *Terror in the Mind of God*, 149.

38 Ibid., 149–50.

39 *Kokutai no Hongi*, 175.

40 Ibid., 176.

41 Ibid.

42 Ibid., 178.

43 Ibid., 179.

44 Ibid.

45 Ibid.

46 Ibid., 181.

47 Hall, *Kokutai no Hongi*, 155.

48 *Fundamentals of Our National Polity*, 183.

49 Ibid., 144–45.

50 Ibid., 147.

51 I will mention in passing here that I spent more than ten years living, working, and studying in Japan from 1974 to 1984. I have had various opportunities to have discussions with Japanese who might be characterized as ultranationalists. I have found that the one thing they continually boast about is that the Europeans (even the German Nazis) could not totally eradicate the value of the individual as the Japanese have done.

52 Ibid., 152.

53 Arendt, *The Origins of Totalitarianism*, 326.

54 Juergensmeyer, *Terror in the Mind of God*, 152.

55 Hall, *Kokutai no Hongi*, 5.

56 Brownlee, *Japanese Historians and the National Myths, 1600–1945*, 134. According to Brownlee,

> In the 1930s, the extirpation of communism and the censorship of liberal expression were accompanied by a positive effort to promote emperor-centered nationalism as an exclusive ideology. Throughout the twentieth century, the Ministry of Education had taught the children of Japan about the divine origins of Japan, the special qualities of its emperor and its people, and the need for each person to contribute sincerely and voluntarily to the greater glory of Japan. In the 1930s, though, this approach proved insufficient. Authorities were shocked by the extent of communist belief among university students, revealed by the presence of students among those arrested in March 1928. Study commissions were set up with a view to educational reform, and comprehensive measures were taken. Among them was the establishment in 1932 of the Research Centre on Japanese Spiritual Culture [Kokumin Seishin Bunka Kenkyujo], a well-funded organization that acquired much prestige.

57 Ibid., 144.

58 Iijima Tadao, "Nihon no Jugaku" in *Kokutai no Hongi Kaisetsu Sosho*, No. 2, ed. Educational Affairs Bureau, Ministry of Education (Tokyo: Cabinet Printing Bureau, 1939), 102.

59 Holtom, *The National Faith of Japan*, 58.

60 Kōno Shozō, "Waga *Kokutai* to Shinto" in *Kokutai no Hongi Kaisetsu Sosho*, No. 3, ed. Educational Affairs Bureau, Ministry of Education (Tokyo: Cabinet Printing Bureau, 1939).

61 Ibid., 1.

62 Ibid.

63 Ibid.

64 Ibid., 3.

65 Holtom, *Modern Japan and Shintō Nationalism*, 56.

66 Kono, "Waga Kokutai to Shintō," 4.

67 Ibid., 2.

68 Ibid., 3.

69 Ibid.

70 Ibid., 4.

71 Holtom, *Modern Japan and Shintō Nationalism*, 19–20.

72 Ibid., 24–25.

73 Ibid., 22.
74 Hoffer, *The True Believer*.
75 Ibid., xii.
76 Ōgushi Toyō, "Teikoku Kempō to Shinmin no Yokusan [The Imperial Constitution and the Subjects' Assistance]," in *Kokutai no Hongi Kaisetsu Sōsho*, no. 7, ed. Educational Affairs Bureau, Ministry of Education (Tokyo: Cabinet Printing Bureau, 1940).
77 Ibid., 21.
78 Ibid., 7.
79 Ibid., 8.
80 Ibid., 6.
81 Ibid., 43.
82 Ibid., 43.
83 Ibid., 51–65.
84 Ibid., 53.
85 Ibid., 53.
86 Ibid., 64.
87 Ibid.
88 I have used the translation in Tsunoda et al., *Sources of Japanese Tradition*, 140.
89 Hisamatsu Senichi, "Waga Fudo, Kokuminsei to Bungaku" [Our Climate, Nationality and Literature], *Kokutai no Hongi Kaisetsu Sōsho*, ed. Educational Affairs Bureau, Ministry of Education (Tokyo: Cabinet Printing Bureau, 1939), 43.
90 Ibid., 60.
91 Ibid.
92 Ibid., 71.
93 Hall, *Kokutai no Hongi*, 82.
94 Ibid.
95 Tsunoda et al., *Sources of Japanese Tradition*, 281.
96 Nippon Gakujutsu Shinkokai, *Manyōshū*, 151.
97 Yamada Yoshio, "Chōkoku no Seishin [The Spirit of the Founding of the Nation]," in *Kokutai no Hongi Kaisetsu Sōsho*, ed. Educational Affairs Bureau, Ministry of Education (Tokyo: Cabinet Printing Bureau, 1939).
98 In the original text of *Kokutai no Hongi*, this word was also pronounced "teikoku."
99 Tsunoda et al., *Sources of Japanese Tradition*, 139.
100 Hall, *Kokutai no Hongi*, 59.
101 Yamada, "The Spirit of the Founding of the Nation," 6.
102 Hall, *Kokutai no Hongi*, 62.
103 Ibid., 62.

104 Yamada, "The Spirit of the Founding of the Nation," 9.
105 Ibid., 14.
106 Ibid., 69.
107 Ibid., 69–70.
108 Ibid., 69.
109 Hoffer, *The True Believer*, 7.
110 Ibid., 7.
111 Ibid., 8.
112 Ibid., 62.
113 Ibid., 63.
114 Yamada, "The Spirit of the Founding of the Nation," 57.
115 Ibid.
116 Ibid., 70.
117 Hall, *Kokutai no Hongi*, 65.
118 Maruyama, "Theory and Psychology of Ultra-Nationalism," 21.

Conclusion

1 Dower, *War without Mercy*, 78–79.
2 Lewis, *The Crisis of Islam*.
3 Ibid., 120.
4 Ibid., 128.
5 Bodansky, *Bin Laden*, 3.
6 Ibid., 4–5.
7 Ibid., xi.
8 This dispute arose from a proposal by Takatomi Senge (1845–1918), chief priest of the Grand Shrine of Izumo, who maintained that O-kuni-nushi-no-mikoto should be added to the official pantheon consisting of Amaterasu Ōmikami and the three creation deities Ame-no-minaka-nushi-no-kami, Takami-musubi-kami, and Kami-musubi-no-kami, who were the center of worship of the Great Promulgation Campaign, a movement by the Meiji government from 1870 to 1884 to articulate a national religion. This was challenged by priests of the Grand Shrine of Ise. The dispute spread throughout Japan.
9 Quoted in Hall, *Kokutai no Hongi*, 6.
10 Yamada, "Shinkoku Nihon no Shimei to Kokumin no Kakugo," 3.
11 Ibid., 2.
12 Ibid.
13 Ibid.
14 Bix, *Hirohito and the Making of Modern Japan*, 306–7.
15 Yamada, "Shinkoku Nihon no Shimei to Kokumin no Kakugo," 8.
16 Ienaga, *The Pacific War, 1931–1945*, 3–12.

17 Ibid., 85.
18 Ibid., 3.
19 Ibid., 86–87.
20 Ibid., 87.
21 Cook and Cook, *Japan at War*, 23.
22 Yamada, "Shinkoku Nihon no Shimei to Kokumin no Kakugo," 5.
23 Ibid.
24 Ibid., 12.
25 Ibid., 9.
26 Aston, *Nihongi*, 131.
27 Yamada, "Shinkoku Nihon no Shimei to Kokumin no Kakugo," 16.
28 Lewis, *The Crisis of Islam*, 138.
29 Ibid.
30 Ibid., 162.
31 Ibid., 164.
32 The Imperial Rule Assistant Political Association (Yokusan Seiji Kai) was formed in 1942 in conjunction with the Imperial Rule Association as the sole legal political party. The Imperial Rule Assistant Political Association itself was formally organized in 1940 following the dissolution of all political parties in the Japanese parliament. Its purpose was guarantee that the parliament was totally cooperative with the political leadership and promote national unity.
33 *Chūō Kōron*, December 1943, 30.
34 An excellent work on the philosophy of the Imperial Way is Satō, *Philosophy of the Imperial Way*, which was written in 1941, at the beginning of the Pacific War. Although his philosophy is not covered in this study, he was a leading ultranationalist scholar of the 1940s. He taught at Kōgakkan University.
35 *Chūō Kōron*, 33.
36 Ibid., 31.
37 Ibid., 32.
38 Ibid.
39 Ibid., 31.
40 Ibid.
41 Ibid.
42 Arjomand, *The Turban for the Crown*, 210.
43 Ibid., 82.
44 Ibid., 85.
45 Ibid., 100.
46 Ibid., 101.
47 Holtom, *Modern Japan and Shintō Nationalism*, 22.
48 Ibid., 22.
49 Ibid., 27.

50 Ibid., 11.

51 Dower, *Embracing Defeat*, 233–34.

52 Holtom, *Modern Japan and Shintō Nationalism*, 153–54.

53 Ibid. 157.

54 Ibid., 158–59.

55 Dower, *Empire and Aftermath*, 278.

56 Holtom, *Modern Japan and Shintō Nationalism*, 162.

57 Dower, *War without Mercy*.

58 Ibid., 289.

59 Ibid., 277.

60 Ibid., 267.

61 Ibid., 273

62 I should point out that the word "fundamentalism" in this study has two meanings. First, it refers to the historical meaning of the word, which dates back to the early part of the twentieth century when American Protestant evangelists sought to clarify the "fundamentals" of the Christian faith in the face of what they perceived to have been the onslaught of secularism and to reassert the truths and doctrines of the inerrant Bible. In a comparable way, the Shintō fundamentalists labored to reassert the Shintō truths and doctrines, integrating them into their interpretations of the Constitution of the Empire of Japan and using them to develop elaborate theories of state. Hozumi Yatsuka, Uesugi Shinkichi, Kakehi Katsuhiko, and other Shintō ultranationalist theorists did all this in the face of what they perceived to be the weakening of the traditional conception of the Japanese state by rational, Western-oriented emperor-as-organ theorists in particular, and by the secularization spreading in Japanese politics and society in general. Second, fundamentalism refers to the fanatical commitment to act in radical ways because of religious conviction.

63 This story is quoted in full from Irokawa, "The Emperor System as a Spiritual Structure," 305–6.

64 Ibid.

65 Ibid., 305.

Select Bibliography

Akita, George. *Foundations of Constitutional Government in Modern Japan 1900*. Cambridge: Harvard University Press, 1967.

Anderson, Benedict. *Imagined Communities: Reflections on the Origins and Spread of Nationalism*. London: Verso, 1987.

Antoni, Klaus. *Shintō und die Konzeption des japanischen Nationalwesens (kokutai): Der religiöse Traditionalismus in Neuzeit und Moderne Japans*. Leiden: Brill, 1998.

———. "Karagokoro: Opposing the 'Chinese Spirit': On the Nativistic Roots of Japanese Fascism." In *Japan in the Fascist Era*, ed. E. Bruce Reynolds. New York: Palgrave Macmillan, 2004.

Arendt, Hannah. *The Origins of Totalitarianism*. San Diego, Calif.: Harcourt Brace Jovanovich, 1973.

Aristotle. *The Politics*, trans. T. A. Sinclair. London: Penguin Group, 1981.

Arjomand, Said Amir. *The Turban for the Crown: The Islamic Revolution in Iran*. New York: Oxford University Press, 1988.

Aston, W. G., trans. *Nihongi: Chronicles of Japan from the Earliest Times to A.D. 697*. Rutland, Vt., and Tokyo: Charles E. Tutle Company, 1972.

Bailyn, Bernard. *The Ideological Origins of the American Revolution*. Cambridge, Mass.: Belknap Press of Harvard University Press. 1967.

Banno, Junji. *The Establishment of the Japanese Constitutional System*, trans. J. A. Stockwin. New York: Routledge, 1992.

Barber, Benjamin R. *Jihad versus McWorld*. New York: Ballantine Books, 1996.

Barshay, Andrew. *State and Intellectual in Imperial Japan: The Public Man in Crisis*. Berkeley: University of California Press, 1988.

Bawer, Bruce. *While Europe Slept: How Radical Islam Is Destroying the West from Within*. New York: Doubleday, 2006.

Bendersky, Joseph W. *Carl Schmitt: Theorist for the Reich*. Princeton: Princeton University Press, 1983.

Berger, Gordon Mark. *Parties out of Power, 1931–1941*. Princeton: Princeton University Press, 1977.

Berman, Harold J. *Law and Revolution: The Formation of the Western Legal Tradition*. Cambridge, Mass.: Harvard University Press, 1983.

Bito, Masahide. "Nihonshijō in okeru Kindai Tennōsei: Tennō Kikansetsu no Rekishiteki no Haikei" [The Modern Emperor System in Japanese History: Historical Background of the Emperor-as-Organ Theory of State]. *Shisō* (August 1990).

Bix, Herbert. "Rethinking 'Emperor-System Fascism': Ruptures and Continuities in Modern Japanese History." *Bulletin of Concerned Asian Scholars* 14, no. 2 (April–June 1982): 2–19.

——. *Hirohito and the Making of Modern Japan.* New York: HarperCollins, 2000.

Bluntschli, Johann Kaspar, *The Theory of the State.* Ontario: Batoche Books, 2000.

Bodansky, Yossef. *Bin Laden: The Man Who Declared War on America.* New York: Forum, 1999.

Bodin, Jean. *Six Books of the Commonwealth*, ed. and trans M. T. Tooley. Oxford: Alden Press, 1951.

Bossuet, Jacques-Benigne. *Politics drawn from the Very Words of Holy Scripture*, ed. and trans. Patrick Riley. Cambridge: Cambridge University Press, 1990.

Brest, Paul. "The Misconceived Quest for the Original Understanding." In *Interpreting the Constitution: The Debate over Original Intent*, ed. Jack N. Rakove. Boston: Northeastern University Press, 1990.

Breuilly, John. *Nationalism and the State.* Chicago: University of Chicago Press, 1994.

Brownlee, John S. *Japanese Historians and the National Myths, 1600–1945: The Age of the Gods and Emperor Jimmu.* Vancouver: University of British Columbia Press, 1999.

Buruma, Ian. *The Wages of Guilt: Memories of War in Germany and Japan.* New York: Farrar, Straus and Giroux, 1994.

Bushidō Gakkai, ed. *Bushidō no Shinzui* [The Essence of Bushidō]. Tokyo: Teikoku Shoseki Kyōkai, 1941.

Butow, Robert J. C. *Tōjō and the Coming of the War.* Stanford: Stanford University Press, 1961.

Byas, Hugh. *Government by Assassination.* New York: Alfred A. Knopf, 1942.

Cahn, Caroline. *Kropotkin and the Rise of Revolutionary Anarchism, 1872–1886.* Cambridge: Cambridge University Press, 1989.

Cambridge History of Japan, The. John W. Hall et al., eds. Volume 6: *The Twentieth Century*, Peter Duus, ed. Cambridge: Cambridge University Press, 1999.

Cannon, Mark W., and David M. O'Brien, eds. *Views from the Bench: The Judiciary and Constitutional Politics.* Chatham, N.J.: Chatham House Publishers, 1985.

Cecil, Robert. *The Myth of the Master Race: Alfred Rosenberg and Nazi Ideology.* London: B. T. Batsford, 1972.

Chamberlain, Houston Stewart. *Foundations of the Nineteenth Century*, trans. John Lees. New York: John Lane, 1912.

Chandler, Albert R. *Rosenberg's Nazi Myth*. New York: Greenwood Press, 1968.

Clausewitz, Carl von. *On War (Vom Kriege)*. Ed. and trans. Michael Howard and Peter Paret. Princeton: Princeton University Press, 1976.

Cohen, Carl, ed. *Communism, Fascism, and Democracy: The Theoretical Foundations*. New York: Random House, 1967.

Coker, F. W. "Organismic Theories of the State: Nineteenth Century Interpretations of the State as Organism or as Person." Ph.D. diss., Columbia University, New York, 1910.

Confucius. *Rongo (The Analects of Confucius)*, trans. Arthur Waley. New York: Vintage Books, 1938.

Cook, Haruko Taya, and Theodore F. Cook *Japan at War: An Oral History*. New York: New Press, 1992.

Craig, Gordon A. *The Politics of the Prussian Army, 1640–1945*. New York: Oxford University Press, 1964.

Crenshaw, Martha. "The Logic of Terrorism: Terrorist Behavior as a Product of Strategic Choice." In *Origins of Terrorism: Psychologies, Ideologies, Theologies, States of Mind*, ed. Walter Reich. Washington, D.C.: Woodrow Wilson Center Press, 1998.

Curtis, Gerald L. *The Logic of Japanese Politics: Leaders, Institutions, and the Limits of Change*. New York: Columbia University Press, 1999.

Daly, James. *Sir Robert Filmer and English Political Thought*. Toronto: University of Toronto Press, 1979.

Doak, Kevin M. *A History of Nationalism in Modern Japan: Placing the People*. Leiden: Brill, 2007.

Dower, John W. *War without Mercy: Race and Power in the Pacific War*. New York: Pantheon Books, 1986.

———. *Empire and Aftermath: Yoshida Shigeru and the Japanese Experience, 1878–1954*. Cambridge, Mass.: Council on East Asian Studies, Harvard University, 1988.

———. *Embracing Defeat: Japan in the Wake of World War II*. New York: W. W. Norton, 1999.

Duara, Prasenjit. "Knowledge and Power in the Discourse of Modernity: The Campaigns against Popular Religion in Early Twentieth-Century China." *Journal of Asian Studies* 50, no. 1 (February 1991).

Dumbauld, Edward, ed. *The Political Writings of Thomas Jefferson*. New York: Liberal Arts Press, 1955.

Dunn, John. *The Political Thought of John Locke: An Historical Account of the Argument of the "Two Treatises of Government."* Cambridge: Cambridge University Press, 1969.

Duus, Peter, and Daniel I. Okimoto. "Fascism and the History of Pre-War

Japan: The Failure of a Concept." *Journal of Asian Studies* 39, no. 1 (November 1979): 65–76.

Dyson, Kenneth H. F. *The State Tradition in Western Europe*. New York: Oxford University Press, 1980.

Emerson, Rupert. *State and Sovereignty in Modern Germany*. New Haven: Yale University Press, 1928,

Fairbank, John K., Edwin O. Reischauer, and Albert M. Craig. *East Asia: The Modern Transformation*. Boston: Houghton Mifflin, 1965.

Ferguson, Niall. *The War of the World: Twentieth-Century Conflict and the Descent of the West*. New York: Penguin Press, 2006.

Figgis, J. Neville. *The Theory of the Divine Right of Kings*. Cambridge: At the University Press, 1896.

Fletcher, Miles. "Intellectuals and Fascism in Early Showa Japan." *Journal of Asian Studies* 39, no. 1 (November 1979).

——. *The Search for a New Order: Intellectuals and Fascism in Prewar Japan*. Chapel Hill: University of North Carolina Press, 1982.

Franklin, Julian H. *John Locke and the Theory of Sovereignty*. Cambridge: Cambridge University Press, 1978.

——. *Jean Bodin and the Rise of Absolutist Theory*. Cambridge: Cambridge University Press, 1973.

Friedrich, Carl Joachim. *The Philosophy of Law in Historical Perspective*. Chicago: University of Chicago Press, 1963.

Fung, Yu-Lan. *A History of Chinese Philosophy*, 2 vols. Princeton: Princeton University Press, 1952.

Geyer, Michael. "The Past as Future: The German Officer Corps as Profession." In *German Professions, 1870–1940*, ed. Geoffrey Locks.

Gluck, Carol. *Japan's Modern Myths: Ideology in the Late Meiji Period*. Princeton: Princeton University Press, 1985.

Gluck, Carol, and Stephen R. Graubard, eds. *Showa: The Japan of Hirohito*. New York: W. W. Norton, 1992.

Gordon, Andrew. *Labor and Imperial Democracy in Prewar Japan*. Berkeley: University of California Press, 1991.

——. *A Modern History of Japan: From Tokugawa Times to the Present*. New York: Oxford University Press, 2003.

Gordon, Harry. *Die Like the Carp*. Melbourne: Cassell Australia, 1978.

Grant, Ruth W. *John Locke's Liberalism*. Chicago: University of Chicago Press, 1987.

Gregor, A. James. *Young Mussolini and the Intellectual Origins of Fascism*. Berkeley: University of California Press, 1979.

——. *Interpretations of Fascism*. Morristown, N.J.: General Learning Press, 1974.

——. *The Ideology of Fascism: The Rationale of Totalitarianism*. New York: Free Press, 1969.

Griffin, Roger. *The Nature of Fascism*. London: Routledge, 1993.

——. *Modernism and Fascism: The Sense of Beginning under Mussolini and Hitler*. New York: Palgrave Macmillan, 2008.

Hadden, Jeffrey K., and Anson Shupe, eds. *Secularization and Fundamentalism Reconsidered: Religion and the Political Order*, vol. 3. New York: Paragon House, 1989.

Hall, Ivan P. *Cartels of the Mind: Japan's Intellectual Closed Shop*. New York: W. W. Norton, 1998.

Hall, Robert K. *Kokutai no Hongi* [Fundamentals of Our National Polity]: *Cardinal Principles of the National Entity of Japan*, trans. John O. Gauntlett. Cambridge, Mass.: Harvard University Press, 1940.

Hamada, Kengi. *Prince Ito*. Tokyo: Sanseido, 1936.

Hane, Mikiso. *Modern Japan: A Historical Survey*. Boulder: Westview Press, 1992.

Hanrieder, Wolfram F. "Alfred Rosenberg: Race, Religion, State Power." Ph.D. diss., Departrment of Political Science, University of Chicago, 1959.

Hardacre, Helen. *Shinto and the State, 1868–1988*. Princeton: Princeton University Press, 1989.

Harootunian, H. D. "Ichiboku Isso ni Yadoru Tennōsei" [An Emperor System in Every Blade of Grass and in Every Tree]. *Shisō* (November 1990).

——. *Things Seen and Unseen: Discourse and Ideology in Tokugawa Nativism*. Chicago: University of Chicago Press, 1988.

——. "Introduction: A Sense of an Ending and the Problem of Taisho." In *Japan in Crisis: Essays on Taisho Democracy*, ed. Bernard S. Silberman and Harry D. Harootunian. Princeton: Princeton University Press, 1974.

——. *Overcome by Modernity: History, Culture, and Community in Interwar Japan*. Princeton: Princeton University Press, 2000.

——. "Review Article: *Hirohito Redux*." *Critical Asian Studies* 33, no. 4 (2001): 609–36.

Hayashi, Saburo, with Alvin D. Cook. *Kogun: The Japanese Army in the Pacific War*. Quantico, Va.: Marine Corps Association, 1959.

Hegel, G. W. F. *Philosophy of Right*, trans. T. M. Knox. London: Oxford University Press, 1967.

——. *The Philosophy of History*, trans. J. Sibree. New York: Dover Publications, 1956.

Henderson, Dan F. "The Evolution of Tokugawa Law." In *Studies in the Institutional History of Early Modern Japan*, ed. John W. Hall and Marius B. Jansen. Princeton: Princeton University Press, 1968.

Hirata, Atsutane. "Tama no Mihashira." In *Nihon Shisō Taikei*, vol. 50. Tokyo: Iwanami Shoten, 1973.

Hitler, Adolf. *Mein Kampf*, trans. Ralph Manheim. Boston: Houghton Mifflin, 1943.

Hiyane, Teruo. "Jiyū Minken Undō no Kokkazō: Suehiro Tetchō no Seiji Shisō" [The Image of Nation in the Civil Rights Movement Era: The Political Thought of Suehiro Tetchō]. *Nihon Seiji Gakkai* (1982): 15–38.

Hobbs, Thomas. *Leviathan*, ed. C. B. MacPherson. London: Penguin Books, 1968.

Hoffer, Eric. *The True Believer: Thoughts on the Nature of Mass Movements.* New York: Harper and Row, 1951.

Hoffman, Bruce. *Inside Terrorism*. New York: Columbia University Press, 1998.

Holmes, Stephen. "The Permanent Structure of Antiliberal Thought." In *Liberalism and the Moral Life*, ed. Nancy L. Rosenblum. Cambridge, Mass.: Harvard University Press, 1989.

Holtom, Daniel C. *The National Faith of Japan: A Study in Modern Shinto.* London: Kegan Paul, Trench, Trubner, 1938.

——. *Modern Japan and Shintō Nationalism: A Study of Present-Day Trends in Japanese Religions*. New York: Paragon Book Reprint, 1963.

Honda, Katsuichi. *The Nanjing Massacre: A Japanese Journalist Confronts Japan's National Shame*, ed. Frank Gibney, trans. Karen Sandness. Armonk, N.Y.: M. E. Sharp, 1999.

Hoshijima, Niro. *Uesugi Hakushi tai Minobe Hakushi Saikin Kempō Uesugi and Dr. Minobe*. Tokyo: Shinseido, 1921.

Hosoka, Masayasu. "Seimen Shōkoga yuso shita Kokko 20. *Bessatsu Rekishi Dokunen Senki Shireezu* 35: 2–26 Jiken to Shōwa Ishin. Tokyo: Shin Jinbutsu Orqi Sha, 1997.

Hoston, Germaine A. *The State, Identity, and the National Question in China and Japan*. Princeton: Princeton University Press, 1994.

Hozumi, Yatsuka. *Kempō Teiyō* [A Handbook on the Constitution]. Tokyo: Yūhikaku, 1910.

——. *Kokumin Kyōiku: Aikokushin* [National Education: Patriotism]. Tokyo: Yuhikaku, 1897.

Huntington, Samuel P. *The Clash of Civilizations and the Remaking of World Order*. New York: Simon and Schuster, 1996.

Hutchinson, John, and Anthony D. Smith, eds. *Nationalism*. Oxford: Oxford University Press, 1994.

Ida, Terutoshi. *Kindai Nihon no Shisō Kōzō* [The Structure of Modern Japanese Thought]. Tokyo: Kikosha, 1976.

——. *Uesugi Shinkichi: Tennōsei Kokka no Benshō* [Uesugi Shinkichi: Discourses on the Emperor System State]. Tokyo: Sanrei Shobō, 1989.

Ienaga, Saburō. *Minobe Tatsukichi no Shisō Shi teki Kenkyū*. Tokyo: Iwanami Shoten, 1964.

——. *Nihon Kindai Kempō Shisōshi Kenkyū* [The Study of the History of Modern Japanese Constitutional Thought]. Tokyo: Iwanami Shoten, 1967.

——. *The Pacific War, 1931–1945: A Critical Perspective on Japan's Role in World War 2*. New York: Random House, 1978.

Ikeda, Satoshi. *Nihon no Uyoku: Hirakareta Nashonarizumu.* Tokyo: Yamato Shobō, 1970.

Imanaka, Tsugimaro. *Seijigaku Tsūron* [An Introduction to Political Science] Tokyo: Taimeido, 1949.

Inada, Masatsugu. *Meiji Kempō Seiritsu Shi* [A History of the Making of the Meiji Constitution], 2 vols. Tokyo: Yūhikaku, 1962.

Ino, Kenji. *Hyōden: Akao Bin: Hankotsu no Kageki Ningen* [A Critical Biography: Akao Bin: The Defiance of a Radical Man]. Tokyo: Ōru Publishing, 1991.

Irokawa, Daikichi. "The Emperor System as a Spiritual Structure." In *The Culture of the Meiji Period,* ed. and trans. Marius B. Jansen. Princeton: Princeton University Press, 1985.

——. *The Age of Hirohito: In Search of Modern Japan,* trans. Mikiso Hane and John K. Urda. New York: Free Press, 1995.

Ishida, Takeshi. *Meiji Seiji Shisō Shi Kenkyū* [A Study of the History of Meiji Political Thought]. Tokyo: Miraisha, 1954.

Itō, Hirobumi. *Commentaries on the Constitution of the Empire of Japan (Kempō Gikai),* trans. Miyoji Itō. Tokyo: Chūō University Press, 1906.

Juergensmeyer, Mark. *The New Cold War? Religious Nationalism Confronts the Secular State.* Berkeley: University of California Press, 1993.

——. *Terror in the Mind of God: The Global Rise of Religious Violence.* Berkeley: University of California Press, 2003.

Kakehi, Katsuhiko. *Kō Shintō Taigi* [The Great Principles of Ancient Shintō]. Tokyo: Shimizu Shoten, 1915.

——. *Kokka no Kenkyū* [A Study of the State]. Tokyo: Shimizu Shoten, 1913.

——. *Kannagara no Michi* [The Way of the Gods as Such]. Tokyo: Naimu Shō Jinja Kyoku, 1926.

——. *Kōkoku Kempō* [The Constitution of the Emperor State]. Tokyo: Akamondo Shoten, 1935.

——. *Dai Nihon Teikoku Kempō no Konpongi* [Fundamental Principles of the Constitution of the Empire of Great Japan]. Tokyo: Kōgakkan, 1936.

Kallis, Aristotle A., ed. *The Fascism Reader.* London: Routledge, 2003.

Kamishima, Jiro. "Mental Structure of the Emperor System." *Developing Economies* 5, no. 4. (December 1967): 702–26.

Kantorowicz, Ernst H. *The Kings Two Bodies: A Study in Medieval Political Theology.* Princeton: Princeton University Press, 1957.

Kasza, Gregory. "Fascism from Below? A Comparative Perspective on the Japanese Right, 1931–1936." *Journal of Contemporary History* 19, no. 4 (October 1984): 607–29.

Kataoka, Tetsuya. *The Price of a Constitution: The Origins of Japan's Postwar Politics.* New York: Taylor and Francis Group, 1991.

Katō, Genichi. *A Historical Study of the Religious Development of Shinto,* Trans. Shoyu Hanayama. New York: Greenwood Press, 1988.

Katō, Shūichi. "Taisho Democracy as the Pre-Stage for Japanese Militarism." In *Japan in Crisis: Essays on Taishō Democracy*, ed. Bernard S. Silberman and Harry D. Harootunian. Princeton: Princeton University Press, 1974.

Kawahara, Toshiaki. *Hirohito and His Times: A Japanese Perspective*. Tokyo: Kodansha International, 1990.

Kay, Richard S. "Constitutional Cultures: Constitutional Law." *University of Chicago Law Review* 57 (Winter 1990): 311–25.

Keene, Donald. *Emperor of Japan: Meiji and His World, 1852–1912*. New York: Columbia University Press, 2002.

Kelly, Duncan. "Revisiting the Rights of Man: Georg Jellenik on Rights and the State." *Law and History Review* 22 (Autumn, 2004): 493–529.

Kern, Paul B. "The New Liberalism in Wilhelminian Germany." Ph.D. diss., Department of History, University of Chicago, 1970.

Kersten, Rikki. *Democracy in Postwar Japan: Maruyama Masao and the Search for Autonomy*. London: Routledge, 1996.

Kim, Hyung Hee. *The Tears of My Soul*. New York: William Morrow and Company, 1993.

Kinoshita, Hanji. *Nihon no Fuashizumu* [Japanese Fascism]. Tokyo: Kokusho Kankokai, 1977.

———. *Nihon Kokkashugi Undō Shi* [A History of the Japan Nationalist Movement]. Tokyo: Keio Shobō, 1939.

Kita, Ikki. *Nihon Kaizō Hōan Taikō* [An Outline Plan for the Reorganization of Japan]. Tokyo: Nishida, 1925.

———. *Kokutairon*. Tokyo: Kita Ikki Itcho Kankokai, 1950.

———. *Kokutairon oyobi Junsei Shakaishugi* [On the Kokutai and Pure Socialism]. Tokyo: Misuzu Shobō, 1959.

———. *Kita Ikki Chosakushu* [The Collected Works of Kita Ikki], vol. 1. Tokyo: Misuzu Shōbō, 1959.

Kojeve, Alexandre. *Introduction to the Reading of Hegel*, ed. Allan Bloom, trans. James H. Nichols Jr. Ithaca, N.Y.: Cornell University Press, 1969.

Kokutai no Hongi [Fundamentals of Our National Polity]. Japanese Ministry of Education. Tokyo, 1937.

Kōsaka, Masaaki, ed. *Japanese Thought in the Meiji Era*, trans. and ed. David Abosch. Centenary Culture Council Series, no. 9. Tokyo: Pan-Pacific Press, 1958.

Koschmann, J. Victor, ed. *Authority and the Individual in Japan: Citizen Protest in Historical Perspective*. Tokyo: University of Tokyo Press, 1978.

Kropotkin, Peter. *Mutual Aid: A Factor of Evolution*. Boston: Extending Horizons Books, 1914.

Kulstein, David I. *Napoleon III and the Working Class: A Study of Government Propaganda under the Second Empire*. San Jose: California State Colleges, 1969.

Kuno, Osamu. "The Meiji State, Minponshugi, and Ultranationalism." In

Authority and the Individual in Japan: Citizen Protest in Historical Perspective, ed. J. Victor Koschmann. Tokyo: University of Tokyo Press, 1978.

Kurosaki, Sadaaki. *Renketsu.* Tokyo: Nihon Kōgyō Shimbun Sha, 1980.

Laqueur, Walter. *Fascism: Past, Present, Future.* New York: Oxford University Press, 1996.

——. *Voices of Terror: Manifestos, Writings and Manuals of Al Qaeda, Hamas, and Other Terrorists from around the World and throughout the Ages.* New York: Reed Press, 2004.

Large, Stephen S. *Emperors of the Rising Sun.* Tokyo, New York: Kodansha International, 1997.

Laslett, Peter, ed. *Patriarcha and Other Political Works of Sir Robert Filmer.* New York: Garland, 1984.

Lebra, Joyce C. *Ōkuma Shigenobu: Statesman of Meiji Japan.* Canberra: Australian National University Press, 1973.

Levinson, Stanford. *Constitutional Faith.* Princeton: Princeton University Press, 1988.

Lewis, Bernard. *The Crisis of Islam: Holy War and Unholy Terror.* New York: Random House, 2003.

Lively, Jack, ed. *The Works of Joseph de Maistre.* New York: Macmillan, 1965.

Lloyd, G. E. R. *The Ambitions of Curiosity: Understanding the World in Ancient Greece and China.* Cambridge: Cambridge University Press, 2002.

Locke, John. *Of Civil Government, Two Treatises,* ed. Ernest Rhys. London: J. M. Dent and Sons, 1943.

Lory, Hillis. *Japan's Military Masters: The Army in Japanese Life.* New York: Viking Press, 1943.

Lubasz, Heinz, ed. *Fascism: Three Major Regimes.* New York: John Wiley and Sons, 1973.

Machiavelli, Niccolo. *The Prince.* New York: New American Library, 1952.

Mackay, Charles. *Memoirs of Extraordinary Popular Delusions and the Madness of Crowds.* 2nd ed. London: Office of the National Illustrated Library, 1952.

Maruyama, Masao. "The Ideology and Dynamics of Japanese Fascism" (1947). In *Thought and Behavior in Modern Japanese Politics,* ed. Ivan Morris. London: Oxford University Press, 1969.

Masayasu, Hosoka. "Seinen Shōko ga Yuso shita Kokka Zo." Remainder of bibliographical information to come.

Masuda, Tomoko. *Tennōsei to Kokka: Kindai Nihon no Rikken Kunshūsei.* Tokyo: Aoki Shoten, 1999.

Matsumoto, Sannōsuke. "Tennōsei Kokka no Ichidanmen: Jakkan no Shisō-shiteki Seiri ni tsuite" [Some Ideological Characteristics of the Modern Japanese Emperor System]. *Nihon Seiji Gakkai* (1982): 1–13.

——. *Tennōsei Kokka to Seiji Shisō* [The Emperor System State and Political Thought]. Tokyo: Miraisha, 1969.

——. *Nihon Kindai Kempō Shisō Shi Kenkyū* [A Study of the History of Constitutional Thought in Modern Japan]. Tokyo: Iwanami Shoten, 1967.

Matsunami, N. *The Constitution of Japan*. Tokyo: Maruzen and Company, 1930.

Matsuzawa, Hiroaki. *Nihon Seiji Shisō* [Japanese Political Theory]. Tokyo: Hoso Daigaku Kyoiku Shinkokai, 1989.

Maxon, Yale Candee. *Control of Japanese Foreign Policy: A Study of Civil–Military Rivalry, 1930–1945*. University of California Publications in Political Science, vol. 5. Berkeley: University of California Press, 1957.

McCormack, Gavan. "Nineteen-Thirties Japan: Fascism?" *Bulletin of Concerned Asian Scholars* 14, no. 2 (April–June 1982).

McGovern, William Montgomery. *From Luther to Hitler: The History of Fascist-Nazi Political Philosophy*. New York: Houghton Mifflin, 1941.

Merari, Ariel. "The Readiness to Kill and Die: Suicidal Terrorism in the Middle East." In *Origins of Terrorism: Psychologies, Ideologies, Theologies, States of Mind*, ed. Walter Reich. Washington, D.C.: Woodrow Wilson Center Press, 1998.

Merriam Jr., C. E. "History of the Theory of Sovereignty since Rousseau." *Studies in History, Economics, and Public Law* 12, no. 4 (1900).

Miller, Frank O. *Minobe Tatsukichi: Interpreter of Constitutionalism in Japan*. Berkeley: University of California Press, 1965.

Minear, Richard H. *Japanese Tradition and Western Law: Emperor, State, and the Law in the Thought of Hozumi Yatsuka*. Cambridge, Mass.: Harvard University Press, 1970.

Minobe, Taksukichi. *Kempō Kōwa* [Lectures on the Constitution]. 4th ed. Tokyo: Yūhikaku, 1914.

——. *Kempō Satusyō* [Essentials of the Constitution]. Tokyo: Yūhikaku, 1923.

Mitsunami, N. *The Constitution of Japan*. Tokyo: Maruzen and Company, 1930.

Miyamoto, Moritaro. *Tennō Kikan Setsu no Shūhen* [The Parameters of the Emperor-as-Organ Theory of State]. Tokyo: Yūhikaku, 1980.

Miyazawa, Toshiyoshi. *Tennō Kikan Setsu Jiken* [The Emperor-as-Organ Theory Affair], 2 vols. Tokyo: Yūhikaku, 1970.

Montesquieu, Baron de. *The Spirit of the Laws*, trans. Thomas Nugent. London: Hafner Press, 1949.

Morris, Ivan I. *Nationalism and the Right Wing in Japan: A Study of Post-War Trends*. Westport, Conn.: Greenwood Press, 1974.

Mosley, Leonard. *Hirohito: Emperor of Japan*. New York: Avon Books, 1966.

Mosse, George L. *The Crisis of German Ideology: Intellectuals Origins of the Third Reich*. New York: Howard Fertig, 1998.

Nagao, Ryūichi. *Nihon Kokka Shisō Shi Kenkyū* [A Study of the History of Japanese State Thought]. Tokyo: Sōbunsha, 1982.

——. *Nihon Hō Shisō Shi Kenkyū* [A Study of the History of Japanese Legal Thought]. Tokyo: Sōbunsha, 1981.

——. *Hozumi Yatsuka Shū* [Hozumi Yatsuka Collection]. In *Nihon Kempō Shi Sōsho* [Japanese Constitutional History Classics], vol. 7. Tokyo: Shinzansha, 2001.

——. *Nihon Kempō Shisō Shi* [Japanese Constitutional History Classics]. Tokyo: Kodansha, 1996.

——. "Hans Kelsen in Prewar Japan." Unpublished paper in author's possession.

Nagel, Robert F. *Constitutional Cultures: The Mentality and Consciousness of Judicial Review*. Berkeley: University of California Press, 1989.

Najita, Tetsuo. *Hara Kei in the Politics of Compromise, 1905–1915*. Cambridge, Mass.: Harvard University Press, 1967.

——. "Some Reflections on Idealism in the Political Thought of Yoshino Sakuzō." In *Japan in Crisis: Essays on Taisho Democracy*, ed. Bernard S. Silberman and Harry D. Harootunian. Princeton: Princeton University Press, 1974.

——. "The New Bureaucrats." Unpublished paper in author's possesssion.

Nietzsche, Fredrich. *Twilight of the Idols and the Anti-Christ*, trans. R. J. Hallingdale. New York: Penguin Books, 1968.

Nippon Gakujutsu Shinkokai, trans. *Manyōshū*. New York: Columbia University Press, 1965.

Nolte, Ernst. *Three Faces of Fascism: Action Française, Italian Fascism, National Socialism*, trans. Leila Vennewitz. London: Weidenfeld and Nicolson, 1965.

Norman, E. H. *The Origins of the Modern Japanese State: Selected Writings of E. H. Norman*, ed. John W. Dower. New York: Pantheon Books, 1975.

Okamoto, Shumpei. "The Emperor and the Crowd: The Historical Significance of the Hibiya Riot." In *Conflict in Modern Japanese History: The Neglected Tradition*, ed. Tetsuo Najita and J. Victor Koschmann. Princeton: Princeton University Press, 1982.

Ortega y Gasset, Jose. *The Revolt of the Masses*. New York: W. W. Norton, 1932.

Payne, Stanley G. *A History of Fascism, 1914–1945*. Madison: University of Wisconsin Press, 1995.

Peattie, Mark R. *Ishiwara Kanji and Japan's Confrontation with the West*. Princeton: Princeton University Press, 1975.

Philippi, Donald L. trans. *Kojiki*. Princeton: Princeton University Press, 1968.

Pittau, Joseph, S. J. *Political Thought in Early Meiji Japan, 1868–1889*. Cambridge, Mass.: Harvard University Press, 1967.

Pollock, Sir Frederick. *Essays in the Law*. Archon Books, 1969.

Proudhon, Pierre-Joseph. *The Principle of Federation and the Need to Reconstitute the Party of Revolution* [Du Principe federatif et de la necsssite de reconstutuer le parti de la revolution], trans. Richard Vernon. Toronto: University of Toronto Press, 1979.

Pyle, Kenneth B. *The Making of Modern Japan*. Lexington, Mass.: D. C. Heath, 1996.

Rakove, Jack N., ed. *Interpreting the Constitution: The Debate over Original Intent*. Boston: Northeastern University Press, 1990.

Rapoport, David C. "Sacred Terror: A Contemporary Example from Islam." In *Origins of Terrorism: Psychologies, Ideologies, Theologies, States of Mind*, ed. Walter Reich. Washington, D.C.: Woodrow Wilson Center Press, 1998.

Reynolds, E. Bruce, ed. *Japan in the Fascist Era*. New York: Palgrave Macmillan, 2004.

———. "Peculiar Characteristics: The Japanese Political System in the Fascist Era." In *Japan in the Fascist Era*. New York: Palgrave Macmillan, 2004.

Rocco, Alfredo. "The Political Doctrine of Fascism." *International Conciliation* 223 (October 1926).

Rommen, Heinrich A. *The Natural Law: A Study of Legal and Social History and Philosophy* [Die ewige Wiederkehr des Naturrechts], trans. Thomas R. Hanley. New York: Arno Press, 1979.

Rosenberg, Alfred. *The Myth of the Twentieth Century: An Evaluation of the Spiritual–Intellectual Confrontations of Our Age*. Newport Beach, Calif.: Noontide Press, 1993.

Rousseau, Jean-Jacques. *The Social Contract*, trans. Maurice Cranston. London: Penguin Books, 1968.

Satō, Masaru. *Nichibei Kaisen no Shinjitsu: Naze Nihon wa Tai Beiei Sensō ni Fumikitta no ka*. Tokyo: Kabushiki Kaisha Kōgakkan, 2006.

Satō, Tsūji. *Kōdō no Tetsugaku* [Philosophy of the Imperial Way]. Tokyo: Asakura Shoten, 1942.

Scalapino, Robert A. *Democracy and the Party Movement in Prewar Japan: The Failure of the First Attempt*. Berkeley: University of California Press, 1967.

Scheiner, Irwin. "Socialism, Liberalism, and Marxism." In Peter Duus, ed., *The Twentieth Century*, Volume 6 of *The Cambridge History of Japan*, John W. Hall et al., eds. Cambridge: Cambridge University Press, 1999.

Scheingold, Stuart A. *The Politics of Rights: Lawyers, Public Policy and Political Change*. New Haven: Yale University Press, 1974.

Schmitt, Carl. *The Crisis of Parliamentary Democracy*, trans. Ellen Kennedy. Cambridge, Mass.: MIT Press, 1988.

———. *Political Theology: Four Chapters on the Concept of Sovereignty*, trans. George Schwab. Cambridge, Mass.: MIT Press, 1988.

———. *Political Romanticism*, trans. Guy Oaks. Cambridge, Mass.: MIT Press, 1986.

———. *The Concept of the Political*. New Brunswick, N.J.: Rutgers University Press, 1976.

Schwab, George. *The Challenge of the Exception: An Introduction to the Political Ideas of Carl Schmitt between 1929 and 1936.* Berlin: Dunker and Humbolt, 1970.

Seika, Tomoyoshi. *Showa Nashonarizumu no Sho Mondai.* Tokyo: Kinseisha, 1995.

Shillony, Ben-Ami. *Revolt in Japan.* Princeton: Princeton University Press, 1973.

Shinya, Michiharu. *The Path from Guadalcanal.* Hamilton, New Zealand: Outrigger Publishers, 1979.

Siemes, Johannes. *Hermann Roesler and the Making of the Meiji State.* Tokyo: Sophia University Press and Charles E. Tuttle, 1968.

Silberman, Bernard S. "The Political Theory and Program of Yoshino Sakuzō." *Journal of Modern History* 31 (December 1959): 310–24.

Skya, Walter. "Fascist Encounters: German Nazis and Japanese Shinto Ultranationalists." In *Japan in the Fascist Era*, ed. E. Bruce Reynolds. New York: Palgrave Macmillan, 2004): 133–53.

Sommerville, Johann P., ed. *Sir Robier Filmer: Patriarcha and Other Writings.* Cambridge: Cambridge University Press, 1991.

Sorel, Georges. *Reflections on Violence*, trans. by T. E. Hume. New York: Peter Smith, 1941.

Sottile, Joseph P. "The Fascist Era: Imperial Japan and the Axis Alliance in Historical Perspective." In *Japan in the Fascist Era*, ed. E. Bruce Reynolds. New York: Palgrave Macmillan, 2004.

Stavrianos, L. S. *The World since 1500: A Global History.* Englewood Cliffs, N.J.: Prentice-Hall, 1966.

Sternhell, Zeev. *Neither Right nor Left: Fascist Ideology in France.* Princeton: Princeton University Press, 1996.

Stone, Geoffrey R., Robert H. Seidman, Cass R. Sunstein, and Mark V. Tushnet. *Constitutional Law.* Boston: Little, Brown and Company, 1991.

Storry, Richard. *The Double Patriots.* Westport, Conn.: Greenwood Press, 1973.

Suzuki, Sadami. *Nihon no Bunka Nashonarisumu* [Japan's Cultural Nationalism]. Tokyo: Heibonsha, 2005.

Szpilman, Christopher W. A. "Kita Ikki and the Politics of Coercion." *Modern Asian Studies* 36, no. 2 (2002), 467–90.

Takahashi, Masae. *Ni-Nijūroku Jiken: Shōwa Ishin no Shisō to Kōdō.* Tokyo: Chūō Kōron Sha, 1965.

Takayanagi, Kenzō. "Kempō Chosakai in okeru Kempō Rongi no Shisōteki Haikei." *Juristo* [The Jurist], no. 309 (1964): 36–46.

Takemoto, Toru. *Failure of Liberalism in Japan: Shidehara Kijurō's Encounter with Anti-Liberals.* Washington, D.C.: University Press of America, 1978.

Tanaka, Stefan. *Japan's Orient: Rendering Pasts into History.* Berkeley: University of California Press, 1993.

Tendō, Tadashi. *Uyoku Undō: 100 Nen no Kiseki: Sono Taitō, Zasetsu, Conmei* [The (Japanese) Right-Wing Movement: A Trajectory of One Hundred Years: Its Rise, Collapse, and Stupor]. Tokyo: Tachibana Shobō, 1992.

Teruhisa, Horio. *Educational Thought and Ideology in Modern Japan: State Authority and Intellectual Freedom*, trans. Steven Platzer. Tokyo: Tokyo University Press, 1988.

Thayer, Nathaniel B. "Race and Politics in Japan." *Pacific Review* 1, no. 1 (1988).

Titus, David Anson. *Palace and Politics in Prewar Japan*. New York: Columbia University Press, 1974.

Tocqueville, Alexis de. *Democracy in America*, trans. George Lawrence. New York: Doubleday, 1969.

Toynbee, A. J., and K. Wakaizunmi. *Life and Death*. Tokyo: Oxford University Press K.K., 1972.

Treitschke, Heinrich von. *Politics*, trans. Blanche Dugdale and Torben De Bille. New York: Macmillan, 1916.

Tsunoda, Ryūsaku, William T. de Bary, and Donald Keene, eds. *Sources of Japanese Tradition*, vol. 2. New York: Columbia University Press, 1958.

Tucker, Robert C. "Towards a Comparative Politics of Movement-Regimes." *American Political Science Review* 55, no. 2 (June 1961).

Uesugi, Shinkichi. *Kokutai, Kempō oyobi Kensei* [The Kokutai, the Constitution and Constitutional Government]. Tokyo: Yūhikaku Shobō, 1916.

——. *Nihonjin no Daishimei to Shinkiun* [The Great Mission of the Japanese and New Opportunities]. Tokyo: Keibunkan, 1921.

——. *Kokumin no Seishinteki Itchi* [Spiritual Unity of the Nation]. Tokyo: Kyoka Dantai Rengokai, 1925.

——. *Nihon no Unmei* [Japan's Destiny]. Tokyo: Nihongaku Fujutsu Kyukai, 1933.

——. *Seijijō no Kokumin Sōdōin* [Politics and National Mobilization]. Tokyo: Nihon Gakujutsu Fukyukai, 1927.

——. *Teikoku Kempō* [The Imperial Constitution]. Tokyo: Nihon Daigaku, 1905.

——. *Kokka Shinron* [A New Thesis on the State]. Tokyo: Keibunkan, 1921.

Vincent, K. Steven. *Pierre-Joseph Proudhon and the Rise of French Republican Socialism*. Oxford: Oxford University Press, 1984.

Walker, Graham. *Moral Foundations of Constitutional Thought: Current Problems, Augustinian Prospects*. Princeton: Princeton University Press, 1990.

Warner, Denis and Peggy, with Commander Sadao Seno, JMSDF (Ret.). *The Sacred Warriors: Japan's Suicide Legions*. New York: Van Nostrand Reinhold, 1982.

Weber, Eugen. *Varieties of Fascism*. New York: Van Nostrand Reinhold, 1964.

Weber, Max. *Economy and Society*, 2 vols., ed. Guenther Roth and Claus Wittich. Berkeley: University of California Press, 1978.

Wetzler, Peter. *Hirohito and War: Imperial Tradition and Military Decision Making in Prewar Japan.* Honolulu: University of Hawaii Press, 1998.

Wilson, George M. *Radical Nationalist in Japan: Kita Ikki 1883–1937.* Cambridge, Mass.: Harvard University Press, 1969.

———. "A New Look at the Problem of Japanese Fascism." *Comparative Studies in Society and History* 10, no. 4 (July 1968).

Wolferen, Karel van. *The Enigma of Japanese Power: People and Politics in a Stateless Nation.* London: Macmillan, 1989.

Yamada, Yoshio. "Shinkoku Nihon no Shimei to Kokumin no Kakugo" [The Divine Mission of Japan and the Resolve of Her People]. *Chūō Kōron* (September 1943).

Yoshino, Sakuzō. "On the Meaning of Constitutional Government and the Methods by Which It Can Be Perfected." In *Sources of Japanese Tradition,* vol. 2, ed. Ryūsaku Tsunoda, William Theodore de Bary and Donald Keene. New York: Columbia University Press, 1958.

Index

WALTER A. SKYA

IS A VISITING ASSISTANT PROFESSOR

IN THE DEPARTMENTS OF HISTORY AND

EAST ASIAN STUDIES AT COLBY COLLEGE

IN WATERVILLE, MAINE.

Library of Congress Cataloging-in-Publication Data
Skya, Walter.
Japan's holy war : the ideology of radical Shintō ultranationalism /
Walter A. Skya.
p. cm. — (Asia-pacific)
Includes bibliographical references and index.
ISBN 978-0-8223-4425-4 (cloth : alk. paper)
ISBN 978-0-8223-4423-0 (pbk. : alk. paper)
1. Shintō and state—History—1868– 2. Religion and state—
Japan—History—1868– 3. Nationalism—Japan—Religious
aspects. 4. Sovereignty—Religious aspects. I. Title. II. Series:
Asia-Pacific.
BL2223.S8S59 2009
320.540952—dc22 2008051089